The

Symmetrical Family

THE SYMMETRICAL FAMILY

BY

Michael Young

Peter Willmott

With a Foreword by Lee Rainwater

PANTHEON BOOKS

A Division of Random House, New York

FIRST AMERICAN EDITION

 Published in the United States by Pantheon Books, a division of Random House, Inc., New York. Originally published in Great Britain as *The Symmetrical Family: A Study of Work and Leisure in the London Region* by Routledge & Kegan Paul Ltd.

Library of Congress Cataloging in Publication Data
Young, Michael Dunlop, 1915–
The Symmetrical Family.

Bibliography: pp. 376–88
1. Hours of labor—London metropolitan area.
2. Leisure—London metropolitan area. 3. Time allocation surveys—London metropolitan area.
I. Willmott, Peter, joint author. II. Title.
HD5168.5.L66Y68 1974 301.5'4'09421
ISBN 0-394-48727-3 73-7009

Manufactured in the United States of America

CONTENTS

MAPS AND TABLES

FOREWORD

Lee Rainwater

Issues relating to work, family relations, and leisure time activities are central to much empirical sociology in the United States. Very seldom have they been so fruitfully drawn together as in this new work by Michael Young and Peter Willmott. Like their earlier *Family and Kinship in East London,* this book seems destined to become a classic of family sociology. But it is much more than that because it uses patterns of family behavior as a vantage point for understanding something of the impact of modern history on human life in the advanced industrial nations. Its importance is greatly enhanced by the systematic way it integrates data from a contemporary social survey with historical materials and with the accumulated knowledge of historians, economists, and sociologists bearing on the authors' principal concern: how the family system has changed over the past two centuries as a result of changing technological and social conditions. The reader has before him, therefore, not simply a research report on London families, but the thoughtful integration by two of Britain's leading social scientists of what they have learned from their own research and from that of their colleagues.

At the most general level, this book can be seen as an intensive exploration of the sociology and social psychology of materialism —an exploration, that is, of the intimate interconnections between the goods and services available to different families in society at any given time (and to all families at different times) and the interpersonal relationships and sense of personal well-being that people in those families have. In its focus on the role of the technology and level of production as the core dynamic of historical changes in patterns of work, family, and leisure over the past two centuries, Young and Willmott's work carries out on a refreshingly specific and concrete level a general charge to sociology made by William F. Ogburn a half-century ago, but not at all well taken up by contemporary American social science theory and research.

The authors find an intimate connection between the dynamic effects of technological change and the tension in democratic society between values of equality and realities of social inequality. The central paradigm of their work was first observed by de Tocqueville in the United States. It has always been more obvious here, and one of the strengths of this book is that it demonstrates how real this dynamic has been in another country, one that most Americans think of as in some sense class-ridden. The authors generalize into the Principle of Stratified Diffusion de Tocqueville's observation that "having shattered the bonds that once held them fixed, the notion of advancement suggests itself to every mind, the desire to rise swells in every heart, and all men want to mount above their station." They observe that as the industrial revolution has run its course, it has been possible to realize the ambition for more of the goods of society: the average person of today enjoys a great deal of what the rich person had yesterday, and the poor man today has most of what yesterday's average man had. Because in this country we have been free of feudal systems of honor, one would think that the far-reaching implications of the Principle of Stratified Diffusion would have been very fully developed by American social scientists. But to a surprising extent the very familiarity of the situation has created disinterest in it to the detriment of our ability to understand both how American society operates and why it has some of its persisting social problems (as I have argued in a recent work on inequality and the social meanings of income).

The Symmetrical Family should make an important contribution to the ongoing debate about modern social stratification in this and other advanced industrial countries. Although it is about London, I think the American reader will recognize events that he can immediately translate into American realities and into their implications for our conceptions of American social stratification.

The tension between equalitarian values and social inequality that Young and Willmott bring so sharply to the fore recalls S. M. Lipset's observations about equalitarian issues in *The First New Nation,* and the more recent theoretical considerations of equality and inequality developed by Talcott Parsons in his paper "Equality and Inequality in Modern Society, Or Social Stratification Revisited." W. Lloyd Warner has dealt with these same issues on the concrete level in his studies of small American communities, particularly in the books influenced by his Midwestern research, *Democracy in Jonesville,* and *American Life: Dream and Reality.* (Young and Willmott's chapter on managing directors also has parallels in descriptions of the American big business elite by Warner and Abegglen, and later by Warner in his research on the role of the American corporation in what he termed "the emergent society.")

The methodological mix of survey and historical analysis makes the case for the Principle of Stratified Diffusion much more powerfully than would either method alone. One is impressed by the extent to which at any given historical period the sense that individuals and families have of choices and constraints that confront them directs the way they construct their styles of life. The qualitative paradigms of this process that Young and Willmott develop are very much like the more rigorously axiomatic perspectives on the same issues of economists such as Gary Becker in his theoretical work on the allocation of time, Staffan Linder in his book on "the harried leisure class," and Richard Easterlin in his cross-national work on happiness. Most striking of all are the parallels between this concrete, empirically grounded work and the theory of consumer behavior developed by James Duesenberry.

The Principle of Stratified Diffusion and its corollary, the growth of the "symmetrical family," go a long way toward providing a perspective for a wide range of empirical studies of the American scene. These theories, developed by Young and Willmott from their explorations of social life in historic and contemporary London, are particularly pertinent in two areas: neighborhood dynamics and suburbanization in the American city and patterns of family relations as these have changed over time and differ among social classes at any one time.

The Symmetrical Family becomes both part of the evidence and a powerful interpretation of the evidence that industrial, and now "post-industrial" development are general processes which produce remarkably similar effects. When put alongside data from other advanced industrial nations it reveals how similar life styles and family life are from one nation to another, even though families in different countries express the general processes in different ways.

Because urban studies and family studies in the United States have been so parochial, Americans understand their society much less well than they might otherwise. Much empirical social science about the American family or the development of the American city seems incomplete because it fails to systematically address the question of the extent to which what seems "typically American" is also typically English or French or Danish—a question that does make a difference. All too often explanations of developments in American social life are offered in terms peculiar to American society without a gesture in the direction of determining whether those same developments are taking place even in other Western countries. The reader will find in this book that many developments in the area of work, family, and leisure that he may have considered "typically American" are just as typically English, and that therefore some of his cherished explanations for them are brought very much into question.

Those who are interested in how the "slow march" and the "growth of the symmetrical family" progressed in the United States will find a very useful dialectic between the ideas developed in this book and historical studies of the American family and the American city—for example, the work of John Demos on the Puritan family, Stephan Thernstrom on the family in nineteeth-century Newberryport, Sam B. Warner, Jr., on streetcar suburbs and more recently on the growth of the major American cities, Richard Sennett on the middle-class family in late Victorian Chicago, and Dorothy Brady on changing patterns of family consumption from the nineteenth to the twentieth century. That dialectic can be continued by comparing the critiques of the modern family and projections into the future of Young and Willmott with those offered from an American perspective by Richard Sennett and by Philip Slater.

Following C. Wright Mills numerous critics of American sociology have noted the constricting, often blinding, effect of the pursuit of "science" rather than substance. Many American sociologists have regarded their English colleagues as either hopelessly lost in classic theory or, in the case of those who like the present authors might vaguely be considered representative of "the Titmuss school," excessively applied, ideological, and methodologically naïve. One sees in this book, as in the earlier work of these authors, the great gains that can come from not taking scientism too seriously. What stands out most about this work is that the authors are really interested in and committed to the people they are studying. Their humanistic commitment shows through on every page. This not only does them credit as human beings but bears an important fruit for their social science by enabling them to see the important in what is apparently mundane. This is not easy for sociologists, who tend instead to interpose theoretical baggage and methodological gimmicks between themselves and the objects of their studies so that their descriptions of social reality often sound more like parodies than science. But Young and Willmott's Londoners, past and present, come alive for the reader, revealing the basic life style and social processes which unite Londoners with Philadelphians or Chicagoans or Denverites. The methodological synthesis also seems to reflect this humanism: the melding of historical and contemporary data, and particularly the easy movement back and forth between quantitative and qualitative analysis, achieve a depiction more true to the dimensionality of their subjects than could any single methodological probe.

At the level of substantive American sociology, I was particularly struck by the parallels between the analysis of the expansion of the London metropolis and what we are now coming to understand of the growth of American cities, in particular, the process of suburbanization and the emptying out of the center city. Young and Willmott quite properly see housing and neighborhood as key realizations of the hoped for style of life each stratum identifies with its present turn according to the rules of the Principle of Stratified Diffusion. They show us that for families to realize new forms of organization, particularly the move from Stage II to III, they must find environments that allow them to constitute the round of life appropriate to that family form. The stratification of these realizations of life chances then becomes the principle by which the cities' residential areas are ordered.

In reading about how the Greater London region takes on social segmentation, I was struck by the parallels to suburbanization and social levels of urban housing in the United States. Their descriptions of London find exact equivalents in the findings of studies now being completed at the Joint Center for Urban Studies, particularly studies being done by Richard P. Coleman as extensions of his earlier work on social class and social geography in Kansas City, Missouri.

On the more intimate scale of the neighborhood, and of old and new life styles within particular urban neighborhoods, there are useful connections between the broad perspective of this work and the rich and fine-grained portraits of particular neighborhoods and suburbs in the United States by Herbert Gans, Bennett Berger, Gerald Suttles, and Ulf Hannerz. A comparison of these American studies with Young and Willmott's perspective on London's growth suggests that a favorite American explanation for rapid and increasing suburbanization—racism and fear of crime—is perhaps less compelling than it has seemed, since much the same development seems to be going on in London, where these two factors are hardly salient. American theories of suburbanization, in recent times at least, have emphasized a "push" theory and a "pull" theory. That is, it is recognized that people move toward the suburbs to seek valued improvements in their living level, but it is also believed that they move away from the central city to escape various kinds of unpleasantness.

There are other, minor but intriguing, parallels which begin to suggest more general theories of neighborhood transition processes. The authors note that immigrants to the city, once rural Englishmen, more recently dark-skinned people from overseas, are inevitably weak in competition for good housing even with people whose economic means are no greater than their own, because of their lesser "social capital." Roger Krohn has described exactly the same process in micro-detail for landlord-tenant relations in two different neighborhoods in Montreal, and Coleman observed much the same process in the Boston Metropolitan Area.

In the end, the most important contribution of this work is to bring squarely into focus the intimate connections between the family's situation in the economy and patterns of social relationships between the marital partners and between them and their children. Any elementary textbook will emphasize the importance of this connection, yet family sociology and the sociology of work tend to proceed along their separate narrow ways barely acknowledging the existence of each other. In large measure this may be a result of a kind of unacknowledged dichotomy between the sociology of "public" behavior and the sociology of "private" behavior. It often seems as if sociologists specialize in one or the other and observe an invisible boundary between them. Certainly it is difficult to point to even one important empirical study of American social life that focuses as systematically as this work does on exchanges between the family and the economic subsystem of society. One can hope that this vibrant example will stimulate additional research that focuses simultaneously on work roles and family roles. The growing interest in achieving a better understanding of wives' employment should also encourage such development.

The concept of the symmetrical family is the fruit of a very incisive reassessment by the authors of a continuing concern of family sociologists to characterize the "modern family." It has its most direct roots in Burgess and Locke's idea of the companionate family and Bott's concept of jointly organized family roles. The analysis of the symmetrical family, the Stage III in contrast to the Stage II family, will add considerably to our understanding of class-related patterns of family organization as described in the work of Komarovsky, Gans, Blood, Lopata, Rainwater, Coleman, and Handel. These contrasts of lower-, working-, and middle-class family life have emphasized differences in American family patterns as a function of the family's position in the contemporary social structure. Young and Willmott show how these contemporary patterns must also be understood as part of an historical process in which the relationship between class and particular patterns of family behavior is constantly changing. The very long time period within which the authors operate allows them to make this case most dramatically, but the same kind of changes can be observed, in much subtler form, over a period of a decade or two. Now that Young and Willmott have spelled out their findings concerning the historical development toward the symmetrical family, I can see that the distinction that Gerald Handel and I drew between "modern" and "traditional" working-class family types around 1960 can best be understood as representing two slightly different points in the long-term historical development from Stage II to Stage III.

The authors suggest that the family is a particularly sensitive vantage point from which to assess how well a given socio-economic system meets the tests of humanity and justice. Their work provides an incisive assessment of both the past and present systems according to this criterion. We see many clues today to suggest that we are on the brink of renewed concern, research, and theorizing about the relationship between individuals, family, and society. *The Symmetrical Family* provides a useful starting point for a new phase of social science concern with society and the family. The authors bring us up-to-date in a most useful way on the effects wrought by technology, equalitarian values, feminism as a concrete family-related expression of equalitarian values, and the revolution in contraceptive technology which allows nearly complete control of fertility (at least on the up side). They suggest that the central focus for understanding the relationship between personal well-being and social institutions might well be the triangle of overlapping commitments among work, family, and leisure. Their conceptions of these matters seem considerably closer to the day-to-day realities of yesterday's, today's, and tomorrow's Englishmen and Americans than much recent social theorizing on these subjects. A great deal of recent American discussion has seemed to take work for granted, to find the family oppressive, and therefore to see a revolution in interpersonal relations as imminent. Although Young and Willmott consider these possibilities, the thoroughness of their analysis of how we have gotten where we are constrains them to see the future as less dramatically different from the present. A new family sociology that builds on this kind of work, with its meticulous attention to how people have lived, do live, and want to live, will in the end make the greatest contribution to social innovations for lives that are more meaningful in mundane human terms.

Finally, this book is an important contribution to the recent American debate about equality versus meritocracy in modern life. Young and Willmott suggest that only if there is a slackening of the appetite for inequality on the part of those at the head of the column of the slow march is it likely that the treadmill quality of that march can be moderated, and its costs in impact on the environment and exacerbation of the differential between the have and have-not nations moderated. Eventually, they argue, "the length of the column has in other words to be shortened, the differences between rich and poor made much less pronounced than they have been at any time in the past." Such a society would allow for greater self-realization by the "less equal" members of even the symmetrical family—the wives and children—as well as by those at the end of the column. The authors suggest that modern industrial societies such as Britain and the United States may have gotten all they can out of material progress, that now the slow march may be going in a circle. Perhaps they are suggesting that a useful social science would help to call off the charade.

References

Becker, Gary. "A Theory on the Allocation of Time." *Economic Journal,* September 1965.

Berger, Bennett. *Working Class Suburb.* Berkeley: University of California Press, 1959.

Blood, Robert M., and D. M. Wolfe. *Husbands and Wives.* New York: The Free Press, 1960.

Blumberg, Rae, and Robert F. Winch. "Societal Complexity and Familial Complexity: Evidence for the Curvilinear Hypothesis." *American Journal of Sociology* 77, no. 5 (March 1972).

Brady, Dorothy. Chapter 3 in Lance E. Davis et al., *American Economic Growth: An Economist's History of the United States.* New York: Harper & Row, 1972.

Coleman, Richard P. "Seven Levels of Housing: An Exploration in Public Imagery." Working Paper no. 20, Joint Center for Urban Studies of M.I.T. and Harvard, 1973.

Coleman, Richard P. *Exploration in Contemporary Meanings of Housing and Neighborhoods.* Forthcoming.

Coleman, Richard P., and Bernice Neugarten. *Social Status in the City.* San Francisco: Jossey-Bass, 1971.

Demos, John. *Little Commonwealth: Family Life in Plymouth Colony.* New York: Oxford University Press, 1970.

Duesenberry, James S. *Income, Saving and the Theory of Consumer Behavior.* Cambridge, Mass.: Harvard University Press, 1949.

Easterlin, Richard. "Does Economic Growth Improve the Human Lot?" In *Nations and Households in Economic Growth: Essays in Honor of Moses Abramovitz,* edited by Paul A. David and Melvin W. Reder. Stanford: Stanford University Press, forthcoming.

Gans, Herbert. *The Urban Villagers.* New York: The Free Press, 1962.

Gans, Herbert. *The Levittowners.* New York: Pantheon Books, 1967.

Gans, Herbert. *People and Plans.* New York: Basic Books, 1968.

Goode, William. *World Revolution and Family Patterns.* New York: The Free Press, 1963.

Handel, Gerald, and Lee Rainwater. "Changing Family Roles in the Working Class." In *Blue Collar World,* edited by Arthur Shostak and William Gomberg. Englewood Cliffs, N.J.: Prentice-Hall, 1964.

Hannerz, Ulf. *Soulside.* New York: Columbia University Press, 1969.

Komarovsky, Mirra. *Blue Collar Marriage.* New York: Random House, 1962.

Krohn, Roger, and E. Berkeley Fleming. "The Other Economy and the Urban Housing Problem: A Study of Older Rental Neighborhoods in Montreal." Working Paper no. 11, Joint Center for Urban Studies of M.I.T. and Harvard, 1972.

Krohn, Roger, and Ralph Tiller. "Landlord-Tenant Relations in a Declining Montreal Neighborhood." *Sociological Review Monographs,* no. 14 (Sociological Studies in Economics and Administration, University of Keele, England), 1969.

Linder, Staffan B. *The Harried Leisure Class.* New York: Columbia University Press, 1970.

Lipset, Seymour M. *The First New Nation: The United States in Historical and Comparative Perspective.* New York: Basic Books, 1963.

Lopata, Helena Z. *Occupation: Housewife.* New York: Oxford University Press, 1971.

Ogburn, William F. *William F. Ogburn on Culture and Social Change, Selected Papers.* Edited by Otis Dudley Duncan. Chicago: University of Chicago Press, 1964.

Parsons, Talcott. "Equality and Inequality in Modern Society, Or Social Stratification Revisited." In *Social Stratification: Research and Theory for the 1970's,* edited by Edward O. Laumann. Indianapolis: The Bobbs-Merrill Co., 1971.

Rainwater, Lee, Richard P. Coleman, and Gerald Handel. *Workingman's Wife.* Dobbs Ferry, N.Y.: Oceana Publications, 1959.

Rainwater, Lee. *Family Design.* Chicago: Aldine Publishing Co., 1965.

Rainwater, Lee, and Gerald Handel. "Persistence and Change in Working Class Lifestyle." *Sociology and Social Research* 48 (April 1964).

Rainwater, Lee. "Making the Good Life: Working Class Families and Lifestyles." In *Blue Collar Workers: A Symposium on Middle America,* edited by Sar A. Levitan. New York: McGraw-Hill Book Co., 1971.

Scanzoni, John. *Opportunity and the Family.* New York: The Free Press, 1970.

Sennett, Richard. *Families Against the City: Middle Class Homes of Industrial Chicago, 1872–1890.* Cambridge, Mass.: Harvard University Press, 1970.

Sennett, Richard. *The Uses of Disorder: Personal Identity and City Life.* New York: Alfred A. Knopf, 1970.

Slater, Philip. *The Pursuit of Loneliness.* Boston: Beacon Press, 1971.

Slater, Philip, and W. G. Bennis. *Temporary Society.* New York: Harper & Row, 1969.

Suttles, Gerald. *The Social Order of the Slum.* Chicago: University of Chicago Press, 1968.

Suttles, Gerald. *The Social Construction of Communities.* Chicago: University of Chicago Press, 1972.

Thernstrom, Stephan. *Poverty and Progress: Social Mobility in a Nineteenth Century City.* Cambridge, Mass.: Harvard University Press, 1964.

Warner, Sam B. *Streetcar Suburbs: The Process of Growth in Boston, 1870–1900.* Cambridge, Mass.: Harvard University Press, 1962.

Warner, Sam B. *The Urban Wilderness: A History of the American City.* New York: Harper & Row, 1972.

Warner, W. Lloyd, *et al. Democracy in Jonesville: A Study in Quality and Inequality.* New York: Harper & Row, 1949.
Warner, W. Lloyd, and James Abegglen. *Big Business Leaders in America.* New York: Harper & Row, 1955.
Wrong, Dennis. "Social Inequality without Social Stratification." *Canadian Review of Sociology and Anthropology* 1 (1964).
Young, Michael, and Peter Willmott. *Family and Kinship in East London.* London: Routledge & Kegan Paul, 1957.

PREFACE TO THE AMERICAN EDITION

It would be quite out of place for a Southern Englishman (even two of them taking courage from each other) to preach to a North American about the global village. The world does not look any more one from London than it does from New York or Chicago. We are all, on each side of the Atlantic, or on each side of the Pacific, caught up both as slaves of society and its masters in the same dynamic processes. These were set in motion by the Industrial Revolution which had its first beginnings in Britain.

The story detailed in this book is illustrated primarily from London, which was the first of the world cities. But it could apply in its broad outline as much to any other society that has stopped being primarily agricultural. When husband, wife, and children worked together on a farm or in handicrafts the family was *the* productive unit even if it did not yield much more than a bare subsistence to its members. When individual wage-employment became almost universal (except for housewives) the family had to give way to a wider division of labor. But in the course of time the family has re-established a new kind of primacy, not as the unit of production so much as the unit of consumption.

In its new role the family has entered into a crucial alliance with technology. The family has provided the incentive that has kept people at work producing ever larger quantities of goods and services. The nineteenth century nightmare of wantlessness which Marx wrote about has been kept at bay. A market of husbands would not, as we shall say again in the last chapter, have been large enough to absorb them. But husbands can go on wanting more, and striving for more, partly because there are others besides themselves to want more for. The most singular characteristic of the family is that it combines altruism with self-interest.

Technology for its part has responded by enlarging not just the flow of goods and services in general but by a more direct acknowledgment of the debt it owes to the smallest and (so far) most enduring human group. The big machines of the factory have labored to produce small machines for the home. Collective has therefore given way to private in transport, in entertainment, in domestic work, as cars have won out against trains and buses, television against cinema and theater, washing machines and refrigerators against laundry and ice factory. It is thus technical invention which has made the home a machine for believing in. If the modern alliance between family and technology has been so stanch, it is in large part because of what the industry of the United States has done for its own country and for the world.

The problems are as familiar as the triumphs. The solidarity of the smallest human group is being increasingly threatened. We are all being "whirled along by the steam-car" of higher material aspirations. One of the greatest social changes of modern times is the move toward symmetry between the sexes. In a sort of cuckoo clock transformation women have whirled themselves out of the home, to work, and men in, to work. The people at the head of the column (an image which keeps on recurring throughout the book) have moved from the state where there was a) one demanding job for the wife and one for the husband, through b) two demanding jobs for the wife and one for the husband, to c) two demanding jobs for the wife and two for the husband. The losses in tranquillity, and in stability for the children, are almost too obvious to need stressing.

Is there any sign of a letup, any sign of a relaxation in the pressures that the mid-century alliance of family and technology has placed upon the human partners in this industrial mission? We have tried to look into the future, and to consider such questions as this, and also to hold them in mind throughout. They are not questions that apply merely to any one of the world's cities.

But why London? We did not choose it; it chose us. But we do not believe it to be such a poor vantage point. We are not joining in the fashionable decrial of the city, this city or indeed any. We love London, to live in. It has also taught us to try and open our eyes to the past, and so suggested the main enterprise we are engaged on in this book—the forming of another kind of alliance, in method this time, between the viewpoints embodied in history and the sociological survey. History is always a pointer to the future. Along with the cities of continents other than the one to which Britain is rejoined, London is the cradle of what will be. If there are any resolutions to the dilemmas of the family, and of the society to which it is so central, they will be found in the cities and their suburbs.

ACKNOWLEDGMENTS

We want first to acknowledge the grants we received for the study at one or other of its various stages from the Nuffield Foundation, the Leverhulme Trust and, above all, the Centre for Environmental Studies. For some subsidiary enquiries we had support from the Sports Council and Post Office Telecommunications.

Although some of them may not like the outcome, we have been greatly helped by many colleagues. On many subjects discussed in this book we have gone well beyond our own knowledge, and have therefore had to seek advice from people more expert than ourselves. The historians were Edmund Cooney, Phyllis Deane, John Harrison, Peter Laslett, Sidney Pollard, Raphael Samuel and John Saville. On urban planning and geography we were helped by David Bryant, Peter Cowan, David Donnison, David Eversley, Ruth Glass, Peter Hall, Emrys Jones, Dick Knowles, Alan Wilson and the members of the London Seminar organized by the Centre for Environmental Studies in 1971 and 1972. The members of the Advisory Committee of our own Institute who read the draft and commented were John Bowlby, Geoffrey Gorer, Geoffrey Hawthorn, Robin Huws Jones, Charles Madge (Chairman), John Peterson and Stephen Schenk. Ronald Blunden of the Office of Population Censuses and Surveys and Judith Calder of the Open University gave advice on sampling. Others who gave comments or advice included Philip Abrams, Brian Allt, A. B. Atkinson, John Barnes, R. M. Belbin, Charles Betty, John Boreham, Michael Burrage, Tom Burns, Ann Cartwright, Albert Cherns, George Cornes, Nicholas Deakin, Norbert Elias, Susan Ferge, Robert Gavron, Ernest Gruenberg, Pat Healey, Tom Lupton, Jean Macdonald, James Meade, Jeremy Mitchell, Louis Moss, Jan Pahl, R. E. Pahl, Stanley Parker, Neil Piercy, Robert Rapoport, Rhona Rapoport, Ann Richardson, H. B. Rodgers, Martin Rein, Alexander Szalai, K. K. Sillitoe, Prudence Smith, Roy Stout, Alan Stuart, A. J. P. Vineall, Marjorie Waite, Robert Weiss, Phyllis Willmott, Sasha Young and

John Ziman. The original members of the Social Science Research Council's Next Thirty Years Committee (of which one of the authors was Chairman) and of the Centre for Environmental Studies' Working Group on Developing Patterns of Urbanization (of which the other author was a member) helped to stimulate the interest in speculation about the future which has generated the main theme of the book.

Our survey of directors was made possible by the support of Sir Richard Powell, Director-General of the Institute of Directors, and Dr Beric Wright, the Medical Director. R. E. Pahl and Jack Winkler, who were studying directors at the same time as ourselves, co-operated with us, especially in allowing us to attend some group meetings that they organized. Roger Jowell, Gerald Hoinville and their colleagues at Social and Community Planning Research helped with the interviewing of directors.

Sydney Urry, former Director of the Institute of Industrial Training at Brunel University, introduced us to the factories in which we made special studies. We are grateful to the managements of these firms and of the district post office and the printing firm described in Chapter VII.

Several people outside our own staff have given crucial assistance. Ian Cullen, of the Joint Unit for Planning Research, was in charge of the computer programming and analyses of the main survey, including the multiple regression in Chapter VIII, and of the time budgets. Elaine Davies, Caroline Clarke and their colleagues at the University of London Computer Centre helped us by carrying out the computer analyses of our main study and time budgets there. P. R. Cox, of the Government Actuary's Office, prepared the calculations used in Chapter IV and presented by him in Appendix 4. James Douglas, Director of the Medical Research Council Unit on Environmental Factors in Mental and Physical Illness, carried out some special analyses for us of his longitudinal study of children born in 1946. Peter Wedge, of the National Children's Bureau, gave us what was then unpublished material from the Bureau's longitudinal study of children born in 1958.

A number of past and present colleagues at the Institute of Community Studies worked on this study. Richard Mills, whose own book on a separate study of young people has already been published, helped in designing our enquiry from its earliest stages on, and took particular responsibility for the time budgets which he describes in Appendix 3. He also joined us in the interviewing, including that in the three firms, along with Timothy Deans. Vic Lanser, after interviewing, supervised the coding of the main questionnaire and liaised with the Computer Centre on the analysis. John Bond did some special interviews with white and immigrant families in Deptford. David Jordan and John Baker did some interviewing, as did Jim Richardson, who also helped in the design of the questionnaire and checked our references. Roger Mitton made the forecasts for the Post Office described in Appendix 5. Wyn Tucker, as skilled and dependable as ever, was the supervisor for the interviewing and analysis. Other people helped at various stages with the administration of the survey or with the analysis: Joan Deane, Dorothy Hills, Jill Jones, Janet Sparrow, Cathy Wallace, David Young and Michael Willmott. We discussed the project at all stages with Peter Marris.

The interviewers on the main survey and its subsidiaries were: Janet Baker, Hazel Bayliss, Olive Betts, Patricia Bunn, Rosemary Catling, Rosalind Claxton, Nathene Cowen, Valerie Crayfourd, Tetra Dixon, Muriel Donald, Shirley Dudman, Juliet Edmunds, Mercia Emmerson, Connie Frost, Frances Gay, Jenny Grey, Freda Hanby, Ruth Harris, Gwen Hawthorne, Christine Healey, Ann Heyno, Yvonne James, Julia Lawrence, Elizabeth Lines, Kristin Mann, Catherine Marr, Rosemary May, Linda Moller, Margaret Morrison, Daphne Moss, Barbara Muggeridge, Janet Powney, Mollie Richards, Ann Scott, Ann Sigaloff, Alan Simons, Barbara Smart, Hilary Smith, Beryl Stanfield, Christine Stebbing, Maila Stevens, Diana Stevenson, Mavis Sutter, Margery Thorne, Stephen Turner, Prudence Vosper, Mary Wake, Olive Wickens, Barbara Wilson, Geoffrey Wilson and Doreen Wohl.

The coders were: Graham Bell, Peter Evans, Douglas Fraser, Sylvia Gains, Julie Green, James Karuga, Lisa King, Malcolm Lomas, Ian Manson, Kate McDonald, Philip Osborn, Carole Powell, Geoffrey Power and Helen Ward.

The typing of the book in its various drafts was done by Irene Allinson, Barbara Caselton, Muriel Eden, Sue Chisholm, Ann Mead, Sheila Morley and Marie Wain. Daphne Piccinelli, as with our earlier books, bore the heaviest responsibility, typing at great speed chapter after chapter of draft after draft.

Above all we want to thank the people in the various samples for giving up their time and putting up with us.

The

Symmetrical Family

Map 1 The London Region

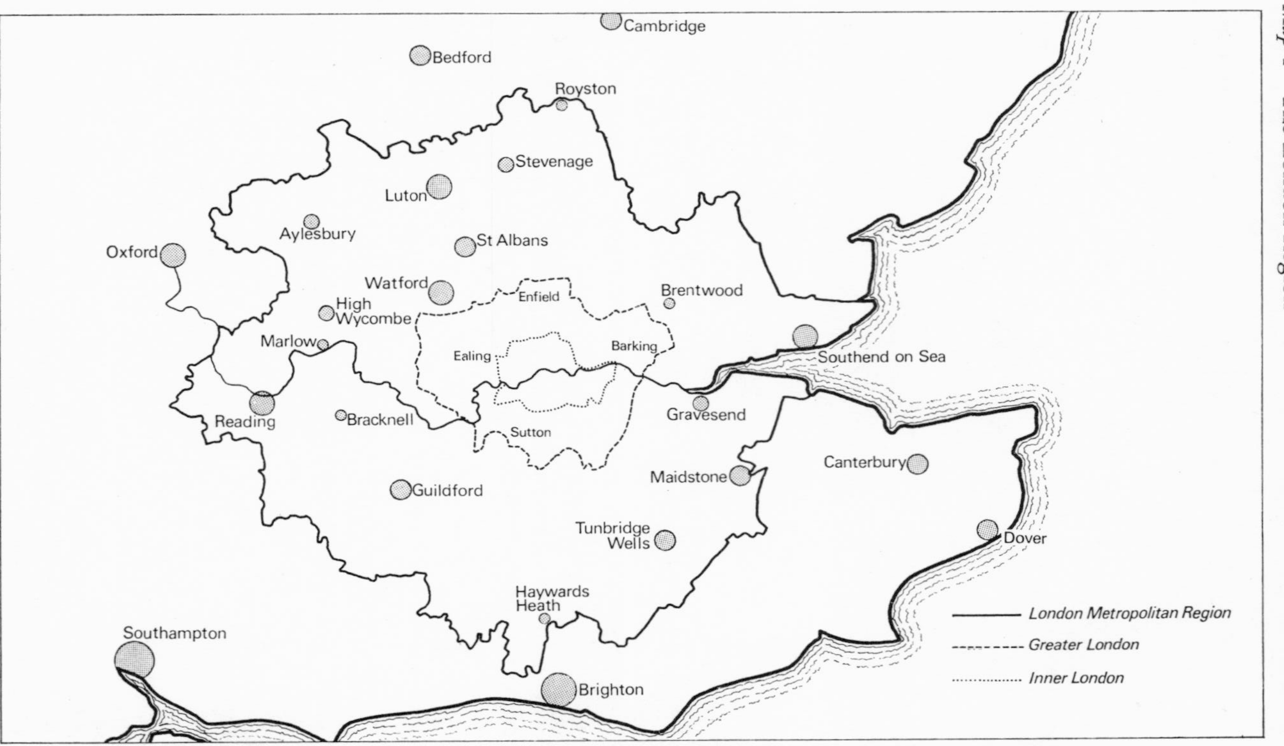

The Outer Metropolitan Area is between the boundaries of Greater London and the Region.

I

THE SLOW MARCH

In our view two of the most promising ways for sociological research to develop are, on the micro scale, through an alliance with anthropology; and, on the macro, with history. In the small studies we have made before in Bethnal Green and other districts we have tried to illustrate the former approach. In this present account of the relationship between work and home we hope to do the same for the latter.[1]

London itself was the prompter. If the present embodies the past in all cities, here it does so with special vividness. The one is there alongside or inside the other in almost every street. For some of the contemporary evidence we have used alongside or inside the historical we have relied on a sample survey of men and women interviewed in 1970. Our province was not just the smaller, more ancient London near the river but the larger Metropolitan Region covering over 4,000 square miles and consisting of Greater London plus the country ring called the Outer Metropolitan Area. When we went out, before seeing individual people, to visit the wards in the twenty-four local authority areas we selected at random for the interviewing,[2] in nearly all of them the past seemed to be crying out to be noticed.

At the centre, we had four wards in Westminster, one of the two Cities that London contains within itself. Near Hyde Park

[1] We are thus following a precedent set by, among others, W. G. Runciman in a previous book in this series, *Relative Deprivation and Social Justice*. Full references to all works cited are given at the end of the book.

[2] The names and addresses of the men and women in the main sample were drawn at random from electoral registers. The methods of selecting areas and people for our various more or less contemporary enquiries – the main sample, the active sportsmen, the managing directors and the studies in particular plants – are described in Appendix 1, and the diary sub-example in Appendix 3. The names of people quoted in the book and of the firms are fictitious and other details have been changed so as to conceal identities.

were some of the wealthiest people in the sample. They lived in flats in large twentieth-century buildings with heavy glass doors laced with black grilles; or in mews cottages built for coachmen and other servants when there were plenty of them and now made so spick and span by their new owners that the paint looked as though it had just been put on and the flowers in their window-boxes or decorative wheelbarrows standing on the cobblestones so fresh that they might have been hurried up from a country house that morning. Contrasts were more sudden than in the suburbs. On the Hyde Park side of Sussex Gardens most of the cars parked at night were new. One minute and many years away, adjoining the street named by a property man of the past, Mr Praed, they were mostly of mid-century design, standing outside cheap hotels and houses so shabby they might not have been painted since Hitler fell. Not far away, near Marylebone Station, run-down homes were being pulled down for redevelopment, a notion as much in vogue as a hundred or two hundred years before.[1] In between the extremes were the large municipal complexes of the welfare state. The one at Churchill Gardens, opposite Battersea power station, actually adorned the river. Others, like those along Edgware Road or in Lisson Grove, were the standardized tower blocks which were less obviously the symbols of the collective life which have inspired architecture in the past than boxes for storage of the living.

The other three of our boroughs in Inner London – Islington, Southwark and Lewisham – all had fewer rich people in them. But gentrification (as Glass[2] called it) was proceeding, the same bountiful State giving aid to the gentry in the form of improvement grants and tax relief. They had been spreading for two decades around Canonbury, in houses built for them in the nineteenth century, then declassed and sub-divided and now being steadily won back. The outer boundaries of their territory had still not been finally drawn. Some empty houses were waiting for the demolition men, their doors and windows blanked off with the

[1] The critics are not new either. 'In future times,' wrote Lady Holland in 1800, 'when this little island shall have fallen into its natural insignificancy, by being no longer possessed of a fictitious power founded upon commerce, distant colonies, and other artificial sources of wealth, how puzzled will the curious antiquary be when seeking amidst the ruins of London vestiges of its past grandeur.' E. Halévy, *A History of the English People in 1815*, Book III, p.429.

[2] R. Glass, 'Aspects of change,' p. xviii.

corrugated iron which is the contemporary equivalent of the plague sign of 1665. At the other end of the same street they were more or less identical except that the stucco instead of being mud-coloured and flaking was shining forth in magnolia or dove-grey. The houses in between were still disputed ground, neither derelict nor restored: it was not certain how far the penicillin would spread to check disease before it led to death. Many of the poorer people who used to live there had been pushed out as they had out of sister-districts like Barnsbury and De Beauvoir Town. Some of them had moved to join Irishmen, Cypriots and West Indians in northern parts of Islington, in street after street of crumbling bays and tiny concreted front yards, empty except for dustbins and the occasional broken milk bottle or Coca-Cola can.

Southwark had a small Canonbury around Camberwell Grove, and also more examples of municipal architecture. Some of the high blocks seemed to have had pieces bitten out of them by a giant on every fourth floor. The concrete was already stained with damp as though the giant in eating the pieces for his dinner had spilled gravy down his front. Next to such a block was a new group, called Gothic Court, in a kind of mock-medieval style, with sharp-angled roofs, blackish bricks, copper over the doorways and small courtyards leading out of each other. Architecture over the last two hundred years has mined the past more or less in sequence so that even new buildings have had the past embodied in them. Classical styles from Greece (which had themselves been repeated in Rome and then in the Renaissance) were repeated again in the seventeenth and eighteenth centuries; Gothic in Victorian times in buildings all the way from St Pancras Station to numberless large family residences; and Tudor, marked by half-timbering, hung tiles, herring-bone brickwork and lavatory windows of coloured glass, in the suburbs of the first half of the twentieth century. After that there was nothing left of a major style to repeat for an encore performance – hence the Modern movement of the 1920s and 1930s. So far, it does not look as though the cycle is going to start all over again, rather that all styles are going to be re-played simultaneously in a general hotch-potch. Gothic Court suggests that even Victorian Gothic may have its counterpart in the architectural supermarket.

Lewisham, stretching from Deptford on the river to the high ridge of Sydenham in the south-west and Beckenham and Sundridge in the south-east, had in it almost a complete range, socially and architecturally. Parts of Deptford were as derelict as anything in London. Many of the houses were condemned. The West Indians who had crowded into them would not be able to stay much longer, along with the native fatherless families, the large families, those with breadwinners out of work or in low-paid jobs. At the other end of the borough, Sydenham was a suburb with plenty of open space near by at Crystal Palace and Dulwich. The impression registered by some of the newly built houses was less that of London's history than of history in other countries to which London is now more closely joined than ever. In a couple of adjoining streets there was an almost pure Cape Dutch bungalow complete with a miniature of itself at the back which looked as if it was meant for the (presumably) non-existent black servants; a terrace with white weather boarding as if from a New England township; a municipal block built while Whitfield Lewis was Principal Housing Architect for the LCC in the 1950s, with his taste for the 'humanist modern' of Sweden and Holland; private flats with rotating wooden pivot frames which lent themselves well to the double-glazing common in the Scandinavia where they originated; and some of the newest detached houses, which were a tentative version of the ranch style with which California has honoured the pioneers of the last century.

In the outer ring of Greater London we had four boroughs in the sample – Enfield and Ealing, Barking and Sutton. In one corner of Enfield was Hadley Wood, ancient but now suburbanized, where, according to one account, 'the children are taken to school not just by one au pair girl but by two', and in another corner Edmonton which had been working-class since the 1870s. The railway came there in 1872. Speculative builders speedily erected three grades of working-class housing which before and after decimalization were still known by some older people as the *5s. 6d.*'s, *6s. 6d.*'s, *7s 6d.*'s, according to the initial rents charged for them. The *5s. 6d.*'s were very like the plain cottages of the mid-century built in the East End – a frill-less miniature of the Georgian houses built for the rich earlier in the century. The *6s. 6d.*'s, also two-up and two-down, added a simple bay window on the ground floor and the beginning of a porch. The *7s. 6d.*'s had more elaborate bay windows, door arches with false keystones, larger porches and tiny classical dentils. There were many similar houses in Ealing – some of them occupied by the Indians and Pakistanis who had settled there, in Southall – as well as a great crop of others built between 1918 and 1939, and, near the old coaching route of St Mary's Road, a few which dated back to the nineteenth and even the eighteenth century. Ealing also had many trees, like other parts of the city. Some of London's trees grow free in the great parks we owe to Henry VIII's love of hunting; others, more gnarled, struggle for life in the midst of offices and factories; many have limbs mutilated by councils who have left only fingers of green to sprout out of the stumps left by the surgeon's saw.

Sutton and Barking were alike in their large inter-war council estates, St Helier and Becontree. The roads ran in neat symmetrical patterns – squares, crescents, circuses and banjoes. The two-storey terraces and semis were monotonously alike. But, as an earlier study showed, in Becontree most of the long-standing residents felt affection for the place and for each other.[1] Sutton had more private houses than Barking. The relatively few built before 1914 reflected the 'battle of the styles' which raged almost as fiercely among the architects of the late nineteenth and early twentieth centuries as it has done since 1945. The struggle used to be between Victorian Baroque, Victorian Dutch, Victorian Jacobean, Victorian Venetian, Victorian Tudor, Victorian Gothic. Between 1918 and 1939 mock Tudor gained such a complete ascendancy as to establish a temporary uniformity.

In the Outer Metropolitan Area, which is such a blend of town and country as to make nonsense of the distinction, we picked two large towns, cities almost, Reading with 120,000 people, Southend with 165,000. Each town sent commuters to the middle of London and gave employment to others in its own factories and offices. Like the metropolis itself, each was ringed by suburbs, which merged into yet other towns and villages. Reading was, more obviously, a communication centre. The old Great Western Railway was there even in the architecture. The Royal Berkshire Hospital and some fine houses in the King's Road were built of Cotswold stone transported by the railway from a tunnel driven through a hill near Bath, and given away free to local builders.

Southend was more dominated by the river than by the railway. It was an amalgamation of the village of Southend, the fishing

[1] P. Willmott, *The Evolution of a Community*, pp. 21, 110.

port of Leigh-on-Sea, and inland the ancient village of Prittlewell. Southend is still the Cockney Paradise for day trippers, mostly working-class people from East London. Many of the residents wished they would stop coming. In 1908 the Mayor said, 'Southend used to be thought of as the place for day-trippers from London. All that is now changing.' It had not changed yet. The impression was that the same sort of people had been coming there for a hundred years to seek the same pleasures: cockles and whelks, penny-gambling and paddling, ghost trains and switchbacks, candy floss and comic postcards like the one of a man saying to a strapping lift girl, 'Have you got room for a small one?' The golden mile was a jumble of brightly lit booths. The green train that trundled to the end of the pier was like an old-fashioned toy. Most visitors were in family parties, usually mum and children, sometimes father, often grandmother. Children and pensioners – with the American term, senior citizen, coming into vogue – could get half-price into many places of amusement.

We drew two other sizeable towns in the Outer Metropolitan Area, Watford with 76,000 people and Brentwood with 60,000. They also had many commuters. Waiting for them when they returned at night from London were lines of cars stretching away from the stations, many with wives and dogs in the front seats. If he was not met by his wife a husband would walk down the line until he found a woman or a dog whom he recognized as a neighbour.

Watford expanded fastest between the wars, and Brentwood after 1945. Watford was therefore more firmly a Tudor town. The Tudor houses went with the coat-of-arms which the council described in the same sort of ancient terms as many others:

> Gules on a pale wavy Argent between two Escallops Or, a pallet wavy Azure charged with a fasces erect of the second, on a chief of the third a hart charged with a saltire also of the third between two harts statant of the first.

Brentwood was again a battleground of styles, but with the international modern predominating. Local residents may, to offset the sameness, have made even more of the differences they saw, or imagined, between people. Those in one group of private houses had given to others just across the road the label of 'the African village'. It was to all appearances, with as many spiky television aerials growing out of the roofs, more or less indistinguishable from their own. The idea was that the women spent a great deal of their time standing in the doorways of their 'huts' shouting to people in other parts of the 'kraal'. But there was no mistaking the identity of some of the larger new houses like those advertised on one board with the prices prevailing at the time:

Shenfield Place Executive Homes
First Phase Release

Mortgages Readily Available   Available for Occupation this Year
Fair prices with de luxe specification as standard

New Design	NHBRC 10 year Guarantee
4 large bedrooms	Central Heating
Open Hardwood Staircase	Wrighton Fitted Kitchen
Fully Insulated Loft	Ground Floor Cloakroom
Coloured half-tile bathroom	Garage with Up and Over Door
Polished Mahogany Doors	Landscaped Front Garden
Separate Study	22 Power Points

Detached Houses
From £12,200   Freehold

The executive homes were not far from others much older, like Hutton Hall. The road that led up to it was lined by houses which looked like great sentry boxes from which the retainers could have once watched the 'big people' driving up to the Hall in their carriages. In Cricketers' Lane was a village butcher wearing a striped apron and a boater.

There were two new towns – Stevenage with 66,000 people, and Bracknell with 37,000. Stevenage had a town centre visited each summer by coach-loads of foreign architects and town-planners who conscientiously photographed the pedestrian shopping piazza, the fountain and the sculptures. The residential areas expressed the shifts of architectural fashion over two decades, the earliest roads with semis and terraced housing giving way to small pedestrian precincts and then to nests of high-density dwellings served by footpaths, the cars being hidden away behind. Whereas Stevenage was mainly an industrial town, Bracknell had more commercial offices, government departments and research establishments, and more of its houses were in traditional cottage or neo-Georgian style.

Marlow was one of the other towns, with as much of a riverside air as Southend seventy miles further down. The difference was that the boat going through Marlow Lock might be a motor cruiser with a smiling blonde in bell-bottom trousers, and the one passing the end of Southend Pier an oil-tanker from the Isle of Grain or a Russian ship from Leningrad. Being so much smaller – 11,000 people – Marlow had more of a sense of unity. The red-brick Georgian houses lining the main street made it look a small country town, as did the strawberries sold by the pound, not in expensive punnets, and the unfrozen ducks and piles of glistening sheep's kidneys at the butcher's. Some of the pubs were still without piped music or juke-boxes. Radiating out from the old town were new estates, the houses more or less identical with those at Brentwood, except for the sense of the river being near. From its bank, at 3 p.m. one wet summer day, could be seen a fisherman on the weir, huge in black waders and oilskins. At 6 p.m. he was still there in the rain, moving restlessly along the wet steps. He had a seemingly empty net wedged between the concrete blocks. He gave up at 9 p.m. as the light was fading. He threw back four small fish, singly and with great deliberation. He then dismantled his rods, emptied his bags of debris, took off his waders and went away along the cat-walk with the bouncy step of a *young* man.

Cuckfield was a rural district in Sussex, with a population of 36,000 strung out over twenty miles from the Surrey border to the edges of Brighton. One of the villages was Hassocks with some bungalows for the retired and semis for the young commuters as well as solid pre-war houses near the station. At the end of a Way or Close were fields and the long dark line of the Downs with Jack and Jill, the two windmills, against the sky. Another village was Horsted Keynes whose name derives from William de Cahaignes; he came 'over' with William the Conqueror. A twin village in Normandy, La Cagnes, has an identical church. There were apple orchards and plums and brooks and copses – Parsons Wood, Oaken Wood, Furzefield Wood, Goddenwick Wood – and no street lights, regarded by the parish council as advance guards of the urban invasion. In Ardingley High Street cottages mingled with larger houses, the White House facing the Red House and the Pink House the Post Office. Copthorne was a sprawling conglomerate of cottages, nineteenth-century family houses and small new ones. A large church stood in a tangle of plants, underneath a procession of planes flying into Gatwick Airport.

These places were connected by a system of roads of which some were even more ancient. De Tocqueville said that in democratic nations 'the woof of time is every instant broken and the track of generations effaced'.[1] This may apply to the links between generations; it does not to the physical framework. The track of Watling Street, which was probably there even before the invasion of Julius Caesar in 55 and 54 B.C., and certainly well before it got that Saxon name, is more or less followed to the south by the M2 to Canterbury and to the north by the M1. Bishopsgate and Shoreditch High Street follow the line of the Roman Ermine Street which went to York. As Hall put it, 'Despite the work of later generations, the basic main road pattern is the gift of the Romans, and has a characteristic Roman simplicity'.[2]

Old words do not have to be demolished before new ones are made. Language is more nearly in perpetual motion than a city, words being constantly re-defined in an even more excited dialectical relationship with other changes in society. But the mark of the past is equally indelible, as it is on one of the strange words, class, that we shall be using a good deal in our description of the citizens of London, both past and present. To lump people, all of whom are unique, into one class or another can be regarded as an offence to human dignity, or, if one is less solemn, simply ridiculous. None of the common distinctions stands up to close scrutiny. One of them is between 'manual' and 'non-manual' and, despite the objections, we shall be driven to follow that convention. But the distinction is not sharp. A surgeon or a shorthand-typist, both described by the Registrar-General as 'non-manual', certainly use their hands, just as 'manual' workers continually use other faculties besides.

If the attempt to distinguish by the combination of skills employed in work is abandoned, it is still possible to make a great leap into the dark and scramble back with a portmanteau term like 'the middle classes'. But what are they the middle of? The

[1] A. de Tocqueville, *Democracy in America*, vol. II, p. 65.

[2] P. Hall, 'The development of communications', p. 52.

way most people talk, there is on that scale apparently nothing either above or below middle. Few would nowadays admit to being 'upper class' and fewer still to being 'lower'.

The modern terminology dates back to the Industrial Revolution which required more people to see themselves as having interests and attributes in common with large numbers of others.

> The concept of 'social class' with all its attendant terminology was a product of the large-scale economic and social changes of the late eighteenth and early nineteenth centuries. Before the rise of modern industry writers on society spoke of 'ranks', 'orders', and 'degrees', or when they wished to direct attention to particular economic groupings, of 'interests'. The word 'class' was reserved for a number of people banded together for educational purposes and more generally with reference to subdivisions in schemes of 'classification'.[1]

The middling people, somewhere between the nobility or higher class and the rest, were from that time on increasingly called the middle classes. To be the middle in some system that had the nobility one rung up[2] was to associate oneself with greatness as well as to claim an opportunity to rise up the ladder oneself.

What, then, were the people at the bottom to be called? They had previously been called the poor or, sometimes, paupers. Gregory King said that in 1688 half the nation were paupers, needing charity if not poor relief to make ends meet.[3] 'For several hundred years the great majority of ordinary people in Britain were known simply as "the poor". A poor man was one who had to work with his hands to support himself and his family.'[4] The middle classes could refer to them as the lower classes, to follow upon the earlier term of lower orders. But

[1] A. Briggs, 'The language of "class" in early nineteenth century England', p. 43. See also R. Williams, *Culture and Society 1780-1950*, p. xv.

[2] At the beginning of the eighteenth century Defoe's hero saw the middle the other way on. 'Mine was the middle state, or what might be called the Upper Station of Low Life, which he had found by long Experience was the best State in the World, the most suited to human Happiness, not exposed to the Miseries and Hardships, the Labour and Sufferings of the mechanick Part of Mankind, and not embarrass'd with the Pride, Luxury, Ambition and Envy of the upper Part of Mankind.' D. Defoe, *Robinson Crusoe*, pp. 2-3.

[3] P. Mathias, *The First Industrial Nation*, p. 200.

[4] J. F. C. Harrison, *The Early Victorians, 1832–1851*, p. 20.

there was nothing to be gained for the poor themselves (or by their sympathizers) from sliding into the slot which the nomenclature of upper and middle pointed down to, and then for thinking of themselves as lower, if there was another tag which would not so obviously smack of inferiority, especially if there was one to hand which would suggest superiority according to a different criterion, that is, whether or not people were working. To be idle, at a time when a true gentleman would not soil himself with 'work', was not as pejorative as it later became. But even in the early nineteenth century plenty of people of all classes except the top held idleness vice. The people at the bottom accordingly gained merit, and turned the tables, by taking advantage of the double meaning of 'industry' and calling themselves the industrial, the industrious or the working classes. The implication was that working people belonged to a two-fold class system in which the other class was the non-working or idle.

The terminology of class can therefore be seen as an attempt to reconcile the not easily compatible – the egalitarian sentiment of democracy and the persistent fact of inequality. By adopting terms derived from different scales of valuation all have been able to edge away from the implication of inferiority. The muddle about 'middle' and the rest was, and is, functional, and will be so as long as the distaste for recognizing that any man is inferior to another co-exists with the truism that in most material respects he is. It is a victory for egalitarian sentiment, or hypocrisy, if one prefers, whenever the Duke of A says he is middle-class because 'we are all middle class now', the businessman that he belongs to the working classes because he has to work too, and the operative (another strange word in a galaxy of circumlocutions) when he denies that, these days, there are any lower classes left. They all know, equally, that inequalities which people are trying to put in some sort of order by their choice of words are still there as the backbone of the system of grading.

That man is a classifying animal, even when he is unsure of his criteria, was once again clear from our own survey. When we asked people in our main sample whether they would call themselves 'middle class' or 'working class', a few did bridle. 'I think they are meaningless titles', said Mr Banks, a thirty-year-old clerk living in Ealing. Mrs Wallace, a forty-year-old Watford housewife, said, 'I can't answer that. I don't think there's the same distinction as there used to be.' Mr Gordon, a physicist at Stevenage, found it difficult to choose between the alternatives: 'According to Vance Packard in *The Status Seekers* I'm in the Limited Success Class'. One wife was just about to say 'working class', her mouth half-open, when her husband, a printer, stopped it with a look and then said, 'What a dumb wife I've got.' She changed in mid-sentence and answered 'middle class', whereupon he nodded, as if to a performing dog, to tell her, yes, that was the right answer. But the overwhelming majority of informants (93 per cent) were prepared, without much hesitation, to accept one or other of our labels. This was similar to the response in Gorer's survey which offered people a longer list of such possibilities; he reported that two-thirds of them chose 'middle' or 'working', and commented: 'Self-assignment by class is clearly congenial to the vast majority of the younger English population.'[1] The binary class system of Britain has been reflected in its binary party system.

We ourselves are evidently even more keen than others on classifying, but had to be more precise than people ordinarily need to be. Every person in the samples had to be assigned to one class or another, whether according to the binary scheme or to the four-class scheme we will come to in a moment. But what criterion were we to use? We could have picked on education as the arbiter, or residence, or power, or wealth, or income. In view of what we say later about the spread of possessions there would have been a good case for using income as the measure. But in the end we decided to adopt occupation as the standard criterion.[2] It suggests the kind of work that people do – something of particular interest to us since we wanted to find out how work affected family life. But it is also often used as an index of 'social class'. Occupational status correlates closely with most of the other possible arbiters, people in the higher occupational classes usually having higher incomes, more wealth, more education, more power and better housing. This aspect of occupation was pointed out in a recent official study of mortality. 'Apart from the

[1] G. Gorer, *Sex and Marriage in England Today*, p. 7.

[2] If, happily, any fellow researchers decide to repeat our study in the early decades of the next millennium in order to show how much our forecasts have erred, they may find occupation less useful as a discriminator than we have. If manual workers are by then a minority, and non-manual an ever-expanding majority, this will not necessarily reduce the differences in power, income, life-style, etc., and new proxies for them may be needed.

possibility of detecting specific occupational hazards, knowledge of a man's profession gives some idea of his income, his intelligence and education, his leisure pursuits, diet, hygiene and other features of his existence.'[1] Sometimes occupation cannot be used in this way; a retired man or a wife not working outside the home do not have occupations of the same sort as others. Even when a married woman is working, her own job may be a poor guide to her social class in the broader sense. A wife with a part-time job in a shop is likely to have a different kind of home background if her husband is a foundry worker than if he is a personnel manager, and probably a different type of shop to work in as well. Except for Table 18 on p. 117, we have for statistical purposes regarded a married woman as having the same occupational class as her husband on the basis of his job. Another rule is that men aged sixty-five or over, whether retired or not, have been classified according to their main occupation before sixty-five, as have single women of sixty or over according to their previous occupation.

We have not used it exclusively. Sometimes the job turned out not to be as crucial as other criteria. In Chapter VIII we show, for example, that the ownership of a car seems to make more difference to the variety of leisure. But, in general, we have taken occupation as the guide. In grouping people into classes we have, as explained in Appendix 1, pp. 298–9, used an adaptation of the Registrar-General's scheme, dividing people into the four of Table 1.

In the text, to avoid repetition, we usually describe professional and managerial people simply as 'managerial' or 'managers': more of them were managers than were professionals. All the 'manual' workers together – that is, skilled, semi-skilled and unskilled – are frequently described as the working class and the others as middle.

What London did even more than thoughts about language was to foster dissatisfaction with the very tool of sociology we are employing. The report of a sample enquiry is usually more like a still photograph than a moving picture. The sociologist of the survey, although he likes to distinguish himself from the his-

[1] Office of Population Censuses and Surveys, *The Registrar-General's Decennial Supplement*, *England and Wales*, *1961*, *Occupational Mortality Tables*, p. 18.

TABLE I *Occupational classes in London Region 1970 (main sample)*

Occupational class	*Examples of occupations*	*Proportions among men and women in main sample*
Professional and managerial	Advertising executive, architect, sales manager, teacher	26%
Clerical	Clerk, commercial traveller, insurance agent, shop assistant	15%
Skilled	Bricklayer, compositor, factory foreman, lorry driver	39%
Semi-skilled and unskilled	Bus conductor, labourer, machine minder, porter	20%
	Total %	100%
	Number	1,865

The number of people is less than the 1928 interviews because information on class was incomplete for 63 people. People have similarly been excluded from some later tables where information about them was inadequate.

torian, is always describing the past. The computer, for all its marvellous appearance of speed, may have even increased the time that elapses between survey and publication. It serves up more information which takes longer to digest. So the report of a survey is always an historical document, but one that is not ordinarily treated explicitly in an historical manner.

But the history is there all the same. Authors themselves alter their minds continuously, if only in small ways. They are bound, when they write up their results, to reflect what has occurred in the society around them in the time since their survey was made. They also cannot avoid having views, mostly gathered from other sources, about how things have changed over much longer periods than that and these are bound to colour the interpretation of their results. However much pegged down by professional convention, the static survey is for ever struggling to take wing.

The informants are likewise constantly recapitulating their own personal histories, which are also part of the common history of society. This double process, individual and collective, cannot be even notionally disentangled without taking up an historical position. The failure to do this, to take a perplexing example, is a frequent source of confusion in dealing with people's age. It cannot be kept out of any survey unless all the people included in it were born at more or less the same time. If they were not, what is one to make of it? If the old are unlike the young in the way they vote, or spend their weekends, or take their holidays, or in anything else, the difference is often attributed to the effects of ageing. The supposition is that they have become like that as they got older. The explanation may not be that at all. Ageing has to be distinguished from historical change – change, that is, which has occurred in the society at large of which people of all ages are members.[1] This can be illustrated from our own survey, which showed – to pick out just two small findings – that older people more often went for walks and were more often satisfied with their jobs. Can it be safely concluded that they were like that only because they were older? Clearly not. Such an unqualified conclusion would be legitimate only if there had been no historical change in these respects since the people, now old, were young. If the assumption is abandoned, the possibility has to be reckoned with that the old people are as they are partly because when they were young they walked more and rode less, or were more satisfied with their jobs than people have since become. They may, as they have grown older, not changed but remained as they started out, while younger generations have started off differently, and also stayed the same subsequently; or, more likely, both influences were at work together. The difference may be due to their birth-date in a sequence of ever-changing centuries as well as to their birth-date alone.

The sociologist is inclined to attribute all age differences to the effect of ageing (thereby upholding the boundaries between his profession and the historian's) and we know that we ourselves have sometimes done this in the book. A precisely opposite error is often made by such older people as look grave and deplore present-day youth, say for their idleness, their promiscuity, their clothes, their lack of a sense of duty, their mania for wrecking telephone boxes; and blame social change for it, along with the

[1] This is notably done by D. Butler and D. Stokes, *Political Change in Britain*, especially chapter 30.

young people themselves. They are condemned because they are said to lack the moral stamina that young people once had. It is implied, if not stated, that the critic (even his whole age group) was quite different when he and his peers were young. The stock defence of contemporary youth is to assert that young people are like that because of their age rather than because of historical change. If the same behaviour can be reported from the past, it suggests that age is responsible and, also, that older people may, through a sort of structural amnesia, have forgotten what they were like when they were young. This is the effect that one of us was hoping to create when he quoted what Walter Besant wrote in 1901 about East End boys:[1]

> The boys gather together and hold the street; if anyone ventures to pass through it they rush upon him, knock him down, and kick him savagely about the head; they rob him as well.

The historical approach is the one we would like to see adopted more often with surveys. Once a doubt has been raised about the respective influence of age and general change, the only way to try and resolve it is to seek evidence about how young and old differed from each other in the past and then compare that with the present. We say 'try'. Data from the past can never be directly comparable with those for the present. The fact that the facts have different references on the map of time makes them different. Anyone wondering why his present state is different from his past cannot be sure, even if he has an excellent memory, how much weight should be put upon his age and how much upon his history. Make comparisons across time and, for the sociologist or historian as much as anyone else, all certainties vanish. All interpretations become more disputable and also more realistic.

Our case is that the attempt made in this book to combine sociology with history is done anyway in almost all survey reports. We want to try and do it more explicitly and indicate how a one-shot survey like ours, made in the spring and summer of 1970, can with some plausibility be put into motion. The major premise is that the contemporaneous (1970 – model) co-exists with the non-contemporaneous. There is a simultaneity of the old and

[1] W. Besant, *East London*, p. 177. Quoted in P. Willmott, *Adolescent Boys of East London*.

the new, or, one might say, of the past and present.[1] Our argument is that what is true of buildings and language is also (though less obviously) true of certain habits of behaviour. All older people, as we have been saying, are as they are partly because they have lived through a particular slice of history. But the ancestry of habits goes much further back than that. The ones who have lived through least history may, paradoxically, in some ways be most affected by it – the young children whose children's subculture is still transmitted by word of mouth. The Opies give many examples. Thus London was for the most part contained in one of Britain's nine main truce-term territories,[2] the territory in which children said 'fainites' when they wanted (and usually got) a respite from a fight – the word probably being descended from medieval English and kept alive by children even though adults no longer have truce terms. Many of their catches have historical origins too. The following rhyme repeated by a London schoolboy, who may have also been a follower of the latest pop music, is, for instance, said to derive from 150 years ago:[3]

> Queen, Queen Caroline,
> Dipped her head in turpentine.
> Why did she look so fine?
> Because she wore a crinoline.

Some people in our survey, as in anyone's observation, appeared to belong to the past more than others. The informant who earned her living from her skill with the sewing machine in her dining-room, the materials being brought in and the finished article taken away by a putter-out in a Vauxhall, was more like the domestic handicraftswoman of the eighteenth century than her neighbours who worked in the modern factories of the Slough Trading Estate. The cockle fisherman of Leigh-on-Sea had a motor on his boat, but he fished the same grounds (which he feared would be irrevocably destroyed by the projected airport at Maplin) as

[1] 'The reality and reliability of the human world rest primarily on the fact that we are surrounded by things more permanent than the activity by which they were produced, and potentially even more permanent than the lives of their authors.' H. Arendt, *The Human Condition*, p. 83.

[2] Showing that children at any rate, if not adults, have accepted rituals for limiting the damage done by aggression in just the same way as animals do. K. Lorenz, *On Aggression*.

[3] I. and P. Opie, *The Lore and Language of Schoolchildren*, p. 21.

other fishermen long before him, and in much the same way, being as much controlled as they by the tides. When we saw him, he was preparing on a Thames-side beach for his night-out at sea as the trains from Fenchurch Street brought home the evening wave of commuters.

The point is no doubt obvious enough not to need further illustration: the present – not only as represented in a survey – always summarizes the past.[1] Yet it is not easy to make very much of it in a systematic way. To bring out the dynamic aspect of the survey data we needed not so much to spot anachronisms here and there as to be guided by some kind of working rules, singly or in combination. What we decided to lean on, as the sturdiest prop we could find, was an idea suggested by an author we have already quoted.

Writing in the 1830s, de Tocqueville believed that the spirit he had noticed in the United States was invincible – invincible, that is, in moral terms, equality being the only legitimating principle which commanded general assent. An 'equality of condition' was therefore the great characteristic of America, and 'the democracy which governs the American communities appears to be rapidly rising into power in Europe.'[2]

> As soon as land began to be held on any other than a feudal tenure, and personal property could in its turn counter influence and power, every discovery in the arts, every improvement in commerce or manufactures, created so many new elements of equality among men. Henceforward every new invention, every new want which it occasioned, and every new desire which craved satisfaction were steps towards a general levelling. The taste for luxury, the love of war, the rule of fashion, and the most superficial as well as the deepest passions of the human heart seemed to co-operate to enrich the poor and to impoverish the rich.[3]

Wealth had become more important than birth or power in determining social standing. 'Men living in democratic times have

[1] Another way of putting the same point is to urge that Maeterlinck's plea, 'There are no dead', should be as much heeded by sociologists as Eileen Power said it should be by historians. *Medieval People,* p. vii.

[2] A. de Tocqueville, vol. I, p. 3.

[3] Ibid., p. 5.

many passions, but most of their passions either end in the love of riches or proceed from it.'[1]

A general social levelling has clearly not occurred, in the housing described earlier in this chapter or in anything else. Each adult has only one vote. Employers do not have such despotic power as they once had. Castes have become classes, and the barriers between the classes in terms of relationships between people who meet each other face to face are not so immense. But, as we suggested when discussing the terminology of class, the endurance with which the distribution of incomes and wealth has resisted change is one of the most striking obstinacies of history. The differences between the classes are not markedly less than they were in the past. In 1970, as in every other year of the century, some people were living in the most miserable poverty, crowded together in stinking rooms or without a home at all, while others had servants, chauffeurs and every luxury that was still exclusive enough to be one. De Tocqueville was 'aware that among a great democratic people there will always be some members of the community in great poverty and others in great opulence'.[2] If one interprets him as stressing the tendency for the poor to follow the rich there is more room for agreement. Then what matters is the spread of ambition – 'Having shattered the bonds that once held them fixed, the notion of advancement suggests itself to every mind, the desire to rise swells in every heart, and all men want to mount above their station; ambition is the universal feeling'[3] – and the enhancement of opportunities for the ambition to be fulfilled. It was this aspect of de Tocqueville's account which Bell (who had a major influence on our thinking about the subject) picked on as describing one of the great engines of social change. 'This, in effect, is the realisation of the promise of equality which underlies the founding of this country and the manifestation of Tocqueville's summation of American democracy: What the few have today, the many will demand tomorrow.'[4] Since we are going to refer to it in various places throughout this book, we shall call this the Principle of Stratified Diffusion, or just the Principle for short. There are plenty of exceptions to it, of

[1] Ibid., vol. II, p. 239.
[2] Ibid., p. 266.
[3] Ibid., p. 258.
[4] D. Bell, 'The year 2000 – the trajectory of an idea', p. 643.

course, like country mansions, grouse-shooting, and the domestic servants whose presence or absence marked, for Rowntree, the decisive boundary between the middle and working classes.[1] But that does not deprive the Principle of its value as a general guide to changes which have occurred since the second half of the nineteenth century and may occur in the future.

The image we are trying to suggest is that of a marching column with the people at the head of it usually being the first to wheel in a new direction. The last rank keeps its distance from the first, and the distance between them does not lessen. But as the column advances, the last rank does eventually reach and pass the point which the first rank had passed some time before. In other words, the egalitarian tendency works with a time lag. The people in the rear cannot, without breaking rank and rushing ahead, reach where the van *is*, but, since the whole column is moving forward, they can hope in due course to reach where the van *was*. Lagged equality – always partial, never including everybody – is the nearest approach there has yet been to equality. The sociologist (or anyone else who imagines himself an observer) is not standing on the side like a general, his hand frozen into an everlasting salute; he is himself grimly hurrying along in the column which is at once in the past, the present and the future.

The source of momentum is not too obscure. Without industrialization the column would not be on the move. People would not have had the opportunity to use their own capacities for improvization to make new lives for themselves. With industrialization, mass production has to some extent created new needs in the same mould for everyone. But this does not wholly explain why people should have remained in the line of march, following each other, instead of scattering as single scouts, nor why the people further back should as they push forward have become so conservative about the objectives if not the means of attaining them. Emulation plays a part. People's aspirations are excited by the sight of those who have more than themselves, though more by those close to them in the ranks immediately ahead whose better fortune they may hope to emulate than by the more distant who are so far off at the front that there is little point in comparing them with oneself. 'Whatever the relative magnitudes of relative deprivation, those near the bottom are likely, even in a society

[1] B. S. Rowntree, *Poverty: A Study of Town Life*.

with an egalitarian ideology, to choose reference groups nearer the bottom than self-conscious egalitarianism would imply.'[1] If that were not so, and the people taken as models were the very rich, all societies of the modern sort would, after freeing aspirations, have been torn apart by revolution long before now. If people had not been more intent on achieving equality with those immediately above them than with those far off the diffusion we are describing would not have been lagged and orderly but sudden and violent. Even as it is, there is a constant tension (as we have been ever more aware since our survey was made) between social justice and the market economy. The one requires acceptance of some equality of condition, or, if not that, at least acceptance of the Principle, without too long a delay between the conception and consummation of an ambition; the other has been held to require income inequality as an incentive to effort and to risk.

There is much more than shabby emulation to each stage of a sequence whereby there has been an advance, say, from the stage of the bicycle through the motor bicycle to the car. No doubt some tastes are transmitted from richer to poorer. But we would put much greater emphasis upon another phenomenon, the similarity of people's needs, and their constancy over time. People in all ranks are like each other. They are all human beings, and more and more recognized as such since the democracy which de Tocqueville was writing about has extended its sway. They are thought of in a modern society as having certain physical needs in common, for food, sleep, shelter, warmth and sex, and many others too, like affection, companionship, self-expression, self-respect, power over their environment, and the need to live for something beyond themselves; and when they place their demands (in so far as they reflect common aspirations) in order of priority, they are apt to agree more or less in their relative assessment. Few people without enough to eat would buy a cine-camera. They agree up to a point about the ways in which such needs are articulated and about the elaboration of means for meeting them, and how to discover ever new needs, because they are members of a society with a common value system shared in varying degrees by rich and poor alike. Their aspirations are from a common stock. Travel, or houses with plenty of space, or swimming

[1] W. G. Runciman, op. cit., p. 27.

pools in the back garden, or colour television, are not things which only the rich like, or the poor want because some of the rich already enjoy them. If they have the opportunity to get them the want will not have to be manufactured as well as the product. What the growth of the national income does is to enable successive layers of people, as they get better off, to satisfy the wishes that, by virtue of belonging to the same society with the same general culture, they have anyway.

The Principle applies most clearly to possessions. One historian, in comparing the sixteenth century with the second half of the eighteenth, said that 'In 1530 the majority of English men and women lived in rural households (mostly mud huts) which were almost economically self-sufficient: they wore leather clothes, and ate black bread from wooden trenchers: they used no forks or pocket handkerchiefs. By 1780 England was being transformed by the factory system: brick houses, cotton clothes, white bread, plates and cutlery were becoming accessible even to the lower classes.'[1] As industrialization has proceeded, the same thing has happened with almost everything that has been thrown on the market, from brass bedsteads to spring mattresses, from open grates to central heating, from linoleum to fitted carpeting. It has been common for new products, like television sets or vacuum cleaners, washing machines or refrigerators, to be first taken up more fully by the rich, and then to spread downwards to encompass more and more of the less well off. The tendency for stratified diffusion in the ownership of products is illustrated for a particular decade by Table 2. By 1967 there were for example more refrigerators and TV sets in the bottom class than there had been in the top in 1956. We are not, of course, asserting that *all* diffusion moves like this. There are examples that go the other way.

But, in general terms at any rate, the same thing has happened with other rights than the right to property. The municipal socialism of the nineteenth century and the welfare state of the twentieth have extended to the many some of the other sorts of privileges once reserved for the few.[2] Formal education was once kept mainly for children with parents who could afford to pay; working-class children have increasingly been able to benefit

[1] C. Hill, *Reformation to Industrial Revolution*, p. 9.

[2] T. H. Marshall, 'Citizenship and social class'.

TABLE 2 *Ownership of household equipment by class in 1956 and 1967 (percentages)*

	Washing machine	*Electric refrigerator*	*Steam iron*	*Electric kettle*	*Food mixer*	*Vacuum cleaner*	*Television*
1956							
Professional and managerial	42	25	10	40	5	83	52
Clerical	29	11	7	36	0	74	50
Skilled, semi-skilled, and unskilled manual	13	4	4	23	0	40	35
All housewives	19	7	5	27	1	51	40
1967							
Professional and managerial	75	73	40	65	35	96	91
Clerical	68	57	37	55	17	91	92
Skilled, semi-skilled, and unskilled manual	56	37	31	42	7	76	89
All housewives	61	46	33	48	13	81	90

These results are from surveys carried out for Odham's Press (now part of the International Publishing Corporation) and originally published under the general title of *WOMAN and the National Market*, 1956 and 1967. The sample size was about 4,000 in 1956 and about 6,000 in 1967. The social class categories, based on the past or present occupations of the heads of households, were differently labelled in the Odham's reports – 'AB' corresponding to what we have called 'Professional and managerial', 'C1' to 'Clerical' and 'C2 DE' to 'Skilled, semi-skilled and unskilled manual'.

from it.[1] Medical care beyond the most primitive kind was likewise once the prerogative of those who could afford it; the National Health Service has brought it to all. Access to public housing, for all the impediments; the old age pension, despite its meanness; welfare benefits of various kinds, for all their inadequacies, show that in a democracy a narrowing can be achieved by political action,[2] if with the usual time-lag. Citizens may still be lower-class; they are not second-class in the way they were. One cannot any longer so convincingly draw the principal distinction that Mayhew did between the well-fed portion of society and the rest. A London at night could still be described as he described it in 1849, not so much the people.[3]

> The noblest prospect in the world, it has been well said, is London viewed from the suburbs on a clear winter's evening. The stars are shining in the heavens, but there is another firmament spread out below, with its millions of bright lights glittering at our feet. Line after line sparkles, like the trails left by meteors, cutting and crossing one another till they are lost in the haze of the distance. Over the whole there hangs a livid cloud, bright as if the monster city were in flames, and looking afar off like the sea by night, made phosphorescent by the million creatures dwelling within it. At night it is that the strange anomalies of London are best seen. Then, as the hum of life ceases and the shops darken, and the gaudy gin palaces thrust out their ragged and squalid crowds, to pace the streets, London puts on its most solemn look of all. On the benches of the parks, in the niches of the bridges, and in the litter of the markets, are huddled together the homeless and the destitute.

Despite the changes, there are obviously many people who are too poor to take much comfort from the fact that they may be somewhat better-off than their parents and better-off than their ancestors in Mayhew's time. Aspirations can sometimes run

[1] The main contemporary issue in the long unfolding of the educational system has been about comprehensive schools. See J. M. Ross, *et al., A Critical Appraisal of Comprehensive Education*.

[2] Briggs quotes Bulwer Lytton as saying that 'While social habits descend from the upper class to the lower class, political principles, on the contrary, are reverberations travelling from the base to the apex of society'. A. Briggs, *Victorian Cities*, p. 359.

[3] E. P. Thompson and E. Yeo, *The Unknown Mayhew*, pp. 101–2.

ahead of fulfilment, and then the downward spread of the fruits of industrialization may actually make things worse for people who can see that others they think of as like themselves are obtaining benefits of which they are deprived. This is particularly liable to happen when inflation removes the stable benchmarks by which advancement can be measured. It always hits hardest at the poor. In or out of inflation, collective action is their best hope of securing what the rich can get as individuals from the market economy.

Whether or not diffusion leaves people dissatisfied depends partly upon the manner in which it operates. If it happens through an increase in the size of the top class, the few then become the many by the top class embracing more people within it. There has certainly been an enlargement of this kind. The trend has been visible in every industrialized country. In our Region and in the country as a whole the proportion of men in the professional and managerial classes has been rising, and that of semi-skilled and unskilled workers falling. If this trend persists, without any acceleration or deceleration, the changes by the end of the century will be something like those shown in Table 3. The differences between the London Region and the rest of the country seem likely to remain. But in Region and country the numbers in the professional and managerial classes may well rise to a third or more of the total by 2001 and the relatively unskilled manual workers decline to one in six or less.

TABLE 3 *Occupational class projections for working and retired men in London Region and United Kingdom*

	London Region			*United Kingdom*		
	1951	1966	2001	1951	1966	2001
Professional and managerial	18%	24%	38%	16%	20%	33%
Clerical and skilled manual	52%	51%	49%	51%	51%	51%
Semi-skilled and unskilled	30%	25%	13%	33%	29%	16%

Sources: Calculations and forecasts based upon Census data for 1951 and 1966. The forecast for the United Kingdom was made for the leisure analysis described in Appendix 5.

In so far as diffusion works solely in this way it will benefit the socially mobile people who move up into the top class that is expanding, but not people in other classes. Nor will it affect them if the increase is in the incidence of new behaviour just within the top class. There is an example of such a change in Chapter V where we suggest that managers have generally been working longer hours, in the week at least, than they did in the past. It is only when diffusion operates by spreading downwards from one class to another that a new pattern will become general.

There can obviously be changes which spread in only one of these ways. But in practice they have usually acted in combination, the one change reinforcing the other. A particular manifestation becomes more common in the top class, embraces more people for the further reason that the top class has been expanding, and, spreading downwards with all the more force, becomes more common in other classes. When that happens the whole society alters in that respect. Whether a change moves through the whole social structure in this way or whether it leaves some people out is, of course, an empirical matter. So is the related question of the speed of the movement, or (as it can be put) the amplitude of the wave-lengths for different kinds of change.[1] The period between the introduction of new consumer durables and something like saturation of the market may be as short as a quarter of a century, even less for some cheaper goods. With family structure the cycles are much longer. It has taken a century for the fall in family size to spread right down the class hierarchy. Other changes in the family may be slower still. We have in this book therefore taken as our span the two centuries or so since the Industrial Revolution began to grip.

If we had the facts we would have liked to interlace age with class. Its importance is also clear. Many changes are taken up first by younger people before being transmitted through society. Fashions in clothes, music and hair-style have, for example, been spread in this way, with the key innovators sometimes not middle- but working-class people. Within their age groups, young working-class earners are often richer than others in the purchasing power they can expend directly on themselves. If new habits spread downwards from richer to poorer people in an age group, that is in accord with the Principle. But what happens subse-

[1] M. Young and J. Ziman, 'Cycles in social behaviour'.

quently is in accord with the other principle, of age. Some relatively large changes in attitude and behaviour take as long as a life-span to permeate the whole society, change being complete only when those who were the youngest have become the oldest. Others, like the new fashions we have mentioned, can spread more quickly, from the younger to the older, without waiting for the bearers of the new behaviour to grow older. Wherever the young have prestige – for instance, in everything in which youth excels, especially to do with sex – they are the 'ruling class', and older people may envy and even emulate them. We have not made much of the age principle in this book. Information comparing people of the same age over time is too sparse. But we look forward to the day when 'trickle down' is mingled with 'trickle up', and the interaction of the two influences elaborated to s how how change works simultaneously downwards from the top to the bottom of the class structure and upwards from the bottom to the top of the age structure.

On our main subject there has been no full history. 'It is a sad comment on British historiography that while we have a great many studies of political parties, trade unions and religious bodies, there is not a single history of the basic social institution of British life, the family. Until some attempt has been made to fill this gap it is impossible to write with assurance about family life in the nineteenth century, or to do more than hazard a few guesses at the nature of the impact of industrialism upon the home.'[1] After Harrison wrote that statement, Anderson went some way towards filling the gap by documenting kinship patterns in one town, Preston, as well as in rural Lancashire and Ireland.[2] The fourfold scheme that we put forward in this book will obviously become more differentiated, the interpretations more sophisticated, when the whole job has been done by historians, rather than sociologists, and changes in family structure related in all their complexity to demography.

But we believe enough is already known to allow a partial reconstruction to be made. By way of preview we should summarize the theme we shall elaborate in later chapters. The process of change, as we are interpreting it, has so far proceeded through

[1] J. F. C. Harrison, *The Early Victorians*, p. 73.

[2] M. Anderson, *Family Structure in Nineteenth Century Lancashire*.

three stages. Even though there is so much in common between family life at each stage, and even though the boundaries between one stage and another are somewhat arbitrary, the rough-and-ready division seems to us useful, as does the generalization, even though it cannot any more than most generalizations do justice to all the evidence. In the first stage, the pre-industrial, the family was usually the unit of production. For the most part, men, women and children worked together in home and field. This type of economic partnership was, for working-class people, supplanted after a bitter struggle by the Stage 2 family, whose members were caught up in the new economy as individual wage-earners. The collective was undermined. Stage 2 was the stage of disruption. One historian has pointed the contrast in this way:[1]

> Women became more dependent upon the employer or the labour market, and they looked back to a 'golden' period in which home earnings from spinning, poultry and the like, could be gained around their own door. In good times the domestic economy, like the peasant economy, supported a way of life centred upon the home, in which inner whims and compulsions were more obvious than external discipline. Each stage in industrial differentiation and specialisation struck also at the family economy, disturbing customary relations between man and wife, parents and children, and differentiating more sharply between 'work' and 'life'. It was to be a full hundred years before this differentiation was to bring returns, in the form of labour-saving devices, back into the working woman's home. Meanwhile, the family was roughly torn apart each morning by the factory bell.

The process affected most the families of manual workers (and not all of these by any means). The trends were different in the middle-class family, where the contrasts for both husbands and wives were somewhat less sharp than they had been in the past. But as working-class people were preponderant most families were probably 'torn apart' by the new economic system. In the third stage the unity of the family has been restored around its functions as the unit not of production but of consumption.

It is clearly not possible, since social history is unlike political or military history, to do more by way of dating than to indicate

[1] E. P. Thompson, *The Making of the English Working Class*, p. 416.

in a rough manner when the successive waves of change started moving through the social structure. The Stage 1 family lasted until the new industry overran it in a rolling advance which went on from the eighteenth well into the nineteenth century. The development of the new industry was uneven as between different parts of the country, coming much later to London than to the industrial north. It also outmoded the old techniques of production more slowly in some occupations than in others. But come it did, eventually, along with many other forms of employment which shared one vital feature, that the employees worked for wages. This led to the Stage 2 family. The third stage started earlier in the twentieth century and is still working its way downwards. At any one period there were, and still are, families representing all three stages. But as first one wave and then another has been set in motion, the proportions in Stage 2 increased in the nineteenth century and in Stage 3 in the twentieth.

The new kind of family has three main characteristics which differentiate it from the sort which prevailed in Stage 2. The first is that the couple, and their children, are very much centred on the home, especially when the children are young. They can be so much together, and share so much together, because they spend so much of their time together in the same space. Life has, to use another term, become more 'privatized'.[1] We shall argue in the next chapter that this trend has been supported by the form taken by technological change.

The second characteristic is that the extended family (consisting of relatives of several different degrees to some extent sharing a common life) counts for less and the immediate, or nuclear, family for more. We have not been able to discover much documentary evidence about kinship patterns in nineteenth-century England. People certainly often lived with or near relatives,[2] and we would expect, for the reasons we give in Chapter III, that daughters more often maintained close links with their parents, and particularly with their mothers, than sons did with theirs. Extended families must have been used for mutual aid. But we doubt, along with Anderson, whether they became so pervasive and so much the arena of women's lives until this century. Our belief is that since the second war, in particular, there has been a

[1] J. H. Goldthorpe *et al.*, *The Affluent Worker in the Class Structure*, p. 97.

[2] See M. Anderson, op. cit., pp. 56–62.

further change and that the nuclear family has become relatively more isolated in the working as in other classes.

The third and most vital characteristic is that inside the family of marriage the roles of the sexes have become less segregated. The difference between two contemporary families of the 1950s, with and without segregated roles, has been well described by Bott.[1]

> There was considerable variation in the way husbands and wives performed their conjugal roles. At one extreme was a family in which the husband and wife carried out as many tasks as possible separately and independently of each other. There was a strict division of labour in the household, in which she had her tasks and he had his. He gave her a set amount of housekeeping money, and she had little idea of how much he earned or how he spent the money he kept for himself. In their leisure time, he went to cricket matches with his friends, whereas she visited her relatives or went to a cinema with a neighbour. With the exception of festivities with relatives, this husband and wife spent very little of their leisure time together. They did not consider that they were unusual in this respect. On the contrary, they felt their behaviour was typical of their social circle. At the other extreme was a family in which husband and wife shared as many activities and spent as much time together as possible. They stressed that husband and wife should be equals: all major decisions should be made together, and even in minor household matters they should help one another as much as possible. This norm was carried out in practice. In their division of labour, many tasks were shared or inter-changeable. The husband often did the cooking and sometimes the washing and ironing. The wife did the gardening and often the household repairs as well. Much of their leisure time was spent together, and they shared similar interests in politics, music, literature, and in entertainment. Like the first couple, this husband and wife felt their behaviour was typical of their social circle, except that they carried the inter-changeability of tasks a little further than most people.

Bott was writing fifteen years ago, and not many families have yet

[1] E. Bott, *Family and Social Network*, pp. 52–3.

got as far as the second couple. Power has not been distributed equally in more than a few families. Division of labour is still the rule, with the husband doing the 'man's' work and the wife taking prime responsibility for the housekeeping and the children. We shall show in Chapter IV that this applies to the majority of families. But the direction of change has, we believe, been from Bott's first to her second type.

Many different terms have been used for the new kind of family that is emerging. Since it has so many facets to it, a single apt word is not easy to find. Burgess and Locke said, a quarter of a century ago, that the family had moved from 'institution to companionship',[1] and their words 'companionship family' have sometimes found favour, although not with us. The members of a family are more (or less) than companions. For the same reason we do not like 'companionate', as employed by Goldthorpe and his colleagues.[2] We have ourselves talked about 'partnership' and the 'home-centred' family,[3] but these words too are open to objection, the former because it is so general as to be applicable to all forms of marriage, and the latter because, although it stresses one of the distinguishing characteristics we have just mentioned, it does not now seem to us to stress the most important of them, the desegregation of roles. The new family could be labelled simply egalitarian. But that would not square with the marked differences that still remain in the human rights, in the work opportunities[4] and generally in the way of life of the two sexes. The term which is best, in our view, is the one used by Gorer, the 'symmetrical family', although the emphasis we want to give is not the same as his. He said that, 'In a symmetrical relationship A responds to B as B responds to A; the differences of temperament, of function, of skills are all minimised.'[5] We think it is closer to the facts of the situation as it is now to preserve the notion of difference but

[1] E. Burgess and H. J. Locke, *The Family: From Institution to Companionship*, p. 22.

[2] J. H. Goldthorpe, *et al.*, *The Affluent Worker in the Class Structure*, p. 108.

[3] M. Young and P. Willmott, *Family and Kinship in East London*, pp. 11–14, 117–120, and P. Willmott and M. Young, *Family and Class in a London Suburb*, pp. 15–27.

[4] Oakley has pointed out how far from equality opportunities are in industry. 'In factories, a division of labour between the sexes is invariably maintained, supported by references to "natural" differences between the sexes and to the economic efficiency that would be lost if the work roles of men and women were interchangeable'. *Sex, Gender and Society*, p. 197.

[5] G. Gorer, op. cit., p. 62.

ally it to a measure of egalitarianism. In this context the essence of a symmetrical relationship is that it is opposite but similar.[1] If all segregation of roles ever disappeared (apart from that minimum prescribed by the dictatorship of a biology from which there is for most people no escape) then one might properly talk about egalitarian marriage. But to be fair to what has happened in this century a term is needed which can describe the majority of families in which there is some role-segregation along with a greater degree of equality than at Stage 2.

We must make it clear, in case we have failed to do so up to now, that we do not think that the Principle of Stratified Diffusion applied until the second half of the nineteenth century to family structure or indeed to much else. It had to wait until the new ideas of democracy had freed people's aspirations and the new products of industry had satisfied some of them. So the middle classes did not lead the movement from the first to the second stage. Their families were not broken up in the way that Thompson described, nor were those of many skilled workers. But the middle classes were the first to enter the third stage, reducing the numbers of their children and adopting other features of the new family. They have been followed by successive strata of the population. The main question posed by the 1970 survey is whether a new, fourth phase is now being initiated in the same class to ripple its way with the same wave-motion through the structure of society in the next century. Before we get to that we need to sketch the history of the family in a little more detail. The emphasis is on the working class who were still predominant in 1970, constituting about 60 per cent of the population, and used to be a good deal more so in a century when the contrasts between the classes were even sharper than in this.[2] In Chapter II we shall describe how home-centredness has been achieved in the setting of London, and in Chapter III how a more symmetrical relationship has been created within marriage.

[1] Amongst those given by the *Oxford English Dictionary* the definition of 'symmetrical' which is nearest, though not identical, to what we have in mind is 'Exact correspondence in size and position of opposite parts; equable distribution of parts about a dividing line or centre. As an attribute either of the whole or of the parts composing it'.

[2] 'In the 1870s eleven-to-twelve-year-old boys from the upper-class public schools were on average five inches taller than boys from industrial schools and at all teen-ages three inches taller than the sons of artisans'. E. J. Hobsbawm, *Industry and Empire*, p. 164.

One limitation that affects all the chapters to come is that on many matters evidence from the past of London did not, as far as we could discover, exist. We have therefore had to draw on the past of the country of which London is a part. To make use of data for London for speculation about the more general future, as we shall also do, is perhaps more justifiable. If our Principle holds, then London, being richer now than the rest of the country, should be more reliable as a pointer – perhaps a warning – than any other district of similar size within it. It is in this respect, if not in others, the leading sector for the country as a whole.

To sum up, the first main idea we have presented in this chapter is that past and future are embodied in the present. The second is summed up in our Principle – that many social changes start at the top and work downwards. The people in the van of the column, to return to our metaphor, should foreshadow what those at the rear will be doing tomorrow, just as those at the rear represent the past of those ahead of them. So if there is a change visible at the upper end of the class spectrum it may well be a portent of a more general change. We have sketched out how we are going to apply these ideas to the family.

II

EXPANSION OF THE METROPOLIS

And now back to London. Throughout the last century people flocked into it, as into other cities. 'And what cities!', said Hobsbawm. 'Smoke hung over them and filth impregnated them . . . the elementary public services – water supply, sanitation, street cleaning, open spaces, etc. – could not keep pace with the mass migration of men into the cities, thus producing, especially after 1830, epidemics of cholera, typhoid and an appalling constant toll of the two great groups of nineteenth century urban killers – air pollution and water pollution, or respiratory and intestinal disease.'[1]

The newcomers to London were mostly poor people seeking work. Some of them maintained the family as a productive unit and carried on their trade in their own homes. They lived on the job, like the weavers who slept either on the ground floor of their homes and worked upstairs, or slept and worked in their 'loom sheds' with their large windows on the first floor. Some of these cottages still survive near Spitalfields. In combining work and home, they were, in much lesser state, like the City guildsmen of previous centuries whose gardens were converted into the courtyards which honeycomb behind Cheapside, Lombard Street and Threadneedle Street. Wren's house by the Bankside power station has its garden still.

Most of the migrants, however, had to work for others and, since London was a pedestrian city, they had to live near enough to their job to be able to walk to it, even if it meant piling one upon the other to do so. In 1801 London already contained about a million people. By 1851 the population had more than doubled. In 1801 people in the most crowded districts of Central London

[1] E. J. Hobsbawm, *Industry and Empire*, p. 67.

were living 149 to the acre; by 1851 the density had risen to 165.[1] Things did not get much better after that. Population rose by natural increase as well as migration, and the space demands of industry and commerce became more and more severe. Over much of the nineteenth century the norm for a working-class family was one room, and even that did not become any easier to find and hold.

A family sharing a room was often a family sharing a bed. Lord Shaftesbury spoke in 1885 about one of the consequences, with a frankness not all that common.[2]

> It is a benefit to the children to be absent during the day, but when they return to their houses, they unlearn in one hour, almost everything they have acquired during the day . . . a friend of mine . . . going down one of the back courts, saw on the pavement two children of tender years, of 10 or 11 years old, endeavouring to have sexual connection on the pathway. He ran and seized the lad, and pulled him off, and the only remark of the lad was 'Why do you take hold of me? There are a dozen of them at it down there.' You must perceive that that could not arise from sexual tendencies, and that it must have been bred by imitation of what they saw.

The sort of housing people had to put up with can be illustrated from Bethnal Green and the neighbouring districts (being those we have ourselves known best over part of the next century) as well as it can from anywhere else. Conditions were no doubt worse here than in other poor areas in the centre, but not much. Engels, writing in 1845, quoted from what the Vicar of St Philip's in Bethnal Green had reported about his parish a year earlier:[3]

> It contains 1,400 houses, inhabited by 2,795 families, comprising a population of 12,000. The space within which this large amount of population are living is less than 400 yards square, and it is no uncommon thing for a man and his wife, with four or five children, and sometimes the grandfather and grandmother, to be found living in a room from ten to twelve

[1] P. Hall *et al.*, *The Containment of Urban England,* vol. I, p. 76.

[2] Quoted in G. S. Jones, *Outcast London*, p. 224.

[3] F. Engels, *The Condition of the Working Class in England,* pp. 35–6. For a general account of housing in London see A. S. Wohl, 'The housing of the working class in London'.

feet square, and which serves them for eating and working in. I believe that till the Bishop of London called the attention of the public to the state of Bethnal Green, about as little was known at the West End of the town of this most destitute parish as the wilds of Australia or the islands of the South Seas. If we really desire to find out the most destitute and deserving, we must lift the latch of their doors, and find them at their scanty meal; we must see them when suffering from sickness and want of work; and if we do this from day to day in such a neighbourhood as Bethnal Green, we shall become acquainted with a mass of wretchedness and misery such as a nation like our own ought to be ashamed to permit. I was Curate of a parish near Huddersfield during the three years of the greatest manufacturing distress; but I never witnessed such a thorough prostration of the poor as I have seen since I have been in Bethnal Green. There is not one father of a family in ten throughout the entire district that possess any clothes but his working dress, and that too commonly in the worst tattered condition; and with many this wretched clothing forms their only covering at night, with nothing better than a bag of straw or shavings to lie upon.

Each 'improvement' thereafter was even more a cause of suffering than some similar ones have been in this century. Builders of railways and roads were the first destroyers. Wherever they could, railway promoters avoided the districts where the wealthy lived so as to ride around their opposition. Instead, their lines were routed through districts like ours, whose protests could be ignored. Its Medical Officer of Health said in 1864:[1]

Owing to the demolition of houses in the neighbouring parishes to make room for railways, a large influx of persons has taken place into our own, and has aggravated the greatest evil with which we have to contend, and that is overcrowding. The parish – always full – is now filled to excess, although a large number of dwellings have been recently erected. Houses even in a bad condition are sure to find occupants, and as there is great difficulty in procuring houseroom, the tenants endeavour to conceal their sanitary wants,

[1] *Tenth Annual Report of the Medical Officer of Health, Bethnal Green,* p. 4. Quoted in G. S. Jones, op. cit., p. 163.

> fearing that they will be compelled to remove while the needful improvements are being made.

Docks were the second agent of destruction. St Katharine Docks in the neighbouring district of Stepney destroyed 1,033 houses in 1828 (as against the 750 that were going to be gained, together with a hotel and a Trade Centre, by restoring the Docks to housing in the 1970s). The third was industry and commerce; they took over and converted what had been homes before. The effects of these various changes upon the stock of housing were especially noticeable in times of depression. The same Medical Officer of Health said in 1867 that 'many families who could ordinarily afford to occupy a whole house have been obliged to let lodgings, others who put up with two rooms have been obliged to put up with one.'[1]

People from overseas added to the pressure. After the Jewish immigration Bethnal Green had to bear some part of the load which spilled over from Whitechapel. Beatrice Webb – Beatrice Potter as she was then, before she married – said in 1888:[2]

> The Jewish coat-making industry is practically concentrated within an area of less than one square mile, comprising the whole of Whitechapel, a small piece of Mile End, and part of St George's in the East. In this quarter thirty or forty thousand Jews of all nationalities and from all countries congregate, and form in the midst of our cosmopolitan metropolis a compact Jewish community. Judisch is a language of the streets, and Hebrew characters are common in shop windows and over doorways. Overcrowding in all its forms, whether in the close packing of human beings within four walls, or in the filling up of every available building space with dwellings and workshops is the distinguishing mark of the district. The percentage of persons per acre rises to 227; the highest at the East End.

No doubt people who lived like this were 'home-centred' in one way: they had to spend much of their time, at night anyway, under the same roof with their family. But people whose standards

[1] *Report of Medical Officer of Health, Bethnal Green,* 1867, p. 4. Quoted in G. S. Jones, op. cit., p. 178.

[2] B. Potter, 'The tailoring trade', p. 46.

were not the lowest must have found it hard to call it a home or to preserve there the old rules and sanctions of the rural communities which many of them had left. For those who emulated Queen Victoria, with her nine children but without her palaces, the room must have been something they were glad to escape from, even the crowded streets a relief. The people in one of the great rookeries of Bethnal Green, as described a few years later by Arthur Morrison in *Child of the Jago*, were off and away whenever they could. Though the air was as polluted by smoke as the water was by the drains, the life with some colour was outside in the streets and courts, not inside. The streets, especially in more prosperous districts, were thronged with peddlers, pickpockets and other thieves, with people hurrying along on foot, and with others trying to hurry by horse or in carriages which were almost as much a threat to pedestrians as cars have since become. It was not true that you could do what you liked in London as long as you did not do it in the street; for there was hardly anywhere else.

The centrifugal movement

Throughout the two centuries a counter-force has been at work. Jobs pulled people in; transport has propelled them out. The richer have always been the first to take advantage of each new technical advance. 'The beginnings of a middle class migration to the new suburbs had been revealed in the middle of the 18th century.'[1] The rich were the only people who could move sitting down. The poor had to travel by foot for a lot longer. Even by the mid-nineteenth century, according to one historian, 'Camberwell was little more than a mile and a half from the City at its closest point, and it must have made its contribution to the 200,000 walkers who were reckoned to file daily into the City along the principal roads in the 1850s.'[2]

But by then the transport improvements, which took people off their feet, were well under way. For the beginning any date is arbitrary. The year 1829 is as good as any other. The horse-bus was introduced then. Although the locomotor was old, what it

[1] G. S. Jones, op. cit., p. 159.

[2] H. J. Dyos, *Victorian Suburb*, p. 69. Dickens said that the 'early clerk population of Somers and Camden Towns, Islington and Pentonville, are fast pouring into the City, and directing their steps towards Chancery Lane, and the Inns of Court'. C. Dickens, *Sketches by Boz*, p. 51.

pulled was new. As Pollins has pointed out,[1] the speed of the bus was about 5 m.p.h. For those who could afford an hour's travelling, settlement was extended to some four or five miles from the centre. The horse-bus was followed by three crucial inventions – the steam, electric and internal combustion engines.

Steam brought the first main line and the first two local railways to London in the 1830s. It was thought that they would affect poorer people most, whether for ill or good depending upon the point of view. The Duke of Wellington was the pessimist. 'Progress be damned,' he said. 'All this will do is to allow the lower classes to move around unnecessarily.'[2] The *Manchester Guardian* was the optimist.[3]

> The birth of this new and cheap means of transit is as if the wings of the wind had been given for a week to the closely confined operative, the hardworking mechanic, and the counter-riveted shopkeeper. They enjoy the needful relaxation from the toil or care or confinement of business; they see new scenes and acquire new tastes for the beautiful in nature, as whirled along by the steam-car, they rush, 'Forth to fresh fields, and pastures new'.

In fact the steam-car did not begin to make mass travel possible until thirty years later. In 1863 the first section of the Underground was opened. In the first decade of this century electric traction further increased the speed and convenience of the Underground trains, and of the trams which had, like the buses, begun by being horse-drawn. Then came the third, the smallest and most crucial of the trio of engines.

One after another these innovations extended the built-up area. In an historical series of maps of it the first ones were like blobs of ink. In 1831 the mass was mostly in the middle where we started this chapter, with threads of black leading out along the main coaching roads and around the villages like Croydon, Barnet and Chiswick. When steam trains added their greater carrying power, growth was still tentacular, near to the railway lines and, especially,

[1] H. Pollins, 'Transport lines and social divisions', p. 34. In the same decade there was also new competition from the river, with steamboats being put into service to carry passengers daily to Greenwich, Woolwich and Gravesend.

[2] R. Arvill, *Man and Environment*, p. 77.

[3] Quoted J. A. R. Pimlott, *The Englishman's Holiday*, p. 95.

their stations: people still had to walk that far.[1] Electric trains again shifted the form. Because of the greater acceleration, stations could be more frequent and, later, motor bus feeder services widened their catchments. Each new railway, up to the Northern Line completed in 1940 and the Victoria Line opened in 1968, has added to the spread. The difference made by the car is that people have been able to untie themselves from the collective. The small machine which has to some extent replaced the big has filled in the spaces between the main radii. The black has spread less like an ink blot and (Green Belt apart) more like a saucer filling with tea, in all directions at once. The old villages and towns of the region have been swallowed up physically, remaining, if at all, as places whose boundaries are not on the map but in people's minds. Many of the communities within the urban fabric can 'be traced back to the original villages which existed when the capital was no larger than present-day Southampton'.[2]

The people who have moved out have left a little more space for those who did not. To cite Bethnal Green once more, in the forty years from 1911 to 1951 the proportion of people living at more than two to a room fell from a third to 3 per cent. Throughout Central London the same thing has happened. At one of the nuclei, in the City of London, the population began to decline in 1851.[3] It was then 127,819. By 1966 it had fallen to 4,850, although the day-time employed population of the Square Mile was 360,000.[4] The same stripping process has gradually enveloped wider and wider areas. Table 4 shows that, taken as a whole, Inner London, until 1965 the County of London, had reached its peak by 1911. By 1981 'Inner London will have a good deal less than three million inhabitants compared with four and a half million fifty years ago.'[5] The ring which constitutes the rest of Greater London reached its peak in about 1951. The mountain has lost height, and right at the centre has become a bowl. The process is expected to continue, with the Outer Metropolitan

[1] P. Hall, *et al.*, op. cit., p. pp. 81–2.

[2] J. H. Forshaw and P. Abercrombie, *County of London Plan*, p. 25. See J. Baker and M. Young, *The Hornsey Plan*, for an account of the way communities continue to exist, and are given importance, in people's minds.

[3] J. T. Coppock, 'A general view of London and its environs', p. 33.

[4] J. H. Dunning and E. V. Morgan, *An Economic Study of the City of London*, p. 34.

[5] *Greater London Development Plan, Subject Evidence – Stage 1: General Strategy and Implementation.*

Area, and the ring beyond that in the Outer South East, continuing to grow both absolutely and relatively.[1] The people of these areas are similarly motivated and similarly motorized.

TABLE 4 *Changes in the population of London from 1861 to 1971*

	Inner London	*Outer Greater London*	*Outer Metropolitan Area*	*London Region*
1861	2,808,000	414,000	1,013,000	4,235,000
1911	4,523,000	2,730,000	1,894,000	9,147,000
1931	4,397,000	3,907,000	1,899,000	10,203,000
1951	3,348,000	4,998,000	3,319,000	11,665,000
1961	3,198,000	4,799,000	4,282,000	12,279,000
1966	3,000,000	4,671,000	4,906,000	12,577,000
1971	2,723,000	4,656,000	5,290,000	12,699,000

Source: Census reports.

The centrifugal movement has always been channelled. The expedition to gain a small territory for a new home has often been within a larger territory which the migrant has explored before venturing out for good. Much of the outward migration has been sectoral, along the main transport routes, rail and road, which radiate from the centre. People mostly go to the nearest place with space for new houses, and quite often, it seems, they are put in mind of it by visiting it beforehand on a trip to the country. They see the trees and the houses, they sniff the air if they get out of their vehicles, they like what they see and smell, and half-decide that if ever they do move, Surbiton or Enfield, Penge or Marlow would be the place for them. Staying in the same sector also means that if children go on with the same school they can travel back to it more easily, and parents to their friends or, if they do not change jobs, to their workplace.

Although we did not expect that sectoral movements would be so common in the car age as they were in the railway age – cars can shuttle between the radials – we thought it was worth seeing

[1] South East Joint Planning Team, *Strategic Plan for the South East.* Also, as well as the main report, see *Studies, vol. 1: Population and Employment.*

how many there were. For this purpose we sliced the map of Greater London into five – the boroughs north of the Thames and east of the River Lea, plus Tower Hamlets; those north of the Thames, west of the Lea and east of Harrow, Brent and Westminster; the remaining boroughs north of the Thames; those south of the Thames and west of Southwark and Bromley; and the remaining boroughs south of the Thames. We extended each boundary into the Outer Metropolitan Area, and then saw whether the people who had moved within the Region during the previous ten years had stayed within the same sector. Detailed information was not available for 10 per cent of the people who had moved. Among the remaining 573, 81 per cent had migrated within the same sector, mainly outwards, the Thames being a particularly crucial barrier. Families had, for example, gone from Islington, Hackney and Tottenham to Enfield,[1] from Poplar and East Ham to Dagenham, from Wandsworth and Wimbledon to Sutton, from North Kensington and Fulham to Ealing, from Harrow and Wembley to Watford, from Stoke Newington and Finchley to Stevenage, from Norwood and Croydon to Caterham.

When people had the chance to move up – up being synonymous with out – many of them moved straight up and out along the shortest route they knew to the place they knew.

> Mrs Jordan was an example of a person who had not yet, but hoped to. She was a 34-year-old Southwark housewife. With her husband, a plumber, and her two young children, she had lived the 12 years of her marriage in three rooms on the top floor of a two-storey Victorian house in a terraced street off the Walworth Road. The house had recently been bought up by the Council who would be demolishing the street within two or three years. Mrs Jordan was pleased – 'We hate this place', she said – but she did not relish the thought of moving into a local council flat. 'We'd prefer a house, with a garden.

[1] The pattern of migration in and out was the subject, for Enfield in particular, of a study of Census data for 1961 and 1966, carried out by the borough's Department of Architecture and Planning. This showed that of the migrants into the borough, 59 per cent had moved from within the same sector as we have defined it; 26 per cent came from Haringey, the next borough 'in' to Central London. Of the people who had left the borough, 35 per cent had moved out within the sector, 22 per cent to Hertfordshire in particular. This analysis, unlike ours, excluded people moving within the borough. *Report on The Changing Nature of Residential Areas*, pp. 11–12.

We'd like more room of course wherever we went - a bedroom for us and one for each of the children, and a dining room away from the kitchen. And I'd love a bathroom; at the moment we use Mum's over the road.' She wanted to move to Eltham or Sidcup, respectively about five and ten miles 'out' from her part of Southwark. 'To me it's nearer the country. You could call it a suburb – fresh air but in easy reach of London. It would be better for the kiddies out there.'

Motor and motive

If transport has supplied the motor for the centrifugal expansion, space has provided the motive. The most sophisticated technology has been harnessed to one of the most primitive drives. Space may not have quite the importance it had in Stage 1 when without land there was in an agricultural society no economic security. But there are other kinds of security that territory can bestow, like security of tenure to a particular house or plot, and the emotional security that comes from being able to control space that others cannot ordinarily turn one out of. A special characteristic of the spatial appetite is that it is not as easily sated as that for food or drink, vacuum cleaners or, perhaps, cars. Even people with a lot would like more.

So important is it that one could, if one made the measurements on a large scale, tease out an index of prestige based on space alone which would tally pretty well with other scales, and perhaps even serve as a general indicator of social class as useful as occupation. We did just that by way of example with three tolerant informants at different levels in the hierarchy of a particular furniture company. The manager had a London house of about 4,600 square feet, a cottage in Sussex of 2,500 and an office of 600 (or 900 if his secretary's suite was added in), making some 8,000 square feet whose entrances and exits he controlled. An accounts clerk had a suburban house of 950 square feet, and an office 'space' of 150, making 1,100 in all, while a machinist had a flat of 550 feet and a work space of 150, or 700 in all. Judged by this ready reckoner, the manager had seven times more prestige than the clerk or eleven times more than the machinist.

The Civil Service had (and has) a particularly famous grading system. At the time of the survey a Permanent Secretary was entitled to an office of 500 to 550 square feet; a Deputy Secretary to 400 to 450; an Under Secretary to 250 to 350; a Principal to 150 to 200; right down to the depths of the Clerical Officer or Scientific Assistant with an allowance of 55 to 65. The ratio was something like eight or ten to one. The University Grants Committee likewise allowed the Vice-Chancellor more than the Professor and the Professor more than the Lecturer below him. Every company, not only the one mentioned above, followed suit. At the top, often literally at the top of the building, was the managing director in a big room whose size could be stressed in various ways, by the secretary being too unctuous about opening the door, by the man himself starting off a little too ostentatiously on the long walk across his large carpet to shake hands, his voice rising too much, ringing around the walls as if to emphasize that the big room had a big man in it.[1] Then came the executives of different levels in their descending order of slot-sizes; the foreman with his desk or cubby hole; and most of the workers with tiny private areas around their machines with invisible boundaries around them which others, if they had any respect, would respect. The houses where they lived roughly accorded with the examples we have given, though there were exceptions, some rich people for instance being prepared to accept a relatively small home with a small garden or none if it was close to Central London; they had sacrificed space for accessibility. But in general people's homes corresponded in size with the scales at work. Some worked, lived and travelled first class; others others. With the homes one difference, in London, was that if they were high up in the air, in blocks of flats, they did not have the same cachet at all. A home territory in the air was far less of a satisfaction than if it was planted on the 'solid' ground, as the phrase sometimes went. An electrician in Ealing lamented about his children – 'Living up here they've never played with the earth, they've never played with a worm.' To play with a worm was self-evidently a natural right of which those perched on a pile of steel and concrete were deprived.

From a tower block the view did not compensate for the psychic vertigo. But a view did add to the value of a house which also had the advantage of being on the ground. Many of the sites with open space in front of them had been appropriated by the

[1] See D. Joiner, 'Office territory', and E. Goffman, *The Presentation of Self in Everyday Life*.

rich. Almost every one of the great common lands of London – Hampstead Heath, Wimbledon Common, Blackheath, Hyde Park, Green Park, Regent's Park, Epping Forest, Hadley Wood, Richmond Park, Ham Common – was public for walking on within the prescribed hours but private all the year round and all the clock round for the views over it. Public property gave a spatial bonus from the community to those who already had private privilege.

A particular kind of space, mobile space, has come to be more important. So dominant was it that as we went around to our informants in our cars, theirs or the garages for them dominated the landscape, sometimes making the houses for the owners into a mere backcloth. They posed a new problem for builders, especially where relatively expensive frontages on to the road were too narrow for garages. In the last century narrow frontages were eked out by the bay window. What Rasmussen[1] called typical Victorian houses (which still stand in a hierarchy of sizes and in great numbers in the inner suburbs) let more light into the long, narrow interiors through this sort of window. In one private estate at Brentwood which was included in our survey the houses backing on each other were packed tight. The speculators did not want their customers to have to leave their cars on the street. The householders were already fearing that one day they might be pushed back off the public space by a line of parking sentries. So the cars had to be put in what would otherwise have been the front gardens, and, to avoid the light being blocked out entirely from the living-room windows, the carports were set off from the houses at a herringbone angle; seen from the end of the two streets, the cars looked like two rows of piglets. In another much grander estate the 'servants' houses' for the three or four cars, with their massive automatic up-and-over doors, were hardly smaller than the adjoining ones for their owners. In the middle of London there were few garages, except for the wealthy. At night, while their drivers slept, the cars rested bumper to bumper along the streets.

The pecking order for parking was even more obvious at work. Outside the main gate to one factory was a row of rectangles, marked out for the Managing Director nearest the door and tailing away to Chief Accountant at the far end. If you saw the

[1] S. Rasmussen, *London: The Unique City*.

spatially elect walking the few steps to his car in the evening he seemed, if he noticed the curious glance, to make a jaunty effort not to look important. The office and manual workers' cars were some distance away, inside a giant compound guarded by a commissionaire who had to check in and out the lesser people in their lesser cars which they had to pay for themselves. A large company at Croydon was like many others in taking the space-user onto the payroll. Members of the Board were given Rover 3.5s, heads of departments Ford Executive Zodiacs, assistant heads Ford Corsairs, other executives Ford Cortinas, salesmen Ford Escorts. All the staff could then read the rank by the armour.

We have been describing a particular value system as it operated more or less at one moment of time, and therefore statically. But any ranking system to which people generally subscribe is, when allied with egalitarianism, a force for change. We asked the people in our survey a few simple questions about space to get an indication of what they hoped a dynamic future might bring them. One question, to the 666 people who wanted to move home, was whether they were after one larger or smaller or about the same. The only surprise – 50 per cent said larger, 28 per cent about the same, and 22 per cent smaller – was that the proportion in the last category was as large as it turned out to be. They were, however, nearly all older people whose children had left home, and who therefore had empty rooms on their hands. It was not only space in the house that people wanted. We asked about gardens: 44 per cent of people who already had gardens wanted larger ones, 35 per cent the same size, 18 per cent smaller, and 3 per cent did not care one way or another. Most people – two-thirds of the potential movers – also wanted to own, so that their property could be as securely bonded to themselves as possible, and they wanted to have space around it as well. The order of desirability for most people ran from a flat to a terraced house, to a semi-detached, to a detached – and preferably with a high degree of detachment, not so much as to be on its own, removed completely from the stimulation of neighbours as friends and enemies, but far enough away so that when in the garden the owners did not feel they 'lived in a goldfish bowl'. 'Look at those houses there, you could hardly call them detached – there's only a few feet between them', said an Enfield bank clerk in disparagement. 'I suppose its quite good here really', reflected a Watford headteacher, 'we've got the open country on one side and our house is detached. But I somehow feel that I would like to have a bit more privacy, to get away from the people on both sides of me. We feel a bit hemmed in here at the sides.' The man who said that 'the semi-detached mentality is a lovely mentality' was a deviant in one way, even if in another – being in a semi-detached himself – he was illustrating the rule that people adjust themselves to what they have and do not hanker too persistently after something that they have little hope of acquiring. Mr Cox, at the summit in a detached, was more full-blooded about it when he said that 'This is my pad, my palace, my only place of habitation, my heaven, plus my wife and children's'.

People knew as they had for a hundred years that, for all but the rich or in other ways fortunate, the only way to get more space was to move outwards. Many people had special reasons for moving, or wanting to move – getting a house near a daughter's, or one with room enough for an aged mother, or because 'I don't like clay soil – it gives people bad feet' (engineering foreman, Gravesend), or a bungalow for an Ealing man with polio who had to go about in a wheel chair. Many others did not want to move at all; the proportion in our sample who wanted to change district was a third, and a fifth among people of 60 or over. Of those who did, a minority, with richer people preponderating, wished to move in from the suburbs of the Greater London area or of the Outer Metropolitan Area to the favoured districts of Inner London. But the majority, as Table 5 shows, wanted to move further out rather than in. They put the usual premium on the value we have been discussing.

TABLE 5 *Present and preferred residence (main sample: people wishing to move out of their present district)*

	Inner London	*Outer Greater London*	*Outer Metropolitan Area*
Further out	79%	74%	58%
Equidistant from centre	14%	16%	26%
Further in	7%	10%	16%
Total %	100%	100%	100%
Number	168	238	172

The desire for space naturally varies with age and marital state, the people who need it most being newly married couples. The great explosive force of the city has therefore been the nuclear family. Before marriage there is no loss in being in or near the centre, rather the reverse. A large number of adults of both sexes have come from all over the country and the world to live near to the job, entertainment and marriage markets of Central London.[1] Marriage changes the situation: private space becomes more important than public. Marriage calls for a house that[2]

> becomes again the centre of people's lives. Space, privacy and storage room – indoors and outdoors – baths, hot water, properly equipped kitchens and a parking space, become urgent necessities. The neighbourhood and the accessibility of its schools, doctors, shops, launderettes and transport services, take on a new importance. If the roof leaks you can no longer escape by moving; if the woman next door bangs angrily on the wall you can no longer simply bang back. You have to live with it – or your wife does – all day. The security and privacy of this home and the right to go on living peacefully in it are the foundations of the family's happiness.

Such a home can be found more cheaply in the suburbs.

Against the advantages of migrating every family that moves has to set the disadvantages. Will the schools be better? As education has increased its influence over people's life chances, this has become a more and more important question. How much will the children suffer if they have to leave their friends? Will the shops be more expensive? Will the traffic be less noisy and less dangerous? Will there be a garden? What will the costs of transport be? Will the amenities inside the home compensate for those that are lost outside it by leaving the inner city behind? Mr Chamberlain, a clerk living in Bracknell, mused to us over the choice he had made.

> Coming from London you're used to bricks and mortar, cement, roads and traffic lights. You're coming out to what was then wilder than it is now. Remember that there wasn't anything here, no cinema, no dance halls, no markets as we

[1] *Greater London Development Plan, Report of Studies*, p. 15.

[2] D. Donnison, *The Government of Housing*, p. 277.

> knew them in London. You could never say of a Saturday, 'Oh, let's go up to town'. You've got to adapt to a new kind of life. You've got to have a car for a start. Also, a funny thing is that you're supposed to be in the country but there are hardly any parks around that you can go to. In London we had Hyde Park and Hampstead Heath of a Sunday. This is supposed to be the country but it's all private. I have that satisfaction – I always go in by train – as you're pulling in to London, of seeing the condition of the houses that back on the railway. When I see that, I say to myself, stop griping. I lived in Hammersmith and it was pretty awful.

Against one disadvantage, Mr Chamberlain and millions like him have always had to set the overwhelming advantage, that, when they needed it most, space inside the house and to an equivalent standard was cheaper further out. Cost was especially important for newly married couples in the financial trough that we shall be saying more about in the next chapter.

The life cycle in relation to housing has been mirrored in the age structure of the region. There have over the centuries, at each period, been disproportionately large numbers of young adults at the two geographical extremes, single near the centre and married on the periphery. New houses built in the suburbs have been filled with young couples and their children, and the bulge in age composition of the districts to which they have gone has moved forward in time with a wave-like motion. In between the two – the furthest in and the furthest out – have been the areas with rather less migrants, which have had time, since their first settlement, to attain a more normal age distribution. People have become free to move again, most further out or a few further in, when their own children have grown up and retirement has released them from dependence upon a job.[1]

The argument so far has been that technology, in the form of improved transport, has allowed the demand for space to manifest itself. A tightly-knit city has been gradually converted into a looser region. Compression has given way to expansion. More people have been able both to remain within the job and collective

[1] 'The over 60 age group has remained a major source of the net loss for the South East.' South East Joint Planning Team, *Strategic Plan for the South East, and Studies, vol. 1: Population and Employment*, p. 26.

life of the city and to gain a purchase on the new provinces because their frontiers have been steadily rolled back. It has happened as much in the expanding cities of the old world as in the expanding territories of the New World. In London richer people have, in accord with the Principle, led the way, and others, too, have gained an advantage from the extra space that transport has brought within their reach. In the last century, before the car, people began moving out of the old East End into places like Leyton and Walthamstow in the 1870s and into Ilford about ten years later.[1] The homes that sprang up in Edmonton when the railway was opened in the 1870s were not alone. In this century the process has been taken further still by the building of municipal estates in the suburbs and of new and expanded towns further out.

The great cross of London

Have all sections of the population taken part in the trek? Some of the poorer people may, as we said in the opening chapter, have been left untouched by the Principle, in this as in other respects. To see whether they have we needed to plot the distribution of social classes in the Region, and to do so for at least two points in time to show what the changes had been.[2] The pattern of urban growth is a subject on which there has been a good deal of theorizing in the past, particularly in the United States, and we should refer to what others have thought before giving our view about what has happened.

The most celebrated generalization was made by the founders of the Chicago school of urban sociology in the 1920s. The map prepared by Burgess and McKenzie pictured Chicago as a series of concentric circles 'which may be numbered to designate both the successive zones of urban extension and the types of areas differentiated in the process of urban expansion'.[3] On this map they built their theory of urban growth in general, not just in their own city. The site of the first settlement became the Central

[1] W. Ashworth, 'Types of social and economic development in suburban Essex', p. 65.

[2] We have profited from some earlier social mapping of London by J. H. Westergaard, whose maps based on the 1951 Census showed the same general pattern. 'The structure of Greater London', pp. 101 and 141.

[3] E. W. Burgess, 'The growth of the city: an introduction to a research project', p. 50.

Business District. When the city was smaller this had been surrounded by a belt of large houses occupied by well-off families. As the city expanded, newcomers – in Chicago mostly immigrants – piled into slums in the centre and then pushed out into the large houses of what then became the Zone of Transition. The third zone, of Workingmen's Homes, was inhabited by workers who had managed to escape from the second one. The fourth, the Residential, was made up of high-class apartment buildings and single-family dwellings. It shaded off into the Commuters' Zone beyond the city limits.

The idea was that poorer people usually started off near the centre and then gradually forced their way outwards, pushing the richer people in front of them, the poor advancing and the rich retreating, the one entering and the other leaving houses originally built for the wealthy. This outward pressure was conceived of as being exerted equally on all parts of the circle, so that the whole expanded concentrically. The analogy drawn by the Chicago theorists was with ecology. They saw people of different classes as trees, beech or pine, which succeeded in invading and driving out other plant species. 'And just as in plant communities successions are the products of invasion, so also in the human community the formations, segregations and associations that appear constitute the outcome of a series of invasions.'[1]

We think they went wrong because they did not take sufficient account of geography. Burgess and his colleagues lived in a city which was geographically an extreme case and, since they did not fully recognize it, their generalization was bound to be at fault. It could only be on flat land that a city could be thought of as expanding in concentric circles. As it was, they neglected topography almost completely and regarded even Lake Michigan as a sort of irrelevance to their ideal scheme, although it made such a bite into the concentric regularity of their maps. Other cities, they seemed to be saying, do not have Lake Michigans, and will expand according to the model displayed. What they should have said was that this will tend to happen – then stating the two chief limiting conditions – *if* the city is (a) without water, that is river, lake or sea, as a primary feature of its environment, and (b) on flat ground.

[1] R. D. McKenzie, 'An ecological approach to the study of the human community', p. 74.

Another American authority produced an almost equally famous monograph on the subject in 1939 which is much nearer to our point of view. Hoyt observed that the expansion outwards of the high-rent areas where the richer people lived was often in rather distinct sectors like those we were discussing earlier. He summarized in nine propositions the considerations that govern the pattern of growth. One of them was that 'The zone of high-rent areas tends to progress towards high ground which is free from the risk of floods and to spread along lake, bay, river, and ocean fronts, where such water fronts are not used for industry.'[1]

For London we ourselves would go a good deal further even than that in stressing the formative power of physical geography (or to put it another way, of the very much drawn-out geological history of the Thames Basin), and, in particular, of water and contours upon the shape the city has taken during the course of its development. The first, in the form of the river, was responsible for the origins of London, the two original settlements being around the fords at the Isle of Thorney, where the Houses of Parliament now stand, and at London Bridge; and thus for the twin cities strung out along the river, the City of London, which became the financial and mercantile centre, and the City of Westminster, which became the seat of kings and parliaments.

The Thames neatly illustrates the double and obverse action of water upon social configuration. It is for the rich a repellent and a magnet, a repellent if the water is also a port and a gateway to the industry that is usually sucked on to a port; a magnet if they can get near to an edge unencumbered by commerce. The Thames below the Pool is (except for the one jewel of Greenwich) a repellent. Lined with docks and industry for fifteen miles, East London has had its back to the river, with the hinterland being for the people who work in the industries and cannot afford to live anywhere except in the low-lying areas nearby. The Thames above the Pool, or at any rate above Westminster, is a magnet. Chelsea, Barnes, Chiswick, Kew, Twickenham, Richmond, are on the route that the royal barges used to take between the palaces of St James, Hampton Court and Windsor; they are all desirable places for people who have the money to make their desires effective and who do not choose the Outer Metropolitan Area.

[1] H. Hoyt, 'The pattern of movement of residential rental neighbourhoods', p. 504.

The 'Chelsea effect' may spread down below the Pool in the next hundred years as the water-port gives way to the airports, and those reaches of the river likewise become more valued for their amenity than for their industrial value. There is the same switch-over, for the same reason, in many other of the world's cities, most of which were established beside water. When it is no longer a necessity, for work, more can be made of it as a luxury, for leisure.

Height is hardly ever ambivalent, unless water makes it so. Where it is not thought an advantage to be high up, as in Rio de Janeiro whose slums are up the hill, it is because the rich have clustered lower down and nearer the sea; but Wellington or Bombay are more typical, with the rich on high ground away from the port. In almost all places in the world where they cannot get near water, the higher classes are literally higher. It is less damp. The soil is better drained. It is free from the noise, fumes and traffic generated by industry. It has better air and less fog. There are finer views. On the heights people command more space in front of their residences even if they do not have parks to look out over.

To be more precise about the effect of height and water we needed a map. Map 2 shows the class geography of Greater London as it was in 1966. The districts shown are the old local authorities before the reorganization of London government. Being smaller than the new boroughs, they provided a finer grain. The distinction we made was between the more middle-class areas, where 25 per cent or more of the population was in the professional and managerial classes, and the more working-class, where 76 per cent or more were in the remaining classes.[1] To compare the map with the Chicago model is also to indicate the differences between our view and theirs.

The map shows that the centre contains a cluster of more middle-class districts – Chelsea, the City, Kensington, Holborn, Paddington, St Marylebone and Westminster. The centre is therefore not just the Central Business District but also very much the Central Residential District, with the advantage for the residents of proximity to water, parks, workplaces and the old

[1] We used 25 per cent or more as the criterion of middle-class character because it represented a rounded-out figure almost the same as the average for the proportion of professional and managerial people in the Region as a whole – which was 24 per cent in 1966. The methods of analysis and the results are described more fully in our paper – P. Willmott and M. Young, 'Social class and geography'.

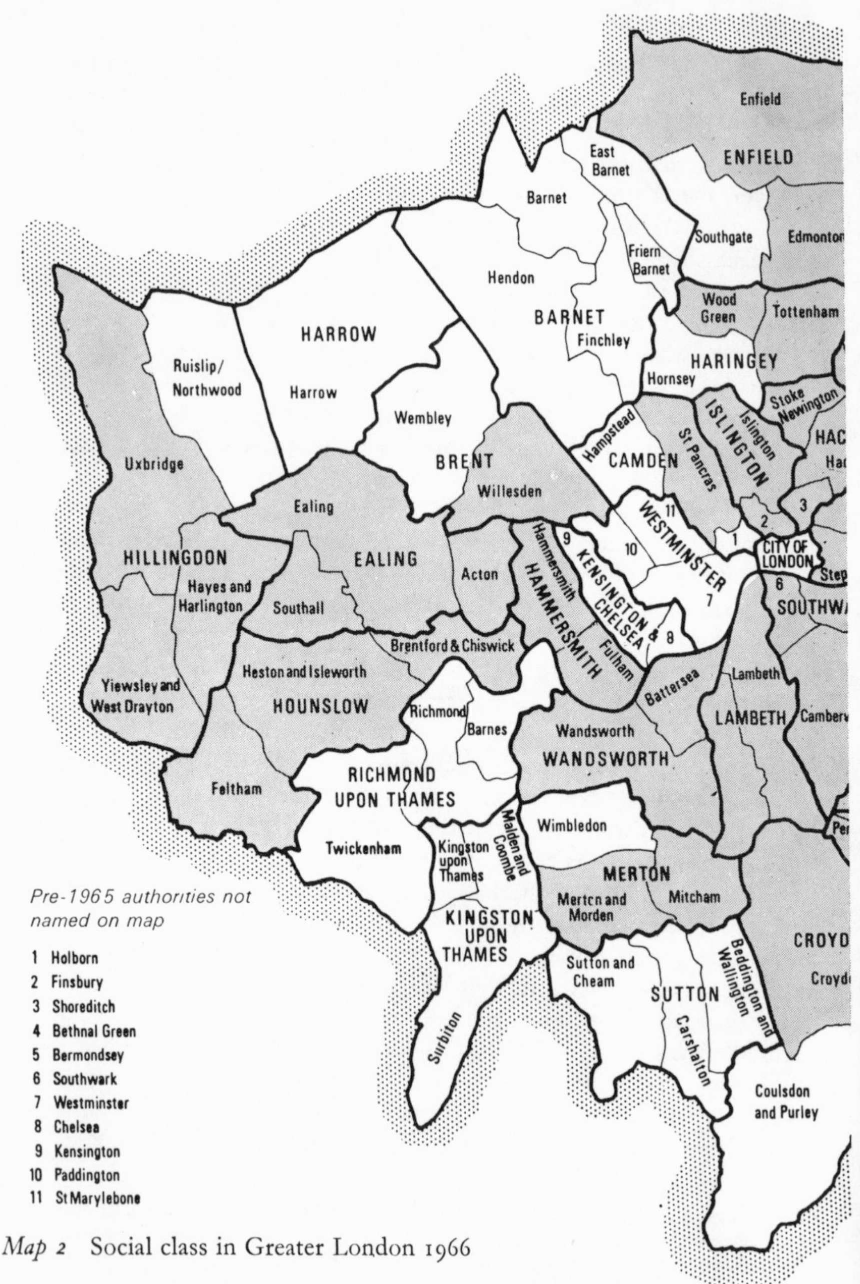

Map 2 Social class in Greater London 1966

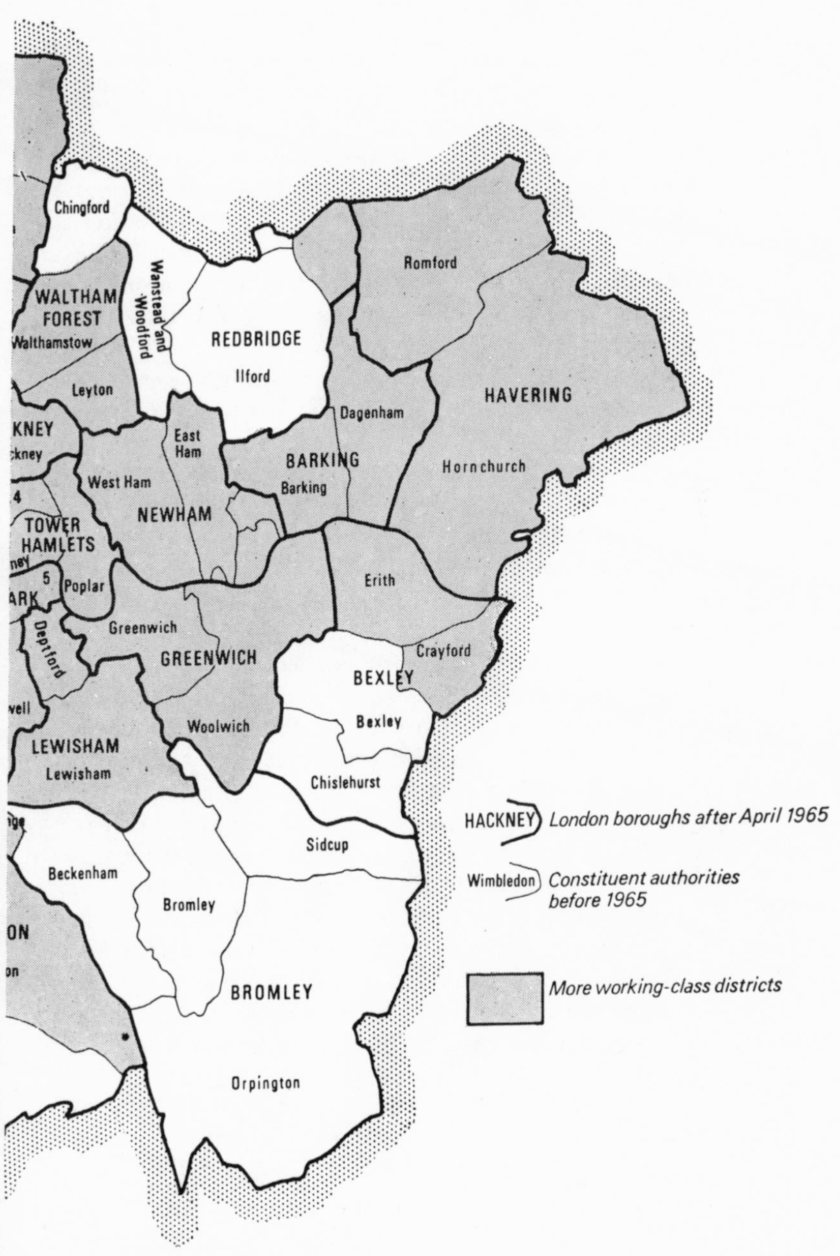

Chingford
WALTHAM FOREST
Walthamstow
Leyton
Wanstead and Woodford
REDBRIDGE
Ilford
Romford
HAVERING
Hornchurch
Dagenham
BARKING
Barking
East Ham
West Ham
NEWHAM
TOWER HAMLETS
Poplar
Greenwich
GREENWICH
Woolwich
Deptford
LEWISHAM
Lewisham
Erith
Crayford
BEXLEY
Bexley
Chislehurst
Sidcup
Beckenham
Bromley
BROMLEY
Orpington
HACKNEY
London boroughs after April 1965
Wimbledon
Constituent authorities before 1965
More working-class districts

buildings which, through the alchemy of a sort of historical snobbery, can confer distinction upon people who live near them.[1] By a backwards extension of the Principle the rich and powerful of the present can gain distinction from association with the ghosts of the rich and powerful from the past. Though it does not show on the map, in four of the districts listed above – the City, Holborn, Paddington and Westminster – there was a gap in the middle of the class spectrum: they had higher proportions of professionals and managers and about average for unskilled workers, but low for skilled and clerks. So, for these four districts, there was some truth in the view which has often been advanced that there has been a measure of class polarization in Central London.

What may happen in the future, to echo what Eversley has said,[2] is that the areas in which the unskilled workers live will become more run-down than ever, and the houses left to them become more overcrowded as richer people take over and convert some of those that had previously been occupied by the poor. The process which we noted before as occurring in Canonbury may, in other words, become still more pronounced in a way that the Chicago school did not allow for. The very growth of London may generate this sort of counter-trend. For the larger the conurbation grows the longer the journeys for people who work in the centre to get back at night to a home in the countryside. The travelling is less burdensome for people who live in the middle during the week and go right out to a second home at the weekends. At the time of our survey it was already more common for well-off people living in Inner London than for those outside it to have second homes in the country. The combination of a first house or flat close to the centre and a second one far away is likely to be even more popular by the end of the century, thus multiplying further the space controlled by the rich at the expense of the poor.

[1] W. Firey (*Land Use in Central Boston*, chap. 2) has shown that the same sort of associations in a city as historically-minded as London helped to preserve Beacon Hill in the middle of Boston.

[2] 'What may happen is that most of the areas of Inner London which are predominantly working class will decline further while the areas which have been, or are becoming, middle class will exert an ever greater attractive power.' D. Eversley, 'Old cities, falling populations and rising costs'. See also R. E. Pahl, 'Poverty and the urban system'.

But the biggest difference from the Chicago scheme is that the more working-class districts form the sign of a cross rather than a circle. It consists of the low-lying districts, shaped by the Thames and its two right-angled tributaries, the Lea and the Wandle, which joins the main river at Wandsworth. The poor of London have been as much limited as the poor of Chicago, or of any other city, by what they could afford. They have had to content (or discontent) themselves with the cheapest accommodation they could find. The difference is that in London the poor have been more obviously subject to another constraint, that of geography. They have pushed east along the unsalubrious Lower Thames, north up the valley of the Lea, south near and not so near to the Wandle, and west along the railway which here as elsewhere (with some exceptions) followed the low ground. It was the same flatness which made the western approaches suitable for the first large airport after Croydon was abandoned. Industry, which in the inter-war years clustered near the Great West Road and Western Avenue, has later been attracted to the new port in the Upper Thames Valley just as it was centuries before to the old one in the Lower Thames. The railway lines that tunnelled through the Northern Heights were the exceptions, and though the poor could be expected to live alongside the line they could not be forced to live in the tunnel itself.

The Zone of Transition is still there but in the cross rather than in a circle. It is most marked in the north. The northern arm of the cross, spreading over into Paddington and North Kensington, was picked out by the Greater London Development Plan (though without calling it part of a cross) as the area where there was excessive overcrowding and sharing of accommodation in houses originally built for richer people. The analogy between classes and species was not wholly inappropriate there. It was least so in the eastern arm, more solidly working-class than the rest, which (since long before Engels wrote) has combined what would have been called slums with the Zone of Workingmen's Homes and in this respect has not changed much. The East End was classified by the Plan as the area with houses in the poorest physical condition but without being overcrowded. Parts of the southern and western arms are a mixture, with bad conditions and too many people.

If the more working-class districts are in the cross, the more middle-class ones are in the four quarters, with Hampstead forming a sort of corridor leading into central London from the north west. Over the centuries the rich have kept to their own sectoral routes, encircling with their houses the old pre-industrial villages, which were already established on relatively high ground in such places as Highgate, Hampstead, Harrow-on-the-Hill, Notting Hill, Campden Hill, Richmond Hill, Sydenham Hill, Blackheath and Buckhurst Hill. Buildings old enough to have special value have combined with height, and usually with the open space we mentioned earlier, to make such districts particularly desirable.

One of the points of such an analysis is that it enables the right question to be asked about the trend. It is not whether the working classes are more concentrated than they were in a circular zone around the centre but whether they are more so in the cross. To answer we compared the figures for 1966 with those from the Census of 1951. The outward drift was very marked. Greater London lost population in all classes, and the Outer Metropolitan Area gained it, as we have already seen. What was most striking, however, was the relative rise over the fifteen years in the concentration of working-class people in the cross, as more and more of them were pushed out of the centre and along its arms. In the cross there was therefore even less of a class mix, and more of a one-class concentration.

Twentieth-century immigrants

This has happened partly because of the new immigrants. The Census of 1966 showed that of the seven and a half million people living in Greater London, two million had been born outside the South-East (an area larger than our Region). About two-thirds of them had come from elsewhere in the British Isles and the remaining third from abroad. Among the latter, immigrants from the Commonwealth – mainly with black or brown skins – amounted to well over half. Being at the rear of the column they are the best indicators of what conditions used to be like for others.

In the last century many immigrants settled in the East End. The Jewish immigrants of whom Beatrice Potter wrote (many of whose descendants have now scattered to Stamford Hill, Finchley and Golders Green) landed by ship in the docks, and stayed nearby, as the Huguenots who made silk-weaving a staple industry had done before them. The Irish who have added so much to the population of London in both centuries did not come to the East End. They came by train, not boat. But their point of arrival left its mark. Many of the later ones took up residence near the two stations where they arrived, Euston (for Islington and Camden Town) and Paddington (for that district and also Willesden). The coloured immigrants have followed and added to the working-class concentration in the south, north and west. The West Indians, when they came, arrived at Waterloo from Southampton and formed a series of settlements in South London, with an early cluster at Brixton; or Euston from Liverpool, and then on into Islington and Finsbury Park. The Indians and Pakistanis who came by air and landed at Heathrow[1] have in quite large numbers also stayed near their point of arrival, especially in Southall and other parts of Ealing.

The story is that the Irishman stopped when he had carried his suitcase as far as he could from Paddington and stayed put for the rest of his life. The housing was cheap, and bad, just because it was near ports, stations and main lines. Most of the immigrants, being poor, have had to go for the low rents. In the middle of this century they have been debarred from waiting lists for council housing in other districts by rules which require so many years' residence, and they have therefore seldom been able to get one of the municipal houses which have benefited people lucky enough to have one of those unlucky nineteenth century Londoners as their ancestor. They are discriminated against by private landlords. They seldom have the sort of family influence with rent collectors of some of the native-born working class. With small resources, of cash or influence, they have no choice, and have to go wherever they can get in, which is for the most part in derelict Victorian houses. These are also quite often scheduled for clearance. In some streets houses boarded up, with old bicycles and

[1] A sociologist has recently given this account of what it was like for one Indian to do so. 'When I arrived in the evening at London airport I looked around to see who had come to meet me . . . Surely some government official must appear at any moment and take me to wherever I was to be accommodated? You see, I was under the impression that if the government issued me a voucher, this meant that they would make all the arrangements for my work and accommodation, just as when I was a soldier the army made all the arrangements as to where we were to go and what we were to do . . . I kept on waiting and still no one called me.' U. Sharma, *Rampal and His Family*, pp. 73–4.

other rubbish thrown into the ground-floor rooms, stand next to others whose brickwork and doors are painted red or yellow or blue. A wall carrying the slogan HOUSE BRITONS FIRST[1] may adjoin a West Indian, Cypriot or Indian shop selling exotic fruits and vegetables, garlic and tins of humous or peppers.

Some of the immigrants in our sample, especially where both wife and husband were at work, had managed to improve their housing and even acquire the resources – by pooling, on a mortgage or by borrowing from a moneylender at high interest rates – to buy some property of their own to live in or to let at expensive rents to their compatriots. Others were like the poor whites among whom they lived. Miss Fernando from Trinidad was an informant in Deptford. She lived with her three children in a 'lodging house', a once-majestic Victorian building which besides her contained fourteen single men and three other small families. She had arthritis and was unable to work. She could not even go outside, since, if she did, her stiff joints would have stopped her climbing back up the rickety stairs. Her income was £12 per week in sickness benefits, family allowances and supplementary benefits. After paying £4 per week for her two rooms she had £8 left for everything else. Her only heating came from a single paraffin heater. It had been knocked over not long before the interview; the fire which broke out was extinguished just in time to prevent the house burning down.

Mr and Mrs Battersby were also from the West Indies – a couple living with their four children in two rooms of a crumbling three-storeyed terrace house in Islington. The other three families in it were also Caribbean. They all shared the kitchen. 'Four women trying to use two stoves is not good', said Mrs Battersby. At night the four-year-old was put into the cot and the baby, aged 18 months, slept with his parents in a way that Lord Shaftesbury would not have approved. By the standards of the last century they were fortunate to have as many as two rooms. By the standards of this they were the unfortunates: 36 per cent of coloured immigrants in Greater London were in 1966 living at

[1] The long-distance immigration has been a spur to short-distance migration by whites. One man, asked why he wanted to move, said, 'If I was to answer that you'd report me to the Race Relations Board.' Others were not so reticent, speaking of the 'creeping black tide', 'the coloureds and Turks and all sorts', or saying 'I'm afraid I'm on the side of Enoch Powell.'

more than 1.5 persons per room as against 3 per cent of the native-born English.[1]

The regional man

The poorest people living in the cross were often doubly deprived, first because they lived there at all, secondly because they could not travel out of it. The more agreeable the district, the easier it was for people to leave. They were the ones who had the means of transport and could afford to use them. This was most true of well-off people in the Outer Metropolitan Area, as is shown in Table 6 (overleaf).

Those with more private resources at their command could also use more fully the roads[2] and public resources of the Region, in rather the same way as the people on the edge of public open space had the bonus we have mentioned earlier. To the poor the Region meant nothing. The rich were the 'regional men', not so much tied to radial journeys in and out of the centre, going further for their work and their leisure, in some ways the twentieth-century counterparts of the nineteenth-century men and women who were forced on to the streets by the cheerlessness of their homes, but doing it from choice. Such people in rural areas were more often urban, in the sense of being able to use more fully the opportunities of urban life, than many of the poorer carless families within a mile or so of Piccadilly Circus. The contrast, to take extremes, can be illustrated by two of our families, the Crawleys and the Wests.

Aged thirty-eight Mr Crawley was a Senior Development Engineer at a plant in Slough. He lived about twenty miles away in a sixteenth-century house, converted out of three former farm cottages, in rural Berkshire. There was a wood at the back of the house and two large farms within about a quarter of a mile. 'The man that way', said Mr Crawley, 'is a weekend farmer. I met him

[1] E. J. B. Rose *et al.*, *Colour and Citizenship*, pp. 133, 139.

[2] Our survey showed that car-owners were naturally more favourable than others to the new motorways proposed for London, and relatively less favourable to more expenditure on public transport. 'A typical advocate of higher expenditure to improve bus services in London is a working-class man, and even more a woman, elderly, with a low income and, of course, no car'. P. Willmott and M. Young, 'How urgent are London's motorways', p. 1038.

at a cocktail party last weekend and we were talking about dining out. He said, "Are you ever down here during the week?" I ask you! This is our home.' Mr Crawley travelled to Slough by car most days, but about once or twice a week had to go to meetings in Central London – to the firm's head office – or to 'a meeting at the Ministry'. One evening during the week before the interview he had, as he put it, 'stayed in Town to have dinner with an old University friend. He lives in Sussex, and it's about the only

TABLE 6 *Occupational class, zone and car ownership (main sample; total number in each category shown in brackets)*

Proportion with one or more cars owned in the household	*Professional and managerial*	*Clerical*	*Skilled*	*Semi-skilled and unskilled*	*All*
Inner London	55% (73)	47% (59)	41% (154)	24% (99)	40% (385)
Outer Greater London	77% (159)	58% (115)	56% (285)	38% (146)	58% (705)
Outer Metropolitan Area, towns	76% (153)	65% (75)	63% (195)	44% (89)	64% (512)
Outer Metropolitan Area, rural areas	84% (102)	92% (26)	75% (84)	52% (48)	76% (260)
London Region	75% (487)	61% (275)	57% (718)	38% (382)	58% (1,862)

chance I get to meet him.' He had, on another evening, gone home after work to collect his wife and then driven her into Central London 'to go to the Festival Hall'. He explained, 'We've got our hi-fi here, but there's nothing quite like hearing it live.' The next Saturday, they planned to go out to dinner at a restaurant in Henley, about ten miles away: 'We're going to meet some friends who used to live near us when we lived in Kensington. They now live at Maidenhead.' There was no trouble about baby-sitting. 'We've got the au pair, you see.'

The Wests had few of the Crawley's advantages. They were in

their early thirties and had four children under eleven. Mr West earned £18 a week as a labourer in a builder's yard. When they got married twelve years earlier, they had first lived for a while with Mrs West's parents in Hackney. 'We found it didn't work,' said Mrs West. 'There wasn't much room anyway, and after a while troubles started blowing up, mainly between my husband and my mother. We put down to move to Harlow New Town. My husband got a job there working for the council and that meant we could get a house. We lived there for four years. It was lovely. I had a big garden and a modern house. But we had to come back because of the work. There's plenty of jobs in these new towns for the more intellectual sort of people – draughtsmen and engineers – but not for people without a trade. My husband was out of work for fourteen months and we had to come back. We tried to get a council flat but in the end we were desperate and all we could get was this.'

'This' was four rooms above an ironmonger's shop in Acton. The West's front door was beside the shop door. Behind it there was a long corridor, with bare cream walls and a single exposed light bulb. The stairs, with a rectangle of grey linoleum on each tread, led up to four rooms. On one floor was a kitchen/dining room and what Mrs West called 'the front room' facing on to the street. The kitchen had an Ascot water heater over the sink which also served as wash basin (there was no bathroom), a modern white gas stove with eye-level grill and transparent door, a tall kitchen cabinet, a red plastic-topped kitchen table and four matching chairs. The other room contained two beds, neither of them as large as standard double size and one much smaller, a two-year-old asleep on it with a dummy in her mouth and a bottle beside her. It was a chilly April day and Mrs West wore thick cream-coloured socks and a long green cardigan over a yellow-and-white flowered dress with an uneven hem. She explained how they used the rooms. 'We watch TV in this room and sleep here. The baby sleeps where she is now and my husband and I in the other bed. The other three children are in one of the rooms upstairs. We don't use the other one because there's damp coming through the walls. You can smell the damp as soon as you go into the room.' The Wests had no car. They had stayed in on every evening but one during the previous week.

Mr and Mrs West had at least been up to 'London' fairly

recently. There were some other people to whom the centre was very far away, as it was to many Bethnal Greeners in the 1840s. A fifty-five-year-old widow in Enfield said, 'Ah, it must be twenty years since I've been up to that part of the country', meaning Central London. A retired seventy-year-old fitter in Dagenham went back even further. 'It was back during the war – that was the last time we went up to the West End. We had a bit of money and went up for drinks. They say you can hardly recognize the place now.' If the trend is (as we think it is) towards the regional man, there are as yet many exceptions.

We have been trying to follow the process whereby the new kind of family has found a home for itself in the sort of city which the Industrial Revolution has produced. The small, mean, comfortless room of the early nineteenth century could not induce the home-centredness which is one of the characteristics of the symmetrical family. Homes with more space in them were needed before most families could turn inwards and these were gained only as the result of a vast upheaval. For two centuries a large part of man's growing productive power has gone into digging great holes in some parts of the world, extracting the minerals and re-fabricating them into cities like London; or pumping out oil from other depths for the transport which can alone keep them functioning. But as the resources have been supplied, and as technology has transformed travel, additional space has been found at ever greater distances from the centre, and without the price being exile.

A minority still live in the kind of housing which would have been more in place in the last century than this, and hemmed in by a topography which goes back much further. But a majority of the citizens of a London which has grown in range and population so many times over the two centuries now have one of the most sought-after rights of citizenship. The column has slowly advanced into the country, with the rich marking the tracks. Those in any class who have been able to follow have one of the most precious possessions of all, the right to an estate which is a support to them and their modern kind of family. Their territory, even their private transport, augments the many other threads in a web of relationships spun by people as eager as ever, perhaps more eager because of all the flux, to create around them the illusion that the present is for ever.

III

GROWTH OF THE SYMMETRICAL FAMILY

Our next subject, touching upon attitudes, is more elusive, partly because attitudes always are, partly because current strivings colour judgments about the strivings of the past. If the present is a summary of the past, the past is also a summary of the present, the one changing as fast as the other. Every shift in current pre-occupations sets off a new interaction with those which are on record from the past, the collective working in the same way as an individual person selectively re-fashioning his personal past in his own memory.[1] The moral judgments of today cannot be segregated from what appear the facts of yesterday. If the front door is barred they creep in the side. But since we happen to be more or less aware of one bias of ours, we want to invite it in. The most vexed question in the protracted debate on the effects of industralization in England has been about the balance of losses and gains to different sections of the population, especially in the period up to 1850; and on that we recognize our bias.

One approach is to ask what would have happened had there been no industry. As the twentieth century has progressed we have become more and more fearful about the population explosion, particularly in Asia. The new Malthusian spirit has added weight, in the interpretation of historians, to the increase in the size of the family, not so much the number born as the number who survived premature death, in the latter half of the eighteenth century. What would have been their fate had a new economic order not been forced upon them? It is easy to sympathize with Ashton's answer, even if it does isolate a particular factor which was linked to a complex of other changes.[2]

[1] See F. C. Bartlett, *Remembering*.

[2] T. S. Ashton, *The Industrial Revolution, 1760–1830*, p. 129.

> The central problem of the age was how to feed and clothe and employ generations of children outnumbering by far those of any earlier time. Ireland was faced with the same problem. Failing to solve it, she lost in the 'forties about a fifth of her people by emigration or starvation and disease. If England had remained a nation of cultivators and craftsmen, she could hardly have escaped the same fate, and, at best, the weight of a growing population must have pressed down the spring of her spirit.

But even though things might (probably would) have been still worse without the new dispensation, they were grievous enough with it. Many people such as Engels and Gaskell, Cobbett and Oastler who could see for themselves what the outcome had been said that the old kind of family had been disrupted. Our bias is the same, which is why we quoted from Thompson in Chapter 1 and refer in various places to the 'break-down' of the family of poor people in Stage 2 – but without, we hope, falling into the ever-open trap of romanticizing what came before. For most people, that too was cruel enough to make glamorizing completely out of place. We will in this chapter (organized as it is in three sections to correspond with the three stages) start with Stage 1 which was a rural more than it was an urban phenomenon and then move on to Stage 2 and Stage 3, with the emphasis throughout on the relationship between the married couple in their capacity as husband and wife as well as parents.

1 *The unit of production*

When we called the pre-industrial family the unit of production we meant that the crucial division of labour was between its members, all of whom were engaged in working such resources as it could command, either for their own immediate consumption or, sometimes, to produce goods for sale. There were, of course, numerous exceptions. Better-off families of the middling sort, though sometimes productive units, were usually not. Then there were many poorer people who did not have any legal or customary rights to land. These were the artisans, ploughmen and labourers who had to work for others for all or part of their time. Many were taken on as farm servants for a year at a stretch at annual hirings. Even when men could work for themselves instead of for wages it did not follow that their womenfolk were equally free. They often had to work, either as domestic servants or on still rougher tasks. 'As servants in husbandry women performed the heaviest tasks of agricultural labour; they served as assistants to masons and bricklayers, as labourers in brickyards and foundries, as load carriers to and from markets, as rag sorters and cutters in paper mills, as cinder sifters and collectors of refuse.'[1] But it was still true that the classic productive unit, setting the norm to which many were able to conform and most others aspire to, was the family itself.

The division of labour was presided over by the husband. He was not just the husbandman. He was the undisputed master, the patriarch[2] of his family, if he had any, including children from other households imported into his own, and including servants. The doctrine of St Paul – 'Wives submit yourself unto your own husbands, as it is fit in the Lord' – was not quite so zealously enforced as in Catholic countries but it was still very much the canon of daily life. Yet the severity of his rule was tempered by the recognition that he needed his wife, and his children, almost as much as they needed him. It was probably the exceptional wife, who was not beaten by her husband, sometimes brutally; and her love, if she had any, was often alloyed with fear of her master. But when so much depended on the person to whom God had joined him, it would have been cutting his own throat to antagonize her too much. Her economic value was her saving, especially if she not only worked herself but also produced for her employer other workers, so putting him in the state recognized in the words of the Psalm – 'Happy is the man who hath his quiver full of children'.

On the larger farms wives supervized not only the maids in the household but the dairy, calves and pigs, garden and orchard. On the middle-sized the wife milked the cows, made the butter and cheese on which the family so much depended, and took to market the dairy products, poultry and eggs. If it was a cheese farm her labours might be arduous indeed – up at 3 or 4 a.m. to milk the cows by lantern, carrying the milk back for the cheese-making to begin, and going through it all once again during the day before

[1] I. Pinchbeck, *Women Workers and the Industrial Revolution, 1750–1850*, p. 2.

[2] See P. Laslett, *The World We Have Lost*, chap. 1.

finishing late in the evening. On the smaller farms, she might have to drive the plough and she certainly helped with the harvest. If her husband was a cottager or squatter and belonged to the increasing numbers of men who had lost their rights to land as the result of enclosure, her part might be even more vital; she would be entirely responsible for tilling a small piece of garden and looking after any livestock they might have while he went to work as a wage labourer. The woman's contribution was so crucial that, to quote a contemporary source in the 1780s:[1]

> I have known instances of the wife's management of the livestock, together with the earnings of herself and her children in hay-time and harvest etc., produce nearly as much money in the course of the year as her husband by all his labours during the same time.

The children were also at work from an early age,[2] the girls helping their mothers and the boys their fathers or, if they had become servants in other people's households, helping the couple at the head of it. 'The school had been, for the most part, an occasional and somewhat irrelevant factor in rural life.'[3] The children learnt by doing what their parents showed them. At six or seven the son of a farming family was taken under the charge of his father, running errands, fetching tools, taking his father's meals out to the fields, and, as he grew older, he was taught the more difficult jobs of tending the animals, shearing the sheep, ploughing the fields and getting in the harvest. Likewise, the mother prepared her daughter for the bearing of children, the cooking, the care of animals, the handicrafts and the work in the dairy:[4]

[1] *Political Enquiry into the Consequences of Enclosing Waste Lands*, 1785, p. 46. Quoted in I. Pinchbeck, op. cit., p. 21.

[2] 'In Ireland, as is usual under conditions of subsistence agriculture, farm labour was mainly provided by the family, with each nuclear family farming its own plot, though probably with assistance at certain times from neighbours and kin. True, some of the larger farms employed labourers regularly or from time to time; there was also a small class of unmarried farm servants who lived with their employers and were considered fairly comfortably placed in comparison with the rest of the population. But, typically, the numerous children assisted the farmer and his wife in the farm work from an early age until marriage.' M. Anderson, *Family Structure in Nineteenth Century Lancashire*, p. 81.

[3] A. E. Dobbs, *Education and Social Movements, 1700–1850*, p. 17.

[4] I. Pinchbeck, op. cit., p. 13, quoting Twamley, *Dairying Exemplified,* 2nd ed., 1787, p. 10.

> Their knowledge was purely empirical and the art of butter and cheese-making was handed down from mother to daughter, with the result that individual practice differed considerably. Twamley, a cheese factor, whose experience of the widely differing methods of dairymen led him to compile a treatise on different usages and their advantages, was well aware of the difficulty of inducing dairymen to adopt new methods, or rules which 'are different from their own, and what hath always been practised by their mothers, to whom they are often very partial, as having been esteemed the best Dairywomen of their time'.

Most people who had a stake in a piece of land, even though it was only a share of common land, also engaged in handicraft production in the home, upon the 'domestic system', as it was called, as did the many people who had no other standby. Capitalists sometimes organized this family method of production where it was making goods for the market and not for the family, and when the husband himself did not organize the buying and selling he was less of a figure than when he did. 'In addition to the factory workers, manufacturing workers and handicraft workers, whom it brings together in large numbers under its direct command, capital sets in motion, through the instrumentality of invisible threads, another army consisting of home workers scattered through the large towns and over the countryside.'[1] But the work of carding and spinning and sometimes weaving, dyeing and dressing cloth, or of manufacturing leather, clay or wood was done in the home, especially by women and children, and especially in the winter when there was less to do in the open. The handicrafts mixed well with the other tasks of the household, with child care and cooking, brewing and baking, because they could be put aside and taken up again when there was a break. The flexibility was later forfeited to the more rigid time-discipline imposed by employers with the costs of capital to worry about. In the century before the arrival of the new industry, to Defoe it was a sign that all was well with the state of England when, 'If we knock'd at the Door of any of the master manufacturers, we presently saw a house full of lusty fellows, some at the dye-vat, some dressing the cloths, some at the loom . . . the women and

[1] K. Marx, *Capital*, p. 497.

children of whom are always busy carding, spinning etc. so that no hands being unemploy'd all can gain their bread, even from the youngest to the ancient; hardly anything above four years old but its hands are sufficient to itself.'[1] So it would have been in the following century. By modern standards almost everyone had a hard life and a short one. Famine and pestilence were everyday companions. But the living, such as it was, and the work done to secure it were shared between the sexes and the age groups within the bounds of the one dominant all-purpose institution.

Such people were the ancestors of later migrants to London. In the first generation many brought some of their country ways with them into the city. Some part of London's past is rural; another is, of course, in London itself, which was, as it is, untypical of the rest of the country, even if it often marks the passage that others will follow. If people who depended for their sustenance primarily upon the wages they earned were a minority in the countryside, it was the other way round in London. Plenty of families were engaged in production. The London baker's household described by Laslett[2] for the seventeenth century consisted of thirteen or fourteen people, some paid journeymen, most unpaid workers of the family, centred around the workshop which was in the house. It was not unlike the households of guild craftsmen. Long after the guilds had gone into decline, and long after the seventeenth century, the domestic system survived in the families of East London weavers and in many other trades. But in London the self-employed, or rather family-employed, were not in a majority.

2 *The spread of disruption*

They were in the country generally and they probably remained so for many years after the factory system began to make headway against the family. The new methods were adopted by only a few industries at the beginning, and their hold, even by the middle of the nineteenth century, was not at all complete. 'Very few large units of industrial employment existed in the early stages, up to 1850, apart from the textile industry, the iron and non-ferrous metal industries, and one or two other trades like glass-making, bleach-making, railway workshops, dockyards and a handful of

[1] D. Defoe, *A Tour Through Great Britain*, vol. III, p. 101.

[2] P. Laslett, op. cit., p. 1.

breweries, paper-making, some mining areas.'[1] It followed that the competition exerted by the new industry against the old family was also slow to take effect, especially because to begin with the family could adapt to the new system by moving *en bloc* inside the new establishments. The man often entered the mills or the mines with his wife and children, supervising their work as he would have done at his home if industry had remained within it. This made the discipline more tolerable until such time as other parents' children and other men's wives came to predominate. At some periods industry encouraged production in the home. 'Industrialization multiplied the number of hand-loom weavers and framework knitters until the end of the Napoleonic wars, thereafter it destroyed them by slow strangulation.'[2]

If industrialization proceeded slowly in the country as a whole, it did so even more in London than elsewhere. In the eighteenth century London had been by far the largest city in Europe, and so remained – the political and commercial capital, the biggest port, with the biggest concentration of population and the biggest concentration of the rich. It was even more the centre of service trades than it is today, with large numbers of domestic servants and large numbers of others supplying goods for the metropolitan demand. As a market for products from all over the country it did a great deal to create a national economy. But it was not a factory centre. By 1851 three-quarters of the people in London employed for wages were still in firms employing five or fewer people.[3] Many of them were relatively skilled workers in industries like cabinet-making, pianos or the watch-making industry of North London which was later wiped out by Swiss competition; trades of this kind allowed men enough of a competence to support their families in a respectable state. Many others were casual workers producing consumer goods subject to strongly marked seasonal demands. The London 'season', originally synchronized with the summer parliamentary session, lasted from May to July. During those months of each year employment in many occupations was at its most brisk, just as it was least so in January. The shifts which people made to switch occupations, as when in the winter Covent Garden porters became pantomime scene-shifters or

[1] P. Mathias, *The First Industrial Nation*, p. 207.

[2] E. J. Hobsbawm, *Industry and Empire*, p. 90.

[3] G. S. Jones, *Outcast London*, p. 374.

flower girls prostitutes, could hold off destitution only at the expense of it for others. The winter, especially if it was a severe one, was as much a trial for many London workers as it had been for their forbears in rural districts. 'It certainly seems true that some of the worst periods of distress in Victorian London were the result not so much of cyclical trade depression as exceptionally hard winters.'[1]

The problems of the poor were accentuated more by their sheer numbers which caused the overcrowding featured in the last chapter and aggravated the competition between themselves ('We was starving one against the other')[2] than by the intrusion of the factory. This meant that the domestic system could survive in manufacturing longer than it had been able to do in Lancashire or Yorkshire, even though in the degenerate form where family labour was cruelly exploited. In some of the trades described at mid-century by Mayhew the family was still the unit of production, but especially so in the 'dishonourable trades' where sweating was at its most rife and a man might be able to survive only by pressing his wife and children into service. In Spitalfields, 'Another circumstance peculiar to the place was the absence of children. In such a street, had the labour of the young been less valuable, the gutters and door-steps would have swarmed with juveniles.' In one house there was a boy at a spinning wheel and a girl at a loom. In another trade, 'A tailor who had a family needed the aid of his wife to assist him in making a living. The woman, in some cases, was absolutely needed to make three-fourths of the garment.' Amongst boot and shoe makers, 'in order to gain a competency at the low-price work, an operative employs his wife'. A table-maker said that, 'Now children have to be put to work very young I have four sons working for me at present.'[3]

But gradually the family lost its productive functions to industry just as it eventually lost some of its educational ones to the school.

[1] Ibid., p. 44.

[2] As one needlewoman told Mayhew. He also described her workshop. 'There was no table in the room; but on a chair without a back there was an old tin tray, on which stood a cup of hot, milkless tea, and a broken saucer, with some half dozen small potatoes in it. It was the poor soul's dinner. Some tea-leaves had been given her, and she had boiled them up again to make something like a meal. She had not even a morsel of bread'. E. P. Thompson and E. Yeo, *The Unknown Mayhew*, p. 140.

[3] Ibid., pp. 108, 201, 239, 388.

Its roles were differentiated and transferred to other institutions in London and elsewhere as they had been in the Lancashire described by Smelser.[1] The family, even with its greatest advantage, cheap labour, could not indefinitely fend off the competition of the new industry which could exert its power from afar by transporting cheaper and sometimes better products into the shops on every street. The new industry had the financial capital. It gradually built up the management.[2] It had the overwhelming advantage of mechanical power. If electricity had come before steam, domestic industry might have survived more fully. Steam-power could not easily be brought into the home. It was tried in the Coventry ribbon industry, but, after a promising start, the experiment had to be abandoned.[3]

The victory of the new economic forces had a series of effects on the family. One of the vital economic ties holding it together was removed when it ceased to be a business partnership. When home and workplace were physically separated, wives and husbands (though not as much as in the Workhouses of the Poor Law) were also physically separated for a good part of their days and weeks, especially when husbands had to work the long hours that were customary. Wives could not see what their husbands were doing and earning (nor husbands, wives) and children could not learn from their fathers by watching them at work. Responsibility for organizing production was surrendered to the owners of capital and their agents, and by them (after the earlier stages of industrialization were over) people were employed not together as members of a family but as individuals for a wage. If the wage was good people could sustain a nineteenth-century version of the 'home-centred' family (without the marital symmetry of the twentieth-century variety). But if the wage was low or irregular the family, no longer held together by its productive arrangements, was liable to fragment.

A man had dependants in a way he had not usually had in

[1] N. J. Smelser, *Social Change in the Industrial Revolution.*

[2] S. Pollard, *The Genesis of Modern Management.*

[3] Bray's hope was only temporarily fulfilled of seeing 'in healthy country districts squares of three hundred or four hundred houses, with as much land attached to each house as each man can cultivate, with a steam engine in the centre of each square, with power conveyed to each house to do all the hard and dirty work, or to work the loom or other machinery.' C. Bray, *Philosophy of Necessity*, 2nd ed., 1863, p. 410. Quoted in J. Prest, *The Industrial Revolution in Coventry*, p. 110.

Stage 1. Wives could also work for wages whenever they could compete with single women in a century when there was a surplus of women over men. They also had to overcome the barrier set up by men trying to keep women off the labour market. If men were unemployed, why should they allow women in, even if such male monopolism kept one's own wife out of work as well as everyone else's? Booth wrote that, 'One has usually but to hold up the finger to secure whatever men are needed.'[1] This situation did not make the conflict between the sexes any the less. In view of this, it is surprising that the proportion of all women who were employed in the country as a whole was maintained as well as it was throughout the last half of the nineteenth century.[2] We do not know how many of these were married women in the country generally, let alone in London. It can never have been easy for married women to get full-time work, especially when they had young children to look after. The virtue of the domestic system was that productive work could be fitted in with the care of children and other household tasks. Such 'part-time' jobs were too rare for many women to be able to avoid dependence upon their men during their childbearing years.

The change in the role of children was still more significant. When the domestic system was supplanted few fathers could employ their children any more. This did not mean they ceased to be economic assets. They might even be more so, supporting their fathers where more jobs were open to them than to adults, partly because they and women too were more amenable than men to the new discipline of wage-labour. But children were eventually forced to become bread-eaters without being bread-winners. Their hours were limited. Their employment was gradually prohibited by law, often against the protests of their parents.[3] And that was followed by the worst blow of all, the growth of education which became compulsory before it became free. Some of the educational reformers were conscious of the loss that, when they achieved their success, many fathers would

[1] C. Booth, *Life and Labour of the People in London*, 2nd series, vol. 5. p. 89. Quoted in G. S. Jones, op. cit., p. 67.

[2] Department of Employment and Productivity, *British Labour Statistics: Historical Abstracts 1886–1968*, pp. 195–7.

[3] One mother said to a Royal Commission, 'I went to the pit myself when I was five years old, and two of my daughters go. It does them no harm. It never did me none.' *Report on Mines*, 1842, XVI, p. 27. Quoted in I. Pinchbeck, op. cit., p. 265.

incur. One hundred years before Ivan Illich[1] and other opponents of formal education wanted to abolish schools and return to something like a pre-industrial pattern, Lord Shaftesbury was not surprised when unskilled working-class people objected to the new schools in the East End of London.[2] He moved an amendment to the Education Bill of 1870 to lower the age of school-leaving from thirteen to ten, urging that 'the extent to which persons in London depended on the labour of their children their Lordships would scarcely be aware of, and it was impossible that a man could maintain wife and family on nine shillings a week, unless he was assisted by such labour.'[3] The amendment was defeated. The separate stage in human life to be known as 'childhood' was officially recognized.

To begin with, it was the family that paid the price for the recognition of a new right to education that almost no one wanted except those who already had it. The parents finally lost the incomes their children might have earned and had thenceforth to contend with a rival in the teacher for the educational role which had once been theirs alone.

Nineteenth-century accounts, in and out of literature, abound with stories of how husbands behaved to those who were no longer their helpmeets in the way they had been before. He had always had the authority bestowed on him by the greater physical force he could wield. 'People are not aware', said Mill, 'how entirely, in former ages, the law of superior strength was the rule of life; how publicly and openly it was avowed.'[4] This law of force was still to a large extent operative even in middle-class families and even more among the poor. The husband could exercise his power more despotically even than in the past because, if they had children,[5] the wife needed him more than he

[1] I. D. Illich, *Deschooling Society*.

[2] 'The new board schools were built in the slums, but the people were not at all grateful; in fact they rose up in their wrath at this interference with their liberty. To be forced to send their children to schools was too much, so they chased away the unfortunate builders, who had to be given police protection while building.' M. and C. H. B. Quennell, *History of Everyday Things in England*, vol. IV, p. 127.

[3] J. L. and B. Hammond, *Lord Shaftesbury*, pp. 257–8.

[4] J. S. Mill, *The Subjection of Women*, p. 35.

[5] Anderson says about Preston in the last century that 'There is also considerable evidence to suggest that bonds of affection were particularly strong between *mothers* and their children, which seems to reflect both the greater role of the mother in the life of the child and also the fact that it was she above all who made sacrifices for her children and she who protected them from their father.' M. Anderson, op. cit., p. 77.

needed her. The marriage was asymmetrical. In the middle of the last century there was good reason for the aspersions on the superiority of man expressed by Engels, Mill or Mayhew. A comment like this was written by the last one of the three in the year of the Great Exhibition, which celebrated the triumph of machinofacture over the old manufacture. But it does not stand alone.[1]

> The costermongers strongly resemble the North American Indians in their conduct to their wives. They can understand that it is the duty of the woman to contribute to the happiness of the man, but cannot feel that there is a reciprocal duty from the man to the woman. The wife is considered as an inexpensive servant and the disobedience of a wish is punished with blows. She must work early and late, and to the husband must be given the proceeds of her labour. Often when the man is in one of his drunken fits – which sometimes last two or three days continuously – she must by her sole exertion find food for herself and him too. To live in peace with him there must be no murmuring, no tiring under work, no fancied cause for jealousy – for if there be, she is either beaten into submission or cast adrift to begin life again – as another's leavings.

Costermongers were, like almost any other occupational group, unusual. But James Mearns in *The Bitter Cry of Outcast London*, James Greenwood in *Seven Curses of London*, Charles Booth in his *Life and Labour of the People in London*, Arthur Morrison in *Child of the Jago*, Walter Besant in *East London*, Medical Officers of Health in their reports, evidence to Royal Commissions, all gave some support to what Aristotle had said more than two thousand years before when he remarked that the only slave a poor man had was his wife. People rubbed along together in adversity partly because it was less wearing, and partly because adversity can unite as well as divide people. But they got on despite circumstances.

Circumstances did not alter all that quickly. There was not a great deal of change in the conditions under which working-class women lived up till the first world war. In 1913 Mrs Pember Reeves quoted a working-class woman in Lambeth who in

[1] H. Mayhew, *London Labour and the London Poor*, vol. 1, p. 43.

praising her husband showed how little she expected of him:[1]

> E's a good 'usbin. 'E ain't never kep' back me twenty-three bob, but 'e's that spiteful Satterday nights I 'as ter keep the children from 'im.

When a man was treated at work with callous disregard of his humanity he could always turn on the troop of scapegoats at home, headed by the person to whom he had promised – 'With this Ring I thee wed, with my body I thee worship, and with all my worldly goods I thee endow.'

If the man did not use the power of his hand he still had the power of the purse. He was *the* breadwinner now, but might refuse to share much more than the bread he won and even in some families take away from her what she earned, if she earned any, as it was his legal right to do. This was not so much because he did not like his family as because he liked other things more. The following story from Mayhew in 1849 became almost a refrain, even though things were worse when wages were still paid at public houses. He was reporting what a tailor told him.[2]

> I myself generally spend half (unless my Missus catches me); and on several occasions I have squandered away in liquor all I earned in the week. My Missus knows my infirmity, and watches me of a Saturday night regularly. She was waiting outside the public house where you picked me up, and there were three or four more wives of journeymen tailors watching outside of the tavern, besides my old woman.

The selfishness of husbands bore with special severity upon their dependants when there were most of them, that is in the early years of marriage, when the family income divided by the number of heads was less anyway, irrespective of what husbands did with it. Outside a few favoured occupations, employees have never yet been paid according to the number of their dependants. It follows that they can hardly avoid downs and ups in their standard of living in accordance with the fluctuations in the number of mouths to be fed and bodies to be clothed and housed. Rowntree pointed out (as Bradlaugh and others had done before him) the cast that this cycle gave to poverty. Few labouring

[1] M. S. Reeves, *Round About a Pound a Week*, p. 16.

[2] E. P. Thompson and E. Yeo, op. cit., p. 194.

people, at the time of his first survey in York,[1] remained all their lives in poverty, at or below the subsistence level that he used to define it. There was a characteristic and systematic cycle with four phases. Before a man married, and in particular before he had children, he was in relative affluence. This was the period

> during which he is earning money and living under his parents' roof; for some portion of this period he will be earning more money than is required for lodging, food and clothes. This is his chance to save money. Then with marriage, and children, poverty will overtake him, as it had overtaken him, for the same reason, when he had been a child. This period of poverty will last perhaps for ten years, until the first child is fourteen years old and begins to earn wages; but if there are more than three children it may last longer.

In a third period there was a repeat of the former time of relative ease when the children ceased to be a burden and, when they were earning, became an asset until such time as they launched themselves on the same undulating path as their parents had taken before them. In a fourth period, when he was too old to work, he descended into the grimmest poverty of all.

What was true of the past remains true today, at least to some degree. Wherever people are on the scale of wealth, they can rarely avoid the same cycle. We asked a question in the 1970 survey about the total joint income of husband and wife before tax. We do not set great store by it, for the reasons that will become apparent in a moment. But the answers, as set out in Table 7, do give some indication of the fluctuations, even allowing for the fact that they all refer to people at one point of time and not to the same people progressing through their own lives. Family allowances and children's tax allowances may have damped down the swings. They have not eliminated them.

The experience of the different classes is not the same. All drop in the period when wives are confined to the home to look after children. The least skilled are relatively the best off in the early adult years when their physical health and strength is at a maximum and before they are overtaken by family responsibilities. They are also exceptional, according to these figures, in that they do not regain the customary plateau in middle life. More or less

[1] B. S. Rowntree, *Poverty: A Study of Town Life*, p. 136.

TABLE 7 *Age, occupational class and income per head (main sample: information from married men and women; average for all ages in each class 100; total number in each class and age group shown in brackets)*

	29 or under	*30–39*	*40–49*	*50–64*	*65 or over*
Professional and managerial	110	87	100	119	68
	(34)	(74)	(74)	(82)	(31)
Clerical	116	107	109	95	61
	(24)	(28)	(36)	(47)	(17)
Skilled	108	100	106	108	60
	(67)	(109)	(117)	(140)	(57)
Semi-skilled and unskilled	121	109	106	105	62
	(27)	(39)	(48)	(81)	(42)

Family allowances have been included. Children of different ages have been treated as fractions of an adult according to the conventions used by the Supplementary Benefits Commission (*Supplementary Benefit Handbook*, p. 67).

uniformly in all classes, old age is a period of relative poverty, though relieved for some by the possession of houses which are both mortgage and rent free, and by the ownership of capital assets which can be drawn on, and for others, if on a lesser scale, by the contributions of children, reversing the income flow of earlier life.

We have gone back to Rowntree and produced these figures of our own about the life cycle in order to emphasize how much families are under financial and other pressure in the early years of marriage. Even if the marriage partnership is also a financial one, some sacrifice can hardly be avoided. But if that condition is not satisfied the sacrifice will be much sharper for some, less for others: it will fall on different members of the family unevenly.

This, we are convinced, is what did happen very generally in Stage 2 of family development. Wives had not ordinarily had money incomes given to them in pre-industrial times, and did not necessarily afterwards. Rowntree himself, and a host of investigators who succeeded him, went astray by assuming that what may have happened in the middle-class families in which they originated also happened in the families that were the objects of their research. Rowntree distinguished 'primary' from 'secondary' poverty. Families were considered to be suffering from the former where their 'total earnings are insufficient to obtain the minimum necessaries for the maintenance of merely physical efficiency'; from the latter where their 'total earnings would be sufficient for the maintenance of merely physical efficiency, were it not that some portion of it is absorbed by other expenditure, either useful or wasteful.'[1] If this lead had been followed and Rowntree and his successors had enquired about the extent of secondary poverty, finding out in detail what money was spent on by all members of the family, they would have had to accept that total earnings are not necessarily any guide to the living standards of women and children.

Unfortunately, they did not do this, or even, it appears, see that the need for it was accentuated by a repeated but incidental finding of their enquiries. The investigators, in the inter-war poverty surveys at Bristol, on Merseyside, in Sheffield, Southampton and in other places, had to try and discover what the husband's income was, in order to be able to decide whether a family was above or below the poverty line. The Bristol survey said of the interviewing that 'on several occasions husbands even ran after them to disclose earnings which they had not wanted to reveal in front of their wives.'[2] The writer meant this to demonstrate how good were relations between interviewers and families; in fact he demonstrated, more revealingly, how bad his understanding was of the internal dynamics of those families. The Merseyside Survey referred in passing to 'the fact that some housewives who were responsible for keeping the budgets would only have knowledge of what was given them to spend, and this sum would not infrequently be less than the aggregate of the family income'.[3] The same mistake was made in repeated family budget enquiries onwards from the one in 1903 which reported that 'the wife frequently does not know what the actual earnings of her husband are, but only the weekly sums he gives her for housekeeping'.[4] The mistake was that, despite this acknowledgment, both then and

[1] B. S. Rowntree, op. cit., pp. 86–7.

[2] H. Tout, *The Standard of Living in Bristol*, p. 24.

[3] D. Caradog Jones (ed.), *The Social Survey of Merseyside*, p. 147.

[4] Board of Trade, *Consumption of Food and Cost of Living of Working Classes in the United Kingdom and certain Foreign Countries*, p. 1.

later the housewife was asked to give details of expenditure of herself *and* her husband, or the husband asked to do so while sitting in the same room as the wife when he did not intend to tell her or the investigator either what he earned or the portion he kept back for himself.

A somewhat fuller knowledge had to wait upon the enquiries done by Soutar and her colleagues in Birmingham[1] and, more notably, upon the only full investigation which focused at all sharply on the issue, made by Madge[2] with the aid of Rothbarth. The picture that emerged from these and other more tangential pieces of research[3] was that in the working classes it was the general practice for husbands not to disclose their earnings – to do so would have been to make it obvious that they were keeping something back for themselves. What mattered even more, they did not increase their allowances to their wives by more than small amounts, if at all, when prices rose or when additional children came. 'It (housekeeping money) is more often a fixed sum than a percentage of his net income. But even if it is a rough percentage it is near enough to a fixed sum.'[4] The same author, in his study of the coalminer, said that 'he would be more willing to give her a treat from time to time than to raise her "wages", just because they are guaranteed, lest she should regard the additional payment as a right. "It is easy to raise them, but it is difficult to lower them if bad times come." '[5] It was not so different in London. The frequent consequence was, of course, that the fall in the standard of life following the arrival of children was borne mainly by the wife and children, and borne not necessarily with complaint but with compliance by many wives who regarded it as her husband's right to spend in the pub if he chose and what he chose as long as, unlike some of the most selfish husbands, he also kept up his payments to her. The selfish ones who gave little or nothing to their families were in every district a warning to wives of how bad their lot could be.

A husband could not dissociate himself entirely from the standard of life inside the home. Outside it he could spend substantial sums out of his earnings on betting, tobacco and beer. But he

[1] M. S. Soutar *et al.*, *Nutrition and Size of Family*.
[2] C. Madge, *War-Time Pattern of Saving and Spending*.
[3] Summarized in M. Young, 'Distribution of income within the family'.
[4] F. Zweig, *Labour, Life and Poverty*, p. 14.
[5] F. Zweig, *Men in the Pits*, p. 96.

slept there and he ate there. The evidence about what he ate, as compared with his dependants, is even more scanty than about the division of cash. What there is suggests that the bread-winner was also the meat-eater. The wife had to give him the best in order to keep up his physical strength, for on that they all relied. If he got ill, the income would (before sick benefit) stop completely. If he could not manage the work any longer, he was liable to get the sack. And of what was left after the husbands had the pick, a good part of the rest went to the children.[1]

> Health Visitors' accounts also speak of the deplorable extent to which the woman will starve herself in order that her children should have a little more or that her labour should be lightened. Nor is this changed even at the times when, for the sake of a coming child as well as for herself, she should be getting a good diet.

This has all been in the past tense. We are ourselves convinced that the conditions of family life have in this respect changed a great deal. The practice was for husbands to keep the figure of their earnings dark, for them to spend a good part of their money upon themselves and for there to be a fairly rigidly defined separation between the things that one or the other would spend money on. There was a man's sphere and a woman's, in spending as in other functions. What makes us think it has changed?

The evidence is not as full as we would like. The welfare state has certainly brought about some redistribution of income from men to women and children now that mothers receive family and other allowances which are paid direct to them rather than to fathers. As mothers were not covered by insurance before, they have also benefited more from the introduction of the National Health Service than have fathers. About the disposal of earned income inside the family, the evidence is more circumstantial. Gorer says that 'more than one wife out of six who receive housekeeping allowances do not know what their husbands earn.'[2] The incidental findings of the various surveys to which we have referred suggest that the proportion of wives ignorant in this respect must have been higher in the past. But since most of the investigators were also ignorant on the same score, and so did not

[1] M. Spring Rice, *Working-Class Wives*, p. 157.
[2] G. Gorer, *Sex and Marriage in England Today*, p. 92.

cast their enquiries in a manner which could have settled the argument, we cannot produce any precise comparison.

Another piece of circumstantial evidence is also from the very family budget enquiries that we have been criticizing. They have shown that people have consistently under-reported their expenditure on alcohol and tobacco, as the main commodities on which husbands spent the part of their income they kept for themselves, when what they say is checked against the figures for sales obtained from the manufacturers and the tax authorities. But the extent of under-reporting has fallen. In 1937–8 people acknowledged only 14 per cent of the actual expenditure on alcohol and 66 per cent of that on tobacco. By 1957–9 they reported 45 per cent of the total for alcohol and 76 per cent of that for tobacco; by 1969–71 60 per cent and 78 per cent respectively.[1] In the fortresses of their own homes where the budget forms are filled in, they have come out with more of the truth. No doubt this is partly because less stigma attaches to either of these drugs, and more to others. Methods of enquiry have improved. But one factor is in our view also that husbands do not need to falsify the information they give in front of their wives because they do not any longer keep it secret from them in ordinary times when the investigation is not proceeding. Being more frank with their wives, they can also be more truthful with the investigators.

These two bits of evidence are by no means conclusive. What is rather more so is the change in the whole pattern of consumption. Expenditure on alcohol and tobacco has (at constant prices) been going down steadily since the beginning of the century.[2] On the other hand, expenditure on things which are to a greater extent shared with the wife and family, such as motoring, entertainment and durable goods (as they are quaintly called) used in the home, has gone up. If expenditure is for joint use, in and around the new sort of home, then there is no point in keeping the income in two rigidly defined and unfairly divided portions. This has especially been so since wives have been able to go out to work in increasing numbers (as we shall show in the next chapter) and earn money for themselves. If they spend *their* money on the home it is not so

[1] The figures are estimates based on a comparison between the Government Social Survey, *Family Expenditure Surveys* and Central Statistical Office, *National Income and Expenditure Accounts*.

[2] D. A. Rowe, 'Private consumption', in W. Beckerman, *The British Economy in 1975*, p. 180.

easy for a husband to refuse to even if he wants to. We expect that when the cohort of people who are marrying now have moved through all the phases of the life cycle the change-over from one financial dispensation to another, from customs more appropriate to Stage 2 to those suitable to Stage 3, will be more or less complete. The ups and downs in relative poverty and prosperity will be jointly shared.

3. *The move towards symmetry*

We have already started speaking about one aspect of the Stage 3 family, the growth of a financial partnership, and we should now say something about the sources of this change, and about other manifestations of the new spirit, which was first evident in the middle classes. Their experience had been if not the opposite at least very different from that of the classes we concentrated on in the previous section. Poor people had been largely dispossessed of such property rights as they had, and the wife of the share she had in exploiting them. The rising middle classes, far from losing their worldly goods, were on the contrary adding to them. The man was as much the master in the families benefiting most from Victorian prosperity. He had the larger houses built for him and his in what has since become the Zone of Transition. But he did not have to withstand the pressure on him of extreme scarcity which constrained his employees to put their own masculine interests so unreservedly first. His wife could be an ornament to his property as well as part of it. She was the mistress of a bevy of maids who needed to be closely supervised if the sort of standards extolled by a Mrs Beeton were to be maintained (her *Book of Household Management* sold two million copies in the one decade of the 1860s[1]). The man's physical comfort, the general good order of the house and the sense of spiritual contentment gained from a consciousness of his own goodness depended upon the circumspection and the affection with which he treated his wife.

But in these same circles the new feminism, nourished by the evangelical insistence on the spiritual worth of the humblest, was beginning to grow. Just as poorer men have struggled to gain some of the privileges of the rich, so have women struggled to secure some of the privileges that formerly belonged to men alone.

[1] O. R. McGregor, *Divorce in England*, p. 64.

This is a basic variant of our guiding Principle. Feminism was in the long run an influence almost as decisive as technology upon the growth of symmetry inside the family. Once it began to be denied that power should be ascribed to rulers solely by their birth into the station of life of a particular family, once elementary democratic rights had been granted to men, or some of them, once slavery had been abolished, once the claims of the new individualism had been acknowledged for men, the same arguments could be used against men by champions of people born into a particular sex and so condemned, by their chromosomes alone, to inferiority in society. The position of women in law was at that time worse than that of slaves. They could not own property. They could not, however much revulsion they might feel, refuse their masters the last familiarity. They had no legal rights to separation from their men nor over their children. However severely a husband beat his wife, she could not, until a reform in the law, free herself from her tormentor. If she ran away she could without right of asylum be forced to return, and, until 1891, when the Court of Appeal decided otherwise in the case of *Regina* v. *Jackson*, he could use physical force to get her back.[1] Mill in 1869 urged 'that the principle which regulates the existing social relations between the two sexes – the legal subordination of one sex to the other – is wrong in itself, and now one of the chief hindrances to home improvement; and that it ought to be replaced by a principle of perfect equality, admitting no power or privilege on the one side, nor disability on the other.'[2]

One by one, leading up to 1928 when women were given votes on the same terms as men, most legal disabilities were removed. Success was achieved because Mill and such unusual men as were of his persuasion were joined by representatives of the underprivileged. An extraordinary band of women, who had gained an education, if only by their own efforts, Miss Nightingale and Miss

1 'The husband there obtained a decree for restitution of conjugal rights. The wife refusing to obey the decree, one Sunday in March 1891, the husband, assisted by two young men, seized her as she was leaving church with her sister and forced her into a carriage. The husband and one of the men got in with the wife, and the carriage was driven to the husband's house, where the wife was shut up and detained. The wife claimed her freedom, and the Court upheld her right to it, and negatived the husband's right to interfere with it. The judgement is a landmark in the law on this head.' S. Coit in Introduction to J. S. Mill, op. cit., p. 25.

2 J. S. Mill, op. cit., p. 29.

Hill, Miss Buss and Miss Beale, Miss Davies and Miss Garrett, many of them refusing to be bound in matrimony to any of their sex's oppressors, led a series of campaigns in the face of far more obloquy than the modern proponents of Women's Liberation. To give one example, Josephine Butler led a bitter and long drawn out campaign against the Contagious Diseases Act which imposed upon prostitutes in garrison towns in England and Ireland compulsory medical examination and compulsory treatment at the hands of male doctors. Her plea was that what was for the first time coming to be widely called the 'double standard' of morality should not penalize women and leave men free. This at a time when the general attitude to sex was one of intense concern certainly, but asserting itself in a contradictory insistence that even piano-legs should have drapings around them for fear of (or in the hope of?) arousing lustful associations; the word 'immoral' was reserved for any books which did not camouflage the subject, and Bishop Wordsworth was able to attack the proposal to legalize the marriage of a widower to his deceased wife's sister in the following obsessional terms. Let this happen, he said, and[1]

> The wife's sister will have ceased to be a sister, and have become almost a stranger. She can no longer enter the house with the same freedom and familiarity as before. Or, if she does, what jealousies and heart-burnings may arise! The wife may be less fair than her sister.

The Bishop gave himself away by his exclamation mark. Yet even in such a prudish atmosphere Josephine Butler was, after twenty years, successful in getting the Contagious Diseases Act repealed, and eventually, in 1907, without destroying the family, a man was allowed to marry his deceased wife's sister, and by 1921 a woman even her deceased husband's brother.

Important as the legal reforms were – perhaps none more so than the placing of the same duty upon parents to send their daughters to school as their sons – they were less a tribute to feminism than was another change which owed little to the State, the reduction in the size of the family. Most women, who had spent the best part of a lifetime in child-bearing and rearing with all its pain and toil, had probably always regarded it as wearisome. But the man, especially if he was humble, delayed in his reaction.

[1] Quoted in D. M. Stenton, *The English Woman in History*, p. 338.

He did not choose to co-operate with his wife in restraint or constraint even if she had got so far as to break free herself from a fatalistic view of her own maternal destiny. Family planning has run repeatedly into opposition from men in the developing countries who, in this respect, are repeating the experience of their sex in England. One of our informants in Bethnal Green told us in the 1950s what things had been like in his father's time:[1]

> The man would spend all his money in the pub, come home and abuse his wife. There was no birth control in those days, I know, but even then there were ways and means not to have children if you didn't want to have them. And if the woman complained, it was hold your noise and give her another baby, and that's the finish.

If the husband's standard of living had been as much dragged down as the wife's by the arrival of the baby which was the result of his insensitivity to her feelings, he would have been more careful, and the reaction of the working classes to the increased population pressure created by falling mortality not so long delayed. But, as we have seen, the full weight of poverty consequent upon a large family fell mainly upon the mother and her offspring. It was no wonder that women used to say, as some still do, of another pregnancy, 'I have *fallen* again.'

The old attitude persists in the assignment of responsibility for the precautions. Even in 1971 Gorer spoke of the 'widespread, if not very articulate belief among the working classes that it is the husband's prerogative to determine whether any form of birth control should be used and that it is unseemly, almost unwomanly, for the wife to take the initiative. Several of our unskilled working-class wives gave verbal approval to the pill if the "husband cannot control himself" (a periphrasis for withdrawal) though they did not themselves use it.'[2] The sheath or condom was still the favoured method amongst working-class people. Mutual discussion between the couple has also remained less common. 'The proportion who had discussed birth control with their husbands before they were married fell from 72 per cent of the mothers with husbands in professional jobs to 17 per cent of those with

[1] M. Young and P. Willmott, *Family and Kinship in East London*, p. 6.

[2] G. Gorer, op. cit., p. 113.

husbands in unskilled jobs.'[1] The initiative has continued to be to a large extent with the man, as it was before.

But the vital statistics show that, however deep-lying men's attitudes, they did eventually shift, and did so very much in accordance with the Principle. Habakkuk considers that there were three main influences on the adoption of birth control. The first was the long-term pressure of increasing population, which may have led some people in competition with others for scarce jobs, especially when they had to wait before securing advancement, to act prudently and defer marriage. A second, of greater importance, was the fall in infant and child mortality which first affected the middle classes. They adjusted to the change when 'the increase in the expectation of life after the middle of the nineteenth century reduced the number of births that were necessary to secure a given number of surviving children'.[2] The third influence was more specific in time. The Bradlaugh-Besant trial of 1877, as far-reaching in its effects as the Lady Chatterley trial in the 1960s, publicized methods of birth control and to some extent made it respectable. Banks[3] believes that the trial made contraception more acceptable in the economic depression which followed it and which would have cut down the standard of living of the middle classes still more if they had not taken steps to sustain it.[4]

The middle classes were the first to be prompted by any of these influences, and they were the first to control births within marriage rather than by the more traditional way of postponing it. 'Middle-class fertility may have started to fall before 1850. Whether this is so or not, there is no doubt that middle-class fertility in the second half of the century fell well in advance of that of the main mass of the population.'[5]

At first the new habits were largely confined to these same classes. The *Fertility Census* of 1911 compared average family size among women married in 1851–61 with those married in 1881–6.

[1] A. Cartwright, *Parents and Family Planning Services*, p. 153.

[2] H. J. Habakkuk, *Population Growth and Economic Development since 1750*, p. 63.

[3] J. A. Banks, *Prosperity and Parenthood*, p. 150.

[4] Technology also played a direct part. 'The invention of the vulcanising process of rubber in the 1840s made possible large-scale production of cheap rubber contraceptives'. D. H. Wrong, *Population and Society*, 2nd ed., p. 56. But more traditional methods of contraception probably remained the most prevalent for a long time after 1877.

[5] H. J. Habakkuk, op. cit., p. 55.

It showed that wives with Professional Class husbands had an average family size which was 86 per cent of the average for all classes at the first date and 72 per cent at the second, while wives of unskilled men had 105 per cent at the earlier and 112 per cent at the later. In time the pattern at the bottom began to change. The gap narrowed. The social classes converged. In the inter-war period, in particular, while family size generally continued to fall more sharply than ever, the reduction was now relatively greater among the wives of manual workers than among the middle classes.[1] Class differences in family size are not, therefore, as marked as in the past.[2] Average family size fell from nearly six at about the middle of the nineteenth century to just over two in 1970, which has been made possible by the spread of contraceptive practices – from the professional class to other non-manual workers, and thence to the skilled, semi-skilled and unskilled.

There may have been yet another change. It seems that in recent decades among at least some sections of the middle classes couples have been having rather *more* children. The evidence is not at all conclusive, but it does suggest that, although class differences in family size are generally smaller than they were, the couples having the largest families have in recent decades been some of those from the top of the occupational scale along with those at the bottom.[3] We cannot throw much light on this subject from our own survey. Large numbers are needed, in order to allow for duration of marriage or for the wife's age, before firm conclusions can be drawn. There were some figures in line with the Census ones. But the numbers were too small and the general pattern of figures too inconsistent for us to specify exactly which people at the top have more-than-average numbers of children. We cannot conclude, not yet anyway, that richer people in the second half of this century are doing what they did in the second half of the last, and inaugurating a new pattern, the opposite of the old. 'While the trend towards smaller families still continues among manual workers, among the professional families it has been not only checked but reversed. May it not be that the middle

[1] D. H. Wrong, op. cit., p. 72.

[2] As D. V. Glass remarked in 'Fertility trends in Europe since the second world war', 'Differences in fertility by socio-economic status now tend to be somewhat narrower than were found formerly' (p. 118).

[3] General Register Office, *Census 1951 – Fertility Report,* pp. xlix–li, and *Census 1961 – Fertility Tables,* pp. 112–34, 244–74.

classes who in the 1870s led the country out of the fashion of small families are now leading us back to big families?'[1] This could happen, particularly if the late 1970s proved to be a period of economic expansion after the relative stagnation of the previous decade.

Whatever happens in the future, it is clear that the reduction in fertility in the past has already brought about an immense change. Titmuss summed it up in this way for the period up to 1951:[2]

> It would seem that the typical working-class mother of the 1890s, married in her teens or early twenties and experiencing ten pregnancies, spent about fifteen years in a state of pregnancy and in nursing a child for the first year of its life. She was tied, for this period of time, to the wheel of childbearing. Today, for the typical mother, the time so spent would be about four years. A reduction of such magnitude in only two generations in the time devoted to childbearing represents nothing less than a revolutionary enlargement of freedom for women brought about by the power to control their own fertility. This private power, what Bernard Shaw once described as the ultimate freedom, can hardly have been exercised without the consent – if not the approval – of the husbands.

Fifteen years was not the maximum period of confinement to the home. The children had to be looked after well beyond the first year of life. The mother's last child would often not have left school until she was in her mid-fifties, by which time she would be as active all over again in her role of grandmother. The new grandmother is a different figure just because she has not practised her craft continuously throughout her life.

Stress on conjugal family

The size of families would not have been limited unless husbands were prepared to co-operate, and if the size of families had not been limited husbands would not have found their homes as congenial as they have eventually done. The result would not have

[1] H. J. Habakkuk, op. cit., p. 69.
[2] R. M. Titmuss, 'The position of women', p. 91.

been achieved as fully as it has without the second of the changes we mentioned in Chapter 1, the separation of the immediate, or nuclear, family from the extended family. We believe that this extended family had a particular pattern to it, being mother centred, this because it was largely created as a protective device against the insecurities inherent, for women, in the Stage 2 family. The evidence, such as it is, comes mainly from 'oral history', that is from the reports about the past we have gathered in various surveys of our own and from comparisons between older and younger people which for once do, to our minds, reveal a secular rather than just an age change. We would agree with Anderson that the system of mutual aid around which this kind of extended family was built probably flourished most fully in the early part of the twentieth century.[1]

The thesis, drawn out through several books,[2] was that when husbands could not be relied upon, women, after a time-lag for acclimatization to city life, eventually built up an organization in their own defence and in the defence of their children. This they did in what became a common mode of reaction in many societies where the conjugal tie was weak, from the West Indies and the Southern States to the Republic of South Africa and the industrial cities of Europe and North America. They created an informal women's trade union. There was only one out of the many kin relationships that they could stress, between the mother and her daughter, the Demeter tie as we called it, to distinguish it from the Oedipus conflict between son and father. Ever since the father had to move out of the home to work, it has been easier for daughters to build on this tie because they have in their mothers a model

[1] 'I would suggest that it was probably only after the introduction of the old age pension transferred much of the economic burden of old age from kin, and above all in the interim period when economic problems caused by other critical life situations began to be eased by the beginnings of that bureaucratical system that we now call the Welfare State to the point where kinship aid was not very costly per capita in cost terms (though still costly in time which was not so scarce, at least for women), that a really strong affective and non-calculative commitment to the kinship net could develop and "traditional" community solidarity become possible.' M. Anderson, op. cit., p. 178. On the same point Hobsbawm said that 'So far as the working class is concerned, as we shall see what is called its "traditional" way of life is if anything more recent still. It is hardly found complete anywhere before the 1880s.' E. J. Hobsbawm, op. cit., p. 6.

[2] M. Young and P. Willmott, *Family and Kinship in East London;* P. Willmott and M. Young, *Family and Class in a London Suburb;* P. Townsend, *The Family Life of Old People;* P. Marris, *Widows and Their Families.*

whom they can copy.[1] This bond was accentuated well into adult life. Daughters lived near their mothers, or with them, even after they were married.

Propinquity made support easier. Mothers could give their daughters and their grandchildren a feeling of security. More tangibly, they could look after the children if the daughter got the chance of a job, and could pass on money or gifts in kind in their capacity as co-ordinators for the extended families which they headed. The more people that belonged to it, that is, the more daughters and daughter substitutes there were, the more effective was the large family as an insurance. If someone was down on her or his luck, someone else might be in the opposite state, and therefore able to contribute, directly or through the intermediary of the grandmothers, to the welfare of the needy. The trade union also worked better as a friendly society if different people in it were at different phases in the life cycle of poverty and prosperity already referred to in this chapter. A person in an up phase could help another in a down. When people were old the flow of services as well as income would be reversed, and the young do for the old what the old had done for the young.

This sort of structure – weak on the family of marriage, strong on the family of origin – tended to perpetuate itself. Husbands were often squeezed out of the warmth of the female circle, and took to the pub as their defence against the defence. They had to put up with mothers-in-law who were constantly interfering, as the man might see it, with the arrangements in his own home. His wife could seem more her daughter than his wife, and both of them belonged to a group which did not award men a high place in its order of values. He could find himself undermined, in a hundred ways, subtle and unsubtle. He could be pushed into becoming an absentee father, so bringing on the insecurity which the extended family in this form was established to counter.

If so self-reinforcing, why has the system of balances and counter-balances been transformed? Everything else that has been mentioned in this chapter, and the last, and will be in the next, has played a part. If we had to plump, we would give special promi-

[1] 'It is possible from an early age to initiate girls directly into many important aspects of the adult feminine role. Their mothers are continuously about the house and the meaning of many of the things they are doing is relatively tangible and easily understandable to a child.' T. Parsons, 'Age and sex in the social structure of the United States', p. 90.

nence to the higher standard of life and to migration. On the first we agree, once again, with Anderson.[1]

> Since the Second World War, by contrast, we have apparently seen further changes leading to some eclipse of the most solidary and normative kinship bonds. In terms of this analysis I should attribute this change on the one hand to some decline in the frequency of critical life situations as health improved, family size declined, and the scourge of unemployment was reduced, and on the other to an increase in people's ability to meet these crises for themselves through increased wages and increased benefits and services from the Welfare State.

As for homes, new ones have been built for immediate families with young children in them, not for extended families in housing clusters like those that are common in Africa and Asia. There is no modern counterpart of the extended family compound found in the 'turnings' and courts of London. The young couples have had to, or have chosen to, move to new houses and away from relatives. Husbands have often been the most willing because it meant that their wives would be wrested away from the influence of their Mums. Without proximity, the woman's trade union is not one. Mother next door, or in the next street, is one thing. She can be visited ten times a day for gossip and exchange of services. Mother ten miles away, even two miles away, is a more distant presence, called on in emergencies but no longer hour-by-hour. Even where the generations have not been physically separated, the declining influence of grandmothers – for instance, in finding rented housing for their daughters or in advising them on health and child care – has helped to turn the trio of mother-daughter-husband into a duet.

Less segregation of roles

These various historical processes are still working their way through the social structure which means that, in many if not all respects, they have had a fuller effect on the families of richer than poorer people, and of younger rather than older. With poorer and with older people the vestiges of Stage 2 are still very much

[1] M. Anderson, op. cit., p. 178.

apparent. But the great majority of married people in our sample were members of the dominant type of new family.

In Stage 2 families there was segregation of roles in many more ways than those to do with money. If husbands did any 'work' at all at home the tasks that they, and their wives, thought proper to them were those to which male strength and male manual skill lent themselves. It was not a man's place to do woman's work any more than the other way round. All that has now changed. Wives are working outside the home in what is much less of a man's world than it used to be. The reader who will turn forward to Table 13 in the next chapter will see the pattern for our sample.

Husbands also do a lot of work in the home, including many jobs which are not at all traditional men's ones – which is one reason why the distinction between work and leisure is now a great deal less clear for men than it used to be. It never was very distinct for women. There is now no sort of work in the home strictly reserved for 'the wives' even clothes-washing and bed-making, still ordinarily thought of as women's jobs, were frequently mentioned by husbands as things they did as well. The extent of the sharing is probably still increasing. The latest reading that we have is recorded in Table 8. What husbands did in detail varied according to occupational class. The people at the top helped rather less than others with house-cleaning, for instance. But taking all forms of help into account it was still true that fewer semi-skilled and unskilled workers contributed at all in this sort of way.

The relationship can also be looked at in another way. Table 9 shows that on weekdays men spent more time with colleagues than they did with family. But take account of the weekend and the picture changes. If the week is treated as a whole the immediate family wins out in the competition for time against its main rival, people at work.

They shared their work; they shared their time. But if the trend was towards it, most married couples were obviously still a long way from the state of unisex that some young people had arrived at. There were many roles which were still primarily the prerogative of one sex or another, particularly in the classes which were not so far on in the process of change. In 1970 the general rule in working-class families with cars was still that the husbands were the drivers and the wives passengers, like the children. But

TABLE 8 *Occupational class and husband's help in the home (main sample: married men working full-time)*

Reported help to wife at least once a week	*Professional and managerial*	*Clerical*	*Skilled*	*Semi-skilled and unskilled*	*All*
None	14%	13%	14%	24%	15%
Washing up only	16%	7%	13%	12%	13%
Other tasks (cleaning, cooking, child care etc.), with or without washing up	70%	80%	73%	64%	72%
Total %	100%	100%	100%	100%	100%
Number	171	70	236	107	585

TABLE 9 *Average hours spent with immediate family compared to others (diary sample: married men aged 30 to 49)*

	Weekday	*Saturday*	*Sunday*	*Total for week*
Family	5·7	8·7	9·5	46·7
Family together with friends or relatives	0·5	1·9	2·3	6·7
Total with family	6·2	10·6	11·8	53·4
Work colleagues without family	7·1	2·6	1·0	39·1
Friends or relatives without family	0·7	1·1	0·8	5·4
Alone	2·1	1·1	0·7	12·3
Total waking hours accounted for	16·1	15·4	14·3	110·2
Number of men	203	197	197	—

In this and later tables time is expressed not in hours and minutes but in hours and tenths of hours. The total for the week has been calculated by multiplying the sample weekday by five and adding the two weekend days. Time has been excluded for which there was no record about who was present with the diarist.

this role, too, was well on the way to being shared. Mr Barwick, a carpenter in Sutton, described what he did at 7 p.m. one Saturday.

> I took Beryl out for a driving lesson just to polish up on turns in the road etc. The kids enjoy Mum driving for a change. Beryl's driving is a bit of a thing in the family at the moment. There is a bit of a competition going on with Dot, one of our friends who is learning as well. There was the usual inquest on the phone tonight after the lessons they had both had.

Just as it was in some families still thought rather strange for women to be drivers, it was in virtually all not expected that men should do more than *help* their wives at the work of child-rearing and housekeeping. The primary responsibilities for home and work were still firmly with one sex or the other, as we shall see in the next chapter.

Miniaturization of machines

The symmetrical family would not have developed as it has without the aid of technology, which has been responsible for the last change we want to mention in this chapter. If technology had made it impossible to operate within the small frame of the home – if it had turned out that consumption had to be, like production, organized in large groups such as Robert Owen thought could be the salvation of mankind in his mill at New Lanark and in his community at New Harmony in Hampshire, and the builders of the *kibbutzim* in Israel likewise in this century – then the family would perhaps have bent to technical necessity. As it is, technology has played new tunes on the same old theme of the primacy of the primordial.

It was not like that in Stage 2 of our scheme. People were thrust into an industrial economy before the houses and consumer goods to put in them had properly arrived. Almost the only luxury was provided in the tavern, and this was largely reserved for men. Along with their work-mates they could find in the warmth and conviviality of the pub some comfort to compensate them for the harshness of their working conditions, as well as abatement for the thirst which the hardness of the work stimulated. The week-ends could, as incomes grew, be so uproarious that absenteeism on 'St Monday', as it was known even in the nineteenth century, was much higher than on any other day. The homes could not compete. They were small. They were full of wailing infants, at any rate where the parents did not keep them quiet (and sometimes stunt them for life) by feeding them with the opium-derived 'Godfrey's Cordial'. The Temperance Reformers, whether religious or secular, sometimes had success with their fearful stories of nemesis for the drinker which were the nineteenth-century counterpart of the statistics about lung cancer which the doctors and their allies have been producing in this. But often not. The space that mattered most for the husband used to be the collective space of the alehouse. As the amount of private space has increased there has been more physical room for the husband at home, more comfort and more room for receiving friends.[1]

The water, before it was piped into an individual supply, used to come from a collective well or stand-pipe in the street or on the landing of one of the tenements built by the Peabody, Guinness, Sutton and other philanthropic housing trusts. The washing was done in communal wash-places. If people took baths at all, they did so in the public slipper-baths. The entertainments were also collective long after a public hanging on Tyburn Hill, near where the Marble Arch now stands, ceased to be the greatest sight in London, drawing crowds of a hundred thousand. The street-markets were an entertainment, as they and football and horse-racing, almost alone of the collective spectacles of the past, still are. The city burst out on Bank Holidays as it had long before when archery practice had been compulsory. Transport was collective. The music hall was collective, as was its successor, the cinema. And for a time it looked as though the big would go on getting bigger, outside as well as at work. In the 1930s Llewellyn Smith drew from his survey the conclusion that[2]

> the supply of some of the more important forms of amusement has become mechanised, with consequent results which,

[1] Not like it was for the locomotive fitter described in an interwar survey. 'We do sometimes entertain a few friends, and on these occasions we have to dismantle our beds so as to make room for dancing or games that might be played.' H. L. Smith, *The New Survey of London Life and Labour*, vol. IX, p. 410.

[2] Ibid., pp. 7–8.

> *mutatis mutandis*, bear some analogy to those which follow the mechanisation of industrial processes. The most characteristic instrument of popular entertainment today is the cinema, of which the first beginnings under the name of the 'bioscope' were referred to by Charles Booth. Today the 258 cinemas within the County of London, with their 344,000 seats and their repeated performances, are capable of entertaining a quarter of the whole population on any one day.

The extent of the change is obvious. What kept people out of the home (and especially husbands with their superiority of command over the money) was the absence of attraction within it. A city of small workshops was also a city of mass life. In this century a city of large factories and offices is also a city of miniature life on the family scale. It is as though the giant of technology has laboured only with one end, to produce tiny reproductions of itself, like the car of the last chapter, and so to make up for the damage it did to the family in the past. Gas-light and electric light were inventions as crucial as piped water; at least husbands could see the faces of their wives after dark without too great an expense. The fractional horse-power motor was another key invention, powering home-laundries, home ice-makers, tiny cold stores, floor cleaners and cooking aids. The average housewife has been given 'about the same amount of mechanical assistance (about two horsepower) as was deployed by the average industrial worker around 1914'.[1] These inventions have, perhaps, done more for the wife than for the husband. But he has been just as absorbed as she by the machines which have brought entertainment into the home, starting with the gramophone and ending (so far) with colour television, and more so than she by the new style of do-it-yourself handicraft production with its power tools and extension ladders and stick-on tiles and emulsion paints. All in all, the machine has by mimicking man, from his fingers to his brain, enabled modern man to mimic his forbears. A partnership in leisure has therefore succeeded a partnership in work.

We do not know how much time people used to spend in and out of the home. But we do know what people who completed the diaries said about their custom in 1970. The figures are in Table 10. We very much doubt whether, before homes became

[1] R. Banham, 'Household godjets', p. 100.

Home, men at any rate would have passed more than half their time there.

TABLE 10 *Proportion of total time spent at home by husbands and wives (diary sample: married men and women aged 30 to 49: total number of people shown in brackets)*

	Weekday	*Saturday*	*Sunday*
Men	55% (203)	66% (197)	76% (197)
Women working outside the home	71% (132)	75% (127)	83% (127)
Women not working outside the home	87% (76)	82% (73)	87% (74)

In this chapter, which has been complementary to the previous one, dealing with other aspects of the same process, we have been sketching out the manner in which family patterns have changed in the last two centuries. The pre-industrial family in which husbands, wives and children were partners in production (if far from equal partners) was in the end unable to resist the force of a much wider division of labour than could be managed within its tiny compass. The new economy did not smoothly incorporate the old or produce a new moral or any other sort of order by which the family could be sustained. Only slowly, and after a great deal of suffering of which women and children were the victims even more than men, has a different sort of integration been achieved around the functions of the family as a unit of consumption rather than production. Various changes, starting first in the middle classes, have been both interacting causes and consequences of the general transformation. The struggle for women's rights has gradually changed the mental climate, as well as bringing material benefits like family allowances to the aid of wives and children; and each victory has set off a campaign for another. Just because their husbands have been willing to co-operate in the process, the limitation of families has emancipated women more than anything else, and as success has been achieved both wives and children have become more rewarding to co-operate with. The acquisition of better homes has (except for those left out of the general advance) made it more worthwhile for husbands to spend money on them, and their occupants. There is then less reason for a sharp segregation of incomes. And if contraception and more tolerant husbands enable wives to go out to work, they can win for themselves a measure of financial independence.

IV

THE WORK OF MARRIED WOMEN

We put contraception high on our list of the changes which have fostered the new family. The toughness is still there without which the sex (and the species) would not have endured the hardships to which women were subjected before and by industrialization; it accounts for their greater longevity now that maternal mortality is such a fraction of what it once was.[1] The toughness is no longer so much needed for survival. Some of it can be devoted instead to the tandem of jobs, one inside and the other outside the home.

Women have done this with such success that in Britain the proportion of all wives in paid work went up from 10 per cent in 1911 (as it remained in 1931) to 26 per cent in 1951 and 42 per cent in 1971.[2] The pioneers had to brave the resistance of husbands and other women, and the remains of it are still there. In 1965 a national survey found that 32 per cent of husbands 'disapproved' of their wives going out to work, 6 per cent on the specific ground that 'a woman's place is in the home'.[3] More husbands disapproved if their wives were not working (46 per cent) than if they were (14 per cent). Some of our husbands were the same.

> I don't agree with it. I've got three children and I think the wife's place is in the home. My wife says she wants to go out to work and meet people, but I don't think it right. When the children come home from school they need to have somebody around to encourage them. (Fitter, Lewisham)

Several women agreed; and showed how far controlled they were

[1] The biological and other handicaps of men are discussed in A. Oakley, *Sex, Gender and Society*, chap. 1.

[2] General Register Office, *Census of 1911 – Occupations and Industries*, vol. X, Part I, p. cxxviii, *Census 1931 – General Report,* p. 163, Central Statistical Office, *Social Trends,* no. 2, p. 61, and *Census 1971*—Advanced Analysis, p.1.

[3] A. Hunt, *A Survey of Women's Employment*, p. 185.

by their husbands by such remarks as 'He says I can't go because he likes me to look after the house', or 'I'd like to, but I wouldn't be allowed to. My husband says no', or 'He let me go out to work when the little girl went to school', or 'He'd only agree to a part-time job'. But now husbands mostly 'let' their wives work, and even look forward to the day. His own standard of life will be raised if she is no longer wholly dependent on him. If he does not stand in the way she can join her friends with children of the same sort of age who have escaped out of the home with (as one of them said) 'the joyful sense of all that housework undone'.

Motives were linked to the changes we have been describing. In the 1965 study married women were asked what they thought were the main reasons for going out to work. 'The most frequently named attraction was the financial one: this was named by over four-fifths of those interviewed.'[1] But, to judge by another study in Bermondsey, many working-class wives sought the money principally to support a home-centred style of life:[2]

> The way in which her wages were spent showed that the woman worked neither to meet basic economic needs nor to provide personal pleasures for herself. Money was wanted as a means of raising the family's standard of living. It was used to build up, on a do-it-yourself basis, a more modern and attractive home, to provide more generous food, better footwear and larger wardrobes, to buy durable consumer goods, to give the family a seaside holiday, and to acquire a cheap second-hand car.

This seemed too much the conventional response to the customary criticism of working mothers, that they are neglecting their families. Even so, these were the kinds of things on which the wife's earnings were largely spent. In material terms the whole family benefitted.

The other main reason was to have social contacts outside the home. A young Dagenham wife in our survey, working part-time as a secretary, said 'It's another interest. I enjoy meeting the other women at work.' Mrs Parker of Watford had got a local job as a part-time machinist. 'You miss your children when they leave home. You can talk to your own flesh and blood and when they've

[1] Ibid., p. 181.

[2] P. Jephcott, *Married Women Working*, p. 165.

gone you miss them. You get lonely. You're glad of something to do outside the home.' To quote the national study again – 'nearly two-thirds of those mentioning financial advantages named at least one other advantage. The most important of these were a desire for company and the wish to escape boredom.'[1] A small minority living with mothers-in-law or mothers did it more to escape from social contacts, of a rather particular kind.

However much wives wanted to have paid work, they would not have been able to but for two main changes, the demographic which we shall say a further word about, and the economic which we have hardly yet mentioned.

The life cycle of women's work

Not only have attitudes and practices altered on family limitation. There has also been a fall in the age of marriage. The proportion of all working women who are single has therefore gone down, and the proportion of married up. Both changes are taken account of in Table 11, which was drawn up for us by P. R. Cox.[2] The first column is an 'average' profile for women born in 1850, and the last for women born in 1950 at about the same time that Titmuss was writing the essay quoted earlier. Since these last are now only in their twenties, current trends have had to be extrapolated in order to indicate what may happen to them later on.

TABLE 11 *Changes in the life cycle of women (England and Wales)*

	Date of Birth					
	1850	*1870*	*1890*	*1910*	*1930*	*1950*
Average age at (first) marriage	26	26	26	25	24	22
Average age at birth of first child	28	28	28	27	26	24
Average age when last child aged 11	47	46	44	41	39	37

The woman's age when her last child reached eleven (or will

[1] A. Hunt, op. cit., p. 19.
[2] For a fuller version, and an explanation of the methods, see Appendix 4.

reach eleven) was ten years lower in 1950 than in 1850. Four of these years were accounted for by the earlier ages at which the first child was born, related as that was to the earlier age of marriage, and the other six to the smaller numbers of children after the first. The age of eleven for the child was arbitrary but was as good for illustration as any other.

The extra ten years have freed women from the home that much earlier, and so more of them altogether can go out to work. But the freedom is far from complete. It is no longer subordinated to the interests of husbands as it used to be when wives gave up paid work on marriage.[1] The freedom is still limited by children. Table 12, which is based on our survey, shows how wives balance home and work at the various stages of life. Each column corresponds more or less to a different stage. Before having children, most wives work full-time. The situation is then reversed. When there are young children most wives stay with them, only returning to work, first part-time and then full-time as the children get older. When they are over sixty there is another reversal.

Part-time work

No less significant have been the economic changes. Many more women than did actually work might have been quite willing to in the inter-war years – fertility had fallen enough to make it possible – had the opportunity been there. Even if husbands had been in agreement there were not the jobs for women. The war and post-war economic expansion gave them their chance. Working wives added to the national product,[2] and when labour was scarce many of them were able to use their bargaining power to get the sort of jobs that fitted in best with their families, that is part-time ones.[3]

[1] The older wives in our sample more often stopped work as soon as they married; the younger when they were first pregnant. Among those who were aged twenty-nine and under and had stopped work after marriage, 88 per cent had done so because they were expecting their first child; the proportion among those aged 30 to 49 was 79 per cent and among those aged 50 or over 50 per cent. This finding is not open to our standard objection to age-comparisons, since women of all ages were asked what they had done earlier in their lives.

[2] So sizeable had their contribution become that Beckerman said that 'the rise in employment of married women is by far the most important factor in determining the projection of the labour force into the future'. W. Beckerman, 'The future growth of national product', p. 83.

[3] The steady rise in part-time work is shown in Department of Employment and Productivity, *British Labour Statistics: Historical Abstracts 1886–1968*.

TABLE 12 *Proportion of married women working according to their stage in life (main sample)*

	No children under 16 at home, wives 39 or under	*Youngest child aged 4 or under, wives of all ages*	*Youngest child aged 5–10, wives of all ages*	*Youngest child aged 11–15, wives of all ages*	*No children under 16 at home, wives 40–59*	*No children under 16 at home, wives 60 or over*
Not working	12%	77%	36%	36%	31%	86%
Working part-time	12%	17%	44%	38%	32%	7%
Working full-time	76%	6%	20%	26%	37%	7%
Total %	100%	100%	100%	100%	100%	100%
Number	50	126	114	72	182	106

Part-time means less than thirty hours a week.

This development is clearly of considerable importance. We said in the last chapter that in the Stage 1 family women had been able so readily to combine productive work with household tasks because they controlled the timing of each. They could at their own will leave off one kind of work and turn to the other. Part-time paid work *outside* the home may not dovetail quite as neatly as that. But it often does a great deal better than full-time, particularly when there is a choice of jobs with different hours. In this respect (even if it was checked by the sharp rise in unemployment in the early 1970s) there has been a restoration, in the Stage 3 family, of the Stage 1 pattern. Of the married women in our sample who had stopped work at some point after marriage and re-started later, 70 per cent had taken a part-time job at first.

The prime advantage can be illustrated from the diaries, starting with the mothers with at least one child under five. There were thirty-six of them. Only six of them were doing paid work on the day for which the diary was prepared, and four of these managed by not leaving their homes at all. Three of them (and two others whose children were older) were outworkers and therefore good examples of the past being reproduced in the present. They typed at home, made dresses, boxes or toys. More even than other part-timers, their practice was the same as that of the old domestic system, except that if they were helped at all in their work it was by young children rather than husbands. Though it had disadvantages, low pay being the most obvious, outwork compensated by leaving open the choice about when to do it and when not to. This modern form of the domestic system is not necessarily of only antiquarian interest; in a form very different from that of the past, more the kind of work done in offices than factories, it may become more common among husbands as well as wives in the next century.

The other one of the four, Mrs Adnitt, with five children aged from four to fourteen, had a small grocery shop in her house in a village near Aylesbury. She worked long hours in it and on her accounts. She managed by inter-weaving shop and children, as the start of her day illustrated.

6.45 Let the baker into shop.
7.00 Bathed two youngest children.
7.15 Woke up son for his paper-round.
7.45 Let second baker in.
7.50 Cooked breakfast for other three children.
8.00 Opened shop.
8.30 Sent children to school.

The two other mothers with children under five worked as office cleaners. One of these, whose home was in Islington, got up at 5.10 a.m., worked from 6 a.m. to 8.30 a.m., and at 8.45 a.m. called at her mother's home in the same block of flats 'to collect my daughter for school'. The second cleaner, living in Southwark, had one child at school and one younger; she worked before breakfast in the morning and before the school closed in the afternoon. She took her baby to the office.

Among the 110 women diarists whose youngest child was aged five to fifteen, 71 had paid jobs. Of these 6 worked in the evenings; such care as was needed for their children could be given by husbands who arrived *from* work as they went *to* theirs. They were, for child care, on different shifts. In one family the cycles of the couple were so out of phase that they saw little of each other except at weekends; since the wife worked by day and the husband by night they could have shared a bed, but not together, like the child-workers in the nineteenth century who kept their bunks continually warm by dropping into the place relinquished by the previous sleeper. Three more mothers worked only on Saturday mornings; in two families the husband helped with the children then, in the third a mother-in-law.

The most common way in which young mothers balanced job with family was by working just in school hours. Some were school-meal helpers; one a teacher at the same school as her youngest child; another a headmaster's secretary. Others, though they worked in offices as secretaries or in factories as assemblers or machine operators, started and finished as much to the school timetable as their children. Mrs Dent was a wages clerk in Ealing. Her day went like this:

8.20 Took daughter to school.
8.30 Travelled to work. Then work, lunch-hour and work again.
3.15 Left work.
3.25 Fetched daughter from school.

Mrs Jones, who lived in Tunbridge Wells and worked as a hospital domestic, had more time to spare in the afternoon.

8.15 Children washed and dressed and to school.
8.50 Walked to work.
9.00 Started work. Then work.
2.00 Clocked off.
2.01 Walked home.
2.11 Arrived home, had a snack. Then a rest, then housework until . . .
3.25 Picked up son from school.

These arrangements were sometimes smoothed by the help of relatives. Mrs Darenth was a part-time secretary in Enfield.

> I left work when the first child was expected and a couple of years later they phoned me. My Mum and Mum-in-law – Mum mostly – said they'd look after baby, so I said yes. The children are happy with their Nans. I'm happy at work. Nans are happy to have the children. So everything works out fine for everyone.

Working could, of course, more easily be combined with children when the hours were part-time. Among those with children under five, all except Mrs Adnitt, the shopkeeper, worked much less than thirty hours a week. Among those whose youngest child was between five and ten, few even of the 'full-timers' had a long working week. Only one worked over forty hours. Some of those working thirty hours or just over could still fit in with school, or at least could if the children took themselves to and from it.

Three different arrangements – working at home, having special working hours, or getting help from grandmothers and other relatives – account, separately or in combination, for all but five of the full-timers who were diarists and had children aged ten or under. Each of them was able to manage because, as well as husbands, they had older children. Mrs Perkins of Southend, who worked forty hours a week in a baker's shop, had four children aged between six and twelve. She left for work at 7.45 a.m., having called the children and dressed the youngest, and she arrived home at 5.40 p.m., when she got tea and had it with her family. Aged 34, she had only recently re-started work as 'the children were off hand and we needed the money'. The older children helped with the younger when she and her husband were not there.

Another wife was Mrs Lewis, a night nurse, living in Caterham and with two children aged ten and fourteen. Her husband sometimes also worked on night duty. The diary, after recording that she had worked since midnight, went like this from 6.30 a.m.:

6.30 a.m. Making beds for 35 patients.
7.00 a.m. Preparing for day staff to come on duty.
7.20 a.m. Give report to Day Sister.
7.30 a.m. Off duty, meet my husband and motor home.
7.50 a.m. Prepare breakfast and school clothes for my children.
8.10 a.m. Have breakfast with family.
8.25 a.m. See children off to school bus.
8.30 a.m. Tidy kitchen and living room.
8.50 a.m. Got to bed.

We have been speaking about weekdays. Weekends were a different matter. Some women, as we have said, worked on Saturday. In other families, as Chapter VII will show, the husbands worked on Saturday morning or all through the day or, less often, on Sunday. But in most families both husband and wife were together on Saturday and Sunday if at no other time. Typically, they got up a little later on Saturdays – between 7.30 and 8.00, instead of 7.00 to 7.30 – and later still on Sundays – between 8.30 and 9.00. The wives mostly shopped on Saturday morning, with husband, children or both. Saturday afternoon was taken up with more shopping, watching television or visits to or from friends or relatives. Sunday, with a high point for most in the meal at 1.30 to 2 p.m., was a more wholly 'leisure' day – given over to gardening, house decorations, trips in the car or again visiting relatives or friends.

Another variation was with school holidays. Two of the people with children under five and four of those whose youngest was five to ten completed their diaries at a time when the children were on holiday. At least three of these usually worked; they had school holidays off either because their job was geared to the school – they were teachers or meal helpers – or because, although working as nurses or secretaries, they had made special arrangements with their employers. Others managed holidays, as they did when their children were ill, by giving up one job and returning later to another. For women job turnover was high.

Work loads of men and women

We have seen that mothers could reconcile the needs of family and work more easily because many of them were able to get part-time jobs and, even when they worked longer than thirty hours, often found hours that suited their children. London and the Home Counties may in this, as in so many other ways, offer exceptional opportunities. We do not, however, want to leave the impression that the working mothers in our sample had an easy life. We can get an idea of the load on them from their diaries, bringing in other housewives and husbands as well for the sake of comparison.

What to count as work? According to the way the government looks for statistical purposes at the work of housewives, it does not contribute anything at all towards the National Income. Colin Clark[1] once pointed out how absurd this is. If a number of un-

[1] C. Clark, 'The economics of housework'.

married men employing paid housekeepers decided to marry them the size of the National Income would be automatically reduced; if married men decided to divorce their wives and pay them as housekeepers it would be automatically increased. Clark calculated the 1956 value of housework, using information about the cost of maintaining children and adults in institutions as his criteria. His figures for the value of housework came to £7,000 million, or just under half the National Income. The comparable figure today would be over £20,000 million. The Chancellor would make a sensation if he announced such an addition to the national resources in his next Budget speech.

We could not follow the government and count housework as though it was not work at all. But there was still a problem about which activities of the day fell one side of the line or the other. In going through the diaries, our guide was the set of conventions adopted in the recent Multi-national Time Budget Study.[1] The informants described, in their own words, what they did – feeding the baby, cleaning the gas-stove, dancing to the radio, or whatever it was – and we then classified the activity according to those conventions. Cleaning the gas-stove was, for example, domestic work and thus a household task. Dancing was leisure. In the multi-national study child care and shopping were, by the way, considered also to be household tasks or 'household obligations', as it described them. There are some activities which are neither one thing nor the other, notably sleeping, eating and self-care of one sort and another. These we have called subsistence (in the multi-national study they were described as 'private' or 'physiological needs').

Table 13 presents the first set of comparisons, for work of various kinds, counting household tasks as work. It gives averages for weekdays, Saturdays and Sundays separately; and the figures for the sample weekday have again been multiplied by five and added to the two weekend days to give averages for the week as a whole. Measured in this way, it looks as though rather more work was done by part-time working wives than by men, and more by full-time women than by part-time. Men worked in the home, especially at weekends, just as women did a good deal outside it.

[1] A. Szalai *et al.*, *The Use of Time;* A. Szalai *et al.*, 'The multi-national comparative time budget research project'; F. Govaerts, *Loisirs des femmes et temps libre.* The classification scheme is explained more fully in pp. 340–6 of Appendix 3.

Both kinds of working women, and men, did more work in total than pure housewives.

TABLE 13 *Average hours of paid and unpaid work (diary sample: married men and women aged 30 to 49)*

	Men	*Women working full-time*	*Women working part-time*	*Women not in paid work*
Weekday				
Paid work and travel to work	9·1	7·7	5·0	0·0
Household tasks	0·9	2·7	4·9	7·0
Total work	10·0	10·4	9·9	7·0
Number of people	188	46	55	61
Saturday				
Paid work and travel to work	3·0	1·6	0·8	0·0
Household tasks	3·0	4·9	6·1	5·7
Total work	6·0	6·5	6·9	5·7
Number of people	188	46	55	61
Sunday				
Paid work and travel to work	1·0	0·1	0·5	0·0
Household tasks	2·4	4·7	4·7	4·8
Total work	3·4	4·8	5·2	4·8
Number of people	188	46	55	61
Total for week				
Paid work, travel to work and household tasks	59·4	63·3	61·6	45·5

The treatment of travel to work is discussed on pp. 137-8.

But these comparisons may mislead. The days of many of those whose only work was at home were punctuated with little breaks for chatting or for cups of tea which were not counted as work. Here, for example, were some of the main events in the Sunday calendar of Mrs Mitchell, a clerk's wife in Watford; it centred around what could fairly claim to be the chief British ritual.[1]

> 7.30 a.m. Got up and made my husband, Jim, a cup of tea which he likes very much in bed first thing in the morning. My husband enjoyed his cup of tea very much . . .
>
> 8 a.m. I washed up the breakfast dishes. Then I had a cup of tea with my husband and daughter which we all enjoyed . . .
>
> 8.30 a.m. Pour my second cup of tea. Bam (my Black Labrador) has his cup. Again this is routine for him. He enjoys his cup of tea.
>
> 8.45 a.m. Finished my cup of tea and felt more like a human being so I start dressing . . .
>
> 1 p.m. Made a cup of tea for Jim. He enjoys a cup very much after his dinner. Between us we drink the pot dry and enjoy it very much . . .
>
> 11 p.m. To bed with a cup of tea. Not a routine day. I never have one.

Mrs Mitchell's cups of tea did not rank as work. Her husband probably did not have quite so many on working days, and perhaps he did not spend quite so long in chatting with colleagues in the office where he earned his living as she did with people at home. But we did not ask men to give us a minute-to-minute account of what they did when actually or nominally 'at work'. The descriptions of many of the jobs done would have been too difficult to record. Moreover, such things not recorded as work might actually be so for housewives. A meal, for example, is not counted as work, though some mothers would think that feeding young children was. If finer distinctions had been made, it might have turned out that the husbands did not, by and large, do more work than their at-home wives.

Apart from the two categories of paid work and household

[1] Engels said in 1845 that 'In England and even in Ireland tea is regarded as being just as essential as coffee is in Germany and only those who suffer from the direst poverty give up their tea'. F. Engels, *The Condition of the Working Class in England*, p. 85. In this respect there has been no change, except that 'German' coffee has been gaining on 'Anglo-Irish' tea.

tasks, the rest of the time could be divided between subsistence, leisure and journeys other than to work. The comparison covering all five categories is in Table 14. Wives working full-time did not save on 'subsistence'. They therefore had the least leisure while pure housewives had the most.

TABLE 14 *Average weekly hours spent in different ways (diary sample: married men and women aged 30 to 49)*

	Men	*Women working full-time*	*Women working part-time*	*Women not in paid work*
Paid work and travel to work	49·5	40·2	26·3	70·0
Household tasks	9·9	23·1	35·3	45·5
Subsistence	73·9	76·1	72·5	73·7
Leisure	31·7	25·7	31·2	44·4
Non-work travel	3·0	2·9	2·7	4·4
Number of people	188	46	55	61

As well as relying on the conventions decided on for the multinational study we asked our informants to say whether their various activities were seen by them as 'work', 'leisure', 'a mixture of work and leisure' or 'neither work nor leisure'. When this was done the amount of time spent on work was reduced for everyone, for women because they did not think of it as including some of the things they did in caring for their children, or as covering special meals, like Sunday lunches, dinners or evening dinner parties as distinct from humdrum meals; for men because when they did at home the same jobs as their wives, like washing the clothes or, still more, putting the children to bed, they sometimes did not regard them as work. But when, categorized in this new way, the times were added up, one conclusion at least still stood. Women working full-time still had the least 'leisure' and housewives the most.

We also compared our findings for London with those for the

other places where similar studies were made – Belgium, Bulgaria, France, Hungary, Poland, West Germany, Czechoslovakia, the Soviet Union, the United States and Yugoslavia. The figures, which are reproduced as Table A10 in Appendix 3, should be read with caution because the London data refer only to married people aged thirty to forty-nine, whereas those from the other countries are for all married people aged from eighteen to sixty-four. For what it is worth, the comparison suggests the following broad conclusions:

1. Married men in London spent about average amounts of time on paid work and travel to work and on household tasks.
2. Married women in London who had paid jobs worked relatively short hours on average; part-time work was apparently less common in most other countries. They had as a result more leisure time than in other countries, the most similar being the United States.
3. The London wives without paid jobs spent on average less time on household tasks than housewives in any other country, and they also had more leisure. Again, the closest was the United States.

This comparison had, as we said, to be tentative. But it suggests that wives in London had a rather easier time than in the other countries studied. It also suggests a conclusion about the balance between the sexes. London was like the other places in that wives with paid jobs did more work in total and had less leisure than husbands, while housewives apparently did less work and had more leisure than either. But the London wives with paid jobs had shorter hours and the husbands gave as much help in the home. The outcome was a closer approximation to equality of condition than anywhere else.

Help from husbands

In London, and probably elsewhere, when wives worked outside the home, their husbands more often worked inside it. Table 15 gives the evidence from our survey. In the interests of symmetry it was only fair, as husbands and wives saw it, for the men to do more so that their wives could do less.

TABLE 15 *Husband's help in the home (main sample)*

Reported help by husband at least once a week	*Wife not working*	*Wife working part-time*	*Wife working full-time*
No help	22%	17%	9%
Washing-up only	14%	15%	12%
Other tasks (cleaning, cooking, child-care, etc.) with or without washing-up	64%	68%	79%
Total %	100%	100%	100%
Number	539	320	293

Many of the wives, even with the help of their husbands, had a sense of pressure. We asked all full-time employees whether, offered the choice, they would prefer to have 'more pay' or 'more time off'. Their answers are recorded in Table 16. There are greater differences in the table between single and married women than between men. The married women were concerned about their other job as housewife. Asked what they would do with the extra time, the overwhelming majority said 'looking after the family', 'giving more time to the children', or other things in the home. 'I'd just catch up with the housework', was the aspiration of a married clerk living in Lewisham. The married men, on the other hand, as often chose more pay as more time off.

TABLE 16 *Choice between more pay and more time off (main sample: men and women working full-time)*

	Men		*Women*	
	Single	*Married*	*Single*	*Married*
More pay	57%	49%	51%	22%
More time off	37%	47%	44%	75%
Other answers	6%	4%	5%	3%
Total %	100%	100%	100%	100%
Number	144	522	73	152

If they could not cut down their hours without forfeiting money which they thought they needed, it seemed that most women at least put their paid work into second place. They were not so committed to it, partly because the jobs they had were less absorbing, partly because they did not want to be absorbed in them. As Table 17 shows, wives less often thought of themselves as having 'career ladders', less often thought they had 'a lot of say' at work, less often felt 'pressed' at work, less often had leisure interests linked to their job, less often did overtime and, as an indication that they selected jobs nearer to and thus more convenient for their main workplace, did not travel so far.

TABLE 17 *Involvement in work by men and women (main sample)*

	Men working full-time	*Women working full-time*	*Women working part-time*
Proportion saying that there was a 'career ladder' in their work	58%	40%	25%
Proportion reporting that they had 'a lot of say' at work	63%	49%	32%
Proportion saying they felt 'pressed' or 'sometimes pressed' at work	70%	64%	52%
Proportion reporting some 'link' between their work and their leisure	23%	10%	10%
Proportion who did overtime during previous week	43%	8%	13%
Proportion travelling more than ten miles to their job	19%	5%	1%
Total number	587	168	177

No matter how much work was given second place, conflict remained. Mrs Bennett, a design engineer's wife living near Eton, was not working when we saw her. But she articulated the familiar dilemma, felt as much by those who did not work as by those who did, when she said, 'I'd hate to leave my children to someone else, but I'd love to go out to work and meet different people. I'm a bit torn about it. I want both.' The working wives were asked, as were married men, whether they felt 'that the demands of your work interfere at all with the demands of your home and family'. The proportion who said there were such conflicts was similar among wives working full-time (31 per cent) and husbands (38 per cent), and higher for both than for wives working part-time (17 per cent). The main problems that the wives mentioned were over the care of children, housework and shopping. Mrs Evans, living in Ealing, worked thirty-one hours a week as a domestic in a nearby hospital. Her children were aged six and nine. 'There's a certain amount of work in the home that I don't get done', she said. 'I have meals to get when I get home and there's the washing and ironing. There are always too many jobs. Then there's the tiredness. I get tired and get irritable with the children.' 'I don't have enough time to do all the things at home', said Mrs Brome of Lewisham, who had three children aged between five and ten and worked twenty hours a week as a shop assistant, 'and there are problems with the children – I sometimes think they don't get enough attention from me.'

The kind of work made a difference, as Table 18 shows.

TABLE 18 *Occupational class of wife's job and interference of work with home and family (main sample: married women working full-time)*

	Professional and managerial	*Clerical*	*Manual*
Proportion reporting that work 'interfered' with home and family	58%	30%	22%
Total number	26	76	65

The few married women in full-time managerial jobs more often found that they put strains upon their families. The reason was obvious. Such occupations as retail management, teaching, nursing and social work were more demanding than routine jobs as typists, shop assistants or factory workers. They were also, in the main, more satisfying: wives in them had more 'say' at work, more often said they had a 'career ladder' and more often reported themselves 'very satisfied' with their present job. These wives sought, and sometimes got, the sort of fulfilment and advancement that are commonly enjoyed by men in such jobs.

But their very attractions made for difficulties. 'The family feels neglected', said Mrs Ward, a full-time staff nurse in High Wycombe. 'I tend to put the hospital first. My daughter aged 11 is still too young to be left alone much. I find shopping difficult. I have to buy things on a Thursday to last until Tuesday.' Mrs Johnson, a teacher married to a university lecturer and living in Reading, explained that 'My career is important to me. But there are problems. I can't always get home in time to get meals, and when I am home there's a pile of books to mark. A growing-up family needs a mother who's at leisure with them. I'm so involved in my work that I'm afraid I don't meet that need. I have a guilt complex about it.' In this last family, both husband and wife had 'careers' in which they were fully engaged.[1] She was one of the thirteen wives, out of the twenty-six in this category, whose husbands were also in managerial jobs.

Which way will it go?

More wives have been going out of the home to work. Will more do so in the future or less? Can the Principle be applied? Unfortunately, our own figures do not give a great deal of help. When we compared mothers within classes according to the age of their youngest child, there were no differences large enough to enable us to draw firm conclusions. We therefore had to turn to other evidence based on larger numbers from national samples, and even when we did it was sparse enough to allow for several different interpretations.

[1] See R. and R. N. Rapoport, *Dual Career Families,* for a study where wives were as committed to work (and home) as husbands.

One of the findings of other enquiries was that at all stages of life the higher the class of the husbands, the lower the proportion of their wives who were working. This was shown by the 1966 Census;[1] by Hunt in the study we have mentioned before;[2] by Douglas and Blomfield;[3] and by the National Child Development Study which followed up a cohort of children born in 1958.[4]

If we go by the general rule that we have been advocating, and regard higher-class women as the harbingers of the future, it should follow that fewer wives will go out to work in the future. On one particular ground this seems plausible enough. If one of the chief motives is (as we have said) the money, then higher-class women do not have such a strong spur. As incomes rise in the future, more wives will be as well off as the higher-class ones are now, and hence fewer of them will be driven out to work.

But clearcut as that conclusion would be, we think it would be unjustified. That this is not a straightforward matter like the effect on expenditure patterns of a rise in incomes can be demonstrated by imagining ourselves back in 1950. If we had at that time possessed, say, the Douglas and Blomfield figures we might have forecast that as the poor got richer fewer wives would go out to work. What we have said in this chapter shows how wrong we would have been. Incomes have risen and yet more wives have left the home.[5] In Britain there has apparently been an increase in the employment of married women in every class, including the managerial. The evidence comes from comparing the proportions of working mothers with children born in 1946 and in 1958.[6] It therefore appears that income differences are what matter, not the absolute level of incomes. In order to keep up as best they can with ever-rising aspirations, the poorer wives have at all times a stronger motive to earn. Since in comparison to the generality the poorer do not get any better off over time, the numbers at work will not go down just because all become richer. So if income differences and their effects are more or less

[1] General Register Office, *Sample Census 1966 – Household Composition Tables*, p. 260.

[2] A. Hunt, op. cit., pp. 57, 120.

[3] J. W. B. Douglas and J. M. Blomfield, p. 121.

[4] R. Davie *et al.*, *From Birth to Seven*, Tables A37 and A38.

[5] H. Carter and P. C. Glick, *Marriage and Divorce: A Social and Economic Study*, shows that the same thing has happened in the United States as it has got richer.

[6] J. W. B. Douglas and J. M. Blomfield, op. cit.; R. Davie *et al.*, op. cit.

constants, other influences must have accounted for the long-term changes.

In our explanation of the growth of women's work we would therefore continue to attach importance to the demographic and economic changes which have altered the attitudes and practices of both husbands and wives. The reduction in the age of marriage and in the size of family have released more women for paid work. The economic changes have produced more jobs, particularly part-time, for women in all classes. The proportions of working mothers in part-time as against full-time jobs seem to have been more or less the same in each class. If either the demographic or the economic pattern changed again – if, for example, there was a rise in fertility or a continuation of unemployment – the growth on which we have been focusing could turn into a decline.

There is also another factor that might help to account for the increase – the education of women. The numbers in our own sample were again too small for detailed analysis. The Hunt report suggested that, though the differences were not large, the more educated the women, the more inclined were they to work. Of those whose education went on till nineteen or later, 51 per cent did so, as against 43 per cent of those who stopped earlier.[1] In answer to an opinion question, 48 per cent of the more educated wives said they expected to work until retirement age as against 39 per cent of the others. There is also support from other studies. One is, again, the Douglas longitudinal enquiry. A special analysis of this was carried out for us, to see what influence the education of wives had. This showed that among middle-class wives the most educated more often went out to work before their child was five. Of the middle-class wives who had been to secondary schools and also had a degree or other formal qualification, 32 per cent had started work before the child was five; among the less educated middle-class wives the proportion was 23 per cent. More evidence comes from the Pahls' study of managers and their wives, most of whom were in their thirties with young children living at

[1] H. Carter and P. C. Glick noted in the USA 'a strong correlation between amount of education and percentage of women who worked' (p. 180). There is even stronger evidence from France, where official surveys in 1962 and 1968 showed that at all ages educated wives more often worked outside the home, the increase in wives working over the period being 'certainly linked' to the increase in the proportion of women with educational qualifications. R. Salais and M.-G. Michal, 'L'activité des femmes mariées', p. 33.

home: the proportion of wives who either had a job or planned to get one was 73 per cent among those with higher education of two years or more, 48 per cent among those with less higher education and 31 per cent of those with none.[1] The graduate women studied by Fogarty and the Rapoports were similar in their aspirations; they too were highly committed to the feminist ideal of a vocation outside the home.[2]

> Highly qualified women today are decisively committed to being lifetime workers. Four out of five of those British women graduates of 1960 who are married with children have a firm intention of being in employment, most of them full-time, after their children have grown up, and only 1 per cent have a firm intention *not* to be so. Four out of five also intend to be in employment when their children are between 6 and 12, but in this case most of the employment would be part-time.

This is the trend that we suggest to be of the most importance. When feminism ensured that education was made as much compulsory for girls as for boys, it gained a victory in a long struggle which is far from won. The members of the one sex have slowly gained something nearer equality with the other in educational opportunity and, although more slowly, in the access to careers which education opens up. The numbers of women with education beyond the minimum and with higher education is on the increase and it is likely to continue that way, thereby adding to the proportion of working mothers a steady increment of wives who will hope to get the sort of absorbing jobs we have mentioned. They will have both the appetite and the training for them.

The main point we have been making is that, owing a great deal to the restoration of part-time work, marital symmetry has been enhanced. This is linked with many other changes. If women go out to work, and if in that way their roles are not different from those of men, so much the more difficult is it to preserve segregation in their roles at home. If they also earn money, so much the more difficult is it for men to maintain a rigid division between the financial responsibilities and pleasures of the sexes. If, to be

[1] J. M. and R. E. Pahl, *Managers and their Wives*, p. 132.

[2] M. P. Fogarty and R. and R. N. Rapoport, *Sex, Career and Family*, p. 474.

more general still, women have some economic independence, their social standing is bound to be higher than at either of the two previous stages.

The gain for symmetry has been a loss for home-centredness. The coalition between the three characteristics of the family itemized in Chapter I is not necessarily permanent. Men are evidently back in the home. But the door is a revolving one, men coming in, women going out. If home-centredness is judged by the single – although far from sufficient – criterion of the total amount of time that in a week or a year the couple spend in the home, then there must have been a reduction since the second world war. The number of hours spent in paid work by couples taken jointly has increased, and the total spent at home has decreased.

But time is only one criterion. Commitment to one or other sphere matters more. Most married women are less committed to their paid work. A job is welcome for the money and the company far more than for the satisfaction intrinsic to it. Many of the least psychologically rewarding jobs are reserved for women, as if to ensure that the competitive power of the home remains supreme. But a minority, of more educated wives, do not view their job in that light. They are pledged to it and are liable to be more torn between their two worlds than the women with the misfortune (or fortune, if one likes to look at it that way) to have jobs without such appeal. The minority is likely to grow.

V

MEN'S WORKING HOURS

Does all this mean that, as part of the new switch, men have done less work outside the home, to relieve them in one department of their lives for the sake of the other? There are several different comparisons that can be made with the past. The first is about the number and distribution of working years in a lifetime. Life expectancy at birth for men increased steadily from forty in 1841 to sixty-nine in 1967.[1] More people have been living out the natural span. This has lengthened the working life. Some calculations have been made for two years, 1931 and 1955, relating the proportion of men working at different ages to the Life Tables.[2] For men in England and Wales, life expectation at birth was:

58·7 in 1931
67·5 in 1955

Their working-life expectation was:

40·6 in 1931
45·6 in 1955

So that their non-working life expectation was:

18·1 in 1931
21·9 in 1955

The time spent at work increased, and so did the time not at it. A number of years were lopped off each end of the work-span and added to the two periods of childhood and of retirement. At the beginning were the years of education. Children were still little

[1] General Register Office, *The Registrar-General's Statistical Review of England and Wales for the Year 1967*, part II, p. 10.

[2] Ministry of Labour and National Service, *The Length of Working Life of Males in Great Britain.*

adults to the extent that they also worked, at school rather than at home. But it was a different sort of work from what they did afterwards and was not counted as such in the above figures. The years spent in education were increasing even before the 1870 Act. After it became compulsory, there were still many exemptions. It eventually became binding on all children, and was extended by one year in 1947 and by another in the academic year in which this book went to press. Many, particularly from the better-off classes, stayed on well beyond the minimum. People in the higher classes had shorter working lives because they started in paid jobs later.

At the other end of life there has been a similar change. In the last century people without means could not afford to retire, and did not until failing strength forced them into destitution. Only the rich could afford to give up work before they dropped. Their example was followed when old age pensions, from 1908 on, began to make it possible. At first, these were conditional upon reaching the traditional three score years and ten. Later the age was reduced to sixty-five for men and to sixty for women – usually being younger, wives did not as a consequence have to go on working after their husbands retired. The division of labour which has been carried so far in the economy has been accompanied by a division between labour and leisure over the life cycle.

Despite the embodiment of the Principle in the welfare state, entry to the last period of leisure has been at different points for different classes. This was shown by an official inquiry in 1954;[1] and in our survey, of the 96 men who had retired, 46 per cent in the top class had done so before sixty-five compared with 18 per cent of former clerks, 17 per cent of the skilled, and 11 per cent of the semi-skilled and unskilled. Higher-class men both started work later and finished it earlier.[2]

These changes – longer life, longer education and longer retirement, with the better-off in the lead for each – have altered the arithmetic of the family. The partnership between man and wife, unless broken by divorce or separation, lasts for longer. The marriage of a woman born in 1850 lasted on average twenty-nine years until her husband died; for a woman born in 1950 it is likely

[1] Ministry of Pensions and National Insurance, *Reasons Given for Retiring or Continuing at Work*.

[2] In the USA early retirement has become more and more common, especially amongst richer people. R. Barfield and J. Morgan, *Early Retirement: the Decision and the Experience*.

to be forty-five years.[1] Retirement lasts longer, and as a result when work is over couples have a longer period of shared leisure together. Since women continue to outlive their husbands, it is usually the female who has a subsequent period of enforced retirement from marriage as well as work.[2] All this means that the lengthening of life has made it less homogeneous. Before industrialization people worked more or less continuously from an early age until they died. After it people have used some of their extra years for leisure or for unpaid work, in childhood and in old age, and in the last stage of life men are certainly as much in the home as their wives.

Return to normal?

But that does not quite answer the question with which we started the chapter. There is less pressure on the family after the working life is over. Is there more during it? In the middle years do more people have more time to spend inside their homes? It depends naturally enough upon the dates chosen for comparison. 'If we think', Arendt has said, 'in somewhat longer periods, the total yearly amount of individual free time enjoyed at present appears less an achievement of modernity than a belated approximation to normality'.[3] Is the statement justified? The evidence is thin. Certainly, if the only standard was the day, the facts would be all against Arendt. Here, for instance, is how the Elizabethan Statute of Artificers lent its sanction to custom in 1563.[4]

> And be it further enacted by the authority aforesaid, that all artificers and labourers being hired for wages by the day or week shall, betwixt the midst of the months of March and September, be and continue at their work, at or before five of the clock in the morning, and continue at work, and not depart, until between seven and eight of the clock at night (except it be in the time of breakfast, dinner or drinking, the which times at most shall not exceed two and a half in a day,

[1] See Appendix 4.

[2] This despite the fact that one death to some extent causes another. The risk of a widowed person dying is greater soon after the death of the spouse. M. Young *et al.*, 'The mortality of widowers'.

[3] H. Arendt, *The Human Condition*, p. 114.

[4] Quoted in P. Laslett, *The World We Have Lost*, p. 29.

that is to say, at every drinking one half-hour, for his dinner, one hour, and for his sleep, when he is allowed to sleep, the which is from the midst of May to the midst of August, half an hour at the most, and at every breakfast one half hour). And all the said artificers and labourers, between the midst of September, and the midst of March, shall be and continue at their work from the spring of the day in the morning, until the night of the same day, except it be in time afore-appointed to breakfast and dinner.

The evidence gathered by Bienefeld,[1] in the fullest study yet made of the history of hours, was about industry, not about the agriculture in which most people were employed, but it shows the need to take account of holidays as well as the length of the working day. Bienefeld says that in the mid-fourteenth century there were about thirty-five Saints' days and other holidays, the number in any one year depending on how many fell on a Sunday. The number of them increased up to the Reformation, which began the Protestant process of overthrowing the saints. Including medieval agriculture with industry, Phelps Brown suggested there were rather more holidays than that, amounting in all to between forty and fifty days off in the year, in addition to Sundays. 'The yearly total would then be about 2750 to 3000 hours, an average of about 54 hours a week.'[2] If the working week averaged over the year was as low as this in the middle ages, and the standard day did not change much, the average working year must by the mid-eighteenth century have been raised by the loss in the number of holidays. Bienefeld says that they had been reduced to 'a few days around each of the three major festivals of Christmas, Easter and Whitsunday'.[3]

At all times, the hours worked in agriculture varied by season. At planting and harvest there was intense activity from dawn to dusk, with every hand enlisted, and in between a lessening. Until machines became the pacemakers it was not steady from one day to another. When astronomical cycles set the rhythm, there were more marked ups and downs in activity from one period of the

[1] M. A. Bienefeld, 'A study of the course of change . . .'

[2] E. H. Phelps Brown and M. H. Browne, 'Hours of work'. These figures refer to Europe generally but some evidence suggests they were similar in England. See J. A. R. Pimlott, *Recreations*, p. 13.

[3] M. A. Bienefeld, op. cit., p. 89; see also p. 37.

year to another. If there was less variation over the lifetime there was more over the year.

Within the day the work load could also be varied more easily. This mattered most for children. Although nearly all of them were put to work very young, it was neither as monotonous nor as brutal as it later became.[1]

> In all homes girls were occupied about the baking, brewing, cleaning and chores. In agriculture, children – often ill-clothed – would work in all weathers in the fields or about the farm. But, when compared with the factory system, there are important qualifications. There was some variety of employment (and monotony is peculiarly cruel to the child). In normal circumstances work would be intermittent: it would follow a cycle of tasks, and even regular jobs like winding bobbins would not be required all day unless in special circumstances (such as one or two children serving two weavers). No infant had to tread cotton in a tub for eight hours a day and for a six-day week. In short, we may suppose a graduated introduction to work, with some relation to the child's capacities and age, interspersed with running messages, blackberrying, fuel-gathering or play. Above all, the work was within the family economy and under parental care.

Industrialization broke up the seasonal and daily rhythms as it did the Stage 1 family. It also added to working hours. The day actually worked got longer in textiles and in many other trades where overtime was compulsory. 'The practice of working extra hours is peculiar to no district, and to no description of factory; but it is common to all.'[2] In domestic industry, too, the pressure increased as it had to contend with tougher competition from the new machines. 'Since their fortunes progressively declined during the first half of the nineteenth century, their hours became progressively longer.'[3] In the trades described by Mayhew in 1849, whether or not organized on the domestic system, hours were generally long. The weavers of Spitalfields commonly worked a fifteen-hour day, often on Sundays as well. The cabinet-makers, in the cut-price trade, worked 'seven days – for Sunday work is

[1] E. P. Thompson, *The Making of the English Working Class*, pp. 333–4.

[2] *Factory Commission Report, 1833*, quoted in M. A. Bienefeld, op. cit., p. 172.

[3] M. A. Bienefeld, op. cit., pp. 183–4.

all but universal – each of 13 hours, or 91 hours in all; while the established hours of labour in the "honourable" trade are six days of the week, each of ten hours, or 60 hours in all'. The workers in the London shipyards were there from 6 a.m. to 6 p.m. in summer and from daylight to dusk in winter, and coopers worked from 6 a.m. to 8 p.m.[1]

From about that time the long-term trend began to turn down, partly as the result of legislation. The Saturday half-day off, first introduced by a few enlightened masters for their office employees, spread in the second half of the century and became general for manual workers by 1914. After 1945 the five day week became common.

Without this long-term reduction in the working week, life for most people would have remained work-centred, and home a place for men to sleep in rather than to play in and work in at tasks they could choose for themselves. The new middle-kingdom between paid work and subsistence shown up by the tables in the previous chapter would not have come into existence. The reduction has therefore been another prop to the Stage 3 family.

A levelling off

For extrapolation it makes a lot of difference whether the guide is the long-term trend since the 1850s or the short term since the 1920s. We prefer the latter. The standard working week has dropped since then. The trade unions have succeeded in reducing it more as a way of increasing incomes than of cutting hours. It is overtime that has made a difference. It stayed up even in the period of heavy unemployment in the early 1970s.[2] The week actually worked has thus been more or less maintained. After 1945 actual hours did fall a little. They were 47 in 1946. There were fluctuations up and down but the average was still 45 in 1972. The trend over the last half-century as a whole shows that, though there has been a fall, it has been a small one.

At this level, hours for manual workers may, at the rates of pay prevailing for overtime, have reached a kind of optimum. When people have a choice about the hours they should do, they have

[1] E. P. Thompson and E. Yeo, *The Unknown Mayhew*, pp. 110, 393, 403, 422.

[2] Department of Employment, *Department of Employment Gazette,* February 1973, p. 212.

amongst other things to balance income against fatigue. According to several research studies output per hour stayed steady up to a level of 40–48 and then rose progressively less.[1] If there is a standard hourly rate of pay the employer therefore gets a lesser surplus from each hour worked beyond 48, and if he actually has to pay more at overtime rates for hours in excess of that, so much the less likely is it to be worth his while. The results of some of the early research on munition workers were produced in the first world war and may have made employers more willing to concede the 48-hour standard week in 1918.[2] This is looking at fatigue from the employer's point of view. It is reasonable to think that tiredness sufficient to reduce output per hour is also tiredness sufficient to reduce 'output' at home too, that is, to detract at an accelerating rate from the amount of energy which a man has available for his wife and children. He is unlikely to push up his hours beyond the point where he and his home are affected like this, unless he is paid progressively higher premiums, or to reduce them much below it as long as he can earn more for each one above the standard working week.

The optimum balance is bound to change over time. Aspirations depend mainly upon opportunities. If the standard of living has risen steadily, then people build in to their frame of mind the expectation not that it will remain stable but that the rise will remain stable – that their standard of living will go on rising at the same rate as it has been doing in the past. If it does not, they may be prepared to raise their hours if it will bring them more money, and does not go too far beyond the limit at which fatigue becomes serious. If we are right in this view, hours should remain static if the standard of living of those at work continues to go up at the same rate as it has been doing; should go up if the rise does not conform to expectations, provided the opportunity is there for overtime; and should go down only if the increase in the standard of living accelerates, until the period is reached when this accelerated path sets its own norm. On this basis there should be a further reduction in the actual hours of manual workers only if their real incomes rise a good deal faster than they have so far.

[1] J. D. Owen, *The Price of Leisure*, pp. 31–2, and D. G. Brown, 'Hours and output', pp. 151–3.

[2] For example, H. M. Vernon, *Fatigue and Efficiency in the Iron and Steel Industry*, and E. E. Osborne, *The Output of Women Workers in Relation to Hours of Work in Shellmaking*.

This is, as we say, assuming that most men will be able to get overtime if they wish to, and this assumption may not be justified. Managements may make much more of an attempt than they have made in the past to reduce costs by cutting it down.

TABLE 19 *Average paid and unpaid overtime hours in previous week according to stage in life (main sample: men in full-time work)*

	Single, 24 or under	*Married, 29 or under, no children*	*Married, 29 or under, with children*	*Married, 30–49, with children*	*Married, 50 or over, no children*
Paid overtime	3·8	2·1	8·5	5·6	3·6
Unpaid overtime	0·2	0·9	1·1	2·4	1·0
All overtime	4·0	3·0	9·6	8·0	4·6
Number of people	87	34	39	191	146

Reductions in the standard of living caused by the Rowntree cycle, income per head falling when the wife stops work and starts having children, pose the same kind of problem. The husband tries to maintain the family income as much as he can by working more overtime. Table 19, though liable again to the confusion between the ageing of society and the ageing of its members, suggests that fathers stepped up their overtime and total earnings so as to mitigate the effects of the fall. (At the same ages middle-class men did a good deal of unpaid overtime for different reasons, such as the wish to get promotion.) They did not, as indicated by Table 7 on p. 79, succeed in staving off relative poverty, although they tried. The difference was that they expected it would happen in their early married years and so it was not resented in the way a general drop across all age groups would have been. Husbands and wives knew that they would have to economize, and if they could get a home, they could save money by spending more time in it on forms of leisure which were less expensive than those pursued outside. The couple might even be drawn together by the economizing they had to do in the way that Charles Lamb described in *Essays of Elia* and afterwards look back on penury as the happiest period of their marriage.

Holidays

The drop in hours for manual workers may have levelled off. This is not true of holidays, partly no doubt because the choice between more pay and more time off does not arise. If a worker takes time off in the week, he loses pay. If he takes time off on his official holidays, he does not. There were no paid holidays for manual workers in the early nineteenth century; even the three days off in the year – Christmas Day, Easter and Whit Monday – were not normally paid for.[1] Paid holidays spread slowly after 1918, more rapidly after the Holidays with Pay Act of 1938. In 1970 nearly half the manual workers in our sample had three weeks or more paid holiday, and two-thirds of them were using the time to do what once they could not afford to do at all, go away from home. Holidays abroad had become more common. The proportions going abroad in the previous year were 36 per cent of managers, 14 per cent of clerks, 12 per cent of skilled men and 8 per cent of semi-skilled and unskilled. The Balearic Islands, once for the rich, were no longer exclusively so.

Just to underline the point that holidays are *the* expanding form of leisure time, we give here a forecast of the percentage of workers who will on present trends have paid holidays of various lengths in the year 2001.[2]

	Under four weeks	*Four or more but under six weeks*	*Six weeks or more*
UK 1970	86%	11%	3%
UK 2001	0%	62%	38%

It is not easy to bring together these various statements about hours and holidays. The best we can do is Table 20. The figures are of the number of hours worked annually. The hard facts are

[1] J. A. R. Pimlott, *The Englishman's Holiday*, pp. 83–5, 144.

[2] Calculations for forecast described in Appendix 5.

TABLE 20 *Estimates of the length of the working year of male manual workers in Britain in occupations with relatively high and low annual hours*

		Annual working hours	*Proportion of total waking* year (%)*
Middle Ages	High	3,500	60
	Low	2,750	47
Mid-eighteenth	High	3,600	62
century	Low	2,800	48
Mid-nineteenth	High	4,400	75
century	Low	3,000	51
1906	High	2,900	50
	Low	2,350	40
1924	High	2,550	44
	Low	2,250	39
1946	High	2,440	42
	Low	2,150	37
1972	High	2,340	40
	Low	2,000	34

* This assumes an average of eight hours per day spent sleeping.

Sources:
Middle Ages: E. H. Phelps Brown and M. H. Browne; J. A. R. Pimlott.
Mid-eighteenth century: M. A. Bienefeld.
Mid-nineteenth century: E. P. Thompson and E. Yeo; M. A. Bienefeld.
1906: Board of Trade, *Report of an Enquiry into the earnings and hours of Labour of the Workpeople of the U.K.*
1924 and 1946: Department of Employment and Productivity, *British Labour Statistics: Historical Abstracts 1886–1968.*
1972: Department of Employment, *Department of Employment Gazette,* February 1973, p. 214. The figures are on a different basis from those in the later Table 22, which are for married men in the London Region and include work at home, second jobs and travel to work.

sparse, and unsupported opinion is bound to enter into any such comparisons. All we can say is that our best guess is that there was some rise in hours in the first century of the Industrial Revolution and then a fall which has levelled off somewhat since the first world war.[1] The working week actually worked has not fallen much since the second world war but the working year has, owing

[1] Department of Employment and Productivity, *British Labour Statistics: Historical Abstracts 1886–1968*, Tables 38, 39, 44, 45.

to the extension of holidays, which are being slowly restored to the medieval level. The general answer to the question posed by Arendt is that after a peak in the first half of the nineteenth century hours have not just been restored to pre-industrial levels but are now substantially lower. There is not, however, much sign from the last fifty years that as women have done more work outside the home men have done much less.

The survey information

To go by extrapolation is one way of guessing the future; by the Principle another. For the second method we needed information about people in different classes, not just about manual workers. The sort of people who collect the statistics, as distinct from those for whom the statistics have been collected, have been relatively reticent about themselves. An exception was the official report which showed that in 1968 male manual workers had an average working year of 2,117 hours and non-manual of 1,848.[1] In our survey we asked everyone, irrespective of occupation, to tell us the hours of work they put in at their paid employment, including any extra hours of 'unpaid overtime'. We shall focus here upon married men in full-time jobs and start with examples deliberately chosen to illustrate three of the main sorts that we encountered.

Mr Hastings was a process worker mixing adhesives in the Royal Acetone Company's factory in Hackney. He was thirty-six, married with two young children and living in a council flat in East Ham, a few miles away. His basic working week was 40 hours, with Saturdays and Sundays off and two weeks paid holiday per year. He regularly worked overtime, bringing his working hours up to 47½ and sometimes more. He said:

> The hourly rates are low in this firm, and it's accepted by the management that anyone who wants it can have seven and a half hours overtime a week – an hour and a half a night – to make the money up. Most people do take it. I get a bit more on top of that if I get the chance; I work on Saturday morning or something like that. The week before last I did 14½ hours overtime – that was with staying two extra hours one night

[1] National Board for Prices and Incomes, *Hours of Work, Overtime and Shiftwork*, p. 11.

and working Saturday morning. I think overtime is a necessity. If you've got a growing family you need it. I know that for years my money's only been made up to a decent wage by overtime.

Mr King was a senior accounts clerk at an office near Liverpool Street Station. He was forty, married, with three children; they lived in a mortgaged semi in Brentwood. His basic week was 35 hours – 9.30 to 5.30 with an hour off for lunch; he had all Saturdays and Sundays off and three weeks' annual paid holiday. He never worked overtime:

There's no call for it in my job. Even if there was any need – which there isn't – I wouldn't get paid for it. I can always depend on getting out of the office between 5.30 and 5.35 and catching the 5.42 train from Liverpool Street to Shenfield.

Mr Selby was the general sales manager of a national company producing consumer durables. He was fifty-five, married, with no children at home any longer. He lived in a detached house in the countryside in Surrey and drove to Central London each day in his Rover 3500. He usually arrived in the office at about 9.45 and did not leave before 7 p.m.

'It varies. If I've got to entertain someone or have an evening meeting elsewhere, I leave the office at 7 p.m. Otherwise I stay on until 8 p.m. or later if necessary.' His lunches were usually 'business' ones. 'On the rare occasion that I'm not meeting someone for lunch, I get my secretary to get something sent in to me and I go on working over lunch.' He took reports or journals home to read every night and at weekends. 'If I've got an important paper to draft, it's the only time I can really get down to it. I suppose I did about eight hours at home last weekend and about three hours altogether on weekday evenings.' He was away from home on business 'about forty' nights during the year before the interview, half of them abroad. About holidays, he said, 'I usually manage to take three or four weeks, although I'm sometimes interrupted by a telephone call or cable.'

By adding the various elements of working time and allowing for holidays, we can estimate that, on a rough count, Mr Hastings worked about 2,400 hours a year, Mr King about 1,700 and Mr Selby about 2,800. How typical were they? There are two main ways in which the hours of people in different kinds of job can be compared. One is in terms of averages – showing the mean hours worked per week or per year in each class. The other is in terms of the distribution within the different classes – showing the proportion of people in each who worked, for example, less than 45 hours a week. We shall use both these kinds of measure.

Fifteen per cent of the married men in the main sample did not have 'official' hours at all, that is hours laid down by their employers. These were mainly managerial men, 27 per cent of whom had no official hours; the proportion was 15 per cent among clerical workers and under one in ten among manual. Men without official hours, it turned out, commonly worked a longer average week than those with them, even when overtime, paid or unpaid, was taken into account. This was particularly so among managers. Amongst men who did have official hours, the length of the week varied inversely with class. The lower it was the longer the official working week. The average rose from 38 hours among managerial to 39 among clerical and 41 among manual workers.

Paid overtime beyond the official week was predominantly done by manual workers, especially those with more skill, and unpaid by managers. The manual workers doing long hours, many of them in the hard-pressed stage of the Rowntree cycle, were like Mr Hastings doing it for the money.

> I did seven hours overtime last week. I do it all the time. It's the only way to make a reasonable wage here. (Assembly worker, Dagenham)

> It would be better if you could do without overtime, but you can't. You need the overtime money to go out and enjoy yourself in your leisure. You can have more time off if you don't do overtime but you haven't got the money to enjoy yourself with. (Bus driver, Lewisham)

The managers and professional people did it for other reasons. Here are two who stayed on after others had left:

> My hours are supposed to be from ten to nine until five past five. I arrive every day between about eight and eight-thirty,

> and I never leave before six-thirty or seven in the evening. I come in here one Saturday morning out of two, and sometimes both. Occasionally I look in on a Sunday to see if everything's going as it should be. Last Saturday I worked from nine-thirty until one. Go on – tell me I'm a fool. My wife does. (Computer manager, Brentwood)

> I generally don't leave work till well after 7 and I get home at 8 or 9 in the evening. My work is my hobby. (Chief chemist in food manufacturing company, High Wycombe)

Hours spent at home on work for the employer were also brought into this reckoning. They were mainly done by the same managerial men. The chief chemist just quoted said:

> I always take work home. I read 50 different journals, perhaps spend ten hours a week reading them. I need to. For instance if *Which?* has come out and I see something that is wrong in there I have to follow it up. The same thing may apply with other magazines. Reading one of the journals one might pick up a quite new lead. An important part of my job is to know what to read. My sensitivity to all influences – technical, social, etc. – that might affect the company is one of the assets that I have.

There were also senior people who made a point of not taking work home. 'I avoid it', as one manager living at Marlow said, 'It's better to make a complete break. Anyway if you can't do it at the firm, there's something wrong.' But for many the house was almost a branch office: two in every five managers had worked at home during the week before the interview. The average for the week was 2.2 hours; among clerks it was less than one hour and among manual almost nothing. Motives apart, middle-class men more often had the kind of work which could be done at home – reading, drafting reports, mulling over problems. They also more often had enough space – even if they did not all have a 'study' to work in.

Another kind of work was that done on second jobs. Mr Jeffreys, a young married man in Sutton, worked ordinarily as a motor mechanic but had in the previous month put in an additional sixteen hours as a bass guitarist in a pop group. Mr Mitton, a sixty-year-old storeman in Enfield, had done a few hours gardening for a nearby 'family of nobs'. Mr Glass, a shop under-manager living in Islington, had worked three nights a week as manager of a snooker hall. Others had written TV scripts, marked examination papers, done freelance window cleaning, repaired radio sets. But in all classes the proportions who admitted spending time on 'moonlighting', bearing in mind that the earnings of some were tax-free, were relatively small.[1] Some of those who were not declaring their second incomes to the tax authorities may not have let on to us either. What we were told is summarized in Table 21.

TABLE 21 *Occupational class and second jobs (main sample: married men working full-time)*

	Professional and managerial	*Clerical*	*Skilled*	*Semi-skilled and Unskilled*	*All*
No second job	94%	97%	96%	94%	95%
Worked 1–9 hours on second job in previous month	1%	0%	1%	1%	1%
Worked 10 or more hours on second job in previous month	5%	3%	3%	5%	4%
Total %	100%	100%	100%	100%	100%
Number	173	71	240	110	594

There is a problem about the journey to work. Was it leisure or work? We decided to include it with work. Some people mentioned it specifically. 'I always work on the train,' said Mr Brown,

[1] The proportion of men who admitted second jobs in our sample was 5 per cent among married men working full-time and 7 per cent among all full-time workers. In a national sample in 1970, 6 per cent of men workers had second jobs and 7 per cent of all workers (Department of Employment, 'Family Expenditure Survey: subsidiary occupations', p. 528). Other surveys in Britain have shown higher figures, namely H. B. Rodgers, *The Pilot National Recreation Survey: Report No. 1*, p. 34, in 1965 – 10 per cent – and a Gallup Poll (*Sunday Telegraph*, April 1964) – 17 per cent. These variations are probably mainly due to differences in the definition of second jobs.

a merchant banker whose home was near Haywards Heath and office in the City. 'I have a journey of about an hour and I make a point of reading not only the papers but also any other documents I need to read.' He was obviously very much in a minority. But it seemed to us legitimate to count this particular travel as work, since the time was clearly pre-empted and not available for 'leisure' in general or the family in particular. Also, when men were asked to classify the journey, more labelled it 'work' than any one of the other three categories – 'leisure', 'a mixture' or 'neither'.

The non-manual workers spent more time travelling. About a sixth of professional, managerial and clerical men had a journey of over an hour; among manual workers the proportion was one in twenty. In terms of averages, managers spent about six hours a week travelling to and from work, clerks between five and six hours, and manual workers about three or four.

Two more complications have to be mentioned before we can sum up the differences between classes. One is about nights spent on duty away from home. We did not ask people in the main sample about this, partly because we thought it would have been awkward to ask factory workers whether they had been away from home for this purpose, and we did not want to ask some without asking all. From what people said without being specifically questioned, it seemed that the more senior the man the more likely was he to have been away recently from home on duty. In two of the firms in a pilot enquiry, to which we have given the fictitious names of High Frequency Electronics and Royal Acetone Company,[1] nearly two-thirds of the senior staff had been away during the previous year, but hardly any of the junior staff and none of the works employees.

We did not allow for unpaid holidays or absenteeism, but we did allow for paid holidays. Virtually everybody had the six Bank Holidays off or other days in place. Assuming a five-day week, men in all classes had 1.2 weeks off work on that score. In the main sample as a whole, a few men – 7 per cent – had no other paid holiday and a few more – 3 per cent – only one week. As far as we could judge from their comments, this was usually because they had started a new job and were not eligible for more. 'I hadn't been there long enough to get holiday pay', said a labourer from

[1] See Appendix 1, p. 301, for information about the samples.

Sutton. Unskilled workers, with the highest labour turnover, had the least holidays. For people in general two and three weeks were the most common. The higher the class the longer the annual

TABLE 22 *Average weekly and annual working hours (main sample: married men working full-time)*

	Professional and managerial	*Clerical*	*Skilled*	*Semi-skilled and unskilled*	*All*
Total hours at work in week	48·2	44·7	47·8	47·6	47·5
Hours worked at home	2·2	0·8	0·1	0·0	1·0
Hours on second job	0·4	0·3	0·3	0·3	0·3
Hours spent on journey to and from work	6·1	5·6	4·1	3·5	4·7
Total hours working and travelling to and from work in week	56·9	51·4	52·3	51·4	53·5
Bank holidays in year (in weeks)	1·2	1·2	1·2	1·2	1·2
Paid holidays in year (in weeks)	3·4	2·6	2·5	2·1	2·6
Total weeks worked in year	47·4	48·2	48·3	48·7	48·2
Total hours working and travelling to and from work in year (weekly hours × weeks)	2,697	2,477	2,526	2,503	2,564
Number of people	173	71	240	110	594

holiday. The proportion having three or more weeks ranged down from 75 per cent among managers to 50 per cent among skilled manual workers and 36 per cent among semi-skilled and unskilled.

The various elements for the working week and the working year are brought together in Table 22. The figures are not the same as those in the previous chapter. We do not know the explanation. Part of it may be that the information summarized here is from estimates given by people for the time they had spent working in the previous week or, if that was not 'normal', the last normal week; whereas it was in the last chapter obtained (and multiplied up) from the records for a random day whether or not it was a normal one.

Among the people who had an official working week, this was longer for manual workers. The main effect of adding overtime, unpaid as well as paid, was to leave clerical workers with lower total hours at work than others. Once work at home and travel to work were included, the men at the top end came out as having rather a longer average working week than others. This conclusion still stood after their longer annual holidays were added in. This comparison is of averages. In terms of distributions within classes the general pattern is the same. The proportion doing sixty hours or more in the week was highest among managers, next highest among skilled and semi-skilled manual workers, and least for clerks.[1]

When Veblen was writing in 1899, he thought that the 'abstention from productive work'[2] was the most insistent requirement

[1] Although manual workers in London, as in Britain generally, work longer hours than their counterparts in other European countries and in the USA, this is not true of routine non-manual workers. 'Since normal hours of British non-manual workers are shorter than elsewhere and since they also work comparatively little overtime it follows that their actual hours too are shorter.' National Board for Prices and Incomes, *Hours of Work, Overtime and Shiftworking*, p. 48.

[2] T. Veblen, *The Theory of the Leisure Class*, p. 41. He also said that 'This pervading sense of the indignity of the slightest manual labour is familiar to all civilised peoples, as well as to peoples of a less advanced pecuniary culture. In persons of delicate sensibility, who have long been habituated to gentle manners, the sense of shamefulness of manual labour may become so strong that, at a critical juncture, it will even set aside the instinct of self-preservation . . . A better illustration, or at least a more unmistakeable one, is afforded by a certain king of France, who is said to have lost his life through an excess of moral stamina in the observance of good form. In the absence of the functionary whose office it was to shift his master's seat, the king sat uncomplaining before the fire and suffered his royal person to be toasted beyond recovery' (p. 46).

of the most elevated class. He also believed that the upper leisure class of America was not in America at all but in England. 'In this country, for instance, leisure-class tastes are to some extent shaped on usages and habits which prevail, or which are apprehended to prevail, among the leisure class of Great Britain' (p. 105). The opposite would now more commonly be thought true. Anyway, whatever things may have been like in the past of Britain the highest-status people are for the most part no longer, as they were in the nineteenth century, the leisure class. In 1970 they appeared to have less leisure time than anyone else.

New options for leisure

One of the words most commonly associated with leisure is 'problem'. The conventional idea is that hours have fallen and will fall still further, perhaps producing a three- or four-day week. What will people do with themselves when they have so much time on their hands? 'The difficulties and perplexities arising from a greater number of persons than ever before having means and energy at their disposal to utilize during their free hours, are engaging the attention of educationalists, social workers and all those whose business it is to attend to the working of society',[1] said Durant in 1939, and he has often been echoed since. In terms of hours, the fears (or the hopes, according to the point of view) have not been realized. The decline in hours has levelled off. This could, of course, change, especially if a determined attempt were made to reduce overtime. But at least it has not happened yet.

The decline might come if people could have still longer holidays and, especially, if they were able to have them in new ways. People usually have to take time off in the parcels that are offered to them; the manner in which it is split up is not something they have much influence over. If they did they would perhaps value it more highly and income less. We thought that the questionnaire we used for the main survey would be overburdened if we went into this there. So we confined ourselves to asking about it in the two factories. To begin with we asked people to choose between various ways of taking off an equivalent amount of time – an extra forty-five minutes off each day, or its equivalent in a shorter

[1] H. Durant, *The Problem of Leisure*, pp. 2–3.

week or longer holidays. The answers from the seventy-seven men who replied are summarized in Table 23.

TABLE 23 *Preferred leisure split over a year in two factories*

	High Frequency Electronics	*Royal Acetone Company*
45 minutes off each day	4%	16%
Extra half-day at weekend	28%	32%
Five extra weeks annual holiday	68%	52%
Total %	100%	100%
Number	46	31

There was a clear preference for the five extra weeks. Some people said why. Mr Clark, for instance, would not have liked Friday afternoon off because he would have been pressed into doing the weekend shopping for his wife. Mr Warner would not have liked Friday afternoon either because his wife would be at work then and his children at school. He did not want to spend the afternoon at home on his own. Several said their journeys to work were so long that it would be ridiculous to come all that way for a mere half-day. Several others were against the forty-five minutes because they felt they would not notice such a small addition to their time at home. People who went the other way included one man who wanted forty-five minutes because he would like the extra time with his children before they went to bed, and another who would like to get home earlier because his journey was so long and he was always so tired by it.

The chief arguments for the five weeks were that one would really notice such a large chunk of extra time, one could travel more widely and one's family could be together uninterruptedly. One wife joined in to say that *she* would greatly prefer it because she would then be off work for the greater part of her children's school holidays. This, by the way, does tell against either of the other options. If we had asked working mothers the same question the vast majority would probably have gone for five weeks. Since presumably men and women would like the extra time together, the woman's choice (if it worked out that way) should probably be dominant for general policy.

A further question was about ways in which people would like any extra leisure to be divided over their lifetime – whether they would like an extra week's holiday annually or the equivalent of four periods of three months each, two periods of six months each or one period of one year. One week was the most popular, as Table 24 shows. In each firm, about half the managers opted

TABLE 24 *Lifetime leisure split in two factories*

	High Frequency Electronics	*Royal Acetone Company*
One extra week every year	58%	64%
Three months holiday four times in life	22%	22%
Six months holiday twice in life	4%	7%
One year's holiday in life	16%	7%
Total %	100%	100%
Number	45	28

for 'lifetime holidays' of three months or more, about a third of clerical workers and a quarter of manual. With such small numbers in two sets we cannot be sure that these variations are statistically valid, but since both firms were alike it seems probable that they reflect real differences in preferences.

People were also asked what they would do with the long periods of holiday – the sabbatic leave – if they had it. Long-distance travel was the favourite. It is not something which can be done, or at any rate not well done, within the compass of an annual holiday. Although the question was so hypothetical and may never have been seriously considered before, most of those who favoured travel were fairly clear about when they would go – some when the children were very young so that it would not matter their missing school or they could be left with grand-parents if not taken along, some when the children were of school age so that they could learn a foreign language, some when the children were themselves grown up – and about where they would go.

> I'd go to Canada. My wife's brother and my uncles are out there. Canada has gone right through our family. My mother and father met there. My mother went out there in service and my father worked on a farm. If we liked it there perhaps we'd stay, though I wouldn't risk everything on emigrating without knowing whether we'd like it. (Toolmaker)

> I would take up full-time motor racing and do some of the circuits around Europe. (Salesman)

The travel was quite often to be combined with a job.

> I would spend my three months touring abroad, taking in Madeira and the United States. I'd also take another job which is entirely different from the one I have now. (Chemist)

Mr Taylor remembered that he had been to Germany quite often to visit a firm with which his own had connections. He thought he could easily get a job there for a year and his children would be able to learn German. He warmed to the idea so much during the interview that it almost seemed as though he would do it. Sabbatic holiday had become sabbatic job, and seemed all the more attractive for that.

For Mr Taylor it would have been exceptionally easy to take one; he would come back with valuable additional experience, as would his children when they got back to Maidenhead after a year in Bonn. For most other managers it would not have been so easy. They would have given 'ground in the rat race', and anyway why should the firm consent? What could they possibly gain? A senior manager who was in the sample and keen on the idea from his personal point of view agreed to think about it as a managerial problem. He came to the conclusion that a firm would agree to a sabbatic three months on full pay, say, every five years, only for a quite exceptional man. Even so, the firm's costs would be increased and the man might be tempted away by a competitor during his leave. But if some companies began to offer sabbatic holidays, and in this respect allowed their managers to become a little bit more like Veblen's leisure class, incarnate as they are in university teachers, others might be able to compete in the labour market only by following suit. Trade unions might also decide to seek such additions to holidays as the United Steel Workers Union has done in America;[1] or the government might one day decide to emulate the Australian example.[2] If that happened, total working hours over the life-span might be greatly reduced.

The more likely trend

As things are the more serious present possibility seems to be the opposite one. Weekly hours at any rate may again take an upward turn. Men in professional and managerial jobs have apparently been working the longest, and they are the group whose numbers have been swelling absolutely and as a proportion of the total. As we showed in Chapter 1 they increased between 1951 and 1966 by a third, from 18 per cent to 24 per cent of all the men in the London Region. The likelihood is, therefore, that more people have been working long hours. If the comparison over time was for the hours worked generally in the Region there would probably prove to have been an increase. This is taking men on their own. If working women were included the conclusion would be more emphatic.

The change would naturally be more marked if professional men and managers had been working longer than they used to, as well as longer than people in other classes. We do not know for sure whether they are. As far as we know, no enquiry similar to ours has been made before amongst non-manual workers. All we can do is to record our opinion and mention the three pieces of evidence we rely on. The first is about the past. In the civil service, hours were over a long period about six a day rising to seven in the middle of the nineteenth century,[3] and in other professions like lawyers and surgeons recruited from the leisure class, when

[1] 'Sabbatical or extended vacations were introduced into the mainstream of collective bargaining by the Steelworkers in the negotiations of 1962 and 1963 . . . Under the basic steel contract, 13-week vacations are provided every fifth year for employees in the top half of the seniority roster', 'The growth of longer vacations'.

[2] In all the states of Australia legislation provides for what is called 'long service leave'. In New South Wales, for instance, the Long Service Leave Act, 1955, gives three months' leave on full pay after twenty years' service. Some trade unions have negotiated better terms with employers.

[3] B. V. Humphreys, *Clerical Unions in the Civil Service*, pp. 8, 31, 43; E. Cohen, *The Growth of the British Civil Service 1780–1939*, pp. 30, 147.

Veblen's term really was apposite, the practice was probably not so very different. To judge by our figures, there has been a rise in such occupations since then.

The second piece of evidence, which is about the hours of managers as well as of professional men, comes from what some of those in our samples said to us. Many claimed that hours of work, along with the pressure in general, have been on the upgrade. The increasing complexity of organization has put a bigger load on them. One civil servant, very unlike his nineteenth century counterpart, said that the average number of pieces of paper coming into his in-tray per day was 176 and that he had to take some of them home every night. Even for the relatively small company, relations with the world outside have become more ravelled. Not only are there the suppliers and the customers; there are also the dealings with other bodies which did not have nearly as much impact on business in the last century – the Ministry of this or that, the trade unions, the trade associations. These impressions were the same as those drawn from another small survey.[1] A sample of senior managers were asked whether they worked longer than they did five years ago. They said their hours had gone up on average from 40 to 46, which tallies fairly well with our figure.

The third is from America. The survey just referred to suggested that British managers were being increasingly influenced by their European and American counterparts. If by the latter, what are the implications? One study reported an average week among managers of 62 hours, including business entertainment and business travel.[2] Wilensky summed up his historical review of the United States by saying that: 'With economic growth, the upper strata have possibly lost leisure. Professionals, executives, officials and proprietors have long work-weeks, year-round employment. Their longer vacations and shorter work lives (delayed entry and often earlier retirement) do not offset this edge in working hours.'[3] These various bits of evidence are obviously not decisive.

[1] The survey was made by Kiernan & Co. and reported in the *Financial Times* (9 December 1969), 'Longer hours for executives', p. 13. See also the surveys discussed in Chapter IX, pp. 247–8.

[2] A. Heckscher and S. De Grazia, 'Executive leisure', cited in J. Child and B. Macmillan, 'Managerial leisure in British and American contexts', p. 184.

[3] H. L. Wilensky, 'The uneven distribution of leisure: the impact of economic growth on "free time"', p. 37.

But between them they do to our mind give some support to the opinion that professional and managerial people have been increasing their hours of work as well as their proportionate weight in the labour force of the country.

The initial conclusion of this chapter is that there has not just been a return to the hours worked when the Stage 1 family was dominant, but that they have been reduced well below that level. The restoration of the holidays lost in the Puritan ascendancy has reinforced the effect. When coupled with the lessening of the human energy put into work, the fall has helped to elevate the home-centred family. But this is not the stuff that trends are made of. The process has had a check. It seems that the drop in hours, weekly at any rate, has levelled off and, to answer the question with which we opened the chapter, that men have not been spending less time at work.

The second conclusion is about middle-class men. By and large they have been working longer hours than others, and perhaps longer than they used to. Their numbers have been growing. Are they therefore bent on removing one of the props of the kind of family they helped to bring into being?

VI

ATTACHMENT TO WORK AND HOME

We have been detailing the number of hours done by men in different jobs and the number left over for their families. In this chapter we want to look at the effects of jobs upon the home over and above the sheer amount of time they permitted people to spend there. We are going to argue that people with more control over what they themselves do (and many other privileges as well) are more committed to their work, the one being the consequence of the other. But too much should not be made of the difference. It would be a caricature to portray the working man, with relatively little autonomy, as in it *only* for the money he can get out of it to spend on his home, and the others for their self-fulfilment beyond (or along with) the money; and still more to imply that one is a low purpose, the other high.

The home-centred family may have been restored; but to suggest that, even in the least enviable job, man can live for home alone, with work no more than the means to an end, would be grossly to over-state our thesis. Paradise may have been conceived of as a sort of everlasting saint's day, without toil. But, hard-working angels apart, what were the elect to do with themselves when, like Adam and Eve before the Fall, they had neither to delve nor to spin? The experience of unemployment in this century has shown that such a Paradise could be more like Hell to creatures who did not know how to do nothing with calm minds. One of the most famous studies of the subject was made at Marienthal in Austria in the 1930s. Once unemployed over a long period, the men lost their 'sense of reality', as those responsible for the investigation reported.[1] As is partly the same thing, they also lost their sense of time. The clocks in their homes were not wound. They were unpunctual for their meals. Rationality dis-

[1] M. Jahoda *et al.*, *Marienthal*, pp. 45–77.

appeared from their expenditure. They bought trinkets when they should have bought food. Even though they had on their hands so much time which they no longer bothered to count, and which they could have devoted to reading, they did not do so, and the local library became almost deserted. When they had no attachment to work, they had little or no attachment to leisure either; the one suffered with the other, and, as we shall see in Chapter VIII, it looks as though the opposite also applies – those more attached to work are more attached to leisure as well. The same effects of unemployment, though rather less dramatic, were noted in Britain a few years later,[1] and Wilensky came to a similar conclusion in his study of the lives of 105 men on public relief in Detroit.[2]

Old people no longer in work may attract a sympathy denied to the unemployed, even if they are less often accorded the respect given to them in many more static societies. They are often poorer than they were and more troubled by physical ailments. Townsend has given a vivid account of the grimness of retirement for some working-class people in Bethnal Green. They dreaded it.[3]

> Mr Selwyn was 72 and was worried about his job as a railway labourer. 'I'm only hanging on, just hanging on, like this bit of paper.' And he shook a flimsy bit of paper under my nose. 'I'd sooner be at work but if they retire me I suppose I will have to, then I will have to grin and bear it. I don't want to stand at the corner and watch the other people do it, but I suppose it will come to that.' He recollected with pride the remarks of a foreman who had complimented him on wielding a pick and shovel 'like a young man'. 'He said to me, "If we had some more like you we'd make the railroad go".' He was keen to go on working as long as he could because there was not much for him in life beyond it. 'My father wasn't lazy and I'm not. I want to do a good day's work as long as I can. I want to go on. I don't want to stand on a street corner. What would I do but that? I'd be worse off in every way if I had to sit at home and look at the old girl all day long. I'd have nothing to do and no money.'

[1] The Pilgrims' Trust Fund, *Men Without Work*.
[2] H. L. Wilensky, 'Work as a social problem'.
[3] P. Townsend, *The Family Life of Old People*, p. 139.

Such forebodings were often well founded. Whatever they did, there was little opportunity for self-expression for retired people in that part of London. In our sample for the London Region as a whole many were better off, particularly the middle-class (and a few working-class) people who had while in work developed abiding interests outside it.[1] But as at Marienthal, the absence of work (given the health and energy which it requires) was often regarded as more a curse than a blessing. Men who had gone into retirement were asked what, if anything, they particularly liked about it. Twenty-one per cent of middle-class men and 40 per cent of working-class in our survey said 'nothing'. A former plumber in Southwark said, 'There's too much time on your hands.' Working-class men when retired more often said they were bored: 37 per cent said they were 'often' or 'sometimes bored', compared with 18 per cent of the middle-class men.

People unemployed because there are not enough jobs to go round or because they have retired are usually alike in being short of money. To gain it, or rather the subsistence it buys, and the recognition of worth that an income implies, has ever been the overwhelming reason for work, and some people, if they 'won the Pools', would of course give up thankfully, at any rate until the novelty of not working wore off. But most people in all classes clearly get something more out of it than the money. We asked people whether they would continue to work 'if you didn't need the money'. More middle-class than working-class said 'yes', but nearly two-thirds of the latter also.

Why so? It is clearly not just the strength of social pressure, enormous as that always is: people are supposed to work, and do not ordinarily feel respectable in the eyes of others or of themselves if they do not, just as in previous centuries in certain classes they were not supposed to and did not ordinarily feel respectable if they did. The Puritan ethic in its modern form has swept through all classes. It must therefore claim some of the responsibility for the fact that nowadays even the people who do not need to work for financial reasons do so if they can find something congenial. It has implanted a sense of guilt in people about idle-

[1] An example was Mr Crossman, a retired manager living in High Wycombe, who said, 'I'm fully occupied. I do a tremendous amount of church work. I serve on two church committees and help to run the parish newsletter. Then there's the Community Centre. I've taken an interest in that. I'm on the Committee representing the Church.'

ness which (however fatuous the outcome) is a spur to escape from it.

That cannot be the whole story. The same need is felt in societies touched by other ethics. Work does not just provide social relationships but a chance for self-expression, at however modest a level, and, with almost any product or service, the sense of making or doing something that is a contribution to the good of others. Whether or not labour is, in Marx's term, 'a commodity', it is a link with the collective life. Work also creates a time-ordering of the sort that is necessary not only to social structure. Routines in the way people organize their lives are indispensable to almost everyone. Work may not be essential for that. To provide a counterpoint between effort and relaxation, people invent such structures for themselves, for instance in retirement, when these are not forced upon them. But for most people an element of imposition, of external compulsion over the regularities of their daily lives, seems to make any freedom they have within it more attractive, or (to be negative about it) more bearable. As Uncle Vanya said after everyone had left, as the tinkling of sleigh-bells could be heard when the horses trotted away, 'I feel too sad. I must go to work on something at once. To work! To work!'[1] Work with the characteristics it has acquired in modern society has many detractors, but work altogether almost none. Many have, like Bertrand Russell, pleaded for a reduction in its intensity. He was arguing that men would be liberated to spend their free time less passively if they worked less, not that they would be better off in some spiritual way if only (Nature allowing) they did none at all.[2]

There were certainly very few detractors in our sample, and plenty with relatively unexciting jobs who spoke up the other way. There were, for example, the skilled men.

> I take a pride in my job. I enjoy doing a good piece of bricklaying. I prefer working for a small contractor, as I do now. You can see the job through from start to finish. And I hate to bricklay with a man who doesn't bother about good workmanship. I feel as if I'm hitting my head against a brick wall. (Bricklayer, Tunbridge Wells)

[1] A. Chekhov, *Uncle Vanya*, p. 240.

[2] B. Russell, *In Praise of Idleness and Other Essays*, chap. 1.

> I'm interested in what I'm making. I start off with a drawing, make the tool or jig and then see it work. I always see the finished article. (Toolmaker, near St Albans)

To take another individual example, Mr Branscombe was a carpenter on maintenance in a factory in Deptford. He clocked on at a special decimal clock which was calibrated in periods of six minutes at a jump. By the clock was a pile of cards with job descriptions on them and times: 0.4 meant that it was supposed to take four decimal minutes to complete. To this was added four minutes not in decimal but in ordinary minutes which were counted as 'personal time' for a man to go to the lavatory in or whatever he wanted to do, as though the decimal men recognized that when an ordinary man was out of the control of the management and his time was his own it had to be counted in his way and not theirs. If Mr Branscombe did the job in 0.3 minutes he would have contributed one decimal minute to the carpenters' group bonus. He said it was obviously a daft system sold by an American consultant to the group of which his factory was part. But if the management wanted to play about in this way Mr Branscombe said he just had to lump it, and in some ways it might be better for him because, as no one really thought in this way, it was easier at the expense of the management to lose a decimal minute than an ordinary one.

He picked his own jobs, partly according to how long in ordinary minutes they would take, naturally preferring those where the times allowed were obviously too high. He had a much closer knowledge of the woodwork in the factory than the estimator. He was also influenced by when he would be able to do the work. During the week of the interview he had been making a chart frame for the drawing office between 7.30 and 8.30 on each morning before any of the draughtsmen arrived. On Saturday morning – he was on shifts – he had put up battens and hardboard in the ladies' cloakroom to hide some damp coming through the lavatory wall. On Saturdays the ladies were working at home, not there. In the same week he had made a new sliding window, some nests of lockers, and some door-frames. He was the skilled man who still worked as such. What he did varied little, taking one month with another, whereas it did from one day to another.

The main pleasure was in the relationships. A high point was the midday break, from 12.45 to 1.30. He and his fellow tradesmen did not go to the canteen. The painters made tea in their paint shop and had a game of cards while they were drinking it. 'The painters are good for cards although for work they're a lot of mumpers.' No one in the factory was supposed to make tea except the maintenance men for the drains who smelled so bad they were not allowed into the canteen. But the painters made it and 'the firm provides the tea, the sugar and the milk, although they don't know it'. There was another high point at the beginning of the day. Mr Branscombe got up at 6 a.m. He could not eat breakfast first thing. He waited for Charlie's.

> One winter I saw the lights the other side of the railway bridge as I was going over on my Honda. I noticed the lights each day and then I saw it was a cafe, so I went into Charlie's and now I always stop there for a cup of tea and a couple of slices of toast and meet the same people for a chat. There's Georgie who works around the corner at Marlow's. He's a packer who packs and unpacks machinery and goes off to exhibitions for them, and Bill who's at Jordan's. We don't talk much about work though. It's usually about football, or something like that. I'm always there now by 7 and stay for 20 minutes.

Then there were the unskilled workers. Mr 'Spud' Murphy was one of these. Called a porter, he was not one of the attendants of a machine but of the men and women in a large factory who were. He had to supply them with their material and then take away their finished and waste products. He started at 6.45 stocking up each machine with metal, and collecting trays before the operators arrived at 7.30. Then began the routine of the day. Ten minutes after the machines had begun to hum he went around with his fork-lift truck, taking any full or half-full trays, numbering them, and substituting empty ones. When he had enough, he took them all to the weighing machine. That took about fifteen minutes, as did the next round, which was carrying around the trays of material before he repeated his first task. It was the same every day, every week, every month. Nothing varied, except when there was a welcome breakdown of the machines, or an equally welcome little strike.

Yet Mr Murphy said the job was not too bad. Getting around as he did, he had friends all over the factory. 'Spud', they shouted above the noise, 'Spud this, Spud that', and he stopped for a chat with one of the men, or, still more agreeably, with one of the girls. He knew the English and Irish girls by their first names but could not manage those of the coloured. 'They are a bit complicated.' The friendships made it all more bearable, although the money was what mattered even more. He spent a lot on Saturday nights when he drank until the pubs closed and then went off with a bunch of his Irish friends to one or other house occupied by a similar number of compatriot nurses or factory-girls where they all drank together and moved from bedroom to bedroom, exchanging girls and laughter until it was time to get ready for mass on the Sunday morning.

Satisfaction with work

But even though almost everyone thinks it is better to work than not to, the balance between them varies a lot. This is not an easy topic to enquire about in a general survey. What we did was to ask people several questions about their sense of satisfaction with their work, whether they got most from it or from their leisure, and how often they felt bored by it. The results are in Table 25. They show that on the first and most banal question there was little difference between the classes, which is in line with what we said earlier about aspirations (and, implicitly, satisfactions) depending upon opportunities. The classes did differ in the relative appeal of leisure as against work and, although only a minority admitted to boredom, it was smaller in the higher classes. For working-class men the job was less often, in Dubin's phrase, their central life interest.[1] The main reason seemed to be that they had less control over what happened to them at work. Manual workers less often had before them a career with advancement depending to some extent upon their own efforts. They less often had a say in the day-to-day organization of their working lives. They were more often paced by the machines they served. In all these respects middle-class people generally had more autonomy.

Our question on careers was a general one – 'Would you say that in your line of work there's a career ladder?' Table 26 shows

[1] R. Dubin, 'Industrial workers' worlds: a study of the central life interest of industrial workers', p. 140.

TABLE 25 *Attitudes to work (main sample: married men working full-time)*

	Professional and managerial	*Clerical*	*Skilled*	*Semi-skilled and unskilled*	*All*
Proportion saying they were very satisfied with their job	56%	50%	46%	50%	50%
Proportion saying they got most satisfaction from work or work and leisure combined, rather than from leisure alone	72%	67%	46%	48%	57%
Proportion saying they often or sometimes felt bored at work	19%	34%	38%	42%	32%
Total number	169	70	236	109	584

the class difference. People were, by the way, both more optimistic about future prospects and less satisfied with their jobs if they were younger. More of them wanted a better job than they had and were discontented that they had not got it, perhaps because they had not yet given up hope about it. Older men may have become more resigned and more 'contented'.

Some of our informants thought of a career in the same way as Wilensky, who defined it as a 'succession of related jobs, arranged in a hierarchy of prestige, through which persons move in an ordered, predictable sequence'.[1] Mr Farrow of Brentwood said: 'In my firm they are good about that. If you've got it in you, you can climb right to the top. In five years' time, if I keep going, I should be Deputy Sales Manager for the whole of the South-Eastern Region. I might end up as General Sales Manager, and

[1] H. Wilensky, 'Work, careers and social integration', p. 554.

TABLE 26 *Career ladders at work (main sample: married men working full-time)*

	Professional and managerial	*Clerical*	*Skilled*	*Semi-skilled and unskilled*	*All*
Proportion saying that there was a career ladder	76%	70%	48%	45%	59%
Total number	169	70	238	109	586

even get on the Board – but frankly I don't think that's likely. If I was going to get there, I ought to be higher than I am now, at 35.' In one of the factories where we did a special study many of the managerial staff were similarly aware of a 'succession of related jobs' and endlessly calculated their chances. Success was judged, as Mr Farrow judged it, by the standing of the job reached by a particular age. At each 'stage' (as they liked to think of it) in their careers people were, as anxiously as parents with their children, on the alert for any signs to indicate the progress they had made and the prospects before them. The aspiring executive had to read the oracle repeatedly – at any rate up to his 'career menopause', when he knew, instead of just feared, that he had attained the highest point he would ever reach. The crucial period seemed to be in the late twenties and thirties when the man was, in his other roles as husband and father, also under the greatest pressure. It was then that his fate would be determined according to the acceleration he had built up to. One convention for measuring speed which seemed to be widely credited in the company, and more generally, was that a man enjoying an average kind of ascent should get promotion from one 'tour of duty' to another every three years or so,[1] as he did at his university (if he went to one). It followed that someone who had kept to the rule to begin with and then had to wait four years in his early thirties was slowing down, while

[1] This triennial phenomenon was brought to our notice by Dr H. M. Hugh Murray of the Tavistock Institute of Human Relations. He had observed it in a large industrial organization he had studied and gave us the idea which seemed to be applicable in our factory.

someone else who was getting promotion in two was speeding up. The former would have had his cue to look even more carefully at the advertisements in the Sunday papers. These told the successful man whether his present salary was on the right level by comparison with other jobs of the same sort, but also, more crucially, what openings there might be elsewhere for the man who feared he might be passed over if he stayed put.

The speed of movement depended upon his general 'merit', which was judged by others higher up the ladder. If that had been all there was to it the man might have considered himself more controlled by the career structure than he was in control of it. But he did have some freedom of manoeuvre; he could manipulate as well as be manipulated. To do this he needed information about the ages and past speeds of promotion (as from that he could calculate the likely future chances) of everyone in those parts of the company in which he might be employed. He would then, if he could, avoid being blocked by being immediately junior to a slow-mover because this would mean, however good he was in himself, that he might have to wait longer because there was no job to promote him into. This disadvantage might be offset if it was known that much higher on the same ladder within the firm someone was about to retire or to go to another job; this might mean that all would move up one. If he was completely blocked in one line his best move would be sideways, especially into a department which had been expanding faster than average so that there were more possibilities of promotion. As viewed by any man who was not completely specialized, the metaphor was not so much a ladder as a lattice, although one without all the interconnecting pieces in place. The ideal was to get up such speed that one zigzagged past men older than oneself.[1] A youngish accelerating man might even get spoken about, in a rather hushed voice, as a possible future managing director, and his knowledge of this judgment might do something to make it a self-fulfilling prophecy by filling him out with the confidence which, if he kept it in check in front of the present managing director, would bring him more surely to the prize. When he was firmly tipped for it, he

[1] The tragedy of the older person who is overtaken by the younger, which has such appeal because it eventually happens to everyone, is constantly played out in sport in both real life and a symbolic form: 'Mrs Court and Miss Goolagong are the only Australians to win the title: here was one generation firmly grasping the torch from another' (*The Times*, 3 July 1971, on the Wimbledon of that year).

might have a chance of attracting a 'Praetorian Guard' of other young men who recognized that they would have the best prospects if they gave their personal loyalty, even in a lesser role than their hero, to someone with whom they might rise through the hierarchy, thus fusing a system of personal power into one of bureaucratic power.

This was a large company in a competitive industry, and may not have been typical even for that. The calculations, and the emotions as well as intelligence invested in them, may not usually be so gripping. But something like it was common in industrial and commercial organizations.[1] The game was clearly absorbing, partly because the stakes were even higher than in more ordinary play defined by Huizinga as 'an activity which proceeds within certain limits of time and space, in a visible order, according to rules freely accepted, and outside the sphere of necessity or material utility'.[2] This was in the sphere of necessity, or what men chose to consider as such. The company did as much as it could to make the game worth playing by offering a hierarchy of prizes which taken together gave the loyal and competent member of the staff a standard of living at work, and at the company's expense, which at least matched his standard of living at home: the cars and the name or number plate in the reserved parking lot that were mentioned in Chapter II; the right to a place in the director's dining-room, with all the contacts that brought; the secretary to oneself; the right to attend high-level conferences where there might be other rising stars with whom alliances could be formed; the larger room with the fitted carpet; the placing of one's name higher in the circulation list for trade journals; the drinks cabinet regularly stocked; the move up to the executive floor. The game was more staid and less fraught for many professional people. But even for them work was apt to be absorbing. Their own future depended upon it, and that of their family, 'of course', the aspirants to success would piously assert if they thought about it at all as they arrived home late from another episode in the struggle. 'Business is a rat race, full of Jekylls and Hydes, Jekylls at work and Hydes at home', said one ageing

[1] C. Sofer, *Men in Mid-Career*. However, another study of mid-career managers concluded that 'a firm commitment to achieve "success" is not typical . . . Few men were advancing along a clear and structured career line', J. M. and R. E. Pahl, *Managers and their Wives*, p. 99.

[2] J. Huziinga, *Homo Ludens*, p. 10.

Mr Hyde, 'It's full of pushing, back-stabbing young men.'

Mr Fison, a deputy production manager who commuted to Central London from Reading, was one who did not like this calculated tumbling at all.

> A situation arises when you feel completely competent to handle the trouble on your own. Then you find that your superiors have picked someone else to do it. I find that very irritating. When that happens I come home like a bear with a sore head. In general I suppose you could say that what I don't like about it is the political rat-race. It's the same everywhere in this world. People are jockeying for positions – it's all one-upmanship. People are always trying to get credit for the work that other people have done in order to get promoted. It's not always the best people, I can tell you, who get the top jobs. I've done quite well myself, so it's not sour grapes that makes me say that. I can tell you it's a fact. But it's irritating sometimes, and I have had it happen to me, when you feel you've lost out because of somebody else's one-upmanship.

His wife added:

> It's not so much that he's unpleasant to us. But he will come home and talk the whole problem out – he will talk for two hours on the trot.

Manual workers had shorter ladders to contemplate, and clerical workers ones in between. Some in the former category considered they could rise to chargehand, or foreman if they wished. They remembered people who had done so, and others who had refused promotion when offered.[1] Many expected their standard of life, if unemployment could be held at bay, to continue to advance, not on the steep climb of the successful young executive but at a more gentle if steady rate as a result of the efforts of their trade unions or of competition in the labour market. But most of them knew that there was nothing much they could do individually, only collectively, to get more money, let alone some of the fringe benefits possessed by people in the office.

[1] One who had accepted a foreman's job and then demoted himself explained: 'I packed it in when I found I was doing the firm's worrying for them in the evenings and at weekends.'

It was therefore not surprising that on this ground alone they should invest less of themselves in their work, and have more available for investment elsewhere; nor that those who had more influence over what happened in their lives, even though the strain of it all could be a burden indeed, should behave in the opposite way.

Extent of autonomy

The more senior the managers, the more could they shape not just their future but also what they did from day to day and from hour to hour. Table 27 shows that the men at the top thought they had 'a lot of say' in what happened to them and those at the bottom 'some' or 'none', with variations in between.

TABLE 27 *Degree of influence over use of time at work (main sample: married men working full-time)*

	Professional and managerial	*Clerical*	*Skilled*	*Semi-skilled and unskilled*	*All*
Reported say over the way time used at work					
A lot of say	92%	67%	54%	37%	63%
Some but not much	6%	24%	27%	31%	22%
No say	2%	9%	19%	32%	15%
Total %	100%	100%	100%	100%	100%
Number	170	70	239	109	588

The absence of control over their work, symbolized by the fact that they had to clock in when they arrived there, so handing over their time to their employers, seemed to be more resented than the lack of career prospects. Mr Barrow thought that in his factory he was treated like a child.

With my leisure I can do what I want. I make up my own

mind. If I want to go to the pictures with the wife I go to the pictures. If I want to go to the football match I go to the football match. Here you have to be told. Well, you don't *have* to be, but you are. You're treated like a child. You don't get any chance to say anything about how the job is done. If you try, you're told you're wrong. (Assembly worker, Islington)

Mr Channing was even more straightforward about it, though he was as unable as most people without power to imagine all the constraints limiting the discretion of those with it.

The guv'nors decide how the work has to be done. They know what has to be done and they tell you what to do and how to do it. (Machine minder, Lewisham)

There was also in large companies the sense that the guv'nors who really decided were far off and that their distance itself made it more difficult for men to have a say in what happened to them at the bench, the machine or the counter. Men talked, it is true, about their 'employers', as though they were referring to people. This was, in 1970, still the convention. But men knew that 'the company', even if it still bore the name of the man who began it, and even if it was directed by the holders of particular posts within it, was what employed them. The lower down they were in the hierarchy, the more did the employer seem like a bureaucracy. At the higher levels that we were speaking about earlier the boss struggled to remain a person rather than a rule-bound office-holder, by giving or witholding annual salary increases or fringe benefits, partly according to his own personal discretion, and by being as 'human' as he could in the staff dining-room and in the lift or corridors when he met other members of his 'team'. He could have a better chance of doing this, especially in the eyes of manual workers, when the business was a family business and some of the older men remembered the present boss when he was young. Two centuries after the domestic system of production began to decline, the concept of a family business was for many employees easier to understand and sympathize with than that of a public company owned by completely anonymous stockholders as well as directed by nearly anonymous managers.

The aspirations of many people also still belonged more happily to the old than the new industrial system. To be their own master was their ideal. People wanted to have work which they could put themselves into more fully. 'If you were working for yourself, you'd put more into it than what you would do for the guv'nor' (process worker, Dagenham). 'If I had my own bookies' shop I'd work hard. It would be more like a hobby' (electrician, Enfield). Half the full-time male employees in the sample shared the aspiration to have their own business, in the sense of having at one time 'thought' about it, tried it or actually had one.[1]

Disadvantage of divided labour

Specialization has long been regarded as operating much more to the advantage of middle-class than of working-class people. The expertise it creates is more saleable, partly because it can with the help of the State more securely be monopolized, as in the specialized professions, than it can be by any trade union. The competition of outsiders lacking what are held to be the necessary qualifications can therefore be kept at bay and the fruits of their labours reserved in full measure for those who can put ARIBA, or AMICE, or FRCS, or ARSI, or AMTPI, or AIPM, or AIQS after their names. And it can be highly pleasurable to exercise one's skill if it is accredited, or even if it is unaccredited except by experience. The extension of specialization has often been lamented, but on the grounds that there are too few people devoting their energies to the general problems of an organization, a country, or the world, too few generalists and too many specialists, not on the grounds that the specialists have miserable jobs. The earth as a whole may be crumbling; the creatures burrowing down their holes are not only busy but (it is assumed) beaming. They are thought to have, within the proper bounds, some opportunity for expressing their own personalities.

Not so at the other end of the scale, where the jobs are lower paid, less secure and, as if that were not enough, less rewarding in other ways as well. The responsibility, or much of it, for the 'alienation' of labour has often been attributed to specialization.

[1] Goldthorpe and his colleagues, whose question on this we substantially repeated, found even larger proportions who had 'thought' about it or done it: 73 per cent of their manual workers and 56 per cent of the white-collar workers. J. H. Goldthorpe *et al.*, *The Affluent Worker: Industrial Attitudes and Behaviour*, pp. 131–2.

One of the assaults launched by the young Karl Marx was on the grounds that 'the division of labour implies the possibility, nay the fact that intellectual and material activity – enjoyment and labour, production and consumption – devolve on different individuals, and that the only possibility of their not coming into contradiction lies in the negation in its turn of the division of labour.'[1] The evil was apparent well before mechanization, for instance in Adam Smith's pin factory, where fragmentation of the giant process of making a pin had been subdivided into eighteen different operations 'which in some manufactories are all performed by distinct hands, though in others the same man will sometimes perform two or three of them'.[2] Smith was an upholder of the system as the progenitor of wealth. At the same time he recognized its dark side.[3]

> The man whose whole life is spent in performing a few simple operations, of which the effects too are perhaps always the same, or very nearly the same, has no occasion to exert his understanding or to exercise his invention in finding out expedients for removing difficulties which never occur. He naturally loses, therefore, the habit of such exertion, and generally becomes as stupid and ignorant as it is possible for a human creature to become.

Few modern critics would be so sweeping. But the division of labour, at least for manual workers, has few friends amongst those who wish to increase the satisfaction gained from work rather than just from the consumption of its products.

Work into home

The advantages for the one class, which are also disadvantages for the other, are not clear-cut, of course. But there is not much doubt who is most engaged, with the clerical workers in most respects falling somewhere between the two extremes. The manual worker, in the service trades as well as in factories, ordinarily has less of the prospects which can give some point to present labour; less of the sense of control which enables a man to assert himself; and

[1] K. Marx and F. Engels, *The German Ideology*, p. 44.
[2] A. Smith, *The Wealth of Nations*, vol. 1, p. 6.
[3] Ibid., vol. II, p. 267.

more repetition from day to day. Not many of them could say with a design engineer, 'There's the satisfaction of creating something in your mind, turning it into a drawing and, finally, seeing it take shape as a real piece of hardware'; or with a production manager, 'I enjoy taking a project, starting it from scratch and taking it through to the finished product'. The pleasures were more often like those of playing cards in the paint shop.

But, among those whose work was more satisfying, the corollary was that it intruded into their homes. We are not suggesting that this did not happen at all with manual workers. We said in the last chapter that, hours being less than in Stage 2, so was fatigue less. But it has not disappeared by any means. When men are tired out they may bring home, if not the work itself, some of its consequences. In all classes, there were sizeable proportions who found their work tiring. As Table 28 demonstrates, people nearer the top more often found it mentally tiring and those nearer the bottom more often physically.

TABLE 28 *Work fatigue (main sample: married men working full-time)*

	Professional and managerial	*Clerical*	*Skilled*	*Semi-skilled and unskilled*	*All*
Proportion saying they found their work					
Physically tiring	51%	52%	66%	67%	60%
Mentally tiring	88%	66%	59%	40%	65%
Total number	169	70	239	109	587

In one interview, Mr Campbell, an assembly worker from Dagenham, was trying to remember what he had done the previous evening. His wife was also present.

Mr Campbell: What did I do? I can't remember.
Mrs Campbell: You fell asleep, that's what you did. You went to sleep at half-past six after your tea and at ten you got up off the settee and went to bed.

A few people who would not conventionally be thought of as manual workers also suffered from physical weariness along with the sort more common to their class. Mrs Morrell, who lived near Eton and was the wife of a pilot, had to face it each time he returned home.

> I often say BOAC is his mistress. He gets very tired. The first day home I have learned to keep quiet and not mention any problems. He still has the noise of the jet engines in his ears. His face is white and fatigued. The children run up to him shouting 'Daddy', and they can't take it in when he doesn't respond.

Although work spilled over in all classes, it seemed generally to do so more at the top. Table 29 shows the men's answers to our question about the interference of work with family, bringing together the subject matter of the last chapter, hours, and of this, other kinds of stress. Managers were more aware of conflict, both because of the hours they put in and the pressures associated with them. We come to shiftwork in the next chapter.

TABLE 29 *Occupational class of men and interference of work with home and family (main sample: married men working full-time)*

	Professional and managerial	*Clerical*	*Skilled*	*Semi-skilled and unskilled*	*All*
No interference	47%	60%	69%	75%	63%
Time spent on work instead of with family	36%	18%	16%	15%	22%
Difficulties of shift work	2%	10%	8%	9%	7%
Strain, worry, overtiredness	9%	4%	3%	0%	4%
Other interference	12%	10%	8%	3%	8%
Total number	168	71	237	110	586

Percentages add to more than 100 because some men mentioned more than one kind of interference.

The greater involvement of senior people showed up in the home in two main ways apart from their long hours – in the hold that the problems of their work had over their minds, and in the extent to which home was in direct communication with work. The first is illustrated by what three managers said.

> I think about work continually when I'm at home. If you are digging a flower bed for a couple of hours you can have a marvellous think about some deep problems of organization. You are not necessarily trying to think something through at high pressure; you are just mulling it over. (Computer manager, Brentwood)

> When I'm in the bath or mowing the lawn, I'm often trying to figure out some problem or other. It's happening all the time. (Sales manager, Sutton)

> Five to ten per cent of my home activity is directed towards work. It's mainly current problems, more of a technical or scientific sort, because there are less external influences disturbing you at home. (Service manager, near Burgess Hill)

A manager living at Caterham said he worked best when he was apparently doing nothing.

> If you saw me very happily sitting in the garden with a drink at my side I might be thinking over a problem. If you came along beside me you might be talking to me for ten minutes and I wouldn't hear you, I'd be so concentrated. There is a total commitment to my job. I'd almost say that my work is my leisure.

Such people knew they were not exactly ideal companions for their wives and children.

> I think work does interfere at home. Possibly in my manner. You get drawn down sometimes when you've got problems inside you. It makes you a little more difficult to get on with at home. (Marketing manager, Reading)

> One has problems. You think about them and drift off into a haze and don't pay attention to what your wife is telling you. I said that I never take work home – that's true, not paper

work. But unfortunately it remains in my head. There are the usual domestic problems as a result. (Service manager, near St Albans)

My concern for work interferes with my home. It would be nice if I could switch myself off and cheerfully help my wife with the washing up instead of doing it all with a long face. (Surveyor, Maida Vale)

The second problem arose because some of those who could not make a clean split between the two spheres were only too liable to be interrupted in each. The telephone was the means of trespass. A husband could use it during the day to tell his wife if his plans for the evening had changed; a wife to ask his secretary – the relationship, amity on top, hostility below, between the wife and his secretary has created two of the stock roles in commercial life – to tell him that he should not forget to buy the whisky or that she has to have the car next Tuesday to take a child to the dentist's. When the husband left work he might be quite alone, out of touch, incommunicado for the time it took him to make the journey – unless he was so completely immersed and so important that he had a radio telephone in his car. As soon as he arrived, he was again at the mercy of others.

I get calls at night from the works. There is someone on duty there all the time. Sometimes a telex message comes in after I've left but they telephone me and I 'phone someone in the States or Scotland or wherever it might be to try and answer the question. (Sales manager, Enfield)

I quite often get a 'phone call when I'm sitting at home with my family in the evening. If the computer goes on the blink at 10 p.m. they ring up and ask me what the hell they should do. Sometimes I have to go back. I try to discourage calls at home though. (Computer manager, Brentwood)

Plans for weekends and even holidays were liable to be changed at the last minute because of a sudden creak in the lattice-work upholding the roles of executives, or in the relationship of 'the employer' to the world outside both work and home.

Such men not only worked at home during 'non-working' hours, at evenings or weekends. Sometimes they also did so during working hours on weekdays, staying at home to concentrate on jobs which they could do better, or no less well, there. Avoiding the usual journey was a bonus. There were sizeable numbers of self-employed people, particularly professionals and managers. One in six of the men in our sample in this class counted himself as self-employed. They were mainly people like architects or doctors, management consultants or the proprietors/managers of small businesses. The proportion among skilled workers was under one in ten; they were watchmakers, taxi-drivers, builders or welders with small businesses in which they worked alone or just with one or two others. The number of people working on their own account recorded by the Census has stayed about the same throughout this century.[1] Such men could work at home more or less whenever they pleased. There were also others who, though not self-employed, could exercise their autonomy[2] by not turning up at their office if they so wished or to move between several different places of work. Here is an extract from an internal circular of a research organization which was not studied specifically by us but which is not completely untypical.

> David Donnison – tries to be at home on Fridays.
>
> Brian McLoughlin – normally expects to be at the Centre on Mondays, Tuesdays and Wednesdays. He spends Thursdays at University College, London, and tries to work at home at Manchester on Fridays.
>
> Malcolm Wicks – is at Brunel University on Mondays and Wednesdays and the Centre on Tuesdays and Thursdays. On Fridays he is either at the Centre or elsewhere.

Such people, when they worked at home, could see more of their wives and children as a consequence. The intrusion of work into home could then be a welcome one because it brought with it a

[1] G. Routh, *Occupation and Pay in Great Britain 1906–60*, Table 1.

[2] Another way in which some people could exercise it and escape from the general rule of society was by postponing retirement. People, according to an earlier enquiry, were less likely to retire at sixty-five or any other set age and remained at work well beyond it if they were employers or managers in small establishments, or self-employed farmers, foresters, fishermen or artists. R. M. Belbin and F. L. Clark, 'The relationship between retirement patterns and work as revealed by the British Census', and General Register Office, *Sample Census 1966: Economic Activity Tables*, Part III, Table 27.

person who would not otherwise be there. If the odd day turned into several, and did so for more and more people, the Stage 1 family could make a reappearance in another form.

What will be the outcome?

A still more important question is about the more general trend – are the more absorbing jobs in the ascendant or not? The stock idea about mechanization is that it has abstracted much of the joy from work, fatigue certainly but also pleasure, especially where machines have been substituted for what had previously been human skill. This has obviously been one of its effects. People have been ousted by the machines that can 'spin without fingers' and do hundreds of other operations once done by fingers and hands and arms and feet; but, what is worse, have often still been required as human attendants, using less of their faculties than before in their new capacity. This has been most resented when, as it so often is, the machine is the boss, controlling and pacing the man, dictating to him when he shall do this and when that. If on the other hand the operator is responsible for starting and stopping it, and in between can make it do what *he* wants within the limits of its design, he may (as anyone can observe) become quite fond of the mechanical creature and the job of caring for it, in the way that some people do of the private vehicles which have replaced their feet or the private laundries which have replaced their hands at home. This fondness is obviously less likely to develop, on paid work at any rate, the less skill the operator is called upon to add to the machine–man relationship.

If machines have on balance made some jobs less interesting they have made others more so. The counter-tendency is for automation, which does away with the need for operators, to eat up the less interesting jobs[1] which lend themselves better to it just because the element of human skill has already been largely eliminated from them. As long as the jobs are made redundant and not the men who do them there is nothing but gain. Whether for manual workers the counter-tendency is yet more powerful than the tendency we do not know. Blauner concluded that in the USA 'Automation is eliminating unskilled factory jobs at a faster

[1]G. Friedmann, *Industrial Society*, pp. 173–90.

rate than they are being created by the further deskillization of craft work.'[1] If this is not yet true of Britain, it almost certainly will be.

But about one effect that mechanization, especially in its later stages, has had upon non-manual workers there is much less doubt. It has helped to increase their numbers, relative to those of the manual. The machines, as they have got more complicated, have required more skilled people to design them and more skilled people, too, in the new sphere between manual and non-manual, to maintain them. The factory organization that makes all this possible itself requires more people to re-design and maintain it, and more people to market the goods that it produces. Mechanization is, in other words, one of the influences, if only one, behind the growth in the proportions of middle-class people to which we have made many references already. It has increased the numbers in 'service' occupations within manufacturing industry.

At the same time an even more significant shift in the economy from manufacturing to service industries (if industry be the right word to use at all) has been brought about by the increasing complexity of the society which therefore needs more effort to go into maintaining communication between all its parts; by the propensity of people, as they get richer, to spend a smaller proportion of their incomes upon goods and more upon services; and above all by the faster rise in productivity in manufacturing than outside it.[2] This change may be further accentuated in the future if the ecological threat from manufacturing industry leads to a damping down of production to the benefit of the services which do not give rise to pollution. The long-term tendency of the service sector to expand has often been noticed before. Colin Clark in a well-known statement which drew on what Sir William Petty had said earlier, in 1691, formulated the proposition that 'as time goes on and communities become more economically advanced, the numbers engaged in agriculture tend to decline relative to the numbers engaged in manufacture, which in their

[1] R. Blauner, *Alienation and Freedom*, p. 169.

[2] 'The major explanation for the shift of employment is that output per man grew much more slowly in the service sector than in the other sectors'. V. R. Fuchs, *The Service Economy*, p. 4.

turn decline relative to the numbers engaged in services'.[1] There is not yet any satisfactory definition of 'service' industries or occupations within them, particularly because they are often thought of as the residue after agriculture, mining, manufacturing and construction have been accounted for, so that any alteration in the definition of any of these affects what is left over. Different commentators have not therefore agreed about the extent to which the second half of the Clark proposition has in fact been borne out. There have already been long-term declines in some service occupations, particularly in domestic service, in public transport and for Britain in the shipping industry which used to perform a particular service on so much larger a scale for the rest of the world.[2] But, as we see it, these decreases have been more than counterbalanced by the growth of public administration, of education, health and other social services rendered collectively, and of other professional, information and financial services rendered privately, so that over more than a century the trend has been as Clark suggested.[3]

This is relevant to the theme of this chapter partly because, compared with manufacturing, the growing service sector employs more in salaried jobs. Table 30 shows this for our region It would not have happened on such a large scale unless consumers had been forced, sometimes gladly, sometimes not so gladly, to take over some of the manual work formerly done by paid employees, serving themselves in supermarkets and buses, cafeterias and self-service petrol stations; maintaining the miniaturized machines we may have already made too much of; and driving themselves as amateurs instead of being driven by professionals. But even if unpaid self-service has spread the manual work around this does not alter the fact that the expansion of paid service jobs has absolutely and relatively augmented the

[1] C. Clark, *The Conditions of Economic Progress*, p. 492. Petty had been put in mind of his generalization that 'there is more to be gained by Manufacture than by Husbandry; and by Merchandise than by Manufacture' by the success of Holland as the richest country of his day. Since Petty believed that in terms of countries at any rate the poorer countries would follow the lead of the richest we might, if we had wished to be more insular, leant in Chapter I more upon Petty than on Tocqueville. On the general rule see also S. Kuznets, *Economic Growth*, Lecture 3.

[2] P. Deane and W. A. Cole, *British Economic Growth*, p. 179.

[3] Department of Employment and Productivity, *British Labour Statistics: Historical Abstracts 1886–1968*, Tables 102, 103, 108. Also G. Routh, op. cit., p. 41.

size of the middle class, and with it the interest of the jobs that have to be done.

TABLE 30 *Distribution of labour force between manufacturing and services (main sample)*

	Men		*Women*	
	Manu-facturing	*Services*	*Manu-facturing*	*Services*
Professional and managerial	19%	38%	4%	20%
Clerical	10%	21%	38%	46%
Skilled	49%	24%	19%	6%
Semi-skilled and unskilled	22%	17%	39%	28%
Total %	100%	100%	100%	100%
Number	307	370	134	339

Services are here defined as in Central Statistical Office, *Standard Industrial Classification*, 1968. The seven 'orders' or groups are: gas, electricity and water, transport and communication; distributive trades; insurance, banking, finance and business services; professional and scientific services; miscellaneous services; public administration and defence.

Moreover, jobs in services probably hold more interest on the whole than in manufacturing. On this point we agree with the leading American authority on service occupations in a country which has even more of a service economy than in Britain.[1]

> The transfer from a craft society to one of mass production was said to depersonalize work and alienate the worker. The advent of a service economy implies a reversal of these trends. Employees in many service industries are closely related to their work and often engage in a highly personalized activity that offers ample scope for the development and exercise of personal skill... It may be true that the initial impact of automation is the substitution of machinery and controls (highly impersonal) for work that was formerly done by human labor. Given full employment, however, the major impact of auto-

[1] V. R. Fuchs, op. cit., p. 11.

mation is to eliminate relatively routine, impersonal work entirely, with the result that if one looks at the kind of work people are now doing – the type of work that is growing most rapidly – it is typically of a much more personal character than before.

In case this seems too sanguine a general conclusion, about the life of work if not of home, we should add that for many decades to come a large proportion of men, and even larger of women, will have jobs that lack many of the satisfactions discussed earlier, unless far more serious efforts are made to eliminate the dreary, the monotonous, the degrading from the working lives of people who are forced to do the dirty work for the rest of us.

The argument of the chapter has been that working-class men are less often deeply committed to their jobs. The compensation (as much for their families as for themselves) is that they have more energy left over for their wives and children. In their Stage 3 families, they are more fully home-centred because they are less fully work-centred. They can more easily leave their work behind them when they leave the premises in which it is done. We have contrasted them with those who in these various respects are, if not opposite, at least different in the extent to which they are wedded to their jobs.

This and the previous two chapters point to the same conclusion. Wives have been getting more involved in work, especially when in the kinds of job which have such a hold over men. Husbands in the higher classes have longer hours than in the lower, and probably longer than they used to. They are also more committed to their work so that it more readily spills over into the home. Their numbers are on the increase and, at the opposite extreme, those with little to attach them to the job except the money it offers are gradually decreasing. All this raises a question about the children, to which we shall return in the final chapter. If a growing minority of mothers and fathers, which within a hundred years could become a large majority, have voluntarily entered into a new compact with the collective life, how does it affect their offspring? Are they less subject to control at home, less bound by old disciplines, more out of the thoughts of parents whose attentions are engaged elsewhere, more emancipated, expected to become little adults at an earlier age than they were, but little adults at school rather than little adults at work as in the Stage 1 family? This is another issue about the present which is also about the future.

VII

SHIFTWORK

There were of course some manual workers who were like middle-class ones. They saw no paradox in sacrificing their families to get the money to support them. None the less, the means they had to adopt could be partially self-defeating. In saying this, we are thinking especially of the workers who were prepared to work unusual hours – in the Post Office it is called Unsocial Attendance – for the sake of the additional price put upon their labour.

We are talking again about a minority but one which appears to be growing along with the other minority of managers. The evidence for the country as a whole comes from the report published in 1970 by the National Board for Prices and Incomes. It declared that 'in recent years the underlying upward trend in the percentage of the manual labour force on shifts in manufacturing has been about 1 per cent per annum'.[1] In vehicle manufacture, to pick an industry of importance in the London Region, there was a sharper rise – 13 per cent of all manual workers employed in it in 1954 were shiftworkers, and 38 per cent in 1968. In the chemical industry the increase was almost as great. In paper, printing and publishing it was less, and in food, drink and tobacco a little less again. The rises in various service industries were much the same as in manufacturing. There were no comparative figures to show the trend in transport and communications, only figures for 1968 which specified 39 per cent of their manual employees as shiftworkers. Shiftwork is clearly on a large, and increasing, scale.

[1] National Board for Prices and Incomes, *Hours of Work, Overtime and Shiftworking*, p. 66. What has been referred to as 'the only true socialist measure' of the Paris Commune of 1871 – the decree abolishing nightwork in bakeries – would, if it were generalized, have become more and more difficult to apply since then. See D. Bell, *The End of Ideology*, p. 368.

Technology again the pacemaker

To understand why, and hence to gauge the likelihood of the trend continuing, we need to consider again the role of technology. Conceiving of it not just as technical know-how, with the tools to express it, but also as the productive organization to make those tools effective, we have given it a central place in our account of the changes which have occurred in the family, both in the effect it has had upon the hold of work and in the style of life it has allowed (or forced) people to adopt as consumers. Technology overthrew the domestic system. Technology, by extending the division of labour, dehumanized much of the work done by the less skilled at one end of the social scale and, at the other, raised the demand for people with skills to design and develop products and generally manage and control the new dispensation. Technology, by raising productivity, allowed people to choose more leisure without loss of income. Technology, in the form of better transport, despatched home-centred families over a larger territory without disrupting the connections between one family and another, and one machine and another, which maintain a city over a region as an interacting whole. The large has to some extent supported the small and the small the large. Each twist and turn of technological change has in other words affected the institution which is our chief concern.

Shiftwork brings us to another of its outcomes. In Chapter V we referred to the rhythms of an agricultural society, and especially the seasonal ones to which the working year was adjusted. There was another equally marked beat which also derived from astronomical cycles, the alternation of day and night; and another, the weekly, which was man-made. All three set the tempo of life for Stage 1 families, and two of them at any rate became blurred in a technological age. The machine does not recognize the difference between one season and another, between one week and another, between day and night; it is bent on forcing man to abandon the old syncopation and conform to its own regular beat.

Its great success has so far been achieved with the diurnal distinction. Before the arrival of industry all but the well-off prepared to enter bed with the dusk and to rise with the lark, which meant that they had shorter working hours in the shorter days of winter; this was recognized even in the Statute of Artificers which we quoted. Fuel was scarce, and on the whole more vital for heat – in eighteenth century England the practice of burning dung-cakes instead of using them as fertilizer was as much lamented as it is in modern India[1] – than for light. The lord of darkness had to be obeyed. The coming of the new industrial system changed that; even where artificial light was highly expensive the night was trenched on. Shifts can be considered a sign of humanity. Before they were common, manufacturers simply extended the working day as far as they could in each direction for the one lot of employees. Oastler, who was such a fierce antagonist of the new factory system, and of child labour in particular, recorded his horror at seeing children at work late at night.[2]

> The very Saturday night when I was returning from the meeting, I saw two mills blazing like fury in the valley. Their inmates, poor little sufferers, had to remain there until 11.30 o'clock, and the owner of one of them I found to be a noted, sighing, praying, canting religionist.

With the arrival first of gas and then of electric light, the cost to the capitalists of keeping their factories running into the night was reduced, and the domestication of the new inventions eventually allowed everyone to throw off the tyranny of the sun. The process has continued. Floodlighting allowed greyhound and dirt-track racing to be introduced between the wars and since the last one has illuminated night football as well as Greenwich Palace and St Paul's. It has also extended the hours that can be worked in open-air industries like building whenever there is clement weather (as it is called in that industry) in winter as well as in summer.

Technology can also claim some of the credit for the overthrow of many of the sanctions behind the Sabbath by its enhancement of the gospel of work. The demands of leisure are still thought of by some as too frivolous to deserve priority, and the Lord's Day Observance Society is still a force to be reckoned with by theatrical and sports promoters. But not so by employers. Sunday has had a price put upon it. With the acceptance of double-time for Sundays another barrier to continuous working has been removed.

As for seasonal work, it has obviously not been destroyed altogether. It is still present in agriculture and horticulture (even when

[1] C. Hill, *Reformation to Industrial Revolution*, p. 204.

[2] Quoted in E. P. Thompson, *The Making of the English Working Class*, p. 348.

under glass) in our Region as much as it is elsewhere. The medieval pattern is reproduced even at the centre of London in the hours of park-keepers which are short in the winter and lengthen steadily as the sun rises higher in the heavens. But the great seasonal turn-about is no longer directly linked with agriculture, though it is with the weather, and especially with the academic year which used to be linked to the harvest. The 'Season' which turned prostitutes into flower girls in the last century matters less. The rich do not arrive from their country houses but from overseas. The new crop is of holiday-makers. Tourists begin to arrive in London as the days get longer and the temperature higher, and their numbers are increasing every year. People who work in hotels, restaurants, pubs, shops, entertainment, transport or anywhere at all in the 'tourist industry' have therefore to work longer, and do more shiftwork, in season than out of it, and take their holidays when others are not doing so. Fortunately for the capacity of the city, Londoners pile out (with the peak period for them determined by the school holidays) at more or less the same time as the tourists, from other parts of Britain and overseas, pile in. If it were not for this complementarity the temporal economy would be more disturbed than it is.

Important as the annual changes still are, they are getting less. The equalization of light over the year is being gradually followed by a similar equalization of temperature, with the richer people as usual being first in the move to escape from the dictatorship of the seasons. Richer people are taking more second holidays in periods of the year when prices of package and other tours are lower, and these new habits are extending downwards too. The car has also reduced differences. Only poorer people now go out to visit friends and relatives much more in the summer than in the winter, when it becomes more of a trial to walk through streets which are cold, even though lit, and to wait at bus stops or on station platforms. People with cars merely have to get into them and wait a few minutes till the heater can be turned on to produce the same temperature as in their stationary sitting-rooms.

The new dictator

The trend is clear. Technology has unseated the old controllers. Machines do not worship the sun or other gods. They can function as well by night as by day. The computers which talk to each other at night, their traffic over the telephone system being concentrated, so far, into the hours when the majority of their masters are asleep, are in this like other machines. But in removing one set of controllers, technology has substituted another, itself. It is freed from astronomical rhythms in a way any biological organism, from amoeba to man, is not. Machines are most efficient when they are used as continuously as proper maintenance will allow. The steady increase in the cost of capital equipment used per man has made this requirement more and more stringent. The further mechanization goes, the more critical becomes its cost. Money has to be found to purchase it, and the sooner the new equipment can repay the money invested in it, the lower will be the burden of interest payments. When the rate of interest is high, as it has been for most of the post-war period, it is more than ever profitable to use the equipment to its maximum capacity. Time also matters more because the rate of technological progress is increasing. The most must be got out of the equipment before it becomes obsolete, which may be long before it wears out physically.[1] The way to do this is usually to work it right round the clock. The hourly cost of leaving it idle is just as great for the night as for the day, for Sundays as for weekdays. From the employer's point of view, shiftwork also becomes more necessary the shorter the ordinary working week. The more the working week is cut, the longer will machines be left idle unless other attendants can be found. These, then, are some of the forces behind the steady increase in shiftwork which is helping to maintain the total labour force in manufacturing higher than it would otherwise be. These same forces are, with computerization and other forms of automation, beginning to affect offices (and therefore non-manual workers) as well as factories.

Since people have to be paid more for shifts than for usual hours, it is more worthwhile for employers when the capital per head is large than when it is small. This accounts for some of the differences between industries. The clothing and footwear, leather and furniture industries are, for instance, not so capital-intensive as others. But there are also some other labour-intensive industries in which unusual hours are prescribed not by the requirements of production but by those of consumption. Vital services have to be

[1] R. Marris, *The Economics of Capital Utilization*.

manned on a 24-hour basis – like the police or the hospitals – because the need for them may arise at any hour; in others, like newspapers or the Post Office, some people must work at night so that others can be served early in the morning; and in yet others, like transport, pubs, restaurants, theatres, cinemas and other places of entertainment, people have to work in the evening or weekends when their customers are not, provided their customers are prepared to pay for the extra wages.

Types of shiftwork

To gather an impression of how far the process has gone in our city, and what sort of effects it has had on the family, we have to turn to our own survey. The facts given in the Report of the National Board for Prices and Incomes were for the country as a whole.

To measure the extent of shiftwork we have to start by saying how we defined it. The national figures were collected from employers. There is apparently no general definition of 'shiftwork' – the report we have quoted from did not state one. But there are several generally recognized terms for particular types of manual shiftworkers. The list in Table 31, taken from a 1964 enquiry, shows the names given to the types and the proportions of people covered in the enquiry who were working on each. The categories are mutually exclusive. A worker cannot be simultaneously on more than one type of shift, although a single employer can of course be simultaneously operating several types of shifts in different departments, say a Continuous Three-Shift in the boiler house and the security department, a Double-Day Shift in the machine-shop, and a Permanent Night Shift for maintenance work.

The one common sort not separately identified by this government enquiry was the split shift. Several people in our sample were on one. Mrs Deal was a hospital nurse living in Gravesend. On Mondays she started at 7.45 a.m. and went on till 1.15 p.m. She then had a break until 4.30 when she returned to work for another four hours. On Tuesdays and Wednesdays she started at 7.45 a.m. and went on till 1.15 p.m. On Thursdays she worked from 7.45 a.m. till 4.30 p.m. without a break. Fridays were the same as Mondays, and Saturdays the same as Thursdays. She was never on nights. Mrs Deal had split hours because there were two

TABLE 31 *Types of shift system in use nationally (percentages)*

Alternating Day and Night Shift Two crews, with a lot of overtime, can give 24-hour coverage, but impossible under modern conditions to do so for a seven-day week.	23
Continuous Three-Shift Twenty-four hour, seven-day coverage given normally by employing four crews on a rotating basis to share the popular and unpopular shifts.	22
Discontinuous Three-Shift Three crews provide continuous coverage from Monday to Friday.	19
Double-Day Shift Two crews on a morning and an afternoon shift, with rotation, give coverage for, say, 80 hours a week.	17
Permanent Nights Can be used instead of, or as supplement to, a rotating system.	12
Part-time Evening Shift A Twilight Shift – usually employing women at the end of a normal working day.	7

Source: Ministry of Labour Gazette, April 1965, quoted in *Hours of Work, Overtime and Shiftworking*, p. 58.

periods of peak pressure, when patients were being got ready for the day and when they were being got ready for the night, with a lull in between. Split shifts were for the same reason common in catering – there were chefs, waiters and barmaids among the shiftworkers in our sample – and public transport – for instance, bus drivers and conductors. They were generally disliked. It is not easy to make good use of the time between the two turns on duty. Recruitment is therefore more difficult than for most other forms of shiftwork.

The terms conventional in industry show why the sort of definition given in dictionaries will not serve. The *Oxford English Dictionary* refers to a 'relay or change of workmen', a relay being 'a set of fresh horses substituted for tired ones'. (One of our informants did actually say that what he disliked most about his job was 'the relay'.) Webster refers to 'a set of workmen who work in turn with other sets'. The general idea is simply that they shift their hours from time to time. But in some of the above categories there is no shifting. People on Permanent Nights or Part-Time Evenings, or on Split-Shifts for that matter, do not necessarily change their hours about. The essence is what shift-workers are not: they are not permanent dayworkers. The operational decision was that a person was counted as a shiftworker if he (or she) worked more than thirty hours a week[1] and did not start work between 7 a.m. and midday in the week previous to the interview and in other weeks as well. On this basis the proportions of men shiftworkers in our sample were as shown in Table 32.

TABLE 32 *Men on shiftwork (main sample)*

	Full-time men employees	*Full-time married men employees*
Shiftworkers	17%	20%
Dayworkers	83%	80%
Total %	100%	100%
Number	636	487

Weekend workers

Other people worked unusual hours judged in another way: they did not have the usual five-day week. Some had a basic week of five-and-a-half or six days. Some had a basic five-day Monday-to-Friday week but regularly worked overtime on Saturday or Sunday. Others had a five-day week but a staggered one so that, like some shopkeepers, they had Monday off in place of Saturday.

To estimate the number of weekend workers we first excluded shift-workers, even though some also have to work at week-ends. All people on a Continuous Three-Shift system are also weekend workers by definition, as are some of those on Alternat-

[1] Part-time workers were therefore ruled out from being counted as shiftworkers although this went contrary to the practice of the old Ministry of Labour.

ing Day and Night Shifts and Permanent Nights. Weekend workers for our purpose were people who regularly or sometimes worked at weekends, having unusual hours in that sense, but who did not have unusual hours on any day taken on its own. They always started work, weekday or weekend, between 7 a.m. and midday. The count, dividing shiftworkers from weekend workers and the occupational classes from each other, is in Table 33.

TABLE 33 *Proportions of men on shift and weekend work (main sample: men working full-time)*

	Professional and managerial	*Clerical*	*Skilled*	*Semi-skilled and unskilled*	*All*
Shiftworkers	5%	17%	18%	25%	17%
Weekend workers	21%	17%	31%	31%	27%
Neither	74%	66%	51%	44%	56%
Total %	100%	100%	100%	100%	100%
Number	150	92	261	133	636

Weekend workers were more numerous than those on shifts. Between them they came to nearly half the labour force; in so far as our sample is representative this means that nearly two million men in the London Region are one or the other. More manual workers than non-manual had unusual hours, taking shifts and weekend work together.

The main motive for working unusual hours of either sort was the money, shiftworkers almost always getting higher wages than ordinary day-workers. This accounted for the fact that there were amongst them relatively few young unmarried men and relatively more married, especially if they had large families to support. When people moved into the first trough of the Rowntree cycle, shiftwork, like overtime, gave some of them the opportunity to increase their earnings and so prevent their families' standard of living falling as much as it would otherwise have done. We would from our survey confirm, and extend to shiftwork as well, what the NBPI report said when it commented that 'Financial commitments and hence the incentive to work overtime tend to be greatest during the early years of married life; older men tend to have fewer commitments and tire more easily, and young single men often prefer more leisure time to high overtime earnings.'[1]

The unsocial side of it

We have referred to the costs to the employer of leaving machines idle. What about the costs to the employee of not doing so? Clegg summed up the effects in this way:[2]

> Shift work does not appear to have a generally injurious effect on health, but it breaks up family life and makes domestic arrangements more difficult. It means that at least half of the time (for the double-day shift workers) and two weeks out of three (for the continuous shift workers) leisure time comes during hours when most people are either at work or asleep. Consequently, the shift worker can only join in normal social activities for one week out of two or three, and finds it impossible to make regular arrangements to join in such activities with workers not on shifts.

The comments our own informants made were of two kinds, about the work itself and about the effects on their home life.

Some men liked being on shifts. They were solitaries or they liked having their hours dictated to them by industrial requirements whose force they could appreciate. They could see that they were needed to keep 'the machine' working. There was also sometimes more solidarity between people on the same shift who changed their hours together. This produced a sense of difference from the rest of the factory or depot or office, the social boundaries between them and the others being set by the hours they worked.

Others disliked it just as much, complaining of the emptiness of the factory at night with so few people in it or of the frustration on a fine sunny afternoon of having to go into the greater heat of the works on the 14.00 to 22.00 shift. (Many men in all kinds of jobs used the 24-hour clock as readily as an air pilot.) And more weekend and even more shiftworkers said that they found their work 'very tiring' than did people with usual hours. This was not

[1] National Board for Prices and Incomes, op. cit., p. 25.

[2] H. Clegg, *Implications of the Shorter Working Week for Management*, p. 8.

just the work, and having to adapt from one set of hours to another on a rotating system. More serious was the lack of sleep, which was most keenly felt by fathers in small dwellings with inadequate insulation to shield them from the noise of their children and of neighbours. In other ways, too, the chief problems were at home, as Table 34 shows.

TABLE 34 *Interference of shiftwork with home and family*

	Shiftworkers	*Weekend workers*	*Other workers*
Proportion saying that work interfered with home and family	52%	34%	27%
Total number	95	137	255

The main sort of interference for the rotating people arose out of the continuous switching from week to week, which involved not only themselves but their families. Some men carried their 'shift cycle' in their pocket to refer to when any decision had to be made about what could or could not be done, with or without the family, at some future date. In this they were in marked contrast to those middle-class men who did not know in advance with any exactness what hours they would be working in a week's, let alone four weeks', time. One sort of timetable was as follows:

Shift Cycle at Magnet Engineering

	Monday	*Tuesday*	*Wednesday*	*Thursday*	*Friday*	*Saturday*	*Sunday*
Week 1	14.00–22.00	14.00–22.00	14.00–22.00	—	—	7.00–14.00	7.00–14.00
Week 2	7.00–14.00	7.00–14.00	7.00–14.00	7.00–14.00	7.00–14.00	—	—
Week 3	—	22.00–7.00	22.00–7.00	22.00–7.00	22.00–7.00	22.00–7.00	22.00–7.00
Week 4	22.00–7.00	—	—	14.00–22.00	14.00–22.00	14.00–22.00	14.00–22.00

What the workers at Magnet Engineering, or anyone on the same sort of rotation, could do obviously depended upon which week it was. In much of Week 1 and most of Week 4 they could not go out in the evening or be with their families at home. One man living in Ealing said, 'It's always difficult about meals. You don't eat as you should. You're all haphazard. The wife won't have a meal when she gets in; she waits for me. Then another thing, when I'm on the 2 to 10 shift I don't feel like going straight to bed. She isn't getting her sleep and she feels tired when she has to get up in the morning.' In Week 2 they were back to more or less normal and it was in weeks like these that men would do their best to make up for what they could not do at other times by going out more with their wives in the afternoons and evenings and seeing more of friends, particularly work-friends on the same shift as themselves.

The problem was Week 3 – and for people on Permanent Nights all weeks were like that – and it was almost as awkward for their families as for themselves. Husband and wife (unless, as sometimes happened when there were no young children, the wife too went on to a 'night shift' at home and slept by day) could not sleep together. Mr Babcock, of Lewisham, complained that on his three-week rotation he was away from home 100 nights a year. 'I've only been married for six years, and you know what I mean by that.' Many of the wives felt frightened being alone in the house at nights, and made themselves anxious trying to keep the house quiet while their husbands were asleep in the day, avoiding the use of their vacuum cleaners, trying to hush the children and rushing to the door if anyone rang to stop it happening twice. Cooking also took longer when meals had to be prepared for husbands and children at different times.

The husbands could miss their families as much as their families missed them. Mr Revers, a Watford printer, wrote in his diary:

> Just finishing dinner when Tom had another of his migraine attacks, poor little perisher, the excitement was too much for him. He was sick as a dog all afternoon. Shame really. Don't see enough of him really. Still, that's shiftwork for you!

Mr Jobling's story was similar.

> I think it does fall back on the wife and the children when I'm

working on these shifts, especially the boy. He's always been very attached to me and until some time ago he couldn't even go out with anyone except me. He had to get used to that when I started working shifts. They don't see nothing much of me. (Injection moulder, Barking)

If wives were lonely by night, husbands sometimes were by day, wherever the wives were also out working, on 'usual' hours. Mr James did six weeks on days and then two on nights. His wife was working. 'I hate nights', he said. 'You never see anyone, just come home, have something to eat, potter about a bit, take a book up to bed with me, sleep and go back to work' (Boiler man, Enfield). Some had a reluctance to be seen around in the streets when 'everyone else' was at work because they imagined that other people might think them unemployed. 'They don't believe around here that I go to work' (Compositor, Brentwood). Those who overcame this reluctance at least had the satisfaction of being able to go to their doctor's or to shop at a time when there were no crowds. Several others in the same circumstances did the domestic work to pass the time and help their wives. Mr Soper of Barking was a guard on a tube train on an afternoon shift. His diary read like this, in summary form:

8 a.m.	Got up (wife already off to work)
8–9 a.m.	Pottered around
9–9.20 a.m.	Had breakfast
9.30–10 a.m.	Peeled potatoes
10–11 a.m.	Hoovered
11–11.10 a.m.	Dusted
11.10–12.40 p.m.	Prepared dinner
12.40–1.40 p.m.	Ate it
1.40–2.10 p.m.	Got ready for work
2.30–3.30 p.m.	Read papers
3.30 p.m.	Left for work
4.15 p.m.	Arrived at work
4.20 p.m.	Made cup of tea

A policeman living in Westminster told how his shifts (or reliefs as he called them) affected his family. When he was on late duty he and his wife could never go out together in the evenings. On night duty she had to put up with being alone – she then barred all her doors so thoroughly that when he came back in the morning even he could not get in until he had woken her up and persuaded her he was no thief – and then be quiet when he was getting his sleep. When it was early duty they had their afternoons as well as their evenings together. But the real trial was not so much the regular reliefs as the irregularity superimposed on them. If, for example, he made an arrest at night he was not able to go off duty at 6 but had to wait and appear with the prisoner in court at 10. He might not be out of the court until mid-day. He was not paid for these extra hours but accumulated an entitlement to other hours off 'in lieu' when the chance occurred. But if his wife had been expecting him to go out with her that afternoon she would be disappointed because he would have to sleep instead. Likewise, if a man ran into trouble shortly before the end of his relief, following up a robbery which he had been called to, he could not drop it all just because it was nearly 2 p.m. He had to stay with it until he had finished his part of the investigation. All that he might be able to do was to get a message to his wife by a patrol car, perhaps, telling her he did not know when he would be home. Not many policemen could afford telephones – they were not well enough paid for that. The more frequent demonstrations that have been held in the West End on the Lord's Day in recent years have also caused domestic disturbance, depriving the men and their families of their precious Sundays off.

Leisure compensations

Some of the men who seemed to feel the least hardship were the ones who had leisure enthusiasms which they could pursue on their own. Team-games, as players or spectators, were out, although individual ones were not. Mr Johns, a heating fitter in Southwark, was able to play golf on an almost empty course, although not with as much satisfaction as he would if it had been easier to find weekday opponents. The story of Mr Cloudesley may be worth telling in a little more detail because it shows, by contrast to so many of the others, how someone *could* make the adjustment.

He worked in a pharmaceuticals plant in South London, as a maintenance fitter. About two years previously the factory had introduced a continuous three-shift system. The hours were from

7.30 a.m. to 4.30 p.m., 4.30 p.m. to midnight and midnight to 7.30 a.m. The change from one to the other was every sixth day, each man having two days off, usually in the week but sometimes at the weekend, before he started up again on his new turn. The men could choose whether to go on to the rotating system or stay on the 7.30 to 4.30 hours. Mr Cloudesley decided for the former, partly because of the extra money – his wages went up by £10 a week on average – and partly because it did not interfere too much with his hobby.

This was fishing. He used to go out quite often on his moped for evening fishing and he still did that when he was on the 7.30 to 4.30 shift. 'If it's a fine evening when I get back from work I ask Doris for some sandwiches, drink a cup of tea and I'm off on my bike; Doris will think something's gone seriously wrong if I'm back before dark.' Now he did more local fishing in the daytime too, when he was on the other shifts.

The big difference was at weekends. Mr Cloudesley belonged to the South Battersea Workingmen's Fishing Club. The Club hired a coach every Sunday to take the members to a different water. Mr Cloudesley always used to go every Sunday during the season, until the shiftwork started. Now he could not, except in the weeks when his days off came at the weekends. This nearly led to his dropping out of the club altogether.

> The ordinary cost of the coach is 60p. That allows for a few empty places, but not many. If there are, there will be a loss on the coach. The Club can stand a bit of this out of the surplus it gets when the coach is full, but not often. So what happens? It's a debate which goes on year after year. The idea this year was that every member should pay 25p whether he comes or not. It would be deducted from the full charge for those who did go. They said it was only fair to charge the people who didn't come out and support the Club. They *are* members after all. I agreed with it. If you are going to have rules in the interests of the Club as a whole you've got to be hard about them. You can't make exceptions. If you make any, everyone will soon be one and there won't be any five bobs. But you can't have clubs just run by majority rule either. I told the other members of the Committee that if they did it I'd have to leave. I can only go on two Sundays out of nine

> because of the shiftworking. I couldn't afford to pay for all the times I didn't go. George Niblett was in the same boat. He's the Fixtures Secretary. He said he'd do the Fixtures for the coming season anyway but then he'd have to resign. So the Committee decided against it. They brought in a coach levy of 5p instead. I can afford that.

When Mr Cloudesley had his 'weekend' off in the week he sometimes went out fishing all night by himself. 'You kind of go to sleep in the middle of the night sitting on the bank although not really asleep; but you always wake up with the dawn and feel more lively. You can see a snake that swims through the water, and the voles – they are normally shy but they come out when you're sitting there quietly, especially in the early morning if you've been sitting there all night.' If his shifts did not allow him to have off 14 March, the day before the end of the fishing season, he took it anyway.

> My friend and me, my friend Tom, we always go on the last day of the season. We make a sort of religious occasion of it. This year we went to Sunbury-on-Thames. The river was in flood. But I caught a barbel 22 inches long. The best I've caught. It wasn't much compared to the record. The record on the Thames was in 1800 and something. It's in the anglers' diaries. It was 14 pounds. Tom and me always go on the first day of the season too.

Mr Cloudesley made one sort of adjustment. He was one of the uncommon people whose life was more leisure-centred than family-centred. And, despite what we have said about the difficulties that others experienced, many of them did manage to adjust by keeping to normal timetables as closely as possible, even at the sacrifice of sleep. To judge by their diaries, people on morning shifts did not go to bed much earlier at night than anyone else, and saved their main meal until the evening when they could have it with the other members of their households. People on afternoon shifts got up at about the same time as other members of their family, even if they went to bed later. People on night shifts stayed awake to have breakfast/supper with their families in the mornings, had supper/breakfast with them when they got up in the evening, and at weekends (if they were having one off) they got out of bed for lunch on Saturday, instead of sleeping on as usual, so as to have as much of the day as possible with the others.

Such accounts showed how much people's hours influenced their lives outside work. We could see the long arm of the job more clearly for shiftworkers than for most others. But we usually caught only a glimpse from a distance of the work time-tables that were having this effect. Sometimes people found it impossible to explain the shift system as it operated in their workplace; it was just too complicated, especially when it came to elaborating the link between the hours that they worked and those that everyone else did. Even if they obviously knew it all, and could go on talking at great length, it was very difficult, sitting in their homes and hearing the men say that 'every other week, I change from the early to late turn, having my days off in rotation', or whatever it was, to grasp the story. It was more confusing because each person had a different employer and a unique system in some particular, even if taken together they could be put into certain broad categories possessing common features. So we decided to make two small case-studies of workplaces in the hope of understanding a little better the detailed interconnections there could be between the requirements of work and the families dependent on it for their income. For this purpose we chose two somewhat extreme examples. The first was a small printers' that worked a twenty-four-hour day, often at weekends as well; the second was a Post Office providing a twenty-four-hour service for seven days a week and fifty-two weeks in the year.

A printing firm

Metro Printers occupied a square, red-brick building in a short side street in West London. The speciality was four-colour lithographic printing – art prints, posters, holiday brochures, mail order catalogues, leaflets and free-gift vouchers. They were essentially jobbing printers – 'any job we start today will normally be out in a couple of weeks'. The firm had six four-colour machines – Roland Rekords, produced in Germany. 'They're the Rolls Royce of printing machines', said Mr Attlee, the managing director. About thirty feet long and ten feet high, they were grey-painted and, apart from a film of fine white powder, were clean.

There were side benches, where some preparation was done and small running repairs made. Between the machines were giant sets of shelving, stacked with packets of new paper and piles of printed sheets. Around the floor were huge cans of coloured ink and of cleaning fluid.

The print shop was noisy – not, it was explained, from the machines themselves but from the pumps which operated the banks of hydraulic suckers that separated the huge sheets of paper and fed them into the machine. The sheets rolled into the first set of rollers for printing the first colour, then down to another set for the second, then along, up and down again, for the third and fourth, to emerge ready to be checked for colour quality and for alignment.

Four men worked on each machine. Two were assistants, sometimes described to their irritation as labourers; members of NATSOPA, the general union, their job was to keep the machine supplied with paper. The other two were minders – a first minder and a second, members of the National Graphical Association, the 'skilled' union. An assistant explained the difference between his work and that of the minders. 'We're responsible for the back end of the machine – we feed it with paper – and they're responsible for the front end. They're the craftsmen. It's their job to see the finished product is up to quality.' A second minder said of his senior colleague: 'He's got that bit more experience. He gets paid a bit more and he carries the can if anything goes wrong.'

The firm operated a three-shift system in the print shop. There were two alternating day shifts – 7 a.m. to 3 p.m., and 3 p.m. to 11 p.m. – and a night shift – 11 p.m. to 7 a.m. There were always fewer men on nights – partly because the pay and therefore the costs to the firm were higher, partly because men were more reluctant to work then even for the extra money, partly because the management preferred to keep some machines in reserve, so that if there was a breakdown at night, when machines could not be called in to do repairs, the job could be switched immediately to an idle machine. Normally there were twenty-four men – twelve minders and twelve operatives – on each of the day shifts and a total of eight working permanent nights.

The high capital cost of the machines and the high rent and other overhead costs were the reasons why the firm operated a shift system. Mr Attlee said:

> These machines cost £80,000 each including all the equipment and extras. The way to get a return on a large investment like that is to use it as fully as possible. The greater the turnover the better the value we are getting out of it. If we worked an ordinary day, it would take half an hour to start each machine and about an hour to clean it up at the end. That means in eight hours you would only get six hours production. If you work 24 hours you get virtually 24 hours production. New machines are coming on to the market all the time, so if you're going to get the full value out of an expensive machine like this before it's replaced by another one you've got to use it to the full. Also we have to think about overheads. All the overheads – rent, office costs, everything else – figure in it. We find that the overheads are more or less the same whether we are working an eight hour day on the machines or a 24 hour day.

Despite the advantages of shiftwork, it posed problems. If the print shop had worked an eight-hour day, Mr Archer, the works manager, would not have had to work much longer hours himself. 'As it is,' he said, 'I obviously can't give 24 hour supervision but I tend to stay on late at night to make sure everything's running smoothly. I work a ten-hour day minimum. If anything goes wrong, I stay on later still.' In Chapter V, we advanced some reasons why managers' working hours may have increased. We can now add another. The increase in shiftwork almost certainly has had an effect on some managers, and as it extends will increasingly do so.

What about the effects on the printers? The first and most obvious was on their pay. 'Shift work is worth £10 a week to me,' said one man. He was on day shifts and for night work the addition was greater still. The men thought there were other advantages. One was that they could do more redecorating or repairs in their homes. 'I'm doing the flat right through, decorating one room after another. If I worked from eight to five it would be half-past six in the evening before I could get started. You'd do a couple of hours and then it would be time for bed. This way I can put in a good stint before or after my work here. Today I'll leave at 3 p.m. and I'll go home and get straight into it. I can virtually do a day's work on the flat. I'm really working a double shift – one shift for the firm and one for me.' Other men mentioned that shopping, paying bills or going to the bank were easier and pleasanter when there were less people around.

> Last week we went out to buy a new three-piece suite. We went into the store and we were looked after properly. They give you proper attention, let you take your time. If you try to go on a Saturday everybody's rushing about and you get things sort of pushed on you that you don't really want.

Some men thought there were advantages for the family.

> I'm very close to my son. Every day, according to what shift I'm on, I can take him to school or fetch him. I couldn't do that if I had an eight to five job. He likes it and he'd miss it if I didn't do it. It suits the wife too, because it means she's only got to do the one trip a day.

There were also many disadvantages. The family might be disturbed early in the morning by the husband getting up to go off to work; one man never had breakfast at home – 'not even a cup of tea' – in case he woke someone up. Wives sometimes wanted to stay up later at night than husbands who had to leave home at between 5.30 a.m. and 6.30 a.m., depending on where they lived. 'My wife complains because when I'm on early shift I get tired of an evening,' said one man. 'About nine I start nodding off. She gives me a cup of coffee to try to keep me awake.' Most wives, even so, much preferred the early shift to the late. When the man was at home in the morning the housework might be disrupted. 'She complains that I'm under her feet all the time.' And when the husbands were absent in the evening, 'It affects what you can do, doesn't it. Most of your social life occurs then and if I'm not there naturally she's restricted in what she can do.' The night shift was the least popular. Mr Archer said, 'It's difficult to find people to do nights.' The men who did so were of two main kinds – the unmarried, whose lives were not complicated by family ties, and the young fathers, who stressed the extra earnings. Pay was time-and-a-third for day shifts and time-and-a-half for nights. The men on nights had almost all been specifically recruited for it; they had been offered jobs at Metro only as night workers and, being what in the trade are known as 'money-chasers', had been attracted by Metro's high rates, which could bring them in over £100 a week. One of them saw the decision to take the job as in his family's best interests: 'In one way my family is worse off. That's obvious. But money is essential in the home. If you want to have a happy family life it's got to be based on a decent home. That's what I'm working to get.'

One man's story

To end this account of the printing firm, here is a closer look at an individual worker. Albert Green, aged thirty-three, was a second minder. He was slim, with short-trimmed fair hair, and wearing a clean bib and brace over a blue Aertex shirt. He was married with three young children.

Mr Green had been born in Hammersmith, a few miles from the firm. As he put it, he 'grew up in a slum', but had developed a love of the country from going to stay in Hampshire with his grandmother when he was a child. He had been able to get into printing through an uncle – 'Printing is all family, you know' – and he was glad, because of the relatively high pay. His average wage was around £80 or £90 a week. It was this that had made possible the things he considered essential to family life – his three-bedroomed semi-detached house with garage in Uxbridge ('It's six years old. We bought it new'), his Vauxhall Viva, his holidays abroad – they had gone to Benidorm in Spain the previous summer.

He had moved out 'in two steps'. When he married, his wife, who was also from Hammersmith, had not wanted to move far. 'We went to Ealing – bought a maisonette there. To her *that* was moving out of London. She wanted to be near Mum. You know what women are.' He had always wanted to move further out, and after four years in Ealing she had agreed.

When he was on early shift, Mr Green got up at 5.30 and went downstairs to cook himself something – 'egg and ham, sausages, I give myself a good breakfast.' He always went to kiss his wife goodbye, although she seldom woke up fully. He left the house at 6.15. 'I like being on the road when there are so few other cars about', and another advantage was that he could at that hour always find somewhere to park. When he got home at 3.45 he looked after the youngest child while his wife went to fetch the other two from school, unless he did. His time after that was usually spent in decorating the house, working in the garden or tinkering with the car.

On the late shift he still got up at 7.30 – 'I'm an early riser' – helped to get the children up and had breakfast with the family. The morning could be spent, again, in the house or garden or garage, unless there was shopping to be done. He often drove his wife to the nearby shopping centre or 'popped along to the bank'.

His wife, like those of most of his colleagues, did not like the late shift. The other people living on the estate were mainly young families like them, and they were friendly and helpful to each other. But most evenings Mrs Green was alone. 'I know she doesn't like it but she watches television or does dressmaking – I think that takes her mind off it till I get back at about half-past eleven.'

Mr Green had, in his own words, 'no hobbies: I'm a typical family man'. Most of his free time was spent with his wife and children, either at home, going to the shops, or going out in the car. Once a month, all the year round, they went to visit the two families in Hammersmith. He had one enthusiasm not shared by his wife. 'You could describe me as a football fanatic.' He was a supporter of Chelsea Football Club, had a season ticket and almost always went to Stamford Bridge when the first team was playing at home. 'Sometimes it's a bit awkward if we're working on the Saturday and I'm on the late shift. I can usually get someone to swap round with me.' If he was working on the early shift on Saturday, he tried to 'slip away a bit early'. He also travelled to away matches about once a month during the season. His wife sometimes complained because he spent so much time on football, especially if he had been on late shift that week. 'I can usually talk her round. I say that I could have been much worse – a gambler, a drinker or a womaniser. She doesn't really mind. And it makes the time we are together all the more sweeter.'

A post office

The other little enquiry was in a large post office in South London. Its heart was a block of floors, one above the other, in each of which the post was sorted, both the outgoing mail and the incoming. The floor-space was filled with sorting frames. The men worked not fast but deliberately and methodically, as though they knew exactly what they were doing and even took some quiet pride in it, whether they were on the franking machines or flipping letters into one or other of the boxes in their frame, or wheeling sacks on trolleys, or throwing packets with quick flicks of the wrist and landing them in the mouth of the right sack every time. It was very quiet as the immense quantities of paper jerked on from one station to another in the sorting rooms.

There were several different types of shift for postmen; although some were only sorters or inside men, most of the employees doubled as delivery or collection men on the one hand and sorters on the other. They were divided, in the way people talked about them, into three main types – an early shift or turn which was mostly in the morning, a late shift or turn which was in the afternoon or evening and a night shift. The term 'middle duty' was also used for a few shifts starting between 10 and 12, and a 'through' for a night shift.

The various arrangements of hours were determined by two main influences – what the service required, as laid down by the management, and what the men would put up with. This largely reflected their home circumstances, and, of course, the pay offered for weekday hours between 8 p.m. and 6 a.m. (time-and-a-third) or Sundays (double time).

The postal service required round-the-clock, seven-days-a-week working. Letters were, on the whole, collected during the day, transported by night and delivered by day. The office therefore had to be manned continuously, but with varying numbers of men: there was not an even flow of work throughout the twenty-four hours or over the seven days of the week. The first and much the heaviest delivery was in the morning, just as the heaviest collection by van from pillar boxes was in the late afternoon and evening.

One category of men – forty-six in all – were on a fixed early turn. 'Fixed' meant that they had the same hours on all weekdays, from 5.45 a.m. to 1.27 p.m., and from 5.45 a.m. to 10.15 a.m. on Saturdays, adding up to the standard working week of forty-three hours which was the same for everyone, although most men also did overtime as well, some regularly, others sporadically. These forty-six men began their day in the office by sorting the mail which had arrived from all parts of the country during the night (and had been sorted into walks by the night shift) into the order of addresses on the walks in which the letters would be delivered. The size of the walks was determined by the maximum load which could be carried on a man's back; the rule of the Union of Post Office Workers was that a mail bag should never weigh more than 35 lbs. Men 'over age', who had chosen to stay on after the minimum retiring age of sixty, were limited to 28 lbs., which meant that on the whole their walks were shorter. After they had done the sorting, the men went out at about 7.15 to their particular district, walking along the same streets each day by the same routes.

There were also various fixed late turns, with thirteen men on from mid-day to 8.36 p.m. and another twenty-three from 2.24 p.m. to 10 p.m., and others on similar hours. They were responsible for the most part for the sorting of the mail (collected in the afternoon and evening) into bags destined either for particular counties and large towns or for further sorting overnight in the travelling post offices on the mail trains.

What they began was continued by the fifty-two men on fixed night shifts. The hours for most of them were either from 8.45 p.m. to 6.01 a.m. or 11 p.m. to 7.46 a.m. These men started with the sorting of mail brought in on late collections for despatch that same night and continued with other mail, mainly second class, which would be forwarded during the following day. The men who came on at 11 p.m. had the better of it at night because they had more of their evenings at home and the worst of it in the morning because there was more bustle and they might have to try and get to sleep at the same time as their children were making a noise as they got up to go off to school. Men due to leave at 6.01 a.m. were more likely to get off early on occasion as supervisors would sometimes tell them that if they worked extra fast in a rush period to finish a sort before the early turn came on they could go home as soon as the work was finished.

Another forty-eight men alternated between a short early turn from 6 a.m. to 9.45 a.m. on weekdays and 6 a.m. to 10.15 a.m. on Saturdays, and a long shift from 6 a.m. to 4.45 p.m. on weekdays and 6 a.m. to 2.15 on Saturdays. They rotated daily through the week, with a short shift on one day being succeeded by a long shift on the following day. The rationale of this was that all of the men would be available for the first heavy delivery, whether on the short shift or the long, and half of them would also be available for the third afternoon delivery which the men on the fixed early turn could not do. The change was daily instead of weekly because a week of turns from 6 to 4.45 every day would have been too tiring for anyone. The combination of longs with shorts meant that after a long day there was a short one in which to recover.

As well as the majority of men who were on a regular shift of one kind or another, there were some thirty-six who were on a general or supplementary reserve ready to do a duty which was not covered for any reason. On all shifts there was overtime for those who wanted it. This was supposed to be arranged so that no one would be able to clock up more hours overtime than any other man who wanted to do it. If two men signed for the same particular overtime duty in any week the people in the 'Book Room' (which was the controlling unit) would give it to the man who had worked only, say, 200 hours overtime so far in the year as compared to another who had worked 1,100 hours. The men choosing the really large amounts of overtime, sometimes working by night as well as day, were disliked by the others who did more moderate amounts. They were called 'Overtime Barons', like 'Tobacco Barons' in prisons. Many of those who did '18 months work in 12 months' were said to be immigrants.

Every year or so there was a re-sign for the different shifts organized by the union, which was indeed generally responsible for deciding how many different rotas there would be. The most popular shift, as shown by the decisions of the men about those to opt for, was by and large the fixed early turn. Men had their evenings with their families and their afternoons also at home. Moreover, as their work finished with the completion of the second delivery, they could leave as soon as this was done, which was usually before 1 p.m. Men on inside duties could not leave much before the official times. No one paid attention to the odd minutes – the night shift ending at 6.01 for instance. This was a piece of bureaucratic arithmetic to make the hours total exactly forty-three. One postman who was on indoor duties in a 'Writing Room', as all rooms were called where people were sitting down as distinct from standing up, had hours from 8 to 4.30. He said that he had with such wonderful hours 'reached the Valhalla of Postmen'. But even those on the early turn had done relatively well for themselves and could compare their lot favourably with the less senior men who had had to sign up for the less popular duties.

A few preferred the night shift. One reason for some older men[1] doing it was that people's pensions were related amongst other things to their earnings in their last three years of service. Since night work, from 8 p.m. on, was paid at time-and-a-third, earnings were a good deal higher, and their pensions also. Another reason, for some younger men, was that if they had babies who were asleep a good part of the day and their wives were working, the father could be in the house when the mother was not. This was a working-class variant of the 'dual-career family'. Husbands and wives barely saw each other except when they had their days off together, provided they were not so tired that they had to spend most of their off-days sleeping. Yet another reason was that some men could have a second moonlighting job in the afternoon. Regulations prohibited employees from working for bookmakers, football pool firms, etc., where there could be abuse, but there was no general prohibition of moonlighting in the Post Office as there was in some other jobs.

A postman

One of the postmen was Mr Charles. He had a round, red face and a slightly startled expression. For indoor work he wore a faded brown coat with a crown on the lapel and his badge number on the left breast. His hands rested very quietly on his lap as he explained that he had fourteen years' service, thirteen of which had been on permanent nights. He got to his nearby home each morning at 6.10 a.m., took his wife her cup of tea and went to bed himself. He liked getting to bed at that hour because the city was still quiet. He would not work on the night turn that ended at 7.46 because the noise and light level would be rising by that time and he would not be able to get to sleep. The men on these hours chose them, if they did, because the train or bus service to wherever they had to go was not good at the earlier time. Mr Charles always woke up, having slept well, at about 2 p.m.

He had no children. His wife would have been at a loss for what

[1] This system meant there were more older men on nights in the post office than on other shifts.

to do in the morning while her husband was asleep if she had not had a part-time job five hours a day, mornings only,[1] which allowed her to get home before he woke up in time to reciprocate for his morning service to her by making him a cup of tea to drink in bed. At 2 p.m. he had a snack and, if the weather was fine, went out for a walk with his wife, usually to a park not far away which he regarded as 'part of his back garden'. He liked the afternoons off partly because he could get in his walk when there were not many other people around. His wife also liked it. It was their chief leisure activity, the other being gardening. In the summer Mr Charles would cut his lawn or do a bit of weeding in the afternoon.

When they got back, sometimes doing some shopping on the way, his wife cooked their dinner. They always had it at 6 p.m. After that they settled down to watch the television for a couple of hours until he had to leave for work. One of his regrets about night duty was that he often missed big sports events. He made up for it a bit at 9.50 p.m. when there was the first tea break. A few nights previously he and all the other men had dashed to the canteen in the break to see the last rounds of a heavyweight boxing match on the TV. The younger men, in particular, were also very keen on a TV series on Casanova that was on at that time because there were naked girls in it.

There were other breaks through the night. At 11.30 Mr Charles had a sandwich, at 1.50 a fruit tart and custard and at 3.50 he used to have corn-flakes and milk, which he had now given up because he was putting on too much weight. The quality and variety of food in the canteen was less good at night, partly because there were fewer staff on duty in it – this being a minor disadvantage of night work. If the food had been better his wife would not have had to prepare so many sandwiches and tarts in the afternoon. In the office there was also a kitchen with two urns for tea and a gas stove for men doing their own 'frying up'. This was not used so much by men on the night shift as by men cooking their breakfast between the first and second deliveries. Some men brought not

[1] Another man went on to night shift because his wife already had a part-time job from 9 a.m. to 2 p.m. each day and, as they had their main meal in the middle of the day, when he was on days he had to cook the meal for her, and he did not like doing it. His escape was to go on nights so that she had to get the meal for him, in the afternoon.

only sausages and bacon but liver and chops for their breakfast fry.

Mr Charles did not like leaving his wife at home when she was ill, which she had been shortly before the interview. They were on the 'phone, though, and he could 'phone her at midnight or thereabouts from the office to see how she was, and she could 'phone him if she was taken worse. If he knew in advance that his wife would need him on a particular night, say for visiting some-one in hospital, Mr Charles could always swap duties with a colleague through the Exchange of Duties Book. Another dis-advantage was that it was very difficult to sleep on the night off. There was a rotating night off for all men on this duty, as well as all Saturdays off.

Why, then, did he prefer it on the whole to the other shifts? The main reason was that his life was generally quieter, and he liked a quiet life above all, especially by contrast to the job as a salesman he had had before joining the Post Office. He avoided the 'hustle and bustle of the days'. The office was much busier in the day. At night comparatively few people were there and the few people in it were more friendly. There were no deliveries at night so all the people were in the same building all the time and got to know each other better. Mr Charles also liked going back home in the morning through the dark quiet streets and climbing into his bed next to the warmth of his wife after she had drunk her tea.

How many people will there be like Mr Green, Mr Charles and Mr Cloudesley in the next century? Shiftwork is on the increase. The extra profitability which comes from using ever more expen-sive capital equipment more intensively is a powerful argument. But will a limit be reached well before all employees become shift-workers in manufacturing, in ever more highly mechanized offices and in the growing service sector? There are counter-pressures. The higher wages rise and the shift premiums with them, the more desirable become the fully automated plants which can run with only a few attendants. Already maintenance men are not needed at night in telephone exchanges. If a fault occurs it is automatically recorded for the men who will arrive in the morn-ing. Aristotle said that 'if every instrument could do its own work, if the shuttle could weave and the plectrum pluck the lyre without a guiding hand, foremen would not need workers, nor masters slaves.'[1] It has not happened yet. But the trend is strongly in evidence, as we said in the last chapter. Eventually, the machine which has called men from their rest may put them back to bed again, at night; and yet another full revolution be complete, at any rate for workers in manufacturing.

The other great unknown is whether men in such numbers will continue to put up with unusual hours. This depends upon what happens to the acquisitive society. For the moment, it is clear, they are willing. Just as the managers of the previous two chapters were prepared to allow the one sphere to intrude on the other, so, if the money was good enough, were the manual workers to have their life interfered with by shiftwork. They were not doing it for themselves alone. They were driven by what they thought to be the needs of their families. There was no sign here of a new Ten Hours Movement. Pember Reeves and the others who wrote about Stage 2 families towards the end of the last century would not have recognized the family man who showed he was one by not being in it. He was not in the pub either, but in the print shop or the sorting room.

[1] Aristotle, *Politics*, I, 1253b. Quoted in S. de Grazia, *Of Time, Work and Leisure*, p. 58.

VIII

LEISURE

On shifts we were again illustrating the truism that people's jobs influence everything else they do. The triangle had work at the apex and husband and wife at the base. We are now going to put leisure, not work, at the top. Forty years ago the authors of the second survey of London life and labour (themselves writing forty years after the first) said that 'all the forces at work are combining to shift the main centre of interest of a worker's life more and more from his daily work to his daily leisure'.[1] The amount of leisure time had increased, as compared with the previous century. People's incomes had increased. New industries were selling mass entertainment, and in many ways what was true then has become more so. Has it all added to, or detracted from, the primacy of the family?

Our interest continues to be class – this although we already know from the pioneering surveys mainly on outdoor recreation made by Rodgers[2] and Sillitoe[3] for the country as a whole that it does not make so much difference as age, marriage and sex. Rodgers said that for sports age is vital. 'Some (cycling, the more vigorous team games, athletics, skating) are dominated by the very young and children. Others (tennis, riding, swimming, hiking and hill-walking) persist strongly through the 24–35 age band . . . Some (fishing, camping, golf, the more expensive forms of sailing) show either a peak or a plateau of incidence in the

[1] H. L. Smith, *The New Survey of London Life and Labour*, vol. VIII, p. 36. For an account of mid-nineteenth-century leisure in London and elsewhere, including the growth of such new recreational institutions as the railway excursion, the music hall, the brass band and the association football club, see G. Best, *Mid-Victorian Britain 1851–75*, pp. 198–227.

[2] H. B. Rodgers, *The Pilot National Recreation Survey*. See also *Leisure in the North West*.

[3] K. K. Sillitoe, *Planning for Leisure*.

middle age ranges.'[1] Sillitoe in the same vein said that, 'Amongst young single people the greatest emphasis was given to physical recreation. In fact, for young men, this continued as their outstanding leisure interest into early married life. . . . The changes in leisure habits that accompanied marriage took place more swiftly amongst women.'[2] There were the same kinds of variation in London. Younger people, especially the single and especially men, did more of almost everything – played more, watched sport more, went more to cinemas and other entertainments. The total number of leisure activities that they went in for at least once in the previous year (to use an index that we shall explain more fully later in the chapter) was 18.8 for men aged 29 or under, 16.2 at 30 to 49, 12.6 at 50 to 64, and 8.8 at 65 or over. The figures for women ranged from 16.0 at 29 or under to 7.4 at 65 or over. The reason seems obvious enough, even despite our own strictures in Chapter I. Young people, particularly single, have the necessary energy, time, money and inclination. Since all this is obvious and documented, we have taken it for granted in order to concentrate on our own chief concern.

We shall proceed by way of four preliminary questions:

1 What is leisure?
2 How do leisure activities vary by class?
3 Does work extend into leisure?
4 How do contacts with friends and relatives differ?

And we shall then come to the main one:

5 How does their leisure affect their families?

What is leisure?

Many of our informants seemed to be as puzzled as us, not about work, a good, solid, worthy word that they, and we, understood, but about leisure. If we used it, in explaining what we were about, they would quite often repeat it after us as if we were both playing a sort of nursery game. 'Leisure? What's that?', 'Leisure? No, I don't have any of that', or, 'Leisure? No, my wife keeps me too busy for that', sometimes with a wry smile.

[1] H. B. Rodgers, op. cit., p. 12.
[2] K. K. Sillitoe, op. cit., p. 17.

Parker[1] has recently reviewed some of the definitions employed by other authors. These have ranged from those which would presumably be adhered to by two of the three informants we have just quoted, that is those which treat leisure as a residual activity – 'free time after the practical necessities have been attended to'[2] or 'the time we are free from the more obvious and formal duties which a paid job or other obligatory occupation imposes upon us'[3] – to those which accept that it is something left over but also attempt to put some positive content into it. Kaplan, for example, put so much into it as almost to bury the word (especially in his last sentence rolling all the ingredients together into a single pie) when he asserted that[4]

> The essential elements of leisure, as we shall interpret it, are (a) an antithesis to 'work' as an economic function, (b) a pleasant expectation and recollection, (c) a minimum of involuntary social-role obligations, (d) a psychological perception of freedom, (e) a close relation to values of the culture, (f) the inclusion of an entire range from inconsequence and insignificance to weightiness and importance, and (g) often, but not necessarily, an activity characterised by the element of play. Leisure is none of these by itself but all together in one emphasis or another.

Parker did not mention another view, which is that leisure is a state of mind, of non-activity, as contrasted with the *activity* of work, as expressed, for instance, by Pieper.[5]

> Compared with the exclusive ideal of work as activity, leisure implies (in the first place) an attitude of non-activity, of inward calm, of silence; it means not being 'busy', but letting things happen. Leisure is a form of silence, of that silence which is the prerequisite of the apprehension of reality: only the silent hear and those who do not remain silent do not hear. Silence, as it is used in this context, does not mean 'dumbness' or 'noiselessness'; it means more nearly that the soul's power to 'answer' to the reality of the world is left undisturbed. For

[1] S. Parker, *The Future of Work and Leisure*, chap. 2.
[2] H. P. Fairchild (ed.), *Dictionary of Sociology*, p. 175.
[3] G. A. Lundberg *et al.*, *Leisure: A Suburban Study*, p. 2.
[4] M. Kaplan, *Leisure in America*, p. 22, quoted in S. Parker, op. cit., p. 23.
[5] J. Pieper, *Leisure: the Basis of Culture*, pp. 52-3.

> leisure is a receptive attitude of mind, a contemplative attitude, and it is not only the occasion but also the capacity for steeping oneself in the whole of creation. Furthermore there is also a certain happiness in leisure, something of the happiness that comes from a recognition of the mysteriousness of the universe and the recognition of an incapacity to understand it, that comes with a deep confidence, so that we are content to let things take their course; and there is something about it which Konrad Weiss, the poet, called 'confidence in the fragmentariness of life and history'.

We put questions to our informants which incorporated the word. If for no other reason, the disagreement between the authors drawn upon by Parker, and added to by Pieper, would have made it ridiculous to assume that it meant the same to them as to us, or that they would all concur with each other. We therefore tried to discover what they did mean in the main survey by asking, 'What would you say is the difference between what you'd call work and what you'd call leisure?', as well as by requesting the diarists to label all their activities throughout the day as one or the other, neither or both. We hoped we might, by interpreting what they said, find out something about what they meant by the words.

The first point was that most people seemed to regard the key words as opposites that could properly be distinguished from each other. Leisure and work belonged (although our informants did not put it that way) to the category of words, sometimes called binary, which can be understood only in relation to one another, in this like husband which can only be understood along with wife, or woman, more generally, with man, or indeed any word out of a pair which describes two complementary actors in a role like parent-child or employer-employee, or many kinds of spatial relationship like left-right, up-down, higher-lower, in-out which are also liberally used as metaphors. These words which are lost if alone gather meaning if they have a companion. But two is company, three is none, as shown by the muddle caused by the word 'free' having two antonyms with different meanings, determined and obligatory. None of our informants suggested, like Arendt, that the opposite of work is labour,[1] though some seemed to think the opposite of leisure is obligation.

[1] H. Arendt, *The Human Condition*, p. 9.

The second point was that the words were not mutually exclusive like the examples given or like the binaries resulting from the fundamental fact that human beings are in many respects symmetrical: they have two sides to them, two hands, two eyes, two legs, two breasts, and not one or three or four. One other biological opposition, of sex, is stressed by conventions and, when these change and, say, the clothes which embody the conventional binary message do not declare whether the person wearing these 'words' is a man or a woman, some observers may behave like computers anxiously looking for a program. Work and leisure were not like that. They did not arouse quite the same anxiety. But when a Lewisham postman in the main sample, not one of those who appeared in the last chapter, said that, 'I get more leisure at work than I do at home', and others said the same kind of thing, it was obvious that different criteria were sometimes being used to distinguish between the two words. They could be both opposites in one context and, if the criteria varied, the same in another.

The third point is about these crucial criteria. One of them was to do with payment. What one was paid to do was work. But although most people thought that was so, it was not the sole yardstick. If it were, the housewives discussed in Chapter IV would do none. So as well as payment there was another criterion which had more to do with the original Latin root of the word 'leisure', that is *licere*, to be permitted. The presence of relatively more autonomy, or freedom from obligation, ranked an activity as leisure, its relative absence as work. Hence the use of free time as a common synonym for leisure.

> Work is when you have to do it. Leisure is when you want to do it. (Bricklayer, Ealing)

> In your leisure you define all your own parameters. (Design engineer, near Slough)

Another criterion often mentioned was the degree of pleasure.

> Leisure is for pleasure. Work you think of as a drudge. (Process worker, Barking)

Boredom is not the antonym of pleasure but at least it was often used as though it were.

> Anything which makes you bored after a length of time is work. (Bank clerk, Brentwood)

Given these principal criteria, what the Lewisham postman said makes good sense. In the Post Office he was paid and that made it work, but he felt more free and perhaps had more pleasure there than he did at home. For a manual worker the postman was, however, exceptional. For most there was no ambiguity: what they were paid to do was not notably characterized by either freedom or pleasure. But middle-class people, as we saw in Chapter VI, were more likely to have autonomy in their jobs. They were therefore more inclined to call paid work leisure; for them the two were more often merged. Pleasure was in this context a word they would not often use themselves, preferring 'sense of commitment' or some such puritanical alternative which allowed them the best of both worlds, an alliance of duty and pleasure.

Freedom and pleasure were also employed to distinguish between work and leisure at home. We referred to this in Chapter IV. Women in overwhelming numbers regarded domestic cleaning, washing clothes and washing-up as work. These were jobs generally disliked. As for meals, routine ones were much more of a drudgery than meals for guests or the great weekly ritual of Sunday dinner. One man said he had such a fine Sunday joint that there was enough over for sandwiches for three days. Men for their part often regarded house decoration and repairs as their wives did routine meals. 'The weekend is never long enough for all the commitments' (computer engineer, Tunbridge Wells). 'Leisure time – that's a laugh. When you come home you work' (lorry driver, Ealing). 'As a houseowner, gardening, car washing and decorating are all what I regard as necessary evils, not as leisure pursuits' (service manager, Enfield). 'I've got a list of things that need doing. I ought to relay the concrete. I ought to put up more shelves. The whole place needs repainting and recarpeting' (research chemist, Stevenage). Keenness or at any rate willingness to keep up the aesthetic standards of the house and maintain it in good repair belonged with home-centredness. It might be work, but the same alliance of duty and pleasure (or duty and freedom) that made for middle-class attachment to paid work could also do the same thing for the unpaid. By working at home they would fulfil a double obligation, doing something *for* as well as sometimes *with* the family. Many working-class men got more out of their work at home, even if it was tiring, because they were more free about what to do and how to do it than they were in the other department of their lives.

The fourth point to make about the two words is that they are not collectively exhaustive. The easiest binaries to deal with are the ones already referred to, like male and female: there is not yet a third sex. Work and leisure are less so because of the middle kingdom between them. In the following list we have recorded the labels that were attached by diarists to the chief categories of activity in the multi-national time budget study. Some activities were left unlabelled; the proportion was about 10 per cent over all, rising to 61 per cent for sleep. 'Mixed' meant that 40 per cent or more of all the activities in the batch were labelled as mixed, as neither work nor leisure, or not labelled at all; 'mainly' work or leisure that 50 per cent or more of them were labelled the one or the other, and 'overwhelmingly' that 75 per cent or more were.[1]

Paid work	Overwhelmingly work
Housework	Mainly work
Travel to work	Mixed
Child care	Mixed
Shopping	Mixed
Personal care	Mixed
Eating	Mixed
Sleeping	Mixed
Meals and breaks connected with paid work	Mixed
Adult education	Mixed
Civic and collective activities	Mixed
Non-work travel	Mainly leisure
Entertainment and social contacts	Overwhelmingly leisure
Sports and walking	Overwhelmingly leisure
Other leisure	Overwhelmingly leisure

As seen by our informants, and dealing still in generalities, there was apparently a spectrum from paid work at one extreme to

[1] Appendix 3, p. 346, shows how these categories were combined into the broader ones used earlier.

entertainment, sport and things like TV watching at the other, with a spread in the middle.

We shall follow our informants, regarding work and leisure as mutually exclusive in principle, as distinguished by the three criteria of payment, freedom and pleasure, and not as collectively exhaustive. We shall from now on concentrate on the kinds of activities that were considered 'mainly' or 'overwhelmingly' leisure.

How do leisure activities vary by class?

In general, as we showed in Chapter III (Table 10), married men taken as a whole spent most of their time at home. It was not without reason that men said, 'My family is my hobby', 'My wife and family are my leisure time', 'Because I'm away for longish hours I hand my weekend over to my family. They dictate me.' One diarist said he always stayed home in the evenings, reporting his routine as follows: 'Made love every night. Pinned wife down and then went to bed.' If the men had not been at home so much we should obviously not be able to talk with any justification of the symmetrical family.

But what things did they do, and how did the classes differ? We gave all the informants a series of lists of leisure activities, to which we invited them to add any we had left out, asking them about the last year taken as a whole. The first was about some of the activities done at home. The counts are in Table 35, arranged in descending order of popularity.

Watching television was of course by far the most common activity, if that is the right word to apply to people like Mr Macrae, a storeman in Islington, who said, 'On Saturday we watched television all evening till we went to bed.' Since it was an everyday business, whereas many of the activities listed in Table 35 were done much less, its importance stood out even more from the diaries. The average time spent watching it during the week as a whole (calculated as before by multiplication) is shown in Table 36. This was in the spring and summer months of the survey. In winter it would have been more prominent.[1] Television was also cited as the leisure activity they 'most enjoyed'

[1] Another study found that television viewing was markedly more popular in winter than summer. K. K. Sillitoe, op. cit., p. 41.

TABLE 35 *Home-based activities (main sample: married men working full-time)*

	Professional and managerial	*Clerical*	*Skilled*	*Semi-skilled and unskilled*	*All*
Proportion in class doing activity 12 times or more in previous year					
Watching television	95%	99%	98%	95%	97%
Gardening	70%	62%	66%	50%	64%
Playing with children	59%	63%	66%	59%	62%
Listening to music on radio, record player or tape recorder	65%	70%	52%	44%	57%
Home decorations or repairs	52%	55%	56%	45%	53%
Car cleaning	55%	44%	51%	35%	48%
Reading (books)	67%	63%	33%	28%	46%
Car maintenance	30%	25%	38%	25%	32%
Collecting stamps or other objects	14%	24%	11%	8%	13%
Technical hobbies	10%	7%	10%	4%	8%
Playing cards or chess	9%	14%	8%	4%	8%
Playing an instrument	10%	8%	5%	4%	7%
Handicrafts	5%	6%	7%	7%	6%
Model building	6%	4%	5%	4%	5%
Total number	171	70	237	110	588
Average number of activities done 12 times or more in previous year	5·8	5·9	5·2	4·2	5·3

Technical hobbies, playing cards or chess and handicrafts were activities added by informants to our original list. Activities done by less than one per cent of the men in any class are not shown but have been counted in the averages.

of any they did by one out of five unskilled workers. The proportion was minute in every other class; the others watched it but did not 'enjoy' it as much as other things.

TABLE 36 *Average weekly hours of television viewing (diary sample: married men and women aged 30 to 49)*

	Men	*Women*
Professional and managerial	10·0	9·9
Clerical	12·8	12·2
Skilled	12·9	11·7
Semi-skilled and unskilled	13·3	13·4
All classes	12·1	11·5
Number of people	203	206

Except for reading and gardening the differences between the classes in Table 35 are not marked, and those there are probably did not affect the family much one way or another. Hobbies could obviously cause friction at home – one man making a very large model aeroplane in his small back garden was hardly leaving room to hang the washing – but they were less liable to than ones which took people out of it.

For active sports there was more difference. According to Table 37 people in the higher classes played more. The order of popularity was broadly the same as in the surveys conducted by Sillitoe[1] and Rodgers,[2] which were on this subject more comprehensive in their territorial coverage and in other ways than ours.

Spectators and supporters

Going to watch turned out to be less common than playing. although a majority of the men watched on television. Association football was the most popular, both 'live' (36 per cent had been at

[1] K. K. Sillitoe, op. cit., p. 126.
[2] H. B. Rodgers, op. cit., pp. 6, 9.

TABLE 37 *Activity in sports (main sample: married men working full-time)*

	Professional and managerial	*Clerical*	*Skilled*	*Semi-skilled and unskilled*	*All*
Proportion in each class doing the sport 12 times or more in previous year:					
Swimming	34%	25%	20%	8%	22%
Fishing (all kinds)	9%	3%	9%	5%	8%
Association football	6%	6%	8%	5%	7%
Golf	9%	11%	4%	2%	6%
Table tennis	10%	10%	4%	2%	6%
Cricket	8%	0%	6%	4%	5%
Tennis	8%	7%	2%	0%	4%
Badminton or squash	7%	6%	2%	0%	4%
Sailing	6%	0%	1%	0%	2%
Bowls	2%	3%	2%	3%	2%
Ten pin bowling	2%	0%	2%	1%	2%
Athletics	2%	0%	1%	0%	1%
Rugby football	2%	3%	0%	0%	1%
Horse riding	0%	3%	1%	0%	1%
Motor cruising	2%	0%	0%	0%	1%
Boxing, judo, karate, wrestling	1%	0%	1%	0%	1%
Fencing, archery, shooting	1%	1%	0%	0%	0%
Motor sports	2%	0%	0%	0%	1%
Boating	1%	0%	0%	0%	0%
Water ski-ing	1%	0%	0%	0%	0%
Total number	171	71	239	110	591
Average number of sports done 12 times or more in previous year	1·1	0·8	0·6	0·3	0·7

Sports have been excluded from the table if done by less than one per cent of the men in any class. Examples were ice-skating, rock climbing and gliding, but again these have been included in the averages.

least once[1]) and on television (72 per cent twelve times or more). Fifteen per cent had been to a cricket match (30 per cent had watched cricket twelve times or more on television), and 12 per cent to some kind of motor sport (32 per cent twelve times or more on television). The other popular sports on television were boxing (40 per cent twelve times or more), wrestling (39 per cent), golf (39 per cent), tennis (39 per cent), athletics (36 per cent), horse racing (32 per cent) and rugby football (32 per cent).

Clerical and skilled workers went to football more and managers watched it on television rather less than other people. Managers watched rugby and tennis more often, live and on television. Working-class men more often went to wrestling and more often watched it on television along with boxing and horse racing. But on the whole people's total 'scores' (in terms either of once or of twelve times) for spectator sports or for watching on television did not vary much by class.

Asked whether they were 'a supporter of any particular team or teams', about two men out of five said they were, the great majority of these – nine out of ten – being supporters of professional football teams. There were again no marked differences between the classes. We also enquired of those who 'regularly read a daily newspaper' which part of it they read first. Most men in all classes read one regularly. But the number starting with the sports pages varied. It was 26 per cent among middle-class men and 40 per cent among working-class. This did suggest a greater relative working-class interest in sport.

The final set of activities was neither home-based nor connected with sport. The details are in Table 38.

Working-class men more often played darts. Managers more often went to theatres and evening classes, more often dined out, and more often did 'voluntary work' – a sort of leisure activity, by the way, which rather offends against the earlier distinctions we were making. The cinema was obviously less popular than it would have been some decades earlier. A warehouseman living in Sutton said, 'We don't go to the cinema very often. All they have nowadays is sex and Walt Disney and I can get both of those at home.'

In asking about these various sorts of things, we did not ask

[1] With every leisure activity we first asked people whether they had done it once or more in the previous year.

TABLE 38 *Some other leisure activities (main sample: married men working full-time)*

	Professional and managerial	*Clerical*	*Skilled*	*Semi-skilled and unskilled*	*All*
Proportion in each class doing activity 12 times or more in previous year:					
Going for 'a drive in a car for pleasure'	62%	51%	62%	49%	58%
Going to pub	51%	42%	54%	58%	52%
Going for 'a walk of a mile or more'	56%	63%	41%	36%	47%
Going out for a meal (not lunch)	48%	31%	25%	23%	32%
Playing darts	12%	13%	25%	25%	20%
Attending church	22%	20%	12%	7%	15%
Cinema	16%	20%	8%	13%	13%
Voluntary work	19%	10%	8%	5%	11%
Dancing	12%	14%	10%	12%	11%
Billiards or snooker	6%	10%	10%	7%	9%
Theatre	9%	1%	1%	3%	4%
Evening classes	7%	4%	2%	1%	3%
Caravanning	2%	1%	5%	3%	4%
Museum	5%	4%	1%	3%	3%
Art gallery	5%	3%	0%	1%	2%
Camping	2%	1%	3%	0%	2%
Total number	172	71	239	109	591
Average number of activities done 12 times or more in previous year	3·5	3·3	2·8	2·5	3·0

Activities have been excluded if they were done by less than one per cent of the men in any class, but again incorporated into the averages. These included bingo and political activities.

where people had gone as distinct from what they had done, except for one particular activity, which varied of course from person to person, the one they had 'enjoyed most'. One difference was that on the last occasion more managers had travelled further for whatever it was: 22 per cent of those whose favourite pursuit was outside the home had travelled fifty miles or more as against 11 per cent in other classes.

The findings are brought together and summarized in two different ways in Table 39. Sports watched on television are excluded from the totals, on the grounds that watching television, including sports, had already been counted. The class difference for the activities which were done once or more was larger than for those which were done more often, twelve times or more, during the year. But the general conclusion is that higher-class people did more.

This run of tables has been about husbands. Most wives were less engaged in sport, as spectators or players; they knitted or sewed more than they did anything else except watch television; they less often went to pubs, played billiards, snooker or darts; and in all, outside the home, they did less things than men. It did not, to judge by most of those measures, matter whether they had paid jobs. Those who worked went to restaurants, pubs, cinemas and theatres more than those who did not. But on the crucial point for us the generalization that applied to the husbands applied also to their wives. The point is demonstrated by Table 40 which, repeating part of the previous table for men, also adds the comparable figures for married women of similar ages.

Does work extend into leisure?

The main conclusion from these figures is about the differences not between the sexes but between the classes. Middle-class people played more sport, and went more often to restaurants and to places of entertainment like the theatre. Above all, they had a greater range of activities both in and out of the home. These findings are in line with those from some previous enquiries on both sides of the Atlantic.[1]

[1] BBC Audience Research Department, *The People's Activities*, pp. 136–8; R. Meyersohn, 'Television and the rest of leisure', p. 102; L. Reissman, 'Class, leisure and social participation', p. 76.

TABLE 39 *Division of average numbers of leisure activities (main sample: married men working full-time)*

	Professional and managerial	*Clerical*	*Skilled*	*Semi-skilled and unskilled*	*All*
Once or more in previous year					
Home-based	7·3	7·3	6·6	5·6	6·7
Active sports	2·2	1·3	1·2	0·7	1·3
Spectator sports	1·3	1·1	1·2	0·8	1·1
Other non-home activities	7·5	6·7	5·7	5·0	6·2
Total	18·3	16·4	14·7	12·1	15·3
Twelve times or more in previous year					
Home-based	5·7	5·9	5·2	4·2	5·3
Active sports	1·1	0·8	0·6	0·3	0·7
Spectator sports	0·4	0·3	0·5	0·3	0·4
Other non-home activities	3·5	3·3	2·8	2·5	3·0
Total	10·7	10·3	9·1	7·3	9·4
Number of people	172	69	241	109	591

Why should it be so? An explanation from Meyersohn is that one leisure activity triggers off another. Mr Eldon of Enfield, a painter and decorator, spent a lot of time in his local pub, saying that 'my work is thirsty work and dirty'. Once there, he played dominoes and cribbage, and was an active member of a social club based on it. He went on the club's outings. Mr Wain, a solicitor living in Caterham, had first joined the local golf club to play. After two years he was drawn into organizing some of the club's competitions and then, because he was so efficient, the Club Committee. He was on the Social Sub-Committee and organized –

TABLE 40 *Average number of leisure activities of men and women (main sample: married men working full-time and married women aged 64 or under; number of people in each category shown in brackets)*

	Professional and managerial	*Clerical*	*Skilled*	*Semi-skilled and unskilled*	*All*
Men	18·3	16·4	14·7	12·1	15·3
	(172)	(69)	(241)	(109)	(591)
Women	15·6	14·5	12·8	10·7	13·3
	(157)	(72)	(261)	(105)	(595)

and, with his wife attended – the club's dinner-dances. Thus, a person who has many interests anyway is likely to add to them. But that does not explain why anyone should have more to start with. If we knew why we should be better able to gauge whether leisure is dependent – whether we are just observing once again the influence upon the family of the greater variety of interest in work through the mediation of leisure as one of its creatures – or whether it is also an independent variable, playing its special part in either supporting or undermining the marriage relationship.

Parker has suggested that leisure is often an extension of work.[1] To explore this we asked whether activities were in any way 'linked to the kind of work you do'. The weakness was that the word 'linked' could be interpreted in several different ways; we put it, despite that, because we wanted to follow it up by asking how. Just under a quarter of the married men in full-time jobs said there was such a link, the proportion being higher at the top. Table 41 also distinguishes the main kinds of link as they were reported.

The examples under the heading of 'technical' were of skills being used in the one sphere which were much the same as those in the other. An industrial chemist in Ealing experimented, as a gardener, with fertilizers and fungicides to see which of them would change the colour of flowers in his garden. A laboratory worker in Sutton said that he learnt a good deal about yeast in the

[1] See S. Parker, op. cit., chap. 8.

TABLE 41 *Links between work and leisure (main sample: married men working full-time)*

Kind of links reported	*Professional and managerial*	*Clerical*	*Skilled*	*Semi-skilled and unskilled*	*All*
Technical	9%	1%	16%	6%	10%
Interest	15%	2%	3%	1%	6%
Business-cum-social	7%	1%	1%	1%	3%
Work-based or with work colleagues	2%	5%	2%	0%	2%
Administrative	5%	0%	0%	0%	1%
Other	1%	3%	0%	0%	1%
All reporting some link	39%	12%	22%	8%	23%
No link	61%	88%	78%	92%	77%
Total %	100%	100%	100%	100%	100%
Number	168	65	235	107	575

brewery where he worked and decided to use his knowledge to make not beer but wine, at home. He was secretary of his company's wine-making group and also a member of two local wine-making clubs. His wife did not like wine and did not join in making what she did not like. An experimental engineer living near St Albans said he had the same approach as in his work – if not exactly the same skills – to the systematic trial of plant-grafts in his garden. The hobby of a sound engineer of Islington, hi-fi, was evident from the speakers we heard in every room. A graphic designer of Enfield said that, 'The ideas I try out in my home can often be used in display advertising which I do at work. Likewise in my work I come across ideas which I use in the home.' A horticultural engineering worker near Maidstone maintained vintage lorries as a hobby. 'It's similar to horticultural engineering. Both of them involve engineering maintenance work.' 'It's similar', said a chargehand gas fitter of Watford of his do-it-yourself, 'to what I do in my job. I plumbed in the washing machine. I installed central heating.' The gas fitter was like many other men who used their skills on their homes.

The next group of men were those who said the interest, though not the skills, spilled over. A technical author living near Aylesbury told us that whenever he could he attended aircraft shows and displays. 'It's something that I enjoy. It's directly linked with my position writing maintenance manuals for aircraft.' A car salesman at Gravesend collected old motoring magazines. A fitter at Bracknell read all he could about engineering. A messenger living in Islington working for a publisher of an antique trade paper specially liked visiting museums.

The men who mixed business with social life did it in many different circumstances. An official of a trade association, living at Sutton, went to dances organized by local branches, not because he wanted to but because he had to. A public relations officer of Marlow took people to play golf, to Lords or to rugby matches. Other people spoke of things that they did, not with clients or customers but with colleagues, like playing cricket or darts for the firm's club, serving on a social committee, going fishing with workmates or just drinking with them in the pub.

Administrative experience was also used in all manner of voluntary and trade clubs and organizations. We have noted that higher-status people more often did voluntary work. Table 42 shows that they also more often belonged to clubs and societies and that, when they did, they more often served as officers or committee members.[1] This was sometimes quite deliberately to further their careers. 'I'm a Fellow', said an accountant living near Haywards Heath, 'and a member of the Council of the Institute of Chartered Accountants. That's a very useful thing to be in my business.' More often, they were drawn in to responsibility because it was known they had the right experience. 'When one is fairly successful in one's profession,' said someone who was, an architect living in Maida Vale, 'one seems to get asked to take part in all kinds of committees and organizations. I suppose they think one is likely to be fairly competent, or maybe that one's

[1] This has often been noted before, e.g. T. S. Cauter and J. S. Downham, *The Communication of Ideas*, p. 66; T. B. Bottomore, 'Social stratification in voluntary organisations', pp. 368–9; and P. Willmott and M. Young, *Family and Class in a London Suburb*, p. 91.

name will help.' A civil servant in Islington said that helping to run an old people's home, as he did, was like his job in helping to run a government department. He was not apparently being ironic.

TABLE 42 *Members and officers of clubs (main sample: married men working full-time)*

	Professional and managerial	*Clerical*	*Skilled*	*Semi-skilled and unskilled*	*All*
Officer or committee member of at least one club or association	28%	16%	13%	4%	16%
Active member but not officer or committee member of at least one club or association	41%	35%	36%	32%	37%
Not active member of any club or association	31%	49%	51%	64%	47%
Total %	100%	100%	100%	100%	100%
Number	169	71	235	107	582

These are only examples, drawn from all classes. The transfer of technical skills was rather more common amongst skilled manual workers than amongst others and activities done with colleagues were similar in most classes. With the other kinds of link, the managers had the edge, as Table 41 showed. Their interests, the prostitution of pleasure and the other things we have mentioned multiplied themselves outside work.

The other chief connection between the binaries seems to have been almost the other way on. Many people talked about 'unwinding' or 'relaxing'.

When I'm out sea-fishing I can relax. I don't think about

work or anything. It's crazy really because it's not pleasant. At least a lot of the time it isn't – you might get caught in a storm or something like that. You're getting wet and blown about and wonder if you're going to get back, and yet it's a form of relaxation. (Computer manager, Brentwood)

About once every week I put on shorts and a singlet and run for about four miles in the country round here. It's a relaxation. You push your body and the mind rests. (Marketing manager, near St Albans)

I consciously unwind when I'm gardening. I think it's sensible. In an office you're not active and you have to keep your mind on a particular train of thought. When you're working in the garden you are being active and your mind does not have to be fixed on a particular train of thought. (Works manager, Sutton)

Parker reformulated Dumazedier's[1] three functions of leisure as being the continuation of personal development, entertainment and recuperation. He argued that the extension of work into leisure was associated with the first, 'neutrality' with the second, and an 'opposition' between work and leisure with the third. We would rather say that the people whose work extends outwards are those who most loudly voice the need for recuperation. For many middle-class men it was not satisfied by sitting around in the garden or before the television. Partly, no doubt, because their work was physically less tiring than manual workers', they chose to relax in a non-relaxed way, actively engaged in something in which they could absorb themselves. The one absorption shut out the other temporarily. We did not find in the working classes as many men who were enthusiasts for a sport or hobby, in compensation for the relatively greater dreariness of their work, as we did amongst other classes who (one would think) needed the compensation less. Mr Cloudesley, the fisherman, was an exception.

Disentangling other influences

So much for the job. What about its concomitants, and especially income, education and car ownership? The money that people

[1] J. Dumazedier, *Toward a Society of Leisure*.

got from their employment was obviously a good handmaiden. Among the managers, richer men more often went sailing, played golf and tennis, and went to theatres, art galleries and museums. Likewise, managers with more education were keener on sports, perhaps because they had played them at school; they also read more.

As for the ownership of cars, this appeared to have a more pervasive effect. Within occupational classes the richer and the better educated did not have a much wider total range of activities than other people. But car-owners did: they had consistently higher general scores, as Table 43 shows. Working-class car-owners were like people with cars in other classes. They played sports more, for example, and ate more meals outside their home. It seemed to be true that in general they followed a more middle-class style of life.

TABLE 43 *Average number of leisure activities according to occupational class and car ownership (main sample: married men working full-time)*

	Professional and managerial		*Clerical*		*Skilled*		*Semi-skilled and unskilled*		*All*	
	No car	*Car*	*No car*	*Car*	*No car*	*Car*	*No car*	*Car*	*No car*	*Car*
Once or more in previous year	14·1	18·8	13·2	17·1	12·6	15·7	10·3	13·8	12·1	16·7
Number of people	21	150	18	52	69	168	52	58	160	428

To hold class constant and consider income, education and car-ownership one by one, as we have just been doing, is a perfectly good approach. But it leaves an important question unanswered. These characteristics are not independent of each other. They are interdependent, bound up together. Managers have more money and more education and more of them have cars, and the combined effect of all this is obviously important. But it is still worthwhile trying to disentangle the elements in the combination to see which matters most. The technique we adopted for this purpose was a multiple regression analysis.[1] A very large number of relationships between the four factors, like that between car-ownership and the range of activities *within* classes, were by this means summarized in a single set of indices. Age had to be brought in as a fifth factor because it made more difference than anything else.

The findings are summarized in Table 44. Men working full-time without any of the five attributes as we defined them for the computer analysis – that is not under 30, not with a car, not a manager, not with £2,000 a year or more, not educated beyond 16 – had done a total number of 11.23 leisure activities at least once during the year. The additions to the score made by first one and then another attribute were as listed. The conclusion is that after age – or rather youth – car ownership added most, more so than our other big three, class, income and education.[2]

TABLE 44 *Additions made by five attributes to men's average number of total leisure activities in previous year (main sample: 760 men working full-time)*

Average number of activities of men without any of the five following attributes	11·23
Addition made by	
1 Age 29 or under	3·78
2 Car owned by household	3·23
3 Professional or managerial class	1·93
4 Annual income £2,000 or over	1·71
5 Educated to age 17 or over	1·59

Our index of leisure has its limitations, of course. One of the most vital was that people's scores could be inflated by a kind of

[1] The procedure is outlined more fully on p. 298 in Appendix 1.

[2] A different kind of multiple regression, done for the Leisure Activities Survey of the North West Sports Council, found that the car (measured by whether people had a driving licence) was after age and sex the most important influence upon participation in several of the forms of leisure analysed. On outdoor water sports, for instance, the report concluded: 'Three factors dominate in the explanation of the pattern of participation . . . namely age, sex, and the possession of a driving licence.' *Leisure in the North West*, pp. 184–91.

multiple counting, because car cleaning and repairing were considered separate activities. But when we re-did the regression with both cleaning and repairing left out, the independent influence of the car – adding 1·97 activities – was still about the same as that of class – adding 2·07. With the spread of cars down the income scale in accord with the Principle it looks as though in one respect they have become as important as class. It follows that those who are both poor and without a car suffer from a doubly severe deprivation. There can evidently be no classless society if some but not all members of it are carless. We do not want to overdo it. We have only been talking about the range of activities, which the car can multiply just by adding to a person's geographical stretch. After this finding had emerged we retraced our ground and analysed by car as well as class almost everything we have mentioned so far in the book, and much that we have not, to see whether our findings about occupational class could still stand. Within each class car owners were more likely to call themselves middle class and vote Conservative. But that apart, the main finding stood up. In almost all respects class mattered more than cars. The main conclusion of the chapter so far also stands. The more varied and less routinized work of middle-class people was, in general, matched by their more varied leisure.

How do contacts with friends and relatives differ?

We have been looking at leisure in terms of activities rather than relationships. To add to our account of what people did with their time we needed also to consider them from this second point of view. The one is, of course, usually the other. People on walks are often unaccompanied unless by a non-human animal. But men who competed in sailing races could not do so alone, or avoid the others afterwards in the club house, even if they had wanted to. On their parents' wedding anniversaries people took them out for a treat. Irish porters piled into houses in Islington on Saturday nights. Sustaining such relationships was itself a major leisure activity which we could not list like billiards or sewing.

The information we have on this topic is not at all systematic. Many people obviously belonged to a series of social 'circles', as they would sometimes call them, meaning that their members all knew each other. It seemed that middle-class people belonged to larger numbers of these circles or networks,[1] although the ones they did belong to were not so tightly knit as those of people who had fewer distinct circles in total. Here are a few examples.

> It's mainly relations and they all know each other. There are no others really because my best friend married my husband's brother. (Bus driver's wife, Islington)

> Our friends are mainly local friends and most of them know each other, either through living locally or through meeting here. We have made friends mainly through the children – their children went to the same school. We go round to spend an evening with one family or another occasionally. There are a few couples that the wife and I knew before we were married. (Administrator in nationalized industry, Lewisham)

> They fall into categories. First, there are our Scottish friends living in the London area – they know each other. Then the Caterham friends know each other. They come from the tennis club, the Wives' Fellowship and some are school mothers I've met through my child being at school. And then there are the business friends and my husband's friends – they link up with our Scottish friends, but otherwise the different groups don't know each other. (Accountant's wife, Caterham)

We naturally listened to what people had to say of this kind, but we could not think how to put questions about it in a large survey like ours, which would in our judgment mean sufficiently the same thing to different people to produce properly comparable answers. (At least we could not see how to without confining the survey largely to that.) All we could manage in the time was to ask about particular people, identified as friends or relatives other than those our informants were actually living with, who had been met socially in the week previous to the interview.

The first point was about their sex. We have been arguing that relationships within the family have been becoming more symmetrical, with roles more interchangeable than they were. But there was still a women's world and a men's, in social contacts as in other ways. Table 45 shows that in all classes men had more men friends than women friends and vice versa.

[1] For a discussion of this term see J. Clyde Mitchell, 'The concept and use of social networks'.

TABLE 45 *Sex of friend met socially (main sample: married men working full-time and married women aged 64 or under; total number in each category shown in brackets)*

	Professional and managerial	*Clerical*	*Skilled*	*Semi-skilled and unskilled*	*All*
Men, proportion whose last seen friend was a man	86%	79%	85%	86%	85%
	(166)	(63)	(218)	(98)	(545)
Women, proportion whose last seen friend was a woman	86%	86%	89%	92%	87%
	(152)	(68)	(242)	(93)	(555)

The sheer numbers of relatives and friends are compared in Table 46. Each person is, of course, counted as one; a mother seen four times in the week by her daughter appears only once, so that the table does not give any indication of the amount of time spent with others, nor the number of occasions on which they were seen. For what it is worth, however, it does show that among both men and women the people at the top end of the occupational scale saw more friends and rather fewer relatives. The others, lower down in the scale, were in one sense at least more family-centred, if family is taken for the moment to refer to the extended rather than to the immediate family. The difference between the sexes is also marked, women in general seeing fewer work friends, fewer non-local friends and less people in total.

Table 46 also shows that managerial-class people had more friends living at a distance. Among the friends most recently seen by the men, 19 per cent of those of managers lived twenty miles or more away, compared with 5 per cent among other classes. Their relatives, too, were more dispersed geographically. The proportion of managers' most recently seen relatives living twenty miles or more away was 42 per cent; among clerical men, it was 17 per cent; among skilled, 14 per cent, and among semi-skilled and unskilled, 5 per cent. Managers had therefore to spend more of their leisure time, even travelling by car as they ordinarily

TABLE 46 *Average number of relatives and friends seen in previous week*
(*a*) (*main sample: married men working full-time*)

	Professional and managerial	*Clerical*	*Skilled*	*Semi-skilled and unskilled*	*All*
Local friends (living within ten minutes' walk)	2·8	1·8	2·8	3·8	2·9
Work friends	3·0	0·3	0·8	1·1	1·4
Other friends	5·2	2·1	2·7	2·2	3·3
Total friends	11·0	4·2	6·3	7·1	7·6
Total relatives	2·6	3·2	3·9	3·7	3·4
Total friends and relatives	13·6	7·4	10·2	10·8	11·0
Number of people	168	69	238	107	582

(*b*) (*main sample: married women aged 64 or under*)

	Professional and managerial	*Clerical*	*Skilled*	*Semi-skilled and unskilled*	*All*
Local friends (living within ten minutes' walk)	2·6	1·6	2·5	2·1	2·4
Work friends	0·3	0·3	0·3	0·1	0·3
Other friends	3·4	1·1	1·3	1·3	1·9
Total friends	6·3	3·0	4·1	3·5	4·6
Total relatives	2·9	3·8	3·8	3·3	3·5
Total friends and relatives	9·2	6·8	7·9	6·8	8·1
Number of people	156	70	258	104	588

If work friends lived within ten minutes they were counted in the category of local friends. There were in fact very few such people in any class.

did, in order to meet both friends and relatives. Since they also went further for 'activities' in the way we were treating them before, it follows that higher-class people spent more time altogether on travel during their leisure just as they did on their journeys to work. Among the men diarists, the total average time spent in travel of all kinds during a week ranged from thirteen hours among managers to under eight hours among the semi-skilled and unskilled.

Wives saw rather less people in total than their husbands. But the couple were usually together as they travelled around their networks. This is shown in Table 47 which reports the presence of wives on the last occasion when married men had met a relative or a friend. There was a class difference, if a fairly small one: the middle-class men were more often with their wives. The question for the last section is whether the same could be said of leisure generally as of that part of it which involved friends or relatives.

TABLE 47 *Presence of wife at meeting with relative or friend (main sample: married men working full-time; total number in each category shown in brackets)*

	Professional and managerial	*Clerical*	*Skilled*	*Semi-skilled and unskilled*	*All*
Wife present at last meeting with relative	83% (159)	81% (64)	75% (220)	73% (98)	78% (541)
Wife present at last meeting with friend	68% (164)	60% (63)	58% (214)	51% (98)	60% (539)

How does leisure affect the family?

Nearly all families were home-centred, and some were more so than others. Managers, as we have seen, did more things outside the home. Were there strains caused by their leisure as well as their work, even though when they went visiting they went with their wives?

In some families there certainly were. Mr Simpson of Reading was a skin-diving enthusiast. He went away to the sea almost every weekend during the summer, leaving his wife to spend a good deal of her time with her mother, rather as many husbands in Bethnal Green used once to do with their wives when they went off to the pub rather than the sea. Her diary recorded what happened on the Monday morning. She had gone to bed the night before, leaving a note for her husband on the kitchen table.

6.30 a.m.	Woke up and found that Derek was not home so I phoned Bill (his friend) to say that Derek would not be able to drive him to work this morning. Then went back to bed. Wondered how many other husbands led such free lives!
7.45–8.45	Called the children, cleaned shoes, plaited their hair, gave them breakfast and got their satchels ready. Saw children off to school and waved from the window as they went down the road.
9.20	Derek arrived home – he had apparently missed the tide and had to wait for the next one.
9.35	He had breakfast and then a bath while I set to work washing up the dishes.
10.20	Saw Derek off to work and went upstairs to make the bed.

Mrs Simpson wondered how many other husbands led such free lives. Not many. In all classes married men spent much of their time at home; and for most of the time that they were away, doing the kind of things that we have been discussing, they were also with their families. They took them along when they visited friends or relatives, or (as we shall see) when they engaged in some of the most popular sports, or to watch cricket or rugby matches, or to the theatre, or to a restaurant for a meal, as well, of course, as on the holidays which were for almost everyone times when the family was together. We tried out many different comparisons between classes according to the amount of time that husbands spent with their wives and children when they were out of the home; according to the extent to which husbands had been out with and without their wives; and according to whether the wife accompanied them when they went out to engage in the leisure activity they enjoyed most. Although wives were somewhat less in evidence in the higher classes, the differences were always small.

To try and get further we adopted three other expedients. The first was to re-interview more intensively the small number of diarists who had done at least one kind of sport twelve or more times in the previous year and also recorded it as their most enjoyed activity. Higher-class people were particularly keen on sport, and this could set up tensions of its own, as the Simpson story illustrated. Fifty-one people were re-interviewed, of whom forty-one were men.

As well as men, the top social class was predominant. Among married men in the main sample aged 30 to 49, 29 per cent were managers; among the male sports enthusiasts the proportion was about half (20 out of 41).[1]

The most common sports for managers were sailing (four), golf (three) and tennis (three); among the rest of the men, fishing (five) and swimming (four). The others, including squash, cricket, table tennis, motor racing and ice-skating, were done by one or at the most two people. Clearly some of these could more easily be family affairs than others. Swimming was almost always, as were camping and walking (which in this context did not mean just 'going for a walk'). Tennis, squash or table tennis could, and so could sailing, if the boat was big enough. Golf was played by wives less often than husbands and seldom together. Fishing was predominantly for men and so were motor racing, pistol shooting, cycling, football and athletics, unless the wife and children came along as spectators and supporters.

Some of the ways in which the family could be affected are worth illustrating.

Family takes part:

There's no question of tennis interfering with my family. I make sure it doesn't. My wife loves it and plays too, and our nine-year-old boy is keen. As a matter of fact it was my wife who started me playing tennis again. I used to play at school. When I was first married I was playing cricket, hockey and rugby. They were my games. Then the first baby came and those games didn't fit in with my family life. My wife loved

[1] This was not because of any differences between the diarists and the comparable people in the main sample. In their sex and their social class, the diarists as a whole closely matched the people from whom they were drawn.

tennis and I switched to that. (Manager, chemical company, Marlow)

There's no problem over swimming. It's the opposite. My wife likes to swim herself. So do my two sons and daughter. We all go together. (Wire maker, Stevenage)

Family does not take part but appears to tolerate:
My wife doesn't play golf herself and doesn't come, but she's all for it. She likes to see my card and see how I've done. (Draughtsman, Brentwood)

She's quite pleased, when I go fishing, to get rid of me for an hour or so. She's happy as long as I bring home something to eat. She looks on it as something that keeps me more amenable – something to occupy my mind, like. (Plumber, Southwark)

Family does not take part:
I like sailing very much but my wife and daughter don't like it, so they're left behind. It means that I can't go as often as I'd like. The garden suffers too – they always say you can tell a sailing man by his garden. *Wife commented:* Yes, just look at ours. (Schoolmaster, Gravesend)

My bowls sometimes interferes with the outings or with the household timetable. It's not serious, but it does affect them. (Store manager, Sutton)

Jobs do get neglected at home because of my running. I do cross-country in the winter, track running in the summer and road running in between. My wife thinks a man should have an interest but she sometimes gets fed up. She thinks I'm mad. (Electrician's mate, Dagenham)

The numbers were, as we have said, very small. But they suggested that senior people were more likely than others to be in one of the extreme categories. With them it was rather more common for the family to suffer (if that is not too strong a word) *or* for the sport to be a family affair. In the main sample as a whole nearly two-thirds of managers took part in a sport twelve times or more during the previous year. So the number of families affected must be fairly large. Sport could unite or divide. But Mrs Simpson was clearly not alone. Leisure was sometimes a duel rather than a duet.

Out of the home

The second expedient was to look at men diarists who had, apart from their time at work, spent four hours or more out of their homes on their own during the period for which the diaries were kept. The proportions were roughly similar, about a third, in all social classes. Middle-class men did three main kinds of thing. One was, again, sport:

> Mr Jordan, a pathologist living in Tunbridge Wells, went home for a meal, then drove six miles to his tennis club on a Wednesday evening, played there and talked to friends for just over three hours and then drove home.

> Mr Stewart, a factory manager working in Slough and living in Reading, drove straight from work on Thursday evening to play in a cricket match with colleagues from his firm. He had drinks in a pub afterwards with six of them and arrived home by 10.30 p.m.

Another was cultural activities:

> Mr Greenberg, a school-teacher, went home after school on a Tuesday, had tea with his wife and went out at 7 p.m. He travelled from his home near Aylesbury to Watford and from 7.30 until 9 p.m. 'rehearsed with the Choral Society'. He had a drink afterwards with a friend and arrived back home at 10.30 p.m.

> Mr Posner, a sales manager, on a Thursday evening drove from his home in Gravesend to Rochester, where he played the viola in an orchestra. He was away from home for three and three-quarter hours, about an hour of that being spent in driving to and from the concert.

Others did voluntary work:

> Mr Welsh, a solicitor in High Wycombe, spent three and a half hours on Wednesday evening 'attending a committee meeting' at his local church.

> Mr McPhipps, an insurance broker from Ealing, 'dug out the undergrowth in the Garden of Rest' on Monday and Wednesday evenings, and went to a meeting of the parochial church council on Thursday. His church activities took up about ten-and-a-half hours during a week, of which about half was with his wife or his wife and daughter and the rest alone or with other people.

The manual workers, when away from home and family, were watching or playing football, 'doing repairs for a friend' or in the pub.

> Mr Miller, an Islington electrician, went to the local pub on Friday evening (two hours) and Sunday lunch-time (three hours). On Saturday evening his wife went with him.

The proportions of men who were out of the home may have been much the same in all classes. But the nature of the engagement was not. The impression was that the brokers and solicitors and the like were more fully absorbed and that they were taking their leisure almost as seriously as their work, sometimes with a similar kind of professional attitude. Given that, the long arm of their leisure could intrude into the family as much as that of their job.

The third thing we did was to lean on a question about leisure similar to the one about work referred to earlier. Most people did not consider that the demands of their family 'interfered' with other things they would like to do in their leisure, as Table 48 shows. But managers and clerical workers were more inclined to.

TABLE 48 *Interference of home or family with leisure (main sample: married men working full-time)*

	Professional and managerial	*Clerical*	*Skilled*	*Semi-skilled and unskilled*	*All*
Proportion saying that home or family interfered with leisure	25%	27%	14%	7%	18%
Total number	169	71	237	109	586

Here are four illustrations:

> I would like to play more golf, get more exercise generally. I'd like to go to more functions. But it would be selfish to my family. (Deputy manager, near Aylesbury)

> I'd like to play golf all Saturday and Sunday. I don't like shopping or decorating. My wife doesn't play golf or tennis. (Telephone manager, Caterham)

> I'd like to take up sailing, gliding, ski-ing but it's just not on for a family man. There's no point in starting something you can't finish. My wife hasn't got the interest. So you tend to compromise on something that everyone wants to do. (Commercial artist, Enfield)

> Without four children I could be doing a lot of things I'm not doing now. Every now and again you feel you'd like to rush off and do something different. (Accounts clerk, Ealing)

Some people talked about the constraints that home and children put upon what they could do as a couple, rather than individually.

> It's so rarely that we have any leisure time and even more rare that we can do something together. (Estate agent, High Wycombe)

> Children inevitably put some limitation on what you can do. We haven't been out for six years. We can't go out for the day, because it is too long for the children. For most of the time we are at home at the evenings and weekends. (Draughtsman, Ealing)

If the trends continue

We should now, as we have done before for other subjects, say something about the implications of our Principle of Stratified Diffusion.[1] Leaving detail aside, the main conclusion is that, to judge from the higher classes, leisure will become more varied and more active. Television viewing and other passivities are likely to take up less of people's time. Participation in almost everything else is likely to increase, particularly in the sports

[1] This discussion draws upon the study described in Appendix 5.

which have been spreading their hold downwards ever since the Old Etonians team lost the Football Cup to Blackburn Olympic in 1883.[1] The same thing has happened, and probably will happen, to the search for culture in museums and art galleries, painting and sculpture, playing musical instruments and adult education. Such a projection is very different from the common one that the amount of leisure time will expand dramatically, and that people will increasingly fill it with bingo and television viewing.[2] Apart from holidays, the trends suggest no great increase in leisure time and less passivity rather than more.[3]

It follows that the plans for the environment will need to allow for growth of many different kinds. Among sports, golf, tennis, badminton and squash are likely to become much more popular, along with sailing, water ski-ing, swimming and the other water sports which grew so rapidly in the 1960s.[4] The demand for camping, caravanning, walking and driving in the country will also grow.

All in all, in as well as beyond the London Region, there will be a large extra call upon land for sport and recreation, and for people to travel about on. With the aid of their cars, others will follow the middle classes into more dispersed networks, and fling the outerworks of the Region wider than ever.

If the car is going to matter so much to those who have one, it will matter even more to those without. Given the likely patterns of leisure, and given the emphasis on mobility-by-car that will go with it, the plight of the transport poor will in relative terms become all the worse. Even though there will be less of them, the ascendance of private transport at the expense of public threatens to isolate the minority from the main, moving stream of society.

[1] 'The "gentlemen's clubs" of the home counties and the soccer playing "public schools", which shared the Football Cup between them throughout the seventies, began in the early eighties to meet stiff northern competition.' G. Best, *Mid-Victorian Britain 1851–75*, p. 209.

[2] Herbert Read has, for instance, written of 'the decline of active play – of amateur sport – and the enormous growth of purely receptive entertainment'. 'Atrophied muscles and empty art', p. 89.

[3] A. H. Halsey has, in a review of past trends in leisure, shown that this is what has been happening. 'In general the statistics representing *participation* in sports show an increase in activity over the period for which figures are available. On the other hand figures for *attendances* at sporting events show a very substantial decline since 1950.' 'Leisure', in A. H. Halsey (ed.). *Trends in British Society since 1900*, p. 543.

[4] M. Dower, 'Fourth wave: the challenge of leisure', p. 124.

Without more equality in general and without priority for public transport in particular, more and more kinds of leisure will be shut off from the poor and the car-less, young and, even more, old.

As for the majority, if the trend towards more varied leisure continues unchecked, what is this going to mean for the family? We have seen that most of our informants thought freedom to be one of the endearing characteristics of leisure. It could be excluded by obligation. But as far as we could judge from the very limited evidence we collected, the obligations generated by the family were not resented. Most people spent a great deal of their leisure time at home, and appeared to be content with it, or, if they left the precincts by car, they did so together.

Once again the higher classes hinted at a different outcome. The greater variety that they enjoyed (or suffered) in their working lives went with greater variety in their leisure and a greater geographical spread in their activities and their networks of relatives and friends. They spent more time travelling about, because they had more to travel about to. Most of them strained to prevent the greater complexity from interfering with their families, especially by taking their wives with them when they went out. But some of them brought something of the same sort of professionalism into their leisure as they did into their work, finding the one, particularly if it required skill and devotion, more of a counterpoint to the other. For such people it was sometimes not easy to reconcile their own needs and those of their families. If leisure meant to them not furious activity but what it meant to Pieper perhaps there would have been less of a conflict. But as it was . . .

IX
MANAGING DIRECTORS

Our main sample was as much of a cross-section as possible. We wanted to see how the majority lived. But one minority was specially critical. If it is true that what the rich do today the poor will do tomorrow, it then becomes important to know as much as possible about what they are doing today, especially those who work for their living rather than those who do not have to. The people in the main sample who were at the head of the column were richer than others, and might themselves be guides. But, though richer, few of them would be thought of as 'the rich', at the extreme end of the larger band of better-off people. If we could isolate any people of that type they might be a particularly sensitive indicator, for it may also be true that what the very rich do today the less rich will do tomorrow and so on down. If it had turned out that the very rich were the opposite of the higher-class people of previous chapters, less absorbed in their work or their leisure and more in their families, we would have had to revise all our guesses about what may happen.

The procedure was roundabout. We could not draw a sample of people according to their incomes from any source that is publicly accessible. We had therefore to go for some group whose members would in fact turn out to be rich. We chose managing directors. The nature of the sample is described in Appendix 1. The main qualifications were that the *men* selected should be managing directors (and therefore executive rather than non-executive); members of the Institute of Directors – this was important as the Director-General of the Institute was kindly prepared to sponsor the survey[1] and so make the response rate more satisfactory than it

[1] A technique which has often been used before in management studies. Rosemary Stewart, for example, was given access to members of such bodies as the Institute of Works Managers and the Institute of Marketing, *Managers and Their Jobs*, p. 24.

would otherwise have been; and also listed in the *Directory of Directors*. This last criterion ruled out some of the many small companies whose directors can belong to the Institute. The *Directory of Directors* excludes smaller companies, though without stating expressly what the threshhold is. The fact that the *Directory* did not list home addresses (and the Institute did not always have them) made it impossible to confine the sample to people actually living in the Region. The best we could do was stipulate that the head offices of the companies should be in the Region; 30 of the 190 managing directors lived outside it, though they worked inside, most of them being long-distance commuters into Central London. We cannot tell how representative of 'the rich' are the people who were interviewed. They are probably not representative of members of the Institute of Directors, since the refusal rate was high. Even if it had been a perfect sample of the Institute we would not have been much further forward because no one knows how far a representative collection of directors, let alone of 'the rich', join the Institute. Our people certainly covered a wide range, with at one extreme 29 per cent of them having less than 100 employees and at the other 29 per cent more than 1,000.

The premises in which the men were interviewed (apart from a few seen at home) also covered a range, from old buildings with large, almost empty halls recalling better days by their lack of people – in one there was a Victorian glass case with a stuffed goose right outside the managing director's office – to modern multi-storied blocks fitted out with deep carpets, mobiles, abstract paintings and plenty of the armchairs and coffee tables and drink cupboards with which the office apes the home. Some were specially memorable, like Mr Joliffe's great room with its view over a large part of London. Its wall was covered with green linen. Orange paint set off white woodwork. On the long, wide desk were several beautiful ornaments – a large uncut amethyst on a black base, a round polished piece of mauve silica on a gold filigree mount, a polished egg of brown variegated stone. Coffee was served in white cups with straight fluted sides and black saucers. 'I like to be surrounded by luxury,' he said. Equally striking was the perfectly maintained seventeenth-century building occupied by a merchant bank; the past heads of the business, and of the family, looked down on the interviewer from the portraits on the walls. There were also many offices that were out of the interior decorator's more standard (if most expensive) book – a show of marble, fitted carpets and wrought-iron staircases, with fountains pitter-pattering in the reception hall.

The men themselves were as diverse as the buildings of which they were in command. Yet there was something that many of them had in common. The interview reports kept repeating words like 'large', 'bluff', 'a big man', 'lively looking', 'expansive' – nearly always, at least with those under sixty, conveying a sense of energy and confidence. They were mostly men accustomed to dominate, so raising the question whether the disposition might act as impresario for special relationships at home.

In the light of our chief criterion they were also fairly homogeneous. All earned more than £5,000 a year, whereas in our main London sample only 1·9 per cent and in the country generally at that time only 1·2 per cent of incomes were over that level. Two-thirds of them had more than £10,000 a year, as compared with 0·2 per cent in the country generally.[1] Even these figures might have understated; several of the men recognized this, for example by saying, 'Do you want my income, because that's a bit misleading. You see, I own a large number of shares in this company. We try to pay ourselves no dividends and plough all the profits back. I'm not taking it in income now but there's a very considerable capital appreciation each year.' These were the sort of men who started their morning papers (not like the working-class who began by looking for news about their football teams) by turning to the City sections to see how the shares of their companies had moved in the previous day's trading on the Stock Exchange. Quite apart from capital that would be used as income, many of them had top-hat pension policies, the use of a company flat in London, meals at the company's expense and hotels as well when they were away from home on company business. Four out of five had cars provided by their companies – sometimes as well as cars they owned for the use of their wives, their children or themselves. It was not uncommon to drive to the country station in one car (leaving the other with the wife) and then to be met at Waterloo or Paddington, by a company chauffeur waiting with a rug in his hands by the door of an even larger company car.

How had the directors got where they had? Many went through the war and sometimes that was the turning point. 'Finished up as

[1] Central Statistical Office, *Social Trends*, no. 2, 1971, p. 74.

a Brigadier – I had a good war.' 'When I got on the C.-in-C.'s staff I stuck to him, and as he rose, I rose too.' But most originated in, or married into, well-off families. Fewer of them had clerical or manual fathers than had professional and managerial people generally. This is shown in Table 49; since most of the directors were over 40 the main comparison in this and other tables is between managing directors who were married and the married men from the main sample aged 40 and over, divided into those in the top class and those in other classes. The directors' families had largely determined the sort of work they did, and this whether or not they took over a family business. For a large majority family had provided background, education, money and contacts. For several who did not have the benefit of education, family connections were still of great importance. On the whole this book has been more about the influence of work upon family than the other way round. To redress the balance slightly we sketch the stories of just three of the 'family-made' men, in two of which the war again figures.

TABLE 49 *Social mobility of managing directors*

	Own occupation		
		Main sample: married men aged 40 or over and working full time	
Father's occupation	*Managing directors*	*Professional and managerial*	*Other classes*
Professional and managerial	83%	43%	15%
Clerical	6%	9%	7%
Manual	11%	48%	78%
Total %	100%	100%	100%
Number	174	100	260

Mr Steiner's father had been in the silk business, and when 'to the relief of the teachers' he left his school in East London at the age of fifteen he went straight into his father's company and 'learnt the trade from the bottom to the top and from one side to another'. In 1939 he left for service in the navy and remembers, as the moment which both infuriated and energized him more than any other in his life, his visit after his demob to a company he had sold to in the 1930s. He told them he was ready to do so again. The response was cold. 'We've got to look after the people who looked after us all during the war,' they said. Mr Steiner in his fury turned on them and said that was a fine way for a company which had made lots of money in the war to behave towards someone who had fought right through it. He decided to desert silk and start up in synthetic fibres. His father took an interest in it and the business had been expanding ever since. 'We've taken this business from a 1*s*. 2*d*. share to a 6*s*. 6*d*. share: I suppose that's some measure of success.'

Mr Fowler said his was not a family business but family connections led him into it. For one thing, his mother owned a few shares in the company. For another, the son of Mr Bishop, who founded the company, was articled to Mr Fowler's father, who was a solicitor. Mr Fowler did not want to become a lawyer, so his father said 'I've got his son, why doesn't he have mine!' He started as an office boy, then became a junior clerk, a traveller, a director and then the managing director. When he first took the post the firm's gross assets were £25,000; by 1970 they were £600,000.

Even if family connections had been less important for Mr Dublin, they still mattered a good deal. He was an outsider like so many of the other businessmen who converted ambition into success in Britain in this century, from Samuel Deterding with Shell and Brunner and Mond with ICI to Warburg with his bank and Cohen with his supermarket chain. Mr Dublin had been a medical student in Poland at the beginning of the war. After arriving, he could not continue his studies – he had no money. But he married, and when his father-in-law invited him to join his business he put aside all thought of becoming a doctor and agreed. He quickly became successful, but he was frustrated at not being his own boss and so started up on his own with a 'capital' of £25. His company, which had long since gone public, was worth £6 million in 1970.

Choice of homes

Most of the managing directors were interviewed in their offices.

But some chose to be seen in their homes, so we have some impressions of the kinds of places they lived in, which were also, perhaps, where many other people would like to live if only they too had the means. Some – those with smaller companies and relatively low incomes – lived in four-bedroom detached houses in suburbs like Cheam or Woodford. Others were grander. Mr Milton was managing director of a national durable goods firm. His London home was an eight-roomed flat in Belgrave Square (he also had a Regency house set in ten acres in Wiltshire, where he and his wife spent their weekends, and a flat in Majorca). The interview took place in a large drawing-room with white walls, grey-painted woodwork, dark grey fitted Wilton carpeting and long green velvet curtains. There were two leather-covered Chesterfields, four matching chairs and a square matching footstool, a low circular table with a bowl of yellow flowers and two green leather tubs of cigarettes. Mr Milton put on a record of Beethoven's Violin Concerto as a background to the interview.

Mr Webb, of a City finance firm, lived in a Georgian house in the middle of private woods in the Essex countryside. He had a housekeeper and a 'daily woman', as well as his chauffeur. The house had fourteen rooms – 'I gave up my 23-roomed house a year ago to switch to a smaller one.' Mr Webb was seen in a room overlooking the garden – a croquet lawn was surrounded by shrubs and an arbour of roses from which two bronze wood nymphs peeped out. The walls of the room were lined with books, and the tables, sideboard, mantelpiece and low cupboard all had antique clocks or musical boxes on them. They were Mr Webb's hobby.

Mr Milton and Mr Webb, although unusually rich, illustrate what did seem to be a general tendency towards geographical polarization. Directors – like professional and other managerial people – more often lived right outside the built-up area of Greater London or right inside, near the centre. At the other end of the scale the poor usually had almost no choice, and in so far as they could exercise it at all, it was more determined by the dwelling than by the district.

About a quarter of the managing directors lived in Inner London. The proportion was similar to that among the married men in the main sample, but the directors were, as one might expect, concentrated in particular districts, especially ones with old houses in them: of the forty-three, seventeen were in Westminster (including St John's Wood), fifteen in Chelsea or Kensington, six in Hampstead or Highgate and two in the City of London. Only three lived outside these areas – one in Islington (near to the edge of the City), the other two further afield, at Blackheath and Tulse Hill. Several had for weekday living moved in to the centre once their children were grown up, or all away at boarding school. One man who formerly lived in Haslemere and had moved to Westminster said he could not stand the Portsmouth line any longer. The service had in his view been getting steadily worse for thirty years. Others had moved their offices out into the country or to a country town for the same reason, to save time on commuting. Among those living outside Greater London there was as much selectivity about district as inside, the rural being preferred. Over a third of all the directors lived in villages or open country, compared with about one in eight of the married men of similar age in the main sample.

The directors were asked why they had chosen that place to live. People said that they 'liked' the area, that they had relatives or friends nearby, that it was accessible from their work—whether inside or outside Greater London there was the familiar advocacy of suburbia.

> I don't like to be right out in the sticks. I want to be near enough to the country and fresh air for the children and myself but able to get into town easily as well. (Mr Kingley, Rickmansworth)

> I looked for a pleasant residential area west of my office – because my office is on the west side of London. This seemed the best residential area within easy reach of the office. I can get home in time to see the children in the evening. (Mr Cabshaw, Twickenham)

And there were the equally familiar eulogies of the county:

> I have a basic yearning for peace. It's a good foil to the pace of the working day. It's a complete contrast. (Mr Bull, village in Hertfordshire)

> I said I'd never live in London because I value my fresh air and peace and quiet and things green about me. I abhor cities.

> I *have* to work in one – I have no choice about that. But I don't have to live in one. I occasionally spend a night at the company flat in Montague Street. I don't feel the same as when I wake up in my home in the country. I miss the sound of the birds, the smell of the fresh air. I'm not a whole man without that. (Mr Smethurst, village in Buckinghamshire)

The number of directors who had second houses was comparatively large – 35 per cent with £15,000 a year or more; 25 per cent with incomes between £10,000 and £15,000, and 19 per cent with less than £10,000. Most were in Britain but others abroad, in places like Majorca, Malta or the Canaries. One man had three 'second' homes, in Antibes, Bermuda and Jamaica, going to each of them in turn in the course of a regular business-cum-holiday trip. Quite a number had a third or fourth home in Britain, particularly if the count included ones they owned but parents, children or servants occupied. Many more of them also owned boats – six times as many as the men over forty in the managerial class in the main sample. The proportion who had second 'homes' of all kinds, including large boats and caravans as well as houses, was nearly twice as high amongst those directors living in Greater London as amongst those outside. Most of the people who did not have them were deterred not so much by the cost as by the journey. 'We've got a pool and tennis court at home. There's so much traffic at weekends it's better not to go away.'

The directors possessed more property than other people, not just in homes but generally. The ownership of pets in particular was rather equally distributed as Table 50 shows, except for the most expensive to maintain – dogs. They sometimes had dogs because their homes were so remote, and the directors themselves so often away. 'The place is rather isolated,' said Mr Drew, 'and it's not very nice for my wife to be there on her own, particularly when I'm away for the night. She explained to me when she got the collie that it was a substitute for me.'

So much by way of preliminary. The people were rich, and had the sort of property that went with (and was) wealth. They were therefore the kind of people we were hoping for. Having established that, we can now return to some of the main questions the book has been about – the amount of time given to work, the style of leisure, and the interactions of each with the family.

TABLE 50 *Ownership of pets by managing directors*

		Main sample: married men aged 40 or over and working full-time	
	Managing directors	*Professional and managerial*	*Other classes*
Tropical fish	1%	1%	5%
Goldfish	9%	5%	10%
Cats	27%	25%	19%
Dogs	50%	23%	25%
Guinea pigs	2%	4%	2%
Rabbits	4%	2%	3%
Tortoises	2%	3%	3%
Other	22%	11%	25%
None	28%	45%	42%
Total number	184	103	264

Totals add to more than 100 per cent because some had more than one kind.

Working hours

There have been several previous accounts of managers and some specifically of directors. There was considerable accord about managers' hours. Burns'[1] people worked an average of 41½ hours; Horne and Lupton's[2] 44 hours; the managers reported on by Rosemary Stewart 42¼.[3] The conclusion from Burns and from Horne and Lupton was that the more senior the manager, the longer the hours he worked. The latter said that the average working week was higher by an hour or two for each level that a person came nearer to the chief executive. It should follow that chief executives would work longer, and as much seemed to be the outcome of the only two previous British studies that we know about. Merrett looked at fifty-one directors who were either on the boards of quoted companies or members of the

[1] T. Burns, 'Management in action', p. 48.
[2] J. H. Horne and T. Lupton, 'The work activities of "middle" managers', p. 30.
[3] R. Stewart, op. cit., p. 29.

Institute of Directors. The salaried and professional ones amongst them worked fifty-three hours per week.[1] Copeman found heads of departments working 41¼ hours and managing directors 49½.[2]

TABLE 51 *Average weekly working hours of managing directors*

		Main sample: married men aged 40 or over and working full-time	
	Managing directors	*Professional and managerial*	*Other classes*
Total hours at work in week	44·3	48·4	44·9
Hours worked at home	3·7	2·3	0·7
Hours on second job	*Not asked*	0·3	0·2
Hours spent on journey to and from work	6·5	6·1	4·8
Total hours working and travelling to and from work	54·5	57·1	50·6
Number of people	184	103	264

As for our own investigation, the hours are compared in Table 51. The average for the managing directors was 48 hours, excluding the hours spent travelling. The table repeats the procedure followed in Chapter V. To the hours at work and at home were added those spent travelling to and from work and, for men in the main sample, those devoted to second jobs. Managing directors were not asked separately about this subject. If they had more than one, as did some with several directorships, all were counted as a single occupation. The table shows that in total the

[1] A. J. Merrett, 'How well off are directors?', p. 4.
[2] G. Copeman *et al.*, *How the Executive Spends His Time*, p. 7.

managing directors worked on average more hours than most men in the main sample but, if anything, to set against the previous studies on this, less than the managers. There was a good deal of variation around the averages. At one extreme, a relatively large minority of the older men worked a fairly short week; a quarter of all the directors did less than 40 hours in total (that is including travel and work at home). At the other extreme, over a quarter put in 60 hours or more, a similar proportion to that among the managers in the main sample.

This was not the end of the story. In general, the directors found it more difficult to distinguish work from leisure and, where they could, were more often working in time they did not count as work. There was also the time spent away from home on business to take into account. We asked the managing directors about trips in the last year. Eighty-one per cent of them had been away inside Britain, three out of every five of these for ten nights or more. Several, employed by multi-national companies requiring many trips to meetings in New York or Bonn or Rome, or by companies with large export interests, had been overseas for more than a hundred nights in the year. Travelling was not something that many of them appreciated. It was like being surfeited, month after month, on champagne.

> I think travelling is hell. Some people who travel for their firms get there and go straight to the beach. We arrive at 8 o'clock and spend all day looking round at the crops and talking to the people and then taste 100 samples in the evening. It's only six minutes from my home to White Walton airport where we keep the company plane so it takes only one hour and a half to get to Cognac.

> I get tired easily. I find that the time travelling really knocks me for six. When I last went to Japan I left London on Saturday, arrived Tokyo on Sunday morning, went to the office Monday morning, worked right through to Saturday afternoon when I caught the plane for London, arriving in London on the Sunday, and was in the office here again on Monday morning.

> Going by air against the sun is what makes one tired. Overseas work is exacting as much for the social side as anything else.

Some had to travel abroad not just for their companies but for international organizations they were members of. Mr Joliot was, for instance, president of an international trade association and of its European affiliate, and each of them had several international meetings every year. If being away from home like this were taken into account, together with business receptions and dinners and quasi-business evening meetings, the effect would have been to raise quite sharply the hours of many of them.

Did they think their hours were too long? A minority did not. They considered they were now too short, sometimes as a result of a merger. Mr Banham was regretful about it, saying that if only the interviewer had come two years previously what a story there would have been to tell, of the really long hours he used to work. The majority, in so far as they expressed any views, went the other way, saying how much they were looking forward to 'letting up and having a lot more leisure' or retiring 'to live in Majorca. I'd like to start a minor activity there giving me some remuneration for the amount of work I put in and eventually die a natural death.'

We asked the directors the same questions as the others about their preference for more pay or more time off, if they had the choice. A lot said the question had not much point. More pay was hardly worthwhile because they were already paying penal rates of tax on their marginal incomes. More time off was something they could have if they wished, being their own masters. Of the majority who thought the question could be answered, most favoured more time off.

> Well I certainly don't want any more pay. I've never worried about pay and I don't particularly need any more money now. I suppose the answer must be 'more time off'. I'm trying to cut down the amount of time I spend working. I'd like to spend more time on other things.

What other things? Thirty-nine would have liked to spend more time on sport and physical recreation. 'I'd want to do leisure things well if I had the time. But I would not want to queue up for hours to go sailing. The pleasure is all taken away if someone else is doing it at the same time. If I had more time off I would go sailing when other people aren't.' Twenty-eight said they would like just to be more in the country. 'I'd like to spend more time at my house in Suffolk. Three or four days there every week would make a long weekend.' Twenty-six would have liked to do more things with their families. 'I would spend it at home with my children, in the garden and riding horses.'

Whatever their attitude to the prospect of more leisure in the future, the great majority did not get their main present satisfaction out of it on its own, as Table 52 shows. 'I get no satisfaction from my leisure. I have got a happy family life, and I love my family. But I don't get any real sense of satisfaction out of anything in my life except my work.' They were almost never bored by it, although they were bored quite frequently at home. They felt pressed by work as often as other people of their age. But they did not find it as tiring either physically or mentally;[1] as several of them said, they had other people around them to whom they could delegate if they chose.

> I am under pressure but I am organized in such a way that I don't feel pressurised. This is because I have a very good secretary and first-class talent around me.

Conflicts with home

If work was so central, it was likely to come as much into conflict with the interests of family and home as for some of the men described in Chapters V and VI. Many of the directors were as explicit as the one quoted earlier about work taking precedence. 'In this job,' said the managing director of a large advertising agency, 'the work always comes first. The family has to wait.' 'The business takes priority,' as another man put it; or another – 'Whatever the business needs of me, I give'; or another – 'I let my wife know when I am going to be at home rather than the other way round'; or another – 'Ninety per cent of my time at home is

[1] Much of their work, like that of most managers, especially where their company was changing fast, was spent in talking face-to-face or on the telephone. A previous enquiry showed that 40 per cent of a sample of 2,400 members of the Institute spent up to one-fifth of their time on the 'phone (Institute of Directors, 'The Director observed', p. 86). One of our directors said: 'In general people who succeed in business are the people who like talking to others. My philosophy is this. Everybody is a little world of their own. They are all unique and if a little bit of them rubs off on you, you become a richer person for it. Everybody I know who has been successful in business has got something of that same attitude. I don't believe you can succeed in business without talking a lot.'

TABLE 52 *Satisfaction in work and leisure of managing directors*

		Main sample: married men aged 40 or over and working full-time	
Proportion saying that they got most satisfaction in:	*Managing directors*	*Professional and managerial*	*Other classes*
Work	47%	28%	14%
Work and leisure in combination	43%	42%	38%
Leisure	10%	30%	48%
Total %	100%	100%	100%
Number	178	100	264

wasted on non-productive activity', and he did not want to waste as much as that. Another was in no doubt which member of the triangle had to give way. 'They say that men in my position keep a mistress and a wife. It's true in the sense that the business is a mistress, and it can be a very demanding one.'

Such men, while admitting the difficulties, argued that they were unavoidable. 'If you want to get somewhere in this world you must let your job intrude a little.' 'It's unavoidable if you're in the rat-race. Once you're in it you're on a treadmill.' They often explained that the wife accepted her lot (as some now old-fashioned working-class men used to explain that their wives did not *want* to know how much they earned) as the price of the family's standard of living or the husband's own happiness or both.

> If I had to choose between clinching a deal and my son's speech day, I'd choose business. We wouldn't live the way we do if I didn't work like I do. My wife understands that.

> The work demands deprive my wife and family of something that is immeasurable. The family has material advantages that they otherwise wouldn't have but it's a poor substitute. But they realise that I *must* be active.

> We have organised round the necessity of my job. There was a point in our married life when my wife felt that the demands of my job tended to conflict with married life. We managed to sort that out. My wife realised that I couldn't be complete without being absorbed in my work and that there would be even greater conflict were this not so.

The conflict was evident enough. Table 53 shows that it was more common among the managing directors than among the (in general, less senior) managers in the main sample. Incidentally, a common initial answer to the question about whether they thought there was interference was 'my wife does', often delivered with a not very amused-looking smile.

TABLE 53 *Interference of work with home and family for managing directors*

		Main sample: married men aged 40 or over and working full-time	
	Managing directors	*Professional and managerial*	*Other classes*
Proportion saying that work interfered with home and family	65%	51%	24%
Total number	184	101	264

The more senior among them – those in the biggest concerns, who were also the highest paid and the hardest worked – seemed to have more problems of this sort, and the men in family businesses less. Of the 184 married directors, 33 were the heads of family concerns. Mr Stone, whose real name is that of a famous menswear firm, took over the business from his father. Mr Jackson was running the furniture firm founded by *his* grandfather, and Mr Wimbolt his father's football pool business. Among such men, 35 per cent reported work/home interference; among the remaining 151, 74 per cent. It did not seem as if this was explained by the scale of family concerns, since they included large companies as well as small. Perhaps competition at the top was less and perhaps also the knowledge that the business was in a sense theirs made wives and children more sympathetic. The family was more involved in it. There was less conflict between the two because they were one.

Among the managing directors who did report difficulties, they were much the same in character as those of executives and professionals in the main sample. The pressure was of sheer time. 'I get a series of evening dinners,' said Mr Barclay, 'that keep me out till 10, 11 and 12 at night.' 'I'm away 11 to 12 hours every day,' said Mr Tucker. 'On top of that there's foreign travel. I was away 50 days last year.'

Holidays were (as we have seen with others) liable to be interrupted or cancelled when some crisis unexpectedly flared up.

> We are restricted at times in what we want to do as a family. Often holidays are interrupted by telephone calls. However, I prefer this as it keeps me in touch. I'd rather know what's going on.

> Until last October, I can think of no occasion when arrangements made by my wife did not have to be altered, even going away on holiday.

Inevitably, the daily round was also disrupted.

> I never know where I am going to be on any given evening in a week so we can never go anywhere socially during the week. Mid-week engagements would interfere with my work next day and if I were late I wouldn't be 'with it'. During the week you are a lodger in the house. The kids are in bed at night when you get home and wives feel neglected.

> I don't get home early enough to see my daughter before she goes to bed, so I only see her at weekends.

> One can't see a growing family if one is away from home as much as I am, or coming home late. I don't moan about it. It's the pattern of our family life.

> I have so many business engagements – cocktail parties,

dinners and suchlike. My wife is too much on her own. She said only the other day, 'When are we going to get an evening off together?'

When they were at home they might only be rather nominally so. Some were tired – 'My wife wants to see more of me and to see me less tired in the evenings.' Some explained that they were 'unable to concentrate on the family'. 'There's a mental strain, a pressure on the top man,' said Mr Tucker, 'which I always carry with me.' 'I'm too absorbed,' said Mr Thurston. 'When I am at home the business is still on my mind. I sit and think about it when I should be listening to my family's problems. It must be very irritating for my family.' 'What I feel,' said Mr Dublin, 'is if you are a businessman – by which I mean a successful businessman – all your time is spent on business. In a way you're thinking about business *all* the time; you're never really divorced from it. If I'm at home at the weekend sitting in the garden I'm turning over various new ideas. My business is my life.'

A means of reducing the difficulties was to bring the family into the work even where it was not a family business. One man took his wife to business dinners with him wherever possible. A director who had to spend long periods abroad said, 'My wife sometimes travels with me', though another had found that this did not work – 'It wasn't much fun for her sightseeing on her own while I worked.' Another alternative was to insist on a separation of spheres, particularly at weekends.

> I'm a very happy man. I divorce my working life completely from my domestic life. If I ever have any extra work to do I do it here in the office before I go home. I close my mind to business when I get home. I don't entertain people at home in connection with work. I think that's the right attitude. The man who lives to work is a fool. You should work to live.

Part played by leisure

The conclusion is plain enough so far – that by and large the directors were if anything even more absorbed in their work than other men in senior positions, and therefore had less of their energies left over for their families. But did they make up for the concentration on work by taking up the sort of leisure that could be shared? It is not too easy to interpret such evidence as we had about this, as we said in the previous chapter when we were discussing the same point. Directors had been out more often with their wives in the evenings, but when it was for a 'business dinner' should that be counted as work, leisure or neither? Otherwise, wives were no more in evidence than those of managers generally.

This was, perhaps, partly because the most striking difference between directors and other higher-class people (apart from the even larger numbers of unpaid 'directorships' that they held in a wide range of voluntary organizations) was that they were keener on sports, both as active participants and as spectators. Some of the main contrasts are set out in Table 54. Many directors made almost a cult of exercise, perhaps in part because of the advice given by the Medical Director of their own Institute and by other doctors – 'It is now generally agreed that reasonable physical fitness plays a major role in diminishing the chance of a coronary . . . Additionally, active people tend to be thinner, feel better, and because of this work more effectively.'[1] 'Neglecting wife and family' was almost as bad for the prognosis as neglecting exercise or not neglecting cigarettes, so it was not all that simple for the harassed director to know what to do unless he could persuade his wife, or his children if they were still at home, to come with him to the Solent for sailing, Norfolk for shooting, the Tay or the Itchen for fishing, Knutsford for dog-training, or the Dukeries for hunting.

> People don't realise what a family activity hunting is. It's absolutely marvellous for the whole family to go together. You pit your wits against the fox and there's nothing else to help, except the hounds. People just don't understand what a good family sport it is.

It was not always like that. Many of these men tried to improve their skills in play as they did in work, using and disciplining the energy, which we have already mentioned as one of their main characteristics, in the one sphere as they did in the other. They worked hard and played hard, and, if their wives were not equally determined, they would not be able to keep up.

[1] H. B. Wright and G. Pincherle, 'Profile of the coronary man', p. 334.

TABLE 54 *Activity in sports by managing directors*

Proportion doing each sport 12 times or more in previous year	*Managing directors*	*Main sample: married men aged 40 or over and working full-time*	
		Professional and managerial	*Other classes*
Swimming	59%	30%	17%
Golf	33%	12%	5%
Sailing	20%	5%	0%
Tennis	20%	5%	2%
Table tennis	15%	10%	4%
Fishing (all kinds)	14%	9%	6%
Fencing, archery or shooting	10%	0%	0%
Cricket	3%	5%	2%
Badminton or squash	3%	3%	2%
Boating	1%	1%	0%
Water ski-ing	1%	0%	0%
Ten-pin bowling	1%	0%	0%
Bowls	1%	2%	3%
Total number	184	103	264
Average number of active sports done 12 times or more in previous year	1·9	0·9	0·6

The sports listed are those done by 1 per cent or more of managing directors.

If it's golf, I've got to learn it and do it as well as I can. It's the same with sailing, or piloting my aeroplane. There's satisfaction in it because of the concentration. I want to do things on my own, by myself, just because in my work I'm so dependent on a team. That's partly why I like flying in bad weather. It's more of a challenge. It's more difficult to arrive at the right place at the right time, and, if you do, it's more of an achievement.

We did not ask him whether his wife also enjoyed flying in bad weather. Another director had a photograph of his wife on his office desk but the walls were lined with large pictures of trophies to success, all the boats he had owned during his life, all with girl's names, all scudding the waves of the world, from the 14-foot dinghy he had when he started at the bottom of the business, working his way up as he got richer through a 10-ton cruising yacht and, eventually, to his present Olympic standard 8-metre.

A different partnership

Such being the circumstances, the wife's chief role was to look after the home and the children, and to do so more single-handedly because her partner was less engaged in that side of his life than in the challenge and excitement of the other. 'I'm not at home enough and also I haven't enough time to think about domestic things so that this throws a lot of extra burden on my wife.' She had, it is true, a good deal of other help to make up for the lack of his – a 'domestic', a gardener, a chauffeur. Eighty-eight per cent of the wives had servants, living in or out, and practically all had had some help when their children were young. In one family the *au pair* girls were not sent off until the eldest son of the family looked as though he was going to get his initiation into sex with one of them in the same way that so many 'young masters' did with the servant girls of Victorian England.[1] The wives had help, but they also had a lot of property to look after and duties to perform as hostesses.

The relationship seemed typically to be one of partnership, but of a different kind from that which we have mainly been describing.

> The whole of my career has been based on partnership rather than togetherness. The whole family is geared to this. I let my wife know where I'm going.

If the wife could accept that she was a junior partner, all could be

[1] Though it looks as though Victorian parents may have been in this respect more 'permissive': 'Adolescent boys might be tempted (even tacitly encouraged) into their first amorous adventure by the presence of an attractive housemaid. J. F. C. Harrison, *The Early Victorians 1832–1851*, p. 110.

TABLE 55 *Working wives of managing directors*

		Main sample: married men aged 40 or over and working full-time	
	Managing directors	*Professional and managerial*	*Other classes*
Wife working full-time	2%	25%	24%
Wife working part-time	8%	24%	32%
Wife not in paid work	90%	51%	44%
Total %	100%	100%	100%
Number	180	102	263

well. One director congratulated himself on having an 'understanding and tolerant wife' who had enabled him to give time to his priority, and also someone with great ability with whom he could discuss his business problems in confidence. 'I think I have been very fortunate with my wife.' Another said that he wanted a wife who would stay at home and be calm and passive – a foil to himself; and yet another that you had to have a woman who could cope with her business as the man coped with his. If he made a mistake they would have to go through the divorce courts.[1] Coping, for Mr White, meant that she needed always to be ready to come with him whenever the business demanded.

> She accepts it. She says that she is not a 'golf widow', she's a 'machine tool widow'. But I try to meet that problem. When people ask me out for business dinners, I say 'I'll only come if my wife comes along.' If I go out with customers she must come along with me. When I go abroad, I do endeavour to take her with me. She came to Munich with me recently and

[1] In another survey among directors, 48 per cent said that 'the wife of a busy, successful businessman gets a raw deal'. Institute of Directors, 'The director observed away from the desk', p. 272.

to Milan. I think it's useful when you go abroad to have your wife with you. If the man wants you to go out to dinner with him and you haven't got your wife, he has to leave his wife out. If your wife is there, his wife can come along too. Often wives get to know each other and it's very good for them *and* for business. The one condition in all this is that my wife has got to be prepared to drop everything and come out if I ask her. I'll ring her up and say 'Do you want to come to dinner this evening? Yes or No?' She knows that she's got to make up her mind. She can't mess about. But she accepts that. She's ready to come out at an hour's notice.

A woman could not easily be a companion wherever she was needed if she also had a paid job. The comparison with other people is shown in Table 55. Only 10 per cent of the directors' wives worked in a paid job outside the home compared with about half the wives of other men. They did not need to work, of course, on financial grounds. They also sometimes had husbands who recalled the heads of middle-class Victorian families who thought that *their* wives' place was by the fireside.

The main conclusion of the chapter is that these people were like others in the top classes who have appeared before in the book, only more so. They had more money; they were more absorbed in their work, and in their leisure. They were less home-centred and their marriages seemed to be less symmetrical. They were in some ways like Stage 2 husbands, but at the opposite end of the social scale. If more people have more interesting jobs in the future they will in one way at least become more like the directors. As an extreme case they tended to support the sort of conclusion we have been building up to in previous chapters. We do not on their account have to revise the kind of guesses about the future which are in line with the Principle.

But though we think that other people may well move in the same direction we do not expect them to go so far. This is partly because these men were unusual in their wealth which made them more disposed to be conservative, and Conservative. They were also unusual in their power. However much they delegated, they were the pivots upon which their companies revolved. They were the main decision-makers and co-ordinators. It was therefore not surprising that their families often had to take second place. But the ratio of those with power of this kind will probably not grow in the future; it could even fall if the domination of big organizations in many spheres of life continues to grow.

The directors themselves warned us not to generalize from them when they spoke of the differences that they noticed between themselves and the junior executives in their companies. The common view was that the youngsters were not so committed to one employer as they had been at the same age, the fault being their education, which had given them a sense of belonging to a profession rather than to a particular company. They were more independent-minded. They did not think they were bound to the man who paid their salaries, since they might soon be on their way, stepping delicately upwards from one company to another.

Some of the directors thought that the wives of the young executives were different too. 'Wives have much more influence on their husband's business lives.' 'They marry young and put down roots too early. They don't seem to have the same sense of loyalty to the firm.'[1] It was said that the husbands were more apt to see the dark side of the high life, like a young man in the main sample who said he had recently been to a director's dinner.

> I sat next to the wife of one of our directors. She started talking about her husband's job. She said 'He spends so little time at home, so little time with his family. Never set your sights up there, because if you do your family life will suffer. You might as well not really have a family at all.' I thought to myself 'She's a perfectly ordinary women, and she can't have much of a life. She can't really be happy.' So if you do become too ambitious and climb up too high, you're likely to start to endanger other parts of your life which are important to you. Well, they're important to me anyway.

Mr Cabshaw, one of the directors, made another point: that the wives – the 'modern woman' – would not be content to stay at home, as directors' wives had done in his generation. For his own wife,

> The family's always come first and we've been a very happy

[1] The general view presented in these paragraphs is in line with that of J. M. and R. E. Pahl, *Managers and their Wives*.

family because of it. Of course that doesn't satisfy the modern woman. The modern woman wants to have a job as well as be at home.

The point is worth heeding. The directors' wives had paid jobs less often than others. This is not in contradiction to anything we said in Chapter IV. These wives were not notable for their superior education and the feminist aspirations that go with it. They belonged to a minority who were prepared to settle for a different sort of compromise in an asymmetrical family, married to a dominant man with whose successes they could to some extent identify, very well-off in material terms, home-centred because their husbands were so much the opposite. We do not expect their number will increase. Nor will people like their husbands if one thinks of them only in terms of power. But if one thinks of the men as being extreme less for that and more for the interest that their jobs had for them then there will probably be increasing proportions like them in the future. The implications of that are among the issues we have to try to unravel in our final chapter.

X

TOWARDS THE FUTURE

We cannot say that we are now going to abandon fact for opinion, or the certainties of the past, even of the present, for the uncertainties of the future. There has already been too much speculation for that in the way we have assessed the interaction between past and present. We can only say that we shall in this chapter be still more speculative about the society to which London is a pointer.

But first we must sum up on what has, according to our account, already happened. We have in several places suggested that the Stage 1 family has in some respects reappeared in Stage 3, as though the column which we pictured in the first chapter has been marching in a circle rather than a straight line, with the orders to wheel being given by technology. The old productive family could not compete indefinitely against it and had to yield after a struggle even more bitter in England than in other industrializing countries, from the USA to the USSR, from Germany to Japan, where the same battle was joined at later periods.[1] But at Stage 3 technology has ceased to be the destroyer. It has harnessed inanimate energy from the fossil fuels and put it to work in machines for productive purposes. Human energy has been saved for other ends. After a rise in the early industrial period the hours of work fell to the sort of level they had been at before, and then still further. Husbands and wives therefore did not need to devote so much of their energy to the fatigues of subsistence and have been able to devote more (and more time) to domestic leisure and to domestic work once again shared between each other.

Technology has harnessed the same energy to miniature machines which people control instead of being controlled by,

[1] Some of the similarities in what has happened to the family in different countries are noted in W. J. Goode, *World Revolution and Family Patterns*.

and so has made their homes more satisfying to be in. The domestication of invention has been a long drawn-out process. The technological thrust can be said to have begun in the seventeenth century with the new craft of printing. This made possible individual study of the scriptures at home[1] (and hence the rise of Protestantism) and continued with the individually owned clocks which made people independent of the church bell, the factory whistle and the knocker-up. As we saw in Chapter II, by applying the same energy to the engines of transport, technology has in this century allowed more people to have decent homes within the ever-expanding city region without depriving themselves of access to jobs and amenities.

Husbands are more at work inside the home; wives more outside. Technology in office as well as factory – the typewriter and the telephone have been amongst the small machines which have transformed the office as much as the home – has produced a range of semi-skilled jobs which have been filled by women. There is no symmetry as yet in the opportunities opened for women as against men, only a growth of jobs for them which, though badly paid and monotonous, have at least been adapted to their needs in another way. The approximation to full employment for most of the time since the war has allowed millions of wives to have part-time jobs. Like those they had when the family was the productive unit, these are more compatible with child rearing than full-time.

The two stages are also alike in one vital demographic respect. Before the onset of industrialization population was kept comparatively stable and sustained growth prevented by a combination of the positive check of mortality and the main preventive check of postponing marriage. People did not marry until they could support a household. 'Europeans married late because in western Europe responsibility for the care of the children rested on the husband and wife – as opposed to some wider family group – and marriage was therefore tied to the setting up of a separate household.'[2] The responsibility was joint. After stability was upset by the reduction of mortality, the massive population growth from 1750 on may have continued so long partly because in Stage 2 the tie between husband and wife was weakened. When

[1] C. Hill, *Reformation to Industrial Revolution*, p. 25.

[2] H. J. Habakkuk, *Population Growth and Economic Development since 1750*, p. 11.

Bosanquet could say, as she did in her account of London families in 1899, that 'as the children grow older the chances are that the burden of maintaining the family falls entirely upon the mother',[1] the father had little interest in family limitation. A rough equilibrium was restored only when something more like a joint responsibility was once again exercised for the control of births within or before marriage. The new situation is one in which marriage is more popular than ever. The reduction in the marriage age and the decline in the number of single people at later ages means that proportionately more people than ever before have conjugal families to be attached to. The tracing out of the interaction between fertility and family structure will have to wait until the history of the latter is tackled in depth. But it is at least clear that in its relative stability of population Stage 3 is like Stage 1. A swing to higher growth again in Stage 4 is still a possibility, though a dreadful one.

One sort of symmetry, with wives earning as well as husbands, has been common to the two stages. But there are other sorts which are new, and taken together important enough to justify the adjective to which we have given pride of place. They stem not just from technology but also from the second great agent of change, which we have identified as feminism. At Stage 1 the man was the unchallenged authority; at Stage 3 not. The way the income of the couple was spent and the household run was at Stage 1 no doubt decided by the couple jointly, up to a point. But the supreme power was always his. So when we talk of a re-appearance we obviously do not mean that the organization or functions of the family are just the same but rather that the family in its new form has a place in the structure of society hardly less important than it had before industrialization. Without the symmetry – without, that is, some of the differences between the one and the other stage – the new family would not have brought ever higher proportions of people within its fold and achieved its pivotal role.

We are talking only of trends. Even in all its different versions the Stage 3 family is not now *the* family, universal as well as paramount. At any moment the column is composed of people who are at several different stages of historical development in the way they earn their living, in what they do with what they earn, in

[1] H. Bosanquet, *Rich and Poor*, p. 106.

their beliefs about themselves and their relation to society and the universe, and, on our main subject, in the patterns of their family life. As history unfolds, it does not completely obliterate any stage so much as alter the proportions contained within each. The contingent in the column at Stage 1 has been falling away for two centuries, but there are still a few families in the London Region who would qualify fairly well. Although the proportion at Stage 2 has also been dropping for a century there are still plenty of families today in which Engels and Mayhew would, were they restored to life, notice the resemblances. The changes we have spoken about are, therefore, still in train. They have not worked their way through to extinction. Fertility is not yet as low in the bottom class, nor the sharing of domestic and financial responsibilities so common. There are also many people without the two properties – a decent home and a car – which are the outward marks of the modern family. In relative terms the home-less and the car-less are all the more left out because the majority have them. But the mass at Stage 3 has been increasing steadily. It is proportions we are talking about, even though we could not, without another survey devoted to that purpose and no other, attempt to count the numbers in each category even for some future-present, let alone for the once-present of 1970.

When we argue that the Stage 3 family is more like Stage 1 than Stage 2, are we taking a cyclical view? If it implies that history *must* repeat itself in a spiral, in response to some mysterious forces which are almost beyond explanation, then emphatically not. There is no imperative of destiny which requires events to move in any such way. The forces we have picked out as the chief promoters of change have not been on the scene before. They are new, but the new has in some ways strengthened the old.

If we say this we cannot also wholly accept what has become a common sociological scheme. The historical drift has been regarded as from traditional to modern societies, though the characteristics of each have been distinguished in different ways by different writers. Tönnies's emphasis was on the shift from the informal family and community to formal association;[1] Durk-

[1] F. Tönnies, *Community and Association*.

heim's on that from 'mechanical' to 'organic' solidarity;[1] Weber's on that from the traditional, the magical and the religious to rational and deliberate calculation;[2] and Parson's on the changes summed up in his pattern variables (or binaries as we called such oppositions when discussing the meaning of work and leisure), from 'particularistic' to 'universalistic', from 'diffuseness' to 'specificity', 'affectivity' to 'affective-neutrality', 'ascription' to 'achievement', 'collectivity-orientation' to 'self-orientation'.[3] Though the emphasis varied, one recurring element in each approach was that the family was seen as an almost all-embracing multi-purpose institution in traditional societies standing for the informal, the mechanical and the rest as against their opposites embodied in the more specialized institutions which have been thrown up by and since the Industrial Revolution. If the contrast is the one we made in Chapter III, between the pre-industrial and the industrial, the family as the generalist has clearly lost to the specialist. But we have been saying that it has not surrendered all its economic functions to industry and commerce, all its educational to the school, all its recreational to the entertainment industries, or even all its religious to the Church or to limbo.[4] In some particulars it may not have lost anything. As far as religion goes the family itself may have become more than any other social institution an object of devotion, the beneficiary of a kind of western Confucianism which reveres the descendants more than the ancestors, but like Confucianism also manages without a god, let alone a purely male god. The smaller has become more sacred, the larger less. If once it was the transfer of obligations from family to wider community that was stressed, more recently the trend has been in the opposite direction. To say this is not to assert that the family has at any later time been *the* institution it was or, if the new family is worshipped, to ignore the heretics.

Yet we are not, like the hymn book, contrasting only the pair of ancient and modern. We have, as we have said often before, chosen to be a little more differentiated about the 'modern', dividing it up into two fairly distinct phases. As we see it, the

[1] E. Durkheim, *The Division of Labour in Society*.

[2] M. Weber, *The Theory of Social and Economic Organisation*.

[3] T. Parsons, *The Social System*, pp. 58–67.

[4] An extreme statement of this general view about the losses of the family was contained in W. F. Ogburn and M. F. Nimkoff, *Technology and the Changing Family*, chap. 6.

same sociological scheme which focused on the decline in the importance of the family from Stage 1 on can also help to explain why there has been a revival as Stage 2 has been succeeded by Stage 3.

If, for example, we return to Parsons's terms we can see that a person has a particularistic relationship with another member of his family which is different from that with anyone else. It is unique, not universalistic in the way a doctor's is with anyone who needs him or a manufacturer's with anyone who has the money to buy what he has to sell. A person has very diffuse obligations to other members of his family – 'For better, for worse; For richer, for poorer; In sickness and in health'. To others he has more specific obligations of a contractual or semi-contractual sort. If people are engaged by an employer they have no more than a specific commitment to work for him in return for a wage; they do not feel bound to wheel him about in a bath-chair if he becomes arthritic. A person in an affective relationship to his family is permitted, even encouraged, to express feelings; in many other roles in the modern sector of society he is required to hold them in check. A person has a role ascribed to him by reason of his birth into a particular family, and almost unlimited obligations towards him are accepted as soon as that happens, not arising from his achievements, which in endless competition with others depend upon his talents, his industry or his luck, but from his being of the same 'flesh' and 'blood'. A spouse is chosen in a way that children or parents are not but, once chosen, the roles and the consequent obligations are much the same as if they had been ascribed. A child is not discarded because he stutters or has mouse-coloured hair or cannot pass any exams; a parent because he has committed a crime; a spouse because he or she has failed to get promotion. Finally, though self-orientation may in general be more dominant than collectivity-orientation, the smallest collectively is an outstanding exception. We would ourselves add to Parsons's list a further contrast to do with the duration of ties as seen by an individual passing through society – that between the more and the less transitory. People usually remain family members for a longer time than they are attached to any other institution, and develop stronger loyalties as a result.

The point is that these strengths of the family on one side of the balance sheet (even if on their own they would never have created the new industrial order) are no less strengths in a modern society. They account for the resistance of the family in England and most other countries to the Industrial Revolution, which would not have come about, at any rate not with so much brutality, if there had been a democracy then with universal suffrage including women. They also account for the family's revival. Its advantages offset some of the disadvantages of the sort of society that technology has created. People who are not much valued by their employers, and are paid a wage that shows it, can still be valued at home, their bad and good qualities combining to make up a whole personality, in the round: not a machinist or a park-keeper, a solicitor or a sociologist, but a person. Whether or not leisure activities are a compensation to people who do not fulfil themselves in their work, the family certainly is. As a multi-purpose institution (although not to anything like the same extent the all-purpose one of Stage 1) it can provide some sense of wholeness and permanence to set against the more restricted and transitory roles imposed by the specialized institutions which have flourished outside the home. The upshot is that, as the disadvantages of the new industrial and impersonal society have become more pronounced, so has the family become more prized for its power to counteract them.

In its capacity as consumer the family has also made a crucial alliance with technology. If it had not, the fears of most about the new system expressed at the time it was launching its assault on the family of production might have been realized before now. There was then a lively debate about what was going to keep men at work if their 'needs' could be satisfied with less exertion:[1]

> the main part of the question respecting the wants of mankind relates to their power of calling forth the exertions necessary to acquire the means of expenditure. It is unquestionably true that wealth produces wants, but it is a still more important truth that wants produce wealth. Each cause acts and reacts upon the other, but the order both of precedence and of importance is with the wants which stimulate to industry.

An expedient often proposed, and acted upon, was to keep people so poor that they would be driven to work by the constantly

[1] T. R. Malthus, *Principles of Political Economy*, 2nd ed., pp. 469–70.

renewed fear of hunger. The prices and incomes policy was a primitive one. Young said in 1771 that 'The master manufacturers of Manchester wish that prices might always be high enough to enforce a general industry'.[1] Only if prices could be kept high or wages low would people be restrained from taking off St Monday and St Tuesday in every week in which they had obtained enough money to satisfy the simple and relatively unchanging needs they had inherited from their rural ancestors. The traditional aspirations of a traditional society did not at once yield to the new discontents required for the economy to expand – one reason for the preference, compared to most of this century, for leisure rather than income.

Part of the incentive to effort was supplied by consumer goods when industry began to produce these in larger quantities. But on their own these would not have been enough without the new sort of family. A market of husbands would not have been large enough to absorb them. Husbands and others are no less self-interested than they were, but in the new family their self-interest has been broadened (as compared with Stage 2) to include others in the image or the imagination of the self. People need something to live for beyond themselves. They are more passionate in the pursuit of any goal if to their self-interest can be allied a larger purpose. Modern society in its later manifestations has been short of larger purposes; but at least it would be a great deal more deficient were it not for the family.

No other group can now compare with it for the intensity of feeling it arouses. Its most singular characteristic (as Burke and many others have said before, and will say again) is that it combines altruism with self-interest. So, of course, do all groups but not to the same degree. The two were not so much combined for poorer families in Stage 2; but in this century, with industry needing markets for the consumer goods which it pours out, the two motives have been fused at just the right time for the one institution to feed and be fed by the other. Although each member of most of the families we have caught a glimpse of in these pages is certainly working for himself or herself, it is not for self alone. As Mr Thompson, a building labourer of Dagenham, put it 'Your family are your life, aren't they?' The smallest primary group to which he belongs has therefore acted as the foundation upon

[1] A. Young, *A Six Months Tour Through the North of England*, vol. III, p. 193.

which the vast edifice of twentieth-century industry has been raised. Marx would not accuse the working (or non-working) classes of wantlessness in an age when inflation is generated by the opposite. Individuals go on wanting more partly because there are others besides themselves to want more for. The vehemence of the wife who goes out to work 'for the sake of the kiddies' may be augmented by her ambivalence; but she is very far from being a hypocrite. Nor was a man in a newish council house in Sutton who said to us, while admiring his eight-year-old daughter, that what he most wanted was a little car (now that the bus service had become so bad) in which he could take her on Sundays to see Windsor Castle, Whipsnade and other great national spectacles.

He was underlining the reciprocity between an industrial society and the family. The more united family has provided the incentive for people to exert themselves in the new industrial system, and the new system has made the family more united by giving it some elementary rights in property (including the machines built to the scale of the smallest human group) which are held or at least enjoyed in common by its members. There is no reason to think that people are any the less eager to be their own masters than they ever were – they may, indeed, with the rise of democracy be more so. It is certainly no less attractive for a family to be its own master, and to have something to be master of, than it is for a man. Modern technological society, with all its impersonality, has therefore been underpinned by the oldest, most traditional and least impersonal institution of all. After a long period at odds with each other, the family and technology have achieved a mutual adaptation.

The new family has been built up, painfully. Is it now to be brought down, also painfully? A new Stage 4 to be gained, itself as similar to Stage 2 as Stage 3 was to Stage 1? We have left the question dangling throughout the book. To arrive at any conclusion we must bring together what we have already said about the impact upon the top social strata of the two chief forces we have picked out.

Our first expectation is that, as technology increasingly though slowly replaces the more backbreaking and less interesting jobs, the greater attachment to work of middle-class people will extend downwards. If more jobs provide some opportunity for advancement, some chance for creative expression and, above all, some measure of autonomy,[1] more of the jobs will also spill over into the home. As for working hours, we do not expect many more people than now to have to exert themselves at tasks of co-ordination and management. But we do expect that more people will be like the managing directors in another way in having so much interest in their work that they will not shy away from long hours at it.

It follows that there will be fewer people able to echo Mr Thompson and accept that the family is far and away the main sphere in which they get the chance for self-expression. The home-centred sort of Stage 3 family was predominant in 1970 because the great majority of people were manual workers or in equally routine non-manual jobs. They had no alternative object of allegiance as compelling. If that changes and the majority of people no longer have such emotionally and intellectually unrewarding work, the predominant kind of family will change also. Since the critical minority is already present, it follows that the Stage 4 family is also, on a small scale, and is likely to grow much further. More people will have two poles to their lives instead of one. More people will have to grapple with the tasks of reconciliation between the two.

We also expect that leisure will continue to mirror the influence of work. People with more varied interests on the job have more varied interests off it, and as the one changes so will the other. Upgrading of incomes should add to the effect. Better houses stimulate new interests and allow them to be expressed. Cars and money do the same, and sometimes, as on holiday, they do so for the whole family. Since its members may be most family-centred when they are not at home, the hold of the family may again be responsible for the preference shown in this century for taking more leisure in the form when it can be taken all together.

The centrifugal effect of interesting and well-paid jobs cannot

[1] The following passage from a paper on 'The Future of the Working Classes' read at a Conversazione by Alfred Marshall a century ago can be taken either as another warning against the folly of making this, or any, sort of forecast or (if Marshall's time-table is extended forwards a good way beyond our time) as eminent support for it. 'The question is not whether all men will ultimately be equal – that they will certainly not – but whether progress may not go on steadily, if slowly, till, by occupation at least, every man is a gentleman. I hold that it may, that it will.' Quoted in T. H. Marshall, 'Citizenship and Social Class', p. 69.

easily be avoided. A family confined by its lack of resources to the home is bound to make shift together just as the Stage 1 family had to in order to break out a living from the soil. A family in the first phases of child-rearing is also pegged down by the immobility of infants and their persistent demands for affection and care. But if these two restraints are lifted, the different interests of different people are almost bound to assert themselves and the wife be off to pottery or (as ever) her mother's, the husband to his sailing or golf, the children to pop sessions or dances, and all to their own friends. Chapter VIII recorded how many of the wives' friends were women and the husbands' men. The central point is that the greater the range of interests of each member of the family the more are they liable to be drawn apart, inside but especially outside the home. Also, the more professional they are about their leisure, the more taken up by it are they bound to be, making for a double absorption, in work and in leisure, which can exclude other members of their families. The managing directors with their almost Grecian proclivity for sports could well be a portent.

Chapter VII was another illustration of the power of technology. In 1970 nearly one out of every five husbands in the Region was a shiftworker and by the end of the century the proportion will be higher than that. The more machinery industry has, the more profitable to work it as near to round-the-clock as possible, and in the growing service sector also shiftwork is likely to increase. Fathers are forced to work when other members of their family are at leisure and to take their leisure when other members are at work. The life of the family can hardly be enhanced, even though the motive is to enhance the means for its support. The practice appears to be spreading in a manner directly contrary to the Principle, with the people most affected up to now being manual workers, and office employees following them on behind. The pattern of diffusion may be different, but the consequence of technological change is the same as that for middle-class people: the family's joint life is challenged.

Technology has affected women as much (or almost as much) as it has men. Most working women have belonged to a special kind of proletariat. They have had to do some of the jobs which have been least rewarding in both main senses of the word. Many of them, being 'appendages of the machine', as Marx put it, have also been most alienated from their work in factories, offices and shops. This has been regarded as a blessing rather than a curse by employers who have found that women, with their thoughts elsewhere, can be put on to jobs so monotonous that few men would stand them. The same alienation from work has also been welcomed by those who think that woman's place is in the home, spiritually if not physically. More alienation from work has meant less alienation from home. Technology has arranged a match between the two spheres. But, as we said earlier, the situation is changing. Machines are taking over more of the sort of jobs which unskilled women have done, and women's aspirations for satisfaction in their work are rising, even if they are lagging behind men's. The jobs they will be able to get, and the interest that these evoke, will depend upon the development path taken by technology, by the economy more generally, and by education. If there is not full employment women will be the first to suffer, as they were after 1970.[1] If the advocates of zero growth ever had their way married women would suffer, in economic terms, more than men. When what have been two-income families are reduced to one, it is rarely the husband's that is sacrificed. But if the longer-run trends which have been evident since the war both in the management of the economy and in technological growth re-assert themselves, there should be more, and more interesting, work for women to take if they wish. There will then be a gradual increase in the numbers of jobs that are worth women committing themselves to, and they too will be more drawn out of the home in consequence.

So we come to the second force, of feminism. It may serve again to highlight the importance of the new meanings being given to symmetry in this century to go back to the book we referred to in Chapter III. Mill said:[2]

> When the support of the family depends not on property, but on earnings, the common arrangement, by which the man

[1] The official level of unemployment among women nearly doubled in 1970–1, and concealed unemployment amongst women who dropped out of work without registering may have risen still more. *New Society*, 14 October 1971, quoted in M. P. Fogarty and R. and R. N. Rapoport, *Women and Top Jobs: The Next Move*, p. 70.

[2] J. S. Mill, *The Subjection of Women*, p. 75.

> earns the income and the wife superintends the domestic expenditure, seems to me in general the most suitable division of labour between the two persons. If, in addition to the physical suffering of bearing children, and the whole responsibility of their care and education in early years, the wife undertakes the careful and economical application of the husband's earnings to the general comfort of the family; she takes not only her fair share, but usually the larger share, of the bodily and mental exertion required by their joint existence. If she undertakes any additional portion, it seldom relieves her from this, but only prevents her from performing it properly. The care which she is herself disabled from taking of the children and the household, nobody else takes; those of the children who do not die grow up as they best can, and the management of the household is likely to be so bad as even in point of economy to be a great drawback from the value of the wife's earnings. In an otherwise just state of things, it is not, therefore, I think, a desirable custom that the wife should contribute by her labour to the income of the family.

This is not a predisposition which the modern proponents of Women's Liberation draw attention to in a man who is otherwise one of their few male heroes. In the sort of marriage he was praising there was symmetry between the sexes in respect, love and legal rights but not in the tasks performed within the family, let alone in the work done beyond it. The modern idea of symmetry is clearly quite different: there should be no monopolies for either sex in any sphere. Women should have as much right as men to seek, and to gain, fulfilment out of the home as in it.

We said in Chapter IV that we expected the tendency for women of the top classes to go out to work to grow more marked and spread downwards in counteraction to the opposite tendency for women in other classes to give up monotonous jobs offering few advantages other than money and companionship. We left open the question of how far this tendency was likely to go.

We can now ask – why should there be any stop to it? Of course there will be minorities, and probably an increasing number and variety of them. An important one appeared in the last chapter in the wives of the managing directors. They were like the wives of the much younger managers, described by the Pahls, who thought that[1]

> A housewife – as most of the women in our study took for granted – is expected to subordinate her own interests to the interests of her husband, children and home. Most do this gladly most of the time; but it makes the problem of taking a job more difficult, when a wife is quite unused, both to taking initiative for herself rather than adapting herself to the daily routines of others, and also to doing things solely because *she* wants to.

If the husband has a very demanding job it is hardly possible for the wife to work as well if they also have children. If he earns a great deal of money he can, like Victorian fathers, hire servants to look after the children, but even that will not release her to go out to work if he needs her to keep his house in the sort of order he likes it to be in, to act as hostess and to accompany him when others are acting hosts instead. We would be surprised if this pattern ever disappeared completely. The devotion of a husband to a career, if it goes with scant sympathy for a partner who does not have one, may drive his wife to espouse the same values as himself and follow him, out. But that is exceptional. The more usual arrangement is another sort of complementary relationship, though not a symmetrical one, and for some women it obviously offers a stable and relatively peaceful life, if not the most challenging. But just as it must be a good deal less common now than it was fifty years ago, so would we, bearing in mind the influence of education, expect it to be even less so in another fifty years, even if a few women make up for the loss of the husband-dominated family by reproducing it in reverse. Some wives may go out to a demanding job and leave the husband to look after the home. It will be up to him to try to find out from her secretary at what hour the managing director will be arriving home for dinner with her senior women executives who have suddenly arrived from an overseas branch.

We mentioned in Chapter III the other possibility suggested by the trends in fertility. The picture is unclear. We know that the birth rate is highly susceptible to the state of the economy, at least

[1] J. M. and R. E. Pahl, *Managers and their Wives*, p. 138. Many of these wives had less education than that of their husbands.

in the short run, and a turn-about amongst the wives of professional and managerial men might have been checked by the troubled state of the economy in the last decade and more. If the economic prospects change, so might fertility. Wives who do not relish the thought of staying at home on their own after their children have left it and who shrink from competing in the job market after a protracted absence might instead give point to their lives by protracted maternity. They might in growing numbers prefer to produce children for themselves than goods and services for others. They would be opting against the symmetrical family in its modern form and siding instead with Mill. But although we say it is a possibility we do not think it a probability.

One reason is that this sort of arrangement, though it might have seemed fair to Mill, does not to many women. Nor even does the more symmetrical type of marriage which according to our survey has become predominant. In Chapter IV we described the phasing which has become common, with the wife staying at home for a period while the children were young and then taking up first part-time and then often full-time work. She was primarily responsible for running the home, but with some assistance from her husband. The strains, for the wife in particular, were considerable. Fogarty and the Rapoports have said that in East European countries 'the two-job pattern is still often in practice understood as one job for the husband and two for the wife, who still has to carry the overwhelmingly greater part of the domestic load'.[1] Some London wives certainly felt the same. The wife's burden depends upon how much of it the husband will share. The seesaw can only tilt back if there is someone at the other end; and sometimes he seems to leave her on the ground.

If we did not believe that feminism was such a powerful force we might be ready to accept that the pattern of two-jobs-for-the-wife and one-for-the-husband might last. The morality of the Principle as applied to the two sexes has become too deep-seated an element of the culture shared by both of them to be abandoned now. It could not be, for one thing, without denying to women the educational opportunities which give them the same aspirations, and sometimes the same training, for a vocation in what has been called the 'man's world'. The phrase is bound to become

[1] M. P. Fogarty and R. and R. N. Rapoport, *Women and Top Jobs: The Next Move*, p. 7.

decreasingly appropriate as it is more fully recognized that 'When one sex suffers the other sex suffers also.'[1] Just as work and leisure are becoming merged, so are the man's and woman's worlds. The jobs open to women will increasingly allow them to rise out of the industrial and commercial proletariat in which most of them have been imprisoned so far.

In this century wives have been doing a job outside the home that they did not greatly care for and the husbands a minor job inside the home that they did not greatly care for either – each therefore showing signs of the bonds that held them to the past as well as their partial recognition of the new order which they have been helping to bring into being. By the next century – with the pioneers of 1970 already at the front of the column – society will have moved from (a) one demanding job for the wife and one for the husband, through (b) two demanding jobs for the wife and one for the husband, to (c) two demanding jobs for the wife and two for the husband. The symmetry will be complete. Instead of two jobs there will be four.

Such a new relationship to the world outside the home will affect all that goes on in it, and vice versa. 'If we have children', more wives will say, 'will you look after them as much as I?' And, 'If my career requires a move of house will that count as much as yours?' Such a new marriage compact could produce smaller families and, incidentally, add once again to the attractions of cities like London as the only places where two educated people, living together, could both find fulfilling jobs within reach of their home.

Strains will be inescapable. There will inevitably be more divorces because people will be seeking a more multi-faceted adjustment to each other, with the two outside jobs clicking with the two inside ones; and because the task will be harder, there will be more failures. Chester, reviewing the evidence about recent trends in divorce and other kinds of marital failure, concluded that in total 'breakdown is probably increasing in volume among contemporary marriages. On the basis of speculative estimates . . . perhaps one sixth to one quarter of contemporary marriages may ultimately experience some form of breakdown.'[2]

[1] M. Mead, *Male and Female*, p. 30.

[2] R. Chester, 'Contemporary trends in the stability of English marriage', p. 389.

The trend is not necessarily disastrous. The people we interviewed who had married more than once did not appear any less content than others.[1] But we did not see the children, and it is they and the divorced spouses who do not remarry who are commonly the victims.

There is also a more general question about children. In the sort of life we have been describing, the early years of marriage are also the years of greatest stress. Material goods and services are so much valued that many parents have to, and are willing to, struggle hard in order to stop their standards of living from falling as their families are enlarged by children who are no longer economic assets. Fathers who can earn more by working longer do so; others who can earn more only by getting promotion exert themselves for that. On either count they may therefore be less at home just at the time when they are most needed. If mothers too go out to work as soon as they can they may add to the income but not to the well-being. We have argued that, while almost all families are subject to conflicting loyalties in this period, this is most so in the middle class. The fathers are most likely to bring their other life back home, and if their minds are furrowed with distractions they cannot concentrate their affection and interest wholeheartedly on their children. The varied and active leisure which coincides with the varied and active work and which takes so much time to organize in advance – requiring a good part of each day to be spent planning the detailed timetables of days to come – also draws attention away from the children. These may have to spend more and more time in the company of the only people who will, without always having something else on their minds, engage in the small but gripping activities of their lives. From them they can learn Queen, Queen Caroline dipping her head in turpentine and many other things besides. But there is much of value to civilization that they cannot learn from each other.

Children can therefore suffer from the new dispensation. They may have too little of the time of their fathers. This was what Bronfenbrenner had in mind when he said from the other side of the Atlantic that 'The difference between England and America in

[1] The proportion of second and later marriages was higher among the managing directors (16 per cent) than among men of similar ages in the main sample (8 per cent).

our results is not great, but it is statistically reliable. England is also the only country in our sample which shows a level of parental involvement lower than our own, with both parents – and especially fathers – sharing less affection, offering less companionship, and intervening less frequently in the lives of their children.'[1] Or they can have too little of the time of their mother. On one particular point, educational performance and its relationship to the mother's work outside the home, there is a little evidence from the same National Child Development Study of 16,000 children that we referred to in Chapter IV. From an analysis of variance Wedge[2] concluded that, although social class, size of family and sex were more strongly associated with children's progress in reading and arithmetic and with their 'social adjustment' than was maternal employment, the latter also had an influence. Even after allowing for these other factors, children were, for example, nearly four months behind in reading at the age of seven if their mothers had worked before school was started, and two months behind if they had worked afterwards. Particularly if the work was full-time rather than part-time, the children suffered from an educational and social handicap.

If this kind of thing is already happening so much the more could it in the future. Continuation of the *entente* between the two forces could provide more fulfilment for men and for women (once they have had a brief encounter with their biological urges) in jobs outside the home than inside. The two jobs of the couple outside the home could be more absorbing than the two inside it which have been in the ascendant in this century. A multiplier effect could then be established. Children coming from homes fragmented by the new triumphs of technology and feminism might fail to develop into the kind of people capable of making a centre of peace in the homes that they in their turn would establish for their children to be reared in.

If the family ceases to be a haven for children, could they have another? This is an old dream which has recurred throughout the period we have been spanning. Robert Owen hoped by means of the communes that he established in the first half of his century

[1] U. Bronfenbrenner, *Two Worlds of Childhood*, p. 116.
[2] P. J. Wedge, 'Working Mothers' Children', in preparation.

to eradicate both private property and, more generally still, individualism.[1]

> Separate interests and individual family arrangements with private property are essential parts of the existing irrational system. They must be abandoned with the system. And instead thereof there must be scientific association of men, women and children, in their usual proportion, from about four or five hundred to about two thousand, arranged to be as one family.

The greatest experiment there has ever been on Owenite lines has been conducted in this century, in the *kibbutzim* of Israel. But the tendency has been, partly on economic grounds, to pull back from a more extreme communalism towards the more familiar form both in Israel and in Eastern European countries. So many people have to be paid to do in creches and nurseries the work which mothers would otherwise do unpaid at home, and the parents separated from their children often feel guilty and unhappy. The communes which are urged, and occasionally established, in England do not have Owen's or Israel's sweeping purposes or proportions. They are regarded as a means of sharing on a more fully communal basis than a single family can sustain on its own the burdens and delights of rearing children, and doing so with a fuller symmetry between the sexes than would otherwise be possible. We expect there will be more of them, and that they will be specially attractive to people at some stages of their lives. Alternative forms of housing and alternative styles of communal living[2] are needed as much as more nursery schools. Not every-

[1] Robert Owen, quoted in J. F. C. Harrison, *Robert Owen and the Owenites in Britain and America*, p. 60.

[2] Mishan has urged that there should be a much wider variety of minority provision. For example, 'decent residential areas could be set aside for those backward-looking people who would be glad to abolish the use of all engines outside the home and for eccentrics who would prefer to dwell in areas admitting only horses and horse-drawn vehicles as means of transport' (E. J. Mishan, *The Costs of Economic Growth*, p. 118). This is not unlike what William Morris had had in mind almost a century before. 'Suppose people lived in little communities among gardens and green fields, so that they could be in the country in five minutes' walk, and had few wants, almost no furniture, and no servants, and studied the (difficult) arts of enjoying life, and finding out what they really wanted; then I think we might hope civilisation had really begun' (W. Morris, *On Art and Socialism*, p. 8).

one wants, or will want, to be stuck into the conventional home. But we do not expect that communes and the like will provide for more than small numbers. In view of what has happened in other countries it seems unlikely that any large-scale substitute of this kind will be found for the family.

Our argument has been that the technology which brought the couple back into the home together may, in alliance with feminism, take them out again together. But we do not think this an outcome that people would welcome. The buttresses described earlier as shoring up the Stage 3 family would not vanish. If it failed to nurture children, if people by their own hyper-activity threatened their own inner stability, they would slowly turn the line of march in another direction. But which?

The answer depends in large part upon whether there is to be any slackening in the characteristic emphasis of an industrial society. If there were, and working were valued a little less and not working a little more, both husbands and wives, even with four jobs, could have more free time with each other and with their children. Life would be less hectic. Some of the pressure would be taken off the family once it loosened its alliance with industry. This would happen if in increasing numbers people settled for what they have instead of striving for more. The fear of wantlessness which Young and Malthus and many others voiced in the early period of industrialization later became more of a hope than a fear – the hope that men would one day be released from the treadmill of ever-rising wants, of aspirations always racing ahead of actualities, to cultivate human relationships and the life of the mind. This is the sort of thing that William Morris pleaded for, that Keynes so often had in mind, and that in our day Mishan has urged in saying that 'the continued pursuit of economic growth by Western societies is more likely on balance to reduce rather than increase social welfare.'[1]

But the only too plain fact is that, with a few exceptions, the critics of the affluent society have not been notably lacking in the quality which they say other people should want less of. In 1797 Wilberforce, who was as high-minded as any of the legion that has in recent years sprung up to preach in the same vein, ex-

[1] E. J. Mishan, op. cit., p. 219.

pounded 'the grand law of subordination' for the behaviour of the poor. They were enjoined to realize:[1]

> that their more lowly path has been allotted to them by the hand of God; that it is their part faithfully to discharge its duties and contentedly to bear its inconveniences; that the present state of things is very short; that the objects, about which worldly men conflict so eagerly, are not worth the contest.

That the state of things is very short nobody could disagree. But just as one is entitled to be sceptical about those who espouse the dignity of labour without doing any, so on Wilberforce's last point is one entitled to be about him, or any Galbraithian who follows him, unless they demonstrate from their position of advantage at the head of the column that the objects are not worth the contest in the only way that would be convincing, by giving them up and preferring a more leisurely life to a richer one. If they did that the march might turn in another direction or many different columns be formed in place of the one.

There are still many people as poor as the Battersbys and the Wests who were locked into the sordid housing of the great cross of London. They may not suffer from material privation so harsh as the workers in the dishonourable trades described by Mayhew over a century ago but it is still sharp enough. We would not expect *them* to follow the path of St Francis, or even that of Pieper. They and millions like them at the back of the column have a right to a larger share. The length of the column has in other words to be shortened, the differences between rich and poor made much less pronounced than they have been at any time in the past. If this happened and if the people at the front slackened off a little in the intensity of work a doubly new dynamic might be set off. The hope is that some of them may be prepared to moderate the contest a little, especially if with a growth in technological unemployment scarce paid work has to be shared around more widely and if they are able to disengage themselves from the machinery of production in ways that suit their own individual needs.

Different locksteps are imposed upon different members of the family by the timetabling of the various other institutions to

[1] Quoted in E. P. Thompson, *The Making of the English Working Class*, p. 402.

which they belong. In this respect, except at weekends and on holiday, the family is not the governing institution but the governed. The child has to be at school between certain hours and have holidays at certain times, the wife similarly at her work, the husband at his. The amount of time they can overlap together at home is settled for them rather than by them. The shiftworkers are only the most extreme illustration of a general rule. If people had more choice not only about what they did outside the home but when, the family would be less fragmented and cross-pressured. Part-time work has been so popular with women (and might in future be so with men) precisely because it does enable the demands of the one institution and another to be reconciled according to individual wish. There are also at least three other possibilities.

The first has already been raised. We reported in Chapter V how much people varied in the ways in which they wanted to take their leisure. In particular, it seemed that many would like to have not only longer annual holidays but also the kind of sabbatic leave which has so far been a privilege reserved to university staff. If in this and other ways people had more choice about the way they sliced their leisure they might be glad to have more of it, and so move towards shorter working hours, taking the year (for ordinary holidays) and the lifetime (for the sabbatic) as the span rather than the week or the day.

The second is about the timing not of year or lifetime but of the day. We asked people in the main survey if they would like to start and finish work earlier or later than they did in order to make their travelling easier. Thirty per cent said they would. Amongst the managing directors, who could choose their hours more than most, well over a third arrived after the morning peak and over half left after the peak hours in the evening. The question was to do with the staggering of transport, but easier journeys would be only one of the advantages people would gain from being able to choose their own hours. We hit on some offices which allowed their employees to set their own hours provided that they worked no less over the week as a whole. The women, particularly, were able to fit their work to their home in ways that suited them better than keeping to the standard. Flexible working hours have been tried out on a large scale in Germany, in factories as well as offices, apparently with gains to employers and employees alike.

In one factory the chief advantage recorded by people who could choose when they worked was that they achieved a 'better balance between work and private life'.[2]

The third possibility is the even more flexible timetabling that people can arrange for themselves when they are their own masters, at home. This is one of the advantages (the few advantages many of them would say) that housewives have, and that house-husbands could have if they worked there on more ordinary days. We mentioned this in Chapter VI. The intellectual work which is in the ascendant does not all have to be done in the office. We said earlier that if electricity had been developed before steam-power, and energy brought directly into the home, the domestic system might have survived better than it did. In this century energy *has* been brought directly into the home and may be still further utilized when to the telephone is added the videophone and the computer terminal linked to the library and a whole range of information services. The Post Office could be more and more the modern version of the putter-out. As for education, when Open University is followed by Open School more and more people will be able to make the home their classroom. If the four jobs could be more fully done in one place a new version of the domestic system could spring up after all as a more leisurely or at least a more intimate form of industry than its large-scale counterpart, with family intruding on work more than work on family.

If against that background people chose to take more time off from their ordinary jobs (as in Chapter V we saw many would already like to do) and to mix work with leisure they might be able to break away from the relentless column and move some way towards the 'communist society' which Marx and Engels once imagined. Without giving up their specialization in ordinary work they could become more the all-rounder amateur in their other time.[2]

> As soon as the distribution of labour comes into being, each man has a particular, exclusive sphere of activity, which is forced upon him and from which he cannot escape. He is a

[1] J. H. Bolton, *Flexible Working Hours*, p. 17. Recent evidence has shown that the same practice has also been spreading in Britain. G. Sheridan, 'Flexing time'.

[2] K. Marx and F. Engels, *The German Ideology*, p. 44.

> hunter, a fisherman, a shepherd, or a critical critic, and must remain so if he does not want to lose his means of livelihood; while in communist society, where nobody has one exclusive sphere of activity but each can become accomplished in any branch he wishes, society regulates the general production and thus makes it possible for me to do one thing today and another tomorrow, to hunt in the morning, fish in the afternoon, rear cattle in the evening, criticise after dinner, just as I have a mind, without ever becoming hunter, fisherman, shepherd or critic.

If such unpaid activities were counted as work, as they were when measuring the working hours of housewives, then the total amount of it done would not necessarily be any the less as the result of such a switch. If the measure were the work done, and not the volume of it paid for, then the national income need not go down at all, and might even rise, as paid working hours were reduced. If the measure were satisfaction, then people could get a good deal more of it if they spent more of their time on unpaid jobs in which they could exercise more autonomy. Such work would also be leisure (in one way the word was defined in Chapter VIII). But it would be an illusion to think that the family could advance as a new-style unit of 'production' unless there was at the same time economic growth of the more ordinary kind. The new families of an industrial society could not be self-sufficient; they would require support from outside in terms of energy, of goods and of service on at least as large a scale as in the past, and the poorer ones much more generously so. It follows that people will only be able to spend more of their time on leisure without reducing their standard of living as measured in the orthodox way if productivity per hour grows in the economy at large.

To finish the book we want to raise a still larger issue. What have the scientist, the engineer and the organizer supplied the technology for? For people, inspired by the one ideology, combining family and hedonism, which has (together with feminism) managed to survive intact and even flourish. We do not underestimate the cohesive force it generates. The weakness so far has not been within but without. Family altruism has been too narrow an affair. The other institutions of industrial society, though myriad, have not been sustained by anything like the same loyalty. In the western world even the nation-state has declined. It is no longer the object of veneration which men would trust and, if necessary, die for. The family has been left floating on its own. The set of beliefs and institutions that relate it to the wider collective have become fragile. The paradox of modern society has been that, as people have become more and more dependent upon each other, as the ever expanding division of labour has brought more millions within its net, they have not necessarily felt any the more united to those with whom they were joined by ties of self-interest. They may feel less. The vaster the network of economic relationships, the more dense the communications which bring the problems of the world into every one's front room, the more difficult is it to think of all the others with whom one has to co-operate as people at all. The father at his breakfast table in Southend or Sutton or Slough does not see the labourer from the sugar plantations of Mauritius standing inside the bowl, the Canadian prairie farmer in the cornflakes, the Danish bacon producer on his plate, the Indian balancing on the rim of his tea-cup. Durkheim, writing in 1893, was more optimistic than most sociologists would now be about the tendency for the division of labour of an industrial order to develop its own organic solidarity. 'But if the division of labour produces solidarity, it is not only because it makes each individual an exchangist, as the economists say: it is because it creates among men an entire system of rights and duties which link them together in a durable way.'[1] The system is still there of course. But it has not become more embracing as the interdependence has gone on extending.

In the working classes the family, even at Stages 2 and 3, was often linked to an extended family and the extended family to a local community. Mutual aid[2] was practised not only within but also without the home; and neighbourly socialism was the mother of political socialism. Now the bonds with the extended family

[1] E. Durkheim, *The Division of Labour in Society*, p. 406.

[2] P. Kropotkin took the East End as his model of mutual aid in the 1890s. 'I know families which continually help each other – with money, with food, with fuel, for bringing up the little children, in cases of illness, in cases of death. The "mine" and "thine" is much less sharply observed than among the rich.' *Mutual Aid*, p. 225. Other similar evidence for the East End of the 1920s is given in G. Lansbury, *Looking Backwards and Forwards*, pp. 131–6, and R. Jenkins, *Mr Attlee*, pp. 32–5.

and the community have been weakened. Better health and better social services provided by the large-scale community have made the small family more self-sufficient. Political socialism has lost one of its tap-roots. Nothing fails like success. The middle classes have perhaps moved a little the other way and emulated the trade unions by setting up more and more of the occupational associations which Durkheim rightly predicted would proliferate along with the division of labour. Maintaining them, sometimes on a national, sometimes an international scale, was one of the things that kept several of the men from the last chapter so busy. But these new and old groupings are mostly specialized affairs. The Transport and General Worker's Union or the Institute of Practitioners in Advertising, the British Internal Combustion Engine Manufacturers Association or the National Association of Funeral Directors will not do much to throw up a bridge between one cosy symmetrical family and another, or between all the cosy ones and the much greater numbers in the world who are still at Stage 1, scraping the soil in conditions even less propitious than those in England in 1750. To recall what Ashton said, these others are caught in a population explosion without an industrial revolution to offset it.

Is the symmetrical family then to have very little for its members to live for beyond themselves? Itself even fostering a general social isolationism? Perhaps so. But there is a current of thought as new in this century as feminism was in the last which may in time make something more open, and therefore more viable, out of the new family. It has been set off by a sense of scarcity which has been strangely sharpened by affluence. For the greater part of the period since 1750 the possibilities of economic expansion have seemed limitless, as one country and then another followed the precedent set first by that in which we write and after that, most notably, by the United States. There was no visible brake upon man's power to exploit the resources of his environment. Making his way across new Frontiers, he could people the empty spaces of the world and force them to yield to him their boundless fruits. He could build great cities like London and nourish them from all the corners of the globe. He was master.

That mood has been changing fast. In the affluent countries we are becoming ever more aware that riches bring their own problems, as people consume more of the scarce fuels which have been responsible for all the changes described in this book, add more waste products to an environment whose capacity to absorb them is limited, and generally get more in each other's way. The regional men in their Rovers and Jaguars may be trying to straddle space with more numbers and more horsepower. Their efforts are bound to be self-defeating in the end, at any rate in cities which cannot command the space of a Los Angeles. The car is the symbol of an age. It would have perhaps been welcomed for its destructive power by Malthus as the modern counterpart of pestilence, a new check upon the growth of population. But it will not go on for ever being welcomed by society, as a machine around which no limits of any sort must be imposed. It stands for a kind of progress that must have a stop, or at least a slackening, now that the Frontier exists only in the myth perpetuated by the Western.

The sense of limits is sharpened immeasurably once the car-parks of Heathrow are left behind for the paddy-fields of India. It may not be generally realized that the world's population is increasing by substantially more each year than the present total population of the United Kingdom, but most people know that there has been breakneck growth. In the Third World the need for more resources to prevent consequent starvation is, on a global scale, even larger than it was in Britain in the first century after 1750. World population cannot, on an optimistic view, reach a stable equilibrium for much under a century at a figure of about 8,000 million.[1] There is little chance even of that unless people in the rich countries do much more to help than they have done so far. As long as the existing ideology lasts, then unless there are rewards in material terms for controlling fertility people in the poor countries will have that much less incentive to try. As it is, many of them are not even in the rearguard of the column, and will not be unless they limit their population and we show by our actions that we regard them as being with us.

The assumption underlying this book is that the Principle will continue to operate, although we hope in the context of a much greater equality within this nation and between nations. Our examples have nearly all been drawn from Britain, mostly from one city within it. But if, as things are going on a world scale, the Principle cannot work, what is to happen? Are there to be

[1] D. H. Meadows, *The Limits to Growth*, p. 183.

increasingly bitter conflicts between haves and have-nots asserting their right to join the rest of mankind? The new sense of limits could make people more desperately competitive than ever. Or it could go the other way, producing more of a feeling of unity with all who inhabit the same small planet dependent upon a Nature[1] which cannot be plundered indefinitely. It is not just chauvinism that prompts us to suggest, in a country whose economy has long been excelling in the slow race, that the adoption of a more leisurely style of life bearing a rather closer approximation to the old ideal of the contemplative man could leave more resources free for others, and that a less voracious attitude to our own standard of living could mean that a larger share of what we produce could go to the developing countries. If the world is thought of as a single society all the others will have the same rights of membership as us, and if we regard them in that light we might in the course of helping them also help ourselves. What we have tried to do in this chapter is to introduce another argument, of a kind of self-interest, to support the more general case often made before.

We have in the book as a whole tried to see the Londoners who co-operated in our survey as a part of history. When the builders excavating for new offices near the Bank of England discovered the remains of a temple to Mithras it was not destroyed once again but preserved. Social history does not have to be consciously preserved, because it cannot be wiped out. The only choices are about the future. But the past can enlarge the range of alternatives from which the choices can be made. The pillars of the temple cannot be pulled down. They could be the model for another.

[1] William Morris was in the last century exceptional when, in calling for a recognition of the unity of man with nature, he tilted against 'a life which was always looking at everything, except mankind, animate and inanimate – "nature" as people used to call it – as one thing, and mankind as another. It was natural to people thinking in this way, that they should try to make "nature" their slave, since they thought "nature" was something outside them.' *News from Nowhere* (1892), p. 201.

APPENDIX I

THE SURVEY METHODS

As well as the main survey, we made others, on time budgets, on active sporstmen and sportswomen, on managing directors, and in a number of plants. The time budget enquiry, being the most complex, is described on its own in Appendix 3. There is also the set of leisure forecasts described in Appendix 5. The material on social class and geography, used in Chapter II, comes from some special analyses of Census data for 1951 and 1966; the details are explained elsewhere.[1] In the statistical analysis of the various enquiries, we have followed the normal rules about the interpretation of statistical findings: in general we have drawn attention to differences only if the probability was less than one in twenty that they could have arisen by chance.

Selecting the main sample

We needed something as near as we could get to a cross-section of the adult population of the London Metropolitan Region. If we had simply picked a sample of individual people scattered all over the Region it would have taken far too long (and have been far too expensive) to go and interview them. We had to follow the familiar method and proceed in two stages, first selecting a sample of places in which the interviewing would be concentrated, and then picking samples of people in each place.

We decided that the first-stage sample should be of local authority areas. We wanted to pick ones that would give a proper representation to areas at different distances from the centre of London, in the northern and southern halves of the Region, of different population sizes and with different class distributions.

We began by delimiting four zones – Inner London (the former County of London which since 1965 has been the area of the Inner London Education Authority), the rest of Greater London, and the inner and outer zones of the Outer Metropolitan Area (the former

[1] P. Willmott and M. Young, 'Social class and geography'.

Ministry of Housing had made this division within the OMA). In each zone we separated areas in the north from the south, drawing the line as close to the river Thames as possible but in such a way as to ensure roughly equal population sizes in the two halves of each zone. In the OMA, local authority areas were split into groups according to their population size – those with smaller and those with larger populations. This was not done inside Greater London because there was much less variation in the population size of London Boroughs. The procedure gave us twelve sectors as follows: Inner London North; Inner London South; Outer Greater London North; Outer Greater London South; Inner OMA North, large populations; Inner OMA North, small populations; Inner OMA South, large populations; Inner OMA South, small populations; Outer OMA North, large populations; Outer OMA North, small populations; Outer OMA South, large populations; Outer OMA South, small populations. Within each of the twelve sectors, we listed cumulatively the population totals of the local authorities, after the authorities had been ranked in order according to their social class, this being measured by the proportion of economically active and retired males aged fifteen or over in the five socio-economic groups which roughly corresponded to the managerial class as we described it in Chapter I. We then, within each of the twelve sectors, divided the total population by two, and drew a random number between that number and zero as our starting point. The local authority in whose range in the cumulative list that number fell was the first area selected of the sector; we obtained the second by adding half the total population from the sector and taking the authority in which that number (i.e. the random number plus half the total) fell.

This procedure gave us two areas from each sector, one relatively 'high' in class and the other relatively 'low'. The resulting sample of twenty-four areas, eight in Greater London and sixteen in the OMA, was:

Inner London	Westminster Islington	Lewisham Southwark
Outer Greater London	Enfield Barking	Sutton Ealing
OMA	Brentwood Watford St Albans Rural Stevenage Eton Rural	Southend High Wycombe Marlow Aylesbury Rural Malling Rural

OMA	Gravesend	Reading
	Caterham and Warlingham	Cuckfield Rural
	Easthampstead Rural	Royal Tunbridge Wells

Most of the so-called rural districts deserved the name, though there were exceptions. A part of St Albans Rural District was a suburb on the edge of the town and, more important, Easthampstead Rural District contained – and was dominated by – Bracknell New Town. When in our analysis we divided the OMA into urban and rural areas, we put Bracknell New Town with the former.

The number of people to be drawn in any particular area was determined by calculating the proportion of the total adult population of the Region living in each sector, allocating to that sector its share of the initial sample of 3,000 people, and dividing the number equally between the two areas in the sector. This gave us, for instance, an initial sample of 302 people in Enfield and in Barking and of 56 in Tunbridge Wells and in Cuckfield Rural District. Inside each area we concentrated the interviewing by picking a sample of four wards (in the rural areas, parishes). Because the selection had already taken account of the population size of wards, we interviewed the same number of people in each of the four. In a few areas there were four wards or fewer; in these we drew a straight sample of people from the electoral registers covering the whole area. Thus the sample was of individual men and women, not of households or families.

Response in the main survey

We did not succeed in interviewing all of them. Ten per cent had moved since the registers were compiled; we decided not to try to follow them to their new addresses, even if they still lived in the Region, because we knew from past experience that, though the new addresses would sometimes be known, they would usually not be, and because of the extra travel that many of these follow-ups would involve. Smaller proportions (see Table A1) had died or proved to be living at an address which was a hospital or other institution. (Because of the problems of interviewing what would in any case have been too small a minority to generalize about with much confidence at all,[1] we tried to exclude 'non-private households' of this kind which appeared on the registers, but had not been wholly successful.) Of the remaining people, 20 per cent refused an interview, 2 per cent turned out to be too ill or incapacitated and 5 per cent could not be contacted despite

[1] In 1971, only 3 per cent of the population of the London Region were living in 'non-private households' (Office of Population Censuses and Surveys, *Census 1971 – Preliminary Report*).

repeated calls (of the initial 3,000 people, 13 per cent were called on five times or more). The details are given in Table A1. As the table shows, 1,928 people were interviewed, which was 64 per cent of the initial 3,000 names and addresses and 73 per cent of those who were known to be eligible. The losses were thus considerable;[1] they were much higher than in our earlier surveys in Bethnal Green, where 86 per cent of eligible people were interviewed, and Woodford, where the proportion was 82 per cent. Our experience, which has been similar to that of other researchers, is that it has been becoming more difficult to get people to co-operate in surveys of this kind.

TABLE A1 *Response in main survey*

	Number	*Proportion of all names drawn*	*Proportion of those known to be eligible*
Moved	299	10%	—
Dead	23	1%	—
Not eligible (living in institution)	34	1%	—
Interviewed	1,928	64%	73%
Refused	533	18%	20%
Too ill, deaf, senile	57	2%	2%
Always out, not traced	126	4%	5%
Total	3,000	100% (=3,000)	100% (=2,644)

Rather more people in Inner London than further out had moved; we think this was partly due to demolition for rebuilding, partly to other causes. Of those who were eligible, rather more living in Greater London, and especially Inner London, refused; the proportions were 27 per cent in Inner London, 21 per cent in Outer Greater London and 15 per cent in the Outer Metropolitan Area. Some of the reasons

[1] We had a lower response than the national sample survey of leisure, where the response, like ours, was lower in Inner London than elsewhere. K. K. Sillitoe, *Planning for Leisure*, pp. 249–50.

for refusing were given by people we did see. About the others we cannot of course say anything.

> We are cautious about letting people in nowadays. We've been caught by Mormons, Jehovah's Witnesses, moneylenders and £300 worth of encyclopaedias. (Bus driver, Barking)

> When I saw you I thought 'Is it genuine?' You've got to be on the alert. Three years ago three men wanted to come in and see the gas stove because of converting to North Sea Gas. When I refused and challenged them, they became abusive. Later the police came round – detectives. (Wife of decorator, Ealing)

> We get bothered by so-called Census people about once a week. Most of them try to sell you things in the end. One of them asked to use the toilet! He looked a real troublemaker – long-haired, but not a student. (Bank manager, Watford)

B as in the main sample

The losses were large. Were they so much so that, together with biases in the sample of areas or inadequacies in the electoral lists themselves, they made our sample unrepresentative of the population? There is no sure answer. The best we could do was to compare the sample interviewed in 1970 with the official Census. When we were preparing this book for the press one set of figures available from the 1971 Census was those of the total population in the different parts of the Region. In this respect, despite the higher removals and refusals in Inner London, the Census proportions were similar to those in our sample: Inner London – Census and survey, 21 per cent; Outer Greater London – 37 per cent in the Census and 38 per cent in the survey, OMA – 42 per cent and 41 per cent. Table A2 apart, for our other comparisons we had to turn to the Census of 1966, which covered a 10 per cent sample of the population.

TABLE A2 *Proportions of men and women in London Region (Survey Sample 1970 and Census 1971)*

	Survey 1970	*Census 1971*
Men	48%	48%
Women	52%	52%

TABLE A3 *Ages of men and women in London* Region (*Survey Sample 1970 and Sample Census 1966*)

	Men		*Women*	
	Survey 1970	*Census 1966*	*Survey 1970*	*Census 1966*
17, 18 or 19	4%	7%	3%	6%
20–24	10%	10%	6%	9%
25–29	9%	9%	10%	8%
30–39	18%	18%	15%	16%
40–49	20%	18%	20%	16%
50–59	18%	19%	18%	18%
60–64	7%	7%	9%	8%
65–69	6%	5%	7%	6%
70 or over	8%	7%	12%	13%

TABLE A4 *Marital status of men and women in London* Region (*Survey Sample 1970 and Sample Census 1966*)

	Men		*Women*	
	Survey 1970	*Census 1966*	*Survey 1970*	*Census 1966*
Single	19%	23%	13%	20%
Married	76% }	72% (Married and Separated)	68% }	65% (Married and Separated)
Separated	1% }		2% }	
Widowed	4%	4%	16%	14%
Divorced	—%*	1%	1%	1%

*Only two people.

Table A2 shows that the sample matched the Census in the proportions of men and women. Table A3 shows that the sample contained fewer men aged 17, 18 and 19; also that among women there were in the sample less aged 20 to 24 as well as less of the younger ones. These differences are reflected in the variations according to marital status (Table A4).

We think that the under-representation of young and single people of both sexes was due to two causes. The registers we were working from were the first to include the new voters under 21 – that is, people aged 18, 19 and 20 when the lists were published (15 February 1970) and those who would become 18 during the following twelve months. It is well-known that many of these young people did not put themselves on the registers – though the extent is not established. Secondly, even if they were on the lists, the young people and particularly the single ones were obviously more likely to be out in the evenings and at weekends.

TABLE A5 *Occupational class of working and retired men* in Greater London, Outer Metropolitan Area and London Region (Survey Sample 1970 and Sample Census 1966)*

	Greater London		*Outer Metropolitan Area*		*London Metropolitan Region*	
	Survey 1970	*Census 1966*	*Survey 1970*	*Census 1966*	*Survey 1970*	*Census 1966*
Professional	5%	5%	9%	7%	6%	6%
Managerial	17%	16%	26%	20%	21%	18%
Clerical and Skilled	54%	52%	49%	49%	52%	51%
Semi-skilled	17%	18%	12%	17%	15%	17%
Unskilled	7%	9%	4%	7%	6%	8%

*Survey 1970, aged 17 or over; sample Census 1966, aged 15 or over.

For class, as measured by the occupations of men, the main differences are shown in Table A5. The survey sample included a larger proportion in the top two classes and a smaller at the bottom, among the semi-skilled and unskilled. Both differences were more marked in the OMA. Four years had elapsed between this Census and our survey, and at least some of the variation in class was probably because of the changes over time in the occupational structure to which we have referred in the body of the book.

Analysing the main survey

After the interviews had been completed, the questionnaires were checked and coded. The information was transferred to punch-cards and then on to computer tapes. The main calculations were done on the CDC 6600 computer at the University of London Computer Centre. The information was also regrouped on to various sets of punch-cards, so that analyses could if necessary be carried out by counter-sorter at our own office.

The survey data were mainly analysed in the form of distributions. For hours and numbers of leisure activities averages were also produced. A total of over 6,000 tables were prepared Copies of the computer data for the main and diary surveys have been lodged with the Social Science Research Council's Survey Archive at the University of Essex. Researchers wishing to carry out their own analyses should approach the Survey Archive.

The leisure regression analysis

A particular analysis that we made of the main survey was the multiple regression on leisure mentioned in Chapter VIII. We wanted to find out the relative influence of class, car-ownership and other factors upon the range of leisure. The multiple regression technique was particularly suited to the task, since it shows how one variable (the dependent variable) is related to a set of others (the independent variables). For this particular analysis the dependent variable was the total number of leisure activities done at least once during the year before the interview. We tried to relate this measure to a whole variety of independent variables, including class and car-ownership. In order to reduce this list to the variables which were most strongly related to leisure behaviour, we carried out the regression analysis in a 'step-wise' fashion. This technique involved selecting first the factor which accounted for most of the variance in the dependent variable, and then successively adding in other factors in the order of their significance. At each stage the next variable was introduced which most to our ability to explain the variation in leisure activities.[1] We decided to convert all our independent variables into a binary form so as to avoid such problems as that of relating eight income groups to four social classes. We followed Johnston throughout in our use of binary data.[2] The standard errors for the co-efficients of the five variables in Table 45 were: age, 0.45; car ownership, 0.44; class, 0.51; income, 0.51, terminal education age, 0.57.

Social class groupings

In grouping people into occupational classes for analysis we used

[1] The technique is described in detail in W. J. Dixon (ed.), *Biomedical Computer Programs*, pp. 233–57d.

[2] J. Johnston, *Econometric Methods*, pp. 221–8.

an adaptation of the Registrar-General's five-fold Social Class scheme.[1] We divided one of his classes – III, Skilled – into 'clerical' and 'skilled manual'. Without the split, this class was by far the largest, accounting for half the people in our main sample, and earlier sociological studies had suggested that the distinction within it was a crucial one.[2] But we combined together his classes I and II, and likewise his classes IV and V; this was partly to give us large enough numbers for some of our more complex analyses (and in particular for the analysis of the diaries) but also because the preliminary results had shown that there were enough similarities to justify the amalgamations. This grouping gave the four occupational classes used throughout the book – professional with managerial; clerical; skilled; semi-skilled with unskilled.

The sample of active sportsmen

We now turn to the other samples. The active sportsmen and sportswomen were a sub-sample of a sub-sample – they came from among the diarists described in Appendix 3. We wanted to carry out additional interviews with a relatively small number of people who were active in one or more sports. Since we were primarily interested in the relationship between this interest and their family, the diarists – being married and aged thirty to forty-nine – seemed a suitable group to draw from. Having already shown their willingness to participate in the survey beyond the first interview, they might, we thought, be disposed to do so again. Over nine-tenths of those whom we defined as active sportsmen agreed to this third round.

An 'active sportsman' was defined for our purpose as someone who (as well as having completed a diary) mentioned a sport[3] as the leisure activity that he or she most enjoyed and also had done whatever it was at least twelve times in the previous year. There were fifty-seven such people, of whom fifty-one were interviewed; the six not interviewed were all men – five refused and one was in hospital. Men predominated and, as we have reported in Chapter VIII, there were relatively large proportions of managers among them.

The managing directors' sample

This sample was selected from members of the Institute of Directors. We sought the Institute's sponsorship because we hoped that having

[1] General Register Office, *Classification of Occupations 1966*. This shows, as well as the social class of each occupation, whether it is 'manual' or 'non-manual'.

[2] P. Willmott and M. Young, *Family and Class in a London Suburb;* the point was also noted by F. Bechhofer, 'Occupations', pp. 112, 118.

[3] We were guided by a list of active sports supplied to us by the Sports Council.

it would help to persuade presumably busy people to give up some of their time; and the Director-General kindly agreed. Since there were relatively few women managing directors we confined the sample to men. We set out to select the directors in the following way:

1. We drew an initial list from the *Directory of Directors*. This was done for two reasons. The *Directory* includes directors of only the larger companies (though the exact criterion is nowhere expressly stated). Since we wanted a sample of the rich, we wanted to exclude directors of small companies such as jobbing builders. We were told that the *Directory* was also probably more up-to-date than the Institute's own membership lists. Membership of the Institute is shown in the *Directory* and only those indicated as members were included in our sample lists.
2. We included only managing, deputy managing, assistant managing or joint managing directors. These could be directors either of a separate company or within a group of companies.
3. The addresses of the companies given in the *Directory* from which we picked were all in the London Metropolitan Region.
4. Directors were excluded if they were in companies, mainly large ones, that belonged to the Institute's Medical Scheme. This was because another survey was being made among Institute members in such companies.

On these criteria 650 names of men were selected at random from the *Directory of Directors* and sent to the Institute of Directors. The first approach was a letter from the Director-General. According to the records supplied to us by the Institute, who excluded members who had died or lapsed, 544 letters were sent out. Altogether 232 directors told the Director-General that they were willing to be interviewed, their acceptance forms being posted on to us from the Institute. This was rather more men than we needed, the response being better than we had estimated on the basis of a small pilot enquiry. Only 190 of the 232 men were interviewed, the other 42 being the last to agree to an interview.

It follows from what we have said that we cannot adopt the usual survey procedures for discussing the response or the sample's representativeness. We cannot define the universe from which the people were drawn in any terms other than their being members, limited in the ways we have described, of a particular body. We cannot know what kinds of managing directors were excluded from our original lists because they did not belong to the Institute or were not listed in the *Directory*. In addition, because of the particular procedure that we adopted with the assistance of the Institute of Directors, we know nothing about the high proportion of people who did not respond to the Director-General's letter. We therefore cannot claim that our 190 managing directors were representative of managing directors generally.

Case studies in firms

Before the main survey and the study of directors we carried out studies in two firms. One firm, which we have called High Frequency Electronics, was a research and development firm in electronics whose plant was a few miles outside the built-up area of Greater London. The second, Royal Acetone Company, was a glue factory in an Inner London working-class area. These names, as we have explained in Chapter I, were not their real ones.

Since the numbers in both factories had to be small, we decided to narrow the demographic range of the samples. In each firm we selected, from the records of people at all levels, a random sample of married male employees aged thirty and over. Of the 58 eligible people picked at random at High Frequency Electronics, eight refused and 50 were interviewed. Of the 54 eligible men at Royal Acetone Company, 12 refused and 42 were interviewed.

Our plan was to interview the men first in the factory about their work and then, if they and their wives were willing, at their home about their leisure. Of the 92 men at the two firms who were interviewed at work, 79–86 per cent – agreed to the further interview at home and 68 wives – 74 per cent – also agreed to participate. Some of the results of these studies at High Frequency Electronics and Royal Acetone Company are reported in a separate paper.[1]

Finally, there were the two small studies of establishments operating shift systems. We had postmen and printers in our main sample, along with other shiftworkers. We wanted to observe them in action and try, in however small a way, to make some sense of shiftwork in these two settings. We approached a district post office through the headquarters office, and we looked for and then approached a printing firm working a shift system. Both agreed to participate. Our observation in the two workplaces was supplemented by interviews with seven people at what we have called Metro Printers and nine at the post office.

[1] P. Willmott, 'Family, work and leisure conflicts among male employees: some preliminary findings'.

APPENDIX 2

INTERVIEWERS' INSTRUCTIONS AND MAIN SURVEY QUESTIONNAIRE

This appendix reproduces the questionnaire used in the main survey, together with instructions to interviewers. The instructions that we have included are of two kinds: first, some general notes of advice, and secondly, specific instructions about the questions. As well as the questionnaire that was used with all informants, which we reproduce here, we also had three special questionnaires used with particular kinds of people. The first was for people aged twenty-four or under; this was mainly about their present or past education and their attitudes to work and leisure. The second was for married women who were not working; the main purpose was to put various questions to them about their past work experience and whether they expected to go to work again. The third, for retired people, to find out when they had retired, why, and what they thought about the enforced 'leisure' of retirement. The detailed definitions of the people to whom these various additional questions were put are shown in Question 14 of the main questionnaire.

Interviewers' instructions

I Some general points

1. *The people to interview.* Your task is to interview the people whose names and addresses are on your lists. Some will be single young people, others housewives, others working men, others retired; as you will see, there are special questionnaires for some of these categories. You will need to check that you have the person listed, that the Christian name is right as well as the surname. If the person listed has moved from the address given, don't try to follow him to his new house. No substitutes or proxies are wanted either. We are interested only in interviewing the people who are listed and are still living at the address listed. One further point: we are collecting information only about people living in *private* households: the questionnaire would not be suitable for other people. So if you find that the address listed is a school, nursing home,

hostel or other institution, you should not proceed with the interview. The exclusion applies to staff as well as other residents.

2. *Introducing yourself.* The people to be interviewed will not know in advance that you will be calling. The best practice in our view is to do what you are being asked to, that is introduce yourself and explain what you want on the doorstep. You will have a card from the Institute introducing you as one of our interviewers. You will not necessarily need to show it to everyone, but you should have it ready.

3. *Getting a high response.* A 'high response' is survey jargon for interviewing successfully a large proportion of the people on your lists. It is obviously important to us; if the response is poor we can't be at all confident that we have a proper cross-section, that the information from the interviews does apply to the wider population. But of course everyone is free to refuse an interview if they wish; if after a thorough explanation someone still says 'No', it is best not to press them too hard. We hope that you will be unfailingly courteous and friendly in manner even to people who do refuse.

4. *Recording the response.* You will have to fill in a 'completion record' for every name on your list. This, to be returned with completed interviews, is to help us check what additional material – like supplementary questionnaires or diaries, both of which are explained later – we should have or can expect, and so on. Any refusals or other failures should be noted on the forms. If there is no interview we need detailed information. What is the explanation? Has the house been demolished? Has the person moved or died? Is he or she deaf or for some other reason unable to be interviewed? (But always try to find some way round the problem if you can.) Above all, if it is a refusal try to give us the reason, so that we can decide how best to make a second approach. Did they say: 'Too busy', 'Not interested', 'Don't agree with it on principle'? Also note particularly if you think it might be hopeful for someone else to try: 'Other interviewer might do better'; 'Perhaps a male/female interviewer could try'. We ask this because we shall try to arrange for another interviewer to call back on everyone who refuses to be interviewed by you in the hope of raising the overall rate.

5. *Recording on the questionnaires.* The questions are designed to give precise information on the topics we are interested in. There are four basic ways in which answers can be recorded, depending on the kind of question it is:

(i) If there are a set of code numbers opposite the alternative answers, you ring the appropriate code.

(ii) If the question is 'open', you write in what the informant says.

(iii) Some questions have space to write in information and also to 'code' (an example is the first subsidiary part of Question 1). In these cases you have to both write in *and* code.

(iv) Some questions have to be answered with a number, like a person's age or his time of starting work; with these you put the figures in the boxes provided.

If the question is pre-coded and for some reason none of the alternative answers seem to apply – or the whole thing is more complicated – please explain as clearly as possible on the questionnaire what the exact circumstances are. This will enable us to decide later how to treat the answer. Quite apart from this, we would like you to record people's answers fairly fully, particularly if they say something striking, vivid or amusing. We would like these to be reported verbatim where possible, with quotation marks to show that it is a direct quote. If there is not enough space on the page you should use the back of the previous page, putting an asterisk opposite the question and the question number opposite the remarks quoted. We would also appreciate it if you could record, on the last page of the questionnaire or on a separate sheet, any striking details you observe about the informant, the home or the district.

6. *Need for care and accuracy.* It is important that the information we get on the questionnaires is sound and accurate. So please carry out all interviews carefully and conscientiously – and also write legibly. Will you, by the way, please code and write on the questionnaire in blue or black biro; red and green won't do, as we use them at a later stage to mark the questionnaire. Please check over each interview as soon as possible after you have completed it (in your car if you have one, but preferably not outside the house), so as to make sure that you have filled in everything you should and that the answers are consistent and clear. This is also a good time to add any notes and comments. We should tell you that, as a continuous check on accuracy, we call back on a proportion of each interviewer's informants and re-do some parts of the questionnaire.

7. *Organizing your work.* When you first start on your lists for a particular area you will find it fruitful to make some day-time calls. The best thing is to start in the morning, calling on addresses near to each other. Many people will not be in, but you will sometimes

be able to find out from other members of the family when the subject is likely to be at home. By the first evening you will have made a preliminary round; you may have interviewed a housewife or two, you will have found out that some people have died or moved, you will have made a series of appointments for evenings or weekends. You might be able to spend the second day equally usefully. But soon after that you will have no daytime calls to make; your work will be concentrated in the evenings. We know this may make life difficult for you but we hope you will be willing to organize your time in this flexible kind of way.

II *Notes on the Questionnaire*

Serial number. The serial number of the 'subject' (or 'informant' – both terms mean the person you interview) is given on your list of names and addresses. It should be put in the five boxes at the top right-hand corner of p.1 of the Questionnaire. It should also be put on any supplementary questionnaires used, on the diary form and on the completion record.

Instructions in the questionnaires. Instructions are always in capitals. They are for your guidance and not to be read out.

Question 1 – 'Less than'. The sign '<' means 'less than', as you probably know. So '5 < 10 years' (Code '1') means 'five years or more but less than ten'. Exactly ten years would be coded '0'.

Question 1 – Previous district. The idea here is that you should write in the district or town and code it if you can. The following definitions may help you:

'Inner London' is the area of the Inner London Education Authority (and formerly the LCC). It comprises the London Boroughs of Camden, Islington, Hackney, Tower Hamlets, Greenwich, Lewisham, Southwark, Lambeth, Wandsworth, Hammersmith, Kensington and Chelsea, Westminster and the City of London.

'Outer GLC' is the rest of the London Boroughs – Barnet, Enfield, Haringey, Waltham Forest, Redbridge, Havering, Barking, Newham, Bexley, Bromley, Merton, Sutton, Croydon, Richmond upon Thames, Ealing, Hillingdon, Hounslow, Harrow, and Brent.

'Outer Metropolitan Area' is the country ring of the London Region – the part outside the GLC area. It stretches from Reading to Southend and from Royston to just north of Brighton, and it contains all of Herts and Surrey and parts of Beds, Berks, Bucks, Oxfordshire, Essex, Kent, Hampshire and parts of East and West Sussex.

'Outside London Region' is anywhere else.

Question 1 – 'You (your household)'. This strange phrase, used for the first time here, comes up in a number of questions. It is put like this to remind you that, though the informant may be the owner or tenant or his wife, he or she *may* be a single child living with parents or an aged parent living with children. It will usually be clear whether the right form of the question is 'Did you . . .' or 'Did your parents . . .' or 'Did your son . . .' But if not people usually understand when you ask 'Does your household . . .' (Household itself is defined in the instructions to Question 7).

Question 3 – Age of property. If the subject doesn't know, please make some sort of estimate and put 'E' (for 'estimate') to the right of the number you code.

Question 4 – Type of housing. You don't need to ask this question but can code it from your own observation.

Question 5 – Garden. A garden not attached to the house can be counted as long as it is in the immediate vicinity, but a special note should be made of this.

Question 6 – Second home. This is somewhere the subject can use *without a specific invitation*; it could however be somewhere that the subject has to *arrange* to go to (i.e. it could be a second home shared with other people). The subject's parents' home does not count, though *their* second home (if available to the subject without invitation) obviously does. A 'Dormobile' should be recorded under 'Other (SPECIFY)'.

Question 7 – Household. A 'household' is all the people under the same roof who share the same housekeeping arrangements. So a lodger, who usually cooks in his own room, is not a member of the same household, but a boarder, who eats with the others, is.

Question 7 – Visitors. Visitors should not be included, but people who usually live as a member of the household should be recorded if they are temporarily away from home, e.g. in hospital. 'Visitors' should, however, be included if they have been there for six months or more preceding the interview; people 'temporarily' away should be excluded if they have been away for six months or more preceding the interview. Someone described as living in the household for part of the week should be counted in if it is a married person who usually returns to his spouse in this household at least once a week, or it is another person who usually spends at least four nights a week in this household.

Question 7 – Relationship to subject. The sort of answer we want is: 'wife', 'husband', 'son', 'daughter', 'wife's mother', 'nephew', 'friend', 'boarder'.

Question 7 – Age. We do not need the ages of people who are not related to the subject; if the household was a group of six students sharing, you would need to record only the age of the subject. Note that we want the 'age last birthday'; someone who says he 'will be 70 in July' is 69 not 70. We do not, however, necessarily need the *exact* age of the subject or of other adults in the family, though it is usually quite easy to get. We do need children's ages and the exact age of subjects aged 24 or under. For other people, if necessary you can put the age in terms of age groups – 25/9 (meaning 25–29), 30+ (meaning 30–39), 40+, 50+, 60/4 (meaning 60–64), 65/9 (meaning 65–69), 70+, 80+ (meaning an age of 80 or over).

Question 7 – Sex. M (Code 'U') is 'male'; F (Code 'L') 'female'.

Question 7 – Marital status. We make an important distinction at various points in the questionnaire between married people living with their husbands and others who, though they have been or are married, are not living with their husbands. The codes should be interpreted as follows:

- 'M' – Code 1 – Married and living with spouse. If there is any doubt whether the spouse is 'living' at home, the definition is that given above under 'Question 7 – Visitors', i.e. spending at least one night a week at home.
- 'S' – Code 2 – Single, i.e. unmarried and never having married.
- 'W' – Code 3 – Widowed (widow or widower).
- 'D' – Code 4 – Formally divorced from previous spouse.
- 'Sep' – Code 5 – Separated from spouse; this includes not only those formally 'separated' but anyone who has a spouse but is not living with him or her.

Question 7 – Sons in paid work. If the informant wonders why we want to know about the sons' jobs, the explanation is this. 'We are interested not only in how work affects leisure but also in whether fathers and sons have the same kind of work. We shall be asking about your/your husband's occupation later on.' Note that the same question is put about sons not living at home in Question 68. For the sort of detail we want on occupation, see the instruction on Question 15.

Question 9 – Car. Note the instruction: a light van is counted as a car, as is a car owned by an employer but available exclusively to the employee (the subject or someone else in his household) and thus in effect usable on the household's behalf. Examples are cars put at the exclusive disposal of a manager or salesman.

Question 10 – 'Bungalow' should not be written in under 'Other' but should be coded as a house (usually '2' or '3'). This is on the reasoning that a bungalow is only a special sort of one-storey house. If 'bungalow' is cited as the type of home wanted, check whether it is '2', '3', '4' or '1'. But remember to add, under 'f', that a bungalow was particularly wanted. Note that a bungalow should similarly be coded as a house in Questions 1 and 4.

Question 11 – Introduction. If the question seems abrupt for people not asked Question 10, you can introduce it by saying 'The questions so far have been mainly about your household and your housing . . .'

Question 11 – Branching. If the informant says that he wants to stay in the present district, you simply move on to Question 12. That is simple enough. But if he says he would prefer to move, there is a branch depending on his answer to the second part of the question. If he has 'a particular district in mind' you carry straight on. If, however, he has no particular district in mind, you go to the top of the right-hand column on p. 4 and put all the questions in that column. You will see that, apart from slight changes of wording, the two branches match each other.

Question 11 – 'Prompt'. This instruction which appears twice in both 'branches', is also used with later questions. It always means that the alternatives should be read out.

Question 12 – 'Working'. 'Full-time' work means 30 hours a week or more on average. 'Part-time' means less than 30 hours a week. Someone who works only one hour a week or less is coded as 'not working'. Someone who does casual or freelance work should be judged on the four calendar weeks before the interview: if he did four hours work or less during those four weeks he is counted as 'not working'. Those still employed but temporarily off work through strikes, illness or accident should be recorded according to their normal working hours (and Questions 15–47 should be put as if the subject were working). But those who, though formally employed, have been off work for four weeks or more should be counted as 'not working'.

Question 12 – Past occupations. See instructions on Question 15. If the subject is retired we want to know the 'main' occupation during his working life. If there were two 'main' occupations take the most recent. If he was someone who moved up a promotional ladder, we want the highest rank he reached.

Question 13 – Husband's occupation. To women whose husbands are currently at work, the question is 'What is your husband's occupation?' If the husband has retired or died: 'What was his main occupation?' See notes on Question 12 and Question 15.

Question 14 – Branch to supplementary questionnaires. This is the point at which you have to decide whether the subject qualifies for supplementary questions and, if so, put them to him. There are three supplementary questionnaires:

Questionnaire II – put to *any* subject of 24 or under.
Questionnaire III – put to a married woman (not widowed, divorced or separated) who is neither a full-time student nor working full or part-time.
Questionnaire IV – put to a man or single woman who describes him or herself as 'retired'.

Note that the criterion for Questionnaire II is simply age, whereas Questionnaires III and IV apply to some of the people not working in a paid job. A young man or woman under 24 who is working will be asked Questionnaire II and then Questions 15–47 (about work). A young wife of 24 or under who is neither working in a paid job nor is a student will be asked Questionnaire II, then Questionnaire III and then Question 48 onwards on the main questionnaire. A retired man or single woman will be asked Questionnaire IV and then 'skip' to Question 48 on the main questionnaire. Some people – for instance, a widow without a paid job or a disabled man – will neither be asked a special set of questions nor the questions about work (15–47) but will 'skip' straight to Question 48. It is important to ring the appropriate codes in Question 14, so that we can check whether the subject should have a special questionnaire. If both '2' and '3' apply – i.e. if the subject is 24 or under and a housewife (not working) – ring both '2' and '3'. For every other kind of subject, only one code should be ringed.

Question 15 – Occupation. We are interested in occupation at a number of other points in the interview but particularly so here.

We want to see how 'leisure' relates to 'work' and to do this we obviously need to have a clear idea of what the subject's work is. We ask you to 'write in and code', i.e. to write down the occupation and also to help us in classifying the job by coding whether the person is 'self-employed', etc. You won't, by the way, necessarily have to ask anything in order to code. If the subject says he is a manager or foreman in a particular firm or organisation, you code 'manager' or 'foreman' accordingly. If he might be self-employed, i.e. has not explicitly mentioned an employer already, you should ask 'Are you self-employed?' and, if the answer is 'Yes', 'With employees or without?' The actual expression 'other employee' which applies to the great majority, should never be used. To people who are not self-employed, again if the answer has not already been given, you should say 'Are you a manager or a foreman?' The occupation must be described with precision and detail. For instance, 'manager' is too vague: we would like such descriptions as 'manager of ironmonger's shop' or 'Assistant Regional Sales Manager for pharmaceutical firm'. 'Engineer' is another example; here, apart from getting the detailed title, check whether the subject is professionally qualified and write for instance 'Senior Design Engineer on computer design (professionally qualified)'. With 'Civil Servants', ask for the grade. If the subject just says that he 'works for Smiths', try to find out exactly what sort of work he does.

Question 16 – How paid. You may already know enough to realise that some of the alternatives don't apply; for example, a self-employed architect with a staff of 20 obviously isn't paid by the hour. You would adapt the question for him: 'How are you paid – or rather how do you pay yourself?' But with most employees, you will read out the alternatives. 'Running prompt' means that you go on reading out the alternatives until the informant says 'Yes' or stops you to explain the details. Only one code should be ringed. Code '5' only if the subject receives *all* his pay by some method other than '1', '2' or '4'.

Question 17 – Kind of firm/organisation. This is supplementary to Question 15, to give us some more detail in classifying the subject's 'work'. Note that Question 17 may not always apply as it stands to self-employed people and may therefore need to be adapted.

Question 20 – Collected by firm. If the subject is collected and taken to work by his firm, write this in.

Question 22 – 'Official' working week. Again this may not apply to self-employed people and may need adapting: 'Do you have "official' working hours?' 'Official' means 'the hours laid down in a contract or agreement between employer and employee'. When we say 'exclude lunch hours', we also mean you to exclude the equivalent for workers on night or other shifts.

Question 22 – 'More hours . . . at your place of work'. This includes any work done outside the home, for instance by a travelling salesman. The question is phrased as it is to exclude the hours worked at home (see Question 23).

Question 22 – 'Last week'. This means the last calendar week before the interview, starting on Monday. If the interview is on a Monday, it means from the previous Monday to the Saturday (or Sunday). If the interview is on a Friday, it means from the Monday before last to the previous Saturday (or Sunday). 'Last normal week' is a guide to you; it is intended to exclude a week when, for instance, the subject had time off work because of illness or when there was a public holiday. (You would then ask him about the last full week that he worked.) It is *not* intended to exclude a week when the subject did less (or more) overtime than usual.

Question 23 – Work at home. If the subject has already explained that he works at or from his home, you obviously don't put the question as it stands; just check that you've got it right and ring '9'.

Questions 24 and 25 – Official starting times last week. These two questions, with Question 26, are mainly intended to get details about shift working. We are not interested here in whether someone arrived earlier than their 'official' starting time or left later. In Question 24, you write in the time of starting and ring 'a.m.' or 'p.m.' accordingly. Likewise, if there was any variation, you fill in the times and ring 'a.m.' or 'p.m.' in Question 25.

Question 40 – Work and leisure. An answer like 'I don't think of them as different' should be coded '2', i.e. 'Both equally . . .'.

Question 43 – More than six weeks paid holiday. The Code '6' should be used for holidays of '6 weeks *or more*'.

Question 43 – Grid. In the 'a' column, '1' means 'one week' and '4' means 'four weeks'. The figures do not refer to the *position* of the week in the month. As for the 'b ii' column, if a holiday spreads over more than one month and some part of it was spent at a relative's home, establish which month or months the stay with the relatives occurred and code 'U' or 'L' accordingly for each month covered.

Question 46 – First married. We have put in first because, if the subject has been married previously, we want the answer in relation to her first marriage not her present one.

Question 47 – Wives' paid work. Note that in the subsidiary parts of this question, as well as in the main question, 'work' means paid work and 'working' means doing at least an hour a week or, if casual or freelance, at least four hours in four weeks. Also, in part 'c', 'starting work' means working for at least four weeks continuously.

Questions 48, 54 and 56 – 12 times or more. In all three questions, the frequency ('1–11' or '12+') refers to the total number of days during the 12 months on which the subject did the particular activity. Thus it's not 12 or more rooms decorated or 12 or more books read; it's 12 or more days spent doing some decorations or doing some reading.

Question 48 – Leisure activities at home. Most of the categories are straightforward. 'Listening to music on a record player' also means 'on a gramophone', and with older people it may make more sense if you ask it in that form. 'Read a book, not a magazine' should be read out, because some people tend to count a magazine as a book. 'Playing with children' should be put to everybody; it includes other people's children, like grandchildren, as well as one's own.

Question 49 – Other home activities. Examples of activities that might come up are: amateur radio, toy-making, watch and clock repairs. If people mention entertaining or visiting friends or relatives, do *not* record this; explain that you will be asking some questions about that separately later.

Question 52 – Spectator sports. 'Go to watch' means going specially to watch, not happening to see when doing something else.

Question 54 – Other listed leisure activities. 'Go out for a meal' means in a cafe or restaurant. With both 'meal' and 'pub', 'not for lunch' includes the similar sorts of meals of shift workers. 'Attend church' does include just going once for a wedding or a funeral. 'Go for a walk of a mile or more' and 'go for a drive in car for pleasure' can include journeys to work if specially mentioned.

Question 55 – Active member. If asked, 'active' means attending or going on at least two occasions during the past 12 months. Trade unions and professional organisations are included only if the subject is 'active' in them in his leisure time (i.e. not during his working hours); card membership alone should not be counted.

Question 55 – Firm's clubs. The instruction 'IF WORKING' is to indicate that the 'prompt' about 'firm's clubs' is put only to those who are working in a paid job.

Question 58 – 'How much enjoyment'. We want you to write in what the informant says and also use your own judgment whether he gives an 'enthusiastic' answer or not. It is of course not just the words but the tone as well. The sort of expressions that, in pilot interviewing, we regarded as showing 'enthusiasm' were: 'Cars are the love of my life'; 'What I *really* enjoy is getting away in a small boat'; 'I love the creative aspect of gardening. I'm out there every evening without fail.'

Question 59 – 'Go with'. We are of course not interested just in the people that the subject *travels* with. 'Go with' is intended to include 'do it with', 'play it with', etc.

Question 59 – Who with. '(+ others)' means 'with or without other people'.

Question 60 – Work – leisure links. We would very much like you to 'probe' with this question. In particular, if someone has a leisure activity which seems to you to be linked to his work but does not mention it, ask him explicitly whether he sees it as 'linked'. Examples that we have come across were a dog-clipper who frequently went to dog shows and an actor who often went to the theatre; neither mentioned the 'links' until asked about them.

Question 62 – Daily newspaper. This may seem a strange question to come at this point. If anyone asks you about it, say that you'll explain in a moment; then, *after* you've asked which section of the paper they read first, explain that some people turn first to the sports pages and we want to see what sort of people do so.

Question 63 – Supporters. Note the phrase 'Code main one only'. People may say that there are a number of reasons why they support the team they do – it's near, a relative took them and it's a good team anyway. If so, try to sort out which reason is the 'main' one.

Question 64 – Parents not in same household. If the parents live in the same dwelling, but not in the subject's household, they should be included here. In that case, they will of course have been seen in the last week and one of them will almost certainly be the 'last relative' met socially . . . (Questions 71–7).

Question 65 – Father's occupation. We want the father's occupation (and in Question 67 that of the father-in-law of a married subject) whether he is still alive or not. If he is dead or retired, it's the 'main' occupation you ask about. The reason for the question, as with those on son's occupations (Questions 7 and 68), is, as well as being interested in 'work' and 'leisure', we want to see how far relatives have the same kinds of occupations.

Question 69 – Relatives in last week. We do not want to count young children; only include relatives aged 16 or over. Note that a couple counts as two people.

Question 70 – No relative met in last week. 'Relative' here includes the relatives asked about in Question 64 (parents), Question 66 (parents-in-law) and Question 68 (children or children-in-law). So if one of those *has* been seen in the last week Question 70 is not asked.

Questions 71–77 – Last relative. This question is put to all those who have seen a relative during the last year, whether during the last week (and picked up in Questions 64–9) or less recently. The same applies to the 'last friend' (Questions 82–9).

Question 71 – Last relative. Again parents, parents-in-law, children and children-in-law are included here. Some people do not readily think of their parents or children living away from home as 'relatives'. So you should add a phrase to Question 71. It should read:

> 'I'd like to ask a few questions about the last relative *or member of your family* you met socially . . .'

Question 78 – Friends within ten minutes walk. As with relatives children aged 15 or under should not be included.

Question 80 – Other friends in last week. To avoid being tedious, we haven't repeated the instruction to the informant about counting married couples as two people. But it applies to this question as to Questions 78 and 79.

Question 89 – School/University/College. This refers to the *subject's* own education, not to that of his children, nor to a school, etc. where he might have worked.

Question 91 – Out with husband/wife. This is meant to apply to those occasions when the subject went out with husband or wife alone, whether or not other people were also present. In other words, it is the presence of the spouse that is important. 'Went out', by the way, means not just travelling together, but spending at least two hours together during the course of an evening.

Questions 93, 94, 95 – Family size. We are asking these questions because we want to see how many children people have, expect and 'want' (or think of as an ideal size of family). All this is obviously linked to how husbands and wives spend their 'leisure'. Note particularly that if the subject is a married man the questions are asked about his (present) wife, even if she has been married before; if the subject is a married woman, they are asked about her. In either case, Question 93 includes any children she had by a previous marriage. The 'skip' at the end of Question 93 and the instruction at the start of Question 94 again apply to the *wife* whether she or her husband is the subject.

Question 97 – Central London. Just 'passing through' Central London on the way to somewhere else should not be counted. But if the subject, while 'passing through', deliberately stopped to do something, this *should* be counted. The definition of 'Central London' has to be left to the subject.

Question 110 – Subsidiary question. The subsidiary question (with the emphasis on the *most likely*) should be put not only to those who 'Don't know' ('6') but also to those who say they 'Won't vote' ('5').

Question 112 – Word test. We are hoping to use this as some sort of indicator of people's 'intelligence'. It is basically a vocabulary test, as you can see, and therefore limited in value, but we clearly can only afford to spend a little time on a test and there is some evidence that this one is as good a guide, within broad limits, as much more complicated and lengthy ones. Why do we want some such measure anyway? The reason is that we think that what people do in their leisure may well be related to 'intelligence', particularly when that in turn is related to the kind of job they do and their 'satisfaction' with it. We would, for example, expect that a very able man in a dead end job would not find the work 'satisfying' and might well be very active in his leisure to compensate, being say an officer in a political party or voluntary organisation. If the informant asks why we are doing this test, you could explain: 'We want to find out whether the people who know a lot of the words do different sorts of things in their leisure – do a lot of reading, for instance.' If people are daunted by the list, point out to them that nearly everyone finds some of the words difficult and hardly anybody gets them all right. If the informant says he doesn't know a particular word say: 'Would you just guess then. It's better for us if you do. Will you just pick out the one that seems as if it might be nearest?'*

The Questionnaire

1 First, can you tell me how long you've lived in this house/flat?

Born here	U
20 years or more	L
10 < 20 years	0
5 < 10 years	1
Less than 5 years	2

IF MOVED WITHIN 10 YEARS (1 OR 2) Where did you live before?

WRITE IN

AND CODE

First home since marriage	0
Inner London (ILEA)	1
Outer GLC	2
Outer Metropolitan Area	3
Outside London Region	4

IF LONDON REGION (1–3) (a) What sort of home did you have?

House, detached	2
House, semi-detached	3
House, terrace	4
Flat or m'nette, self-contained, purpose built	5
Flat or m'nette, self-contained, conversion	6
Rooms or 'flat' (not self-contained)	7
Other (SPECIFY)	8

(b) Did you (your household) own that house/flat or rent it? IF RENT Was that from the council or privately?

Own	0
Rent council	1
Rent private unfurnished	2
Rent private furnished	3
Other (SPECIFY)	4

2 Do you (your household) own or rent this house/flat IF RENT Is that from the council or privately?

Own	5
Rent council	6
Rent private unfurnished	7
Rent private furnished	8
Other (SPECIFY)	9

IF OWN (5) OR RENT (6–8) Whose name is it in?

Subject	1
Spouse	2
Subject and spouse jointly	3
Other person	4

3 When was the house/block built?

1840 or earlier	1
1841–1914	2
1918–1939	3
1945–1960	4
1961 or later	5

4 TYPE OF HOUSING (OBSERVE)

House, detached	2
House, semi-detached	3
House, terrace	4
Flat or m'nette, self-contained, purpose built	5
Flat or m'nette, self-contained, conversion	6
Rooms or 'flat' (not self-contained)	7
Other (SPECIFY)	8

5 Have you (your household) got a garden of your own?

Yes	U
No	L

* This word test, intended as a brief means of assessing people's intelligence was borrowed from an American study, whose methods and results are described in J. B. Miner, *Intelligence in the United States*. In the event, the hypothesis mentioned above was not confirmed and, in general, though 'intelligence' (measured in this way) was highly correlated with class, income and education, it did not seem to have any very strong independent influence on family relationships, work or leisure.

6 Have you (your household) got the use of a second home that you can go to for weekends or holidays? I mean, for instance, a house or a caravan or a boat you can sleep in?

No	0
House or cottage	1
Fixed caravan	2
Mobile caravan	3
Boat you can sleep in	4
Other (SPECIFY)	5

7 Can I check up: who lives with you here in your household?

Relation-ship to subject	Age last birth-day	Sex M F	Marital status M S W D Sep
1 SUBJECT		U L	1 2 3 4 5
2		U L	1 2 3 4 5
3		U L	1 2 3 4 5
4		U L	1 2 3 4 5
5		U L	1 2 3 4 5
6		U L	1 2 3 4 5
7		U L	1 2 3 4 5
8		U L	1 2 3 4 5
9		U L	1 2 3 4 5

CHECK So there are____of you altogether?

IF ANY SONS OF SUBJECT AGED 16 OR OVER IN H'HOLD Is he/are they in regular paid work?

Yes	1
No	0

IF YES (1) What is his/their occupation?

WRITE IN FOR ALL

____

____

____

____

8 Have you (your household) any household pets?

	No	0
	Tropical fish	2
	Goldfish	3
	Terrapin	4
	___ Cats	5
	___ Dogs	6
IF ANY	___ Guinea pigs	7
PUT	___ Rabbits	8
NUMBERS	___ Tortoises	9
	___ Other (SPECIFY)	U
	___ ________	
	___ ________	
	___ ________	

9 Have you (your household) a car? INCLUDE LIGHT VAN AND EXCLUSIVE USE OF FIRM'S CAR

No car	0
1 car	1
2 cars	2
3 cars	3

10 IF HOUSE/FLAT IS 'IN SUBJECT'S OR SPOUSE'S NAME' (CODE 1 2, OR 3, Q2) I'd like to ask what you think about moving from here. I'll ask about the *district* in a minute but I want to ask first just about this *house/flat*. Taking everything into account, would you prefer to stay in this house/flat or move to another home?

Stay	0
Move	1

IF 'MOVE' (1) (a) Would you want a house or a flat?

IF HOUSE What kind of house – detached, semi-detached, terrace or don't you mind?

House, detached	2
House, semi-detached	3
House, terrace	4
House, 'don't mind'	1
Flat or m'nette	5
Don't mind whether house or flat	6

(b) Would you want to have a garden?

Yes 1
No 0
Don't mind 9

IF YES (1) AND HAS GARDEN AT PRESENT Would you want the garden to be larger, smaller or about the same size as your present one?

Larger 5
Smaller 2
About the same size 3
Don't care about size 4

(c) Would you want an older house/flat or a more modern one?

Older 1
More modern 4
Same as present 3
Don't care about age 2

(d) Would you want to own or rent? IF RENT From the council or privately?

Own 5
Rent council 6
Rent private 7
Don't mind 8

(e) Would you want the house/flat to be larger or smaller than this, or about the same size?

Larger 3
Smaller 1
About the same size 2

IF LARGER (3) Can you give me any idea of what you would use the extra space for if you had it?

(f) Can you think of anything else about the house/flat that you would particularly want?

Yes 1
No 0

IF YES (1) What?

11 TO ALL (Now about the district) Taking everything into account, would you prefer to stay in this district or move to another district?

Stay 0
Move 1

IF MOVE (1) Have you any other particular district in mind?

Yes U
No T

IF YES (U) (a) What is it?

WRITE IN

(b) Could you tell me. Is that district:

PROMPT Further out 1
Further in to (the centre of) London 3
Or about the same distance from (the centre of) London as this 2

(c) Would you say that district is:

PROMPT More spread out 4
More built up 6
Or one that's about as built up/spread out as this district 5

(d) Is it a district with similar sorts of people to those who live round here, or not?

Similar 1
Different 0

IF DIFFERENT (0) In what ways are they different?

'Better class', more select 1
No (or less) coloured or foreigners 2
More friendly 3
More mixed in class 4
More same age or stage in life as informant 5
More mixed in age/stage in life 6
Other (SPECIFY) 7

(e) Is there anything else about ——(desired district) that makes you particularly want to move there?

Yes 1
No 0

IF YES (1) What?

IF NO DISTRICT IN MIND (L) (a) What sort of district would you prefer? Would you like one that's:

PROMPT Further out 1

Further in to (the centre of) London 3
Or about the same distance from (the centre of) London as this 2

(b) would you like a district that is:
PROMPT More spread out 4
More built up 6
Or one that's about as built up/spread out as this district 5

(c) Would you like a district with similar sorts of people to those who live round here, or not?
Similar 1
Different 0
IF DIFFERENT (0) In what ways would you like the people to be different?
'Better class', 'more select' 1
No (or less) coloured or foreigners 2
More friendly 3
More mixed in class 4
More same age or stage in life as informant 5
More mixed in age/stage in life 6
Other (SPECIFY) 7

(d) Is there anything else about the district that you would particularly want?
Yes 1
No 0
IF YES (1) What?

12 Are you working in a paid job? (And is your husband/wife?)

	Sjt	Sps
Full-time (30 hrs per week or more)	2	2
Part-time (less than 30 hrs)	1	1
Not working	0	0

IF SUBJECT NOT WORKING (a) Are you:
Retired (man or single woman) 3
Off work through illness or disability (man or single woman) 4
Unemployed (man or single woman) 5
Full-time student 6
Housewife 7
Other (SPECIFY) 8

(b) Have you ever worked?
Yes 1
No 0
IF YES (1) What was your (main) occupation?

WRITE IN
AND CODE
Self-employed with employees 1
Self-employed without employees 2
Manager 3
Foreman 4
Other employee 5

13 IF MARRIED, WIDOWED, DIVORCED OR SEPARATED WOMAN What is/was your husband's (main) occupation?

WRITE IN
AND CODE
Self-employed with employees 1
Self-employed without employees 2
Manager 3
Foreman 4
Other employee 5

14 FOR ALL SUBJECTS, CHECK:

	Code
Subject is working in paid job full or part-time and is 25 or over	1 GO ON TO Q 15
Subject is 24 or under	2 Q'AIRE II
Subject is married woman (*not* widowed, divorced or separated) and is neither full-time student nor working full or part-time	3 Q'AIRE III
Subject is man or single woman and is retired	4 Q'AIRE IV

Subject is none of above — 0 GO ON TO Q 48

TO SUBJECTS WORKING FULL- OR PART-TIME

15 What is your occupation?

WRITE IN
AND CODE

Self-employed with employees	1
Self-employed without employees	2
Manager	3
Foreman	4
Other employee	5

IF MAN, 65 OR OVER, OR SINGLE WOMAN, 60 OR OVER Is that much the same kind of work as you have been doing most of your life?

Yes	1
No	0

IF NO (0) What was your main occupation?

WRITE IN
AND CODE

Self-employed with employees	1
Self-employed without employees	2
Manager	3
Foreman	4
Other employee	5

16 How are you paid?

RUNNING PROMPT IF NECESSARY

On an hourly rate	1
On a weekly rate	2
On a monthly or annual salary	4
Other (SPECIFY)	5

17 What kind of firm/organisation do you work for?

18 Where do you work?

DISTRICT OR
TOWN

Work at home	9
No fixed place, travel around, 'all over'	0

IF '9' OR '0' SKIP TO Q 22

19 How long does it usually take you to get to work from here?

0–5 minutes	1
6–15 minutes	2
16–30 minutes	3
31–45 minutes	4
46 minutes – 1 hour	5
Over 1 hour	6

20 How do you usually get there?

Walk	1
Bicycle	2
Moped, motor scooter, motor bike	3
Car	4
Bus	5
Underground	6
Other train	7

WRITE IN DETAILS OF COMBINATION OTHER THAN WALK PLUS ONE OTHER

21 Do you think the time it takes you to travel to work is:

PROMPT

Too long	3
Too short	1
Or about right	2

22 How long is your 'official' working week? (EXCLUDE LUNCH HOURS) By 'official' I mean the hours laid down by your employer.

__________ hrs.

No 'official' hours, self-employed, casual, freelance	9

IF HAS 'OFFICIAL' HOURS Did you in fact put in more hours than that at your place of work last week (LAST NORMAL WEEK), paid or unpaid?

Yes	1
No	0

IF YES (1) How many hours?

__________ hrs. paid

__________ hrs. unpaid

IF NO 'OFFICIAL' HOURS (9) How many hours altogether did you put in at your place of work last week (LAST NORMAL WEEK)?

__________ hrs.

23 During the last week (LAST NORMAL WEEK) did you do any work at home in connection with your job?

Yes 1
No 0
Work *is* at home 9

IF YES (1) About how many hours?

________ hrs.

PART-TIME WORKERS AND SELF-EMPLOYED SKIP TO Q 33

FULL-TIME EMPLOYEES WHO DO NOT HAVE 'OFFICIAL' WORKING HOURS, SKIP TO Q 28

TO FULL-TIME EMPLOYEES (NOT SELF-EMPLOYED) WITH 'OFFICIAL' WORKING HOURS

24 Can you tell me what your 'official' starting time was on the Monday of last week? (LAST NORMAL WEEK) IF DID NOT WORK MONDAY, on Tuesday then?

	hr mins	
Time		a.m. p.m.

CODE: Monday 1
Other day (SPECIFY) 2

25 Was your 'official' starting time the same each day last week?

Yes L
No U

IF NO (U) (a) What times did you start and finish on the different days?

	START	FINISH
Monday		a.m. p.m.
Tuesday	a.m. p.m.	a.m. p.m.
Wednesday	a.m. p.m.	a.m. p.m.
Thursday	a.m. p.m.	a.m. p.m.
Friday	a.m. p.m.	a.m. p.m.
Saturday	a.m. p.m.	a.m. p.m.
Sunday	a.m. p.m.	a.m. p.m.

(b) How do these unusual hours affect your life outside work?

26 Were your starting times last week more or less the same as they usually are in other weeks?

Yes 1
No 0

IF NO (0) How does the arrangement of your working hours vary as between different weeks?

RECORD DETAILS

27 IF STARTED WORK BETWEEN 7 a.m. AND 10 a.m. INCLUSIVE LAST MONDAY OR TUESDAY Would you prefer to start and finish work earlier or later in the day than you do at present so as to make your travelling easier?

Prefer to stick to present time 1
Start and finish earlier 2
Start and finish later 3

28 TO ALL FULL-TIME EMPLOYEES Do you normally have both Saturday and Sunday off work?

Yes U
No 9

IF YES (U) Instead of having them both off, would you prefer to work on Saturday and have Sunday and Monday off, or to work on Sunday and have Friday and Saturday off, so that places would be less crowded for you and travelling easier?

- Monday off, work Saturday 1
- Friday off, work Sunday 2
- Either 3
- Neither 4

29 Suppose at some time in the future you were able to choose either to have more pay or to have more time off for the same pay, which would you choose?

- More pay 1
- More time off 3
- Other answer (SPECIFY) 2

IF MORE TIME OFF (3) What would you do with the extra time off?

30 Have you ever thought of starting up in business on your own?

- Yes 1
- No 0

IF YES (1) Have you ever done anything about it – I mean made any definite plans or anything like that?

- No 1
- Definite plans 2
- Actually had own business 3

31 How long have you worked for your present employer/firm?

- Less than 1 year 0
- 1 year < 5 1
- 5 years < 10 2
- 10 years < 20 3
- 20 years or more 4

32 Apart from your main job, have you in the past month done any other work for pay?

- Yes 1
- No 0

IF YES (1) (a) What kind of work is that?

(b) Roughly how many hours have you put in on this job/these jobs during the last month?

_________ hrs.

TO ALL WORKING FULL- OR PART-TIME

33 (Now I'd like to go back to your main job.) Would you say that in your line of work there's a career ladder?

- Yes 1
- No 0

Comments

34 In your job, how much say do you have over the way you use your time at work? Do you have:

PROMPT
- A lot of say 2
- Some but not much 1
- Or no say 0

35 When you are at work do you feel on the whole that you are pressed for time – that you are being rushed – or do you have plenty of time to do the things you have to do?

- Pressed 3
- Sometimes pressed, sometimes not 2
- Not pressed 1

36 Would you say that you usually find your work:

RUNNING PROMPT
- Very tiring physically 3
- Fairly tiring 2
- Or not tiring 1
- (Sometimes, sometimes not) 0

37 And would you say that you usually find it:

RUNNING PROMPT
- Very tiring mentally 3
- Fairly tiring 2
- Or not tiring 1
- (Sometimes, sometimes not) 0

38 How often do you feel bored at work? Is it:

PROMPT Often 3
Sometimes 2
Rarely 1
Never 0

39 And at home – how often do you feel bored at home? Is it:
PROMPT Often 3
Sometimes 2
Rarely 1
Never 0

40 What do you think you get most satisfaction from – your work or your leisure?
Work 3
Leisure 1
Both equally, 'the combination' 2

41 Taking it all round, how satisfied would you say you are with the job you've got at present?
PROMPT Very satisfied 3
Fairly satisfied 2
Not satisfied 1

42 If you didn't need the money, do you think you would go on working anyway?
'Don't need the money' 1
Would work 2
Wouldn't work 0

43 How many weeks paid holiday did you have in 1969? (COUNT TO NEAREST FULL WEEK: ASSUME 5-DAY WEEK)
1 week 1
2 weeks 2
3 weeks 3
4 weeks 4
5 weeks 5
6 weeks 6
None 0

IF ANY (1–6) (a) Did you take that all in one go?
Yes U
No L

IF YES (U) When did you take it? RECORD IN TABLE
IF NO (L) How did you split it up? RECORD IN TABLE

(*b*) Did you go away?
IF YES (i) Where to?
(ii) Did you stay at a relative's home for any part of the time?

	(a) How many weeks?				(b) (i) Did not go	UK	Eire	Abroad	(b) (ii) Stays rel's home Yes	No
Jan	1	2	3	4	5	6	7	8	U	L
Feb	1	2	3	4	5	6	7	8	U	L
Mar	1	2	3	4	5	6	7	8	U	L
Apr	1	2	3	4	5	6	7	8	U	L
May	1	2	3	4	5	6	7	8	U	L
June	1	2	3	4	5	6	7	8	U	L
July	1	2	3	4	5	6	7	8	U	L
Aug	1	2	3	4	5	6	7	8	U	L
Sept	1	2	3	4	5	6	7	8	U	L
Oct	1	2	3	4	5	6	7	8	U	L
Nov	1	2	3	4	5	6	7	8	U	L
Dec	1	2	3	4	5	6	7	8	U	L

IF TOOK ANY HOLIDAYS IN JULY OR AUGUST Would you have preferred to take all or part of your summer holiday at another time in the year, when holiday places would have been cheaper and less crowded and travelling easier?
Yes 1
No 0

IF YES (1) Why didn't you?
Could not get away from own work 1
Other members of family or holiday party could not get away 2
Children's school holidays 3
Other reason (SPECIFY) 4

SINGLE, WIDOWED, DIVORCED OR SEPARATED PEOPLE SKIP TO Q 48

MARRIED MEN AND WOMEN ONLY

44 Do you feel that the demands of your work interfere at all with the demands of your home and family?
Yes 1
No 0

IF YES (1) In what way?
Long hours 1

CODE ALL THAT APPLY	Shift work	2
	Strain, worry, irritability	3
	Problems with children	4
	Problems with meals	5
	Problems with housework	6
	Problems with shopping	7
	Other (SPECIFY)	8

45 Do you feel that the demands of your home and family interfere at all with other things you would like to do in your leisure?

Yes 1

No 0

IF YES (1) What is it that you would like to do and can't?

MARRIED MEN SKIP TO Q 48

46 TO MARRIED WOMEN Were you working just before you first got married?

Yes 1

No 0

IF YES (1) What was your occupation?

47 Did you give up paid work at some point after you got married?

Yes 1

No 0

IF YES (1) (a) How old were you when you first gave up work?

Age [|]

(b) Why did you give up work at that time?

Was expecting first child 1

Other reason (SPECIFY)

(c) How old were you when you first started work again?

Age [|]

(d) Why did you start at that time?

Youngest child went to school 1

Youngest child was old enough 2

(What age? [|])

Found suitable job 3

Other (SPECIFY) 4

(e) Was that full-time or part-time?

Full-time 4

Part-time 5

IF PART-TIME AND NOW WORKING FULL-TIME

(i) How old were you when you first started working full-time?

Age [|]

(ii) Why did you change then?

48 Now I want to ask about various leisure activities. I'd like to go through this list with you (HAND SUBJECT LIST) and ask for each activity whether you've done it at all in the last 12 months. FOR EACH ACTIVITY DONE About how many times have you done that during the last 12 months? Would you say that you've done it less than 12 times or more?

	How often?		
	12+	1–11	Not
Watching television	2	1	0
Listening to music on record player	2	1	0
Playing an instrument	2	1	0
Home decorations or repairs	2	1	0
Car maintenance or repairs	2	1	0
Car cleaning	2	1	0
Knitting or sewing	2	1	0
Read a book (not a mag)	2	1	0
Playing with children	2	1	0
Gardening	2	1	0

Model building	2	1	0
Collecting stamps or other objects	2	1	0

49 These are all things that people do in or around their home. Can I ask if there are any other leisure activities that you do at home and that you have done in the last year?

Yes 1
No 0

IF YES (1) (a) What?
(b) How often?

What?	How often? 12+	1–11
	2	1
	2	1
	2	1
	2	1
	2	1
	2	1

50 The next part of the list covers sports. I'd like to know if you've actually played or taken part in any of these in the last 12 months?

	How often? 12+	1–11	Not
Swimming	2	1	0
Sailing	2	1	0
Golf	2	1	0
Fishing	2	1	0
Association football	2	1	0
Cricket	2	1	0
Tennis	2	1	0
Table tennis	2	1	0
Bowls	2	1	0
Ten-pin bowling	2	1	0
Athletics	2	1	0

51 Are there any other sports you've actually taken part in during the past 12 months?

Yes 1
No 0

IF YES (1) (a) What?
(b) How often?

What?	How often? 12+	1–11
	2	1
	2	1
	2	1
	2	1
	2	1
	2	1
	2	1
	2	1

52 Now sports you go to watch as a spectator or watch on television.

	Spectator How often?			Watched on TV How often?		
	12+	1–11	Not	12+	1–11	Not
Swimming	2	1	0	6	5	4
Golf	2	1	0	6	5	4
Association football	2	1	0	6	5	4
Rugby football	2	1	0	6	5	4
Cricket	2	1	0	6	5	4
Tennis	2	1	0	6	5	4
Athletics	2	1	0	6	5	4
Motor sports	2	1	0	6	5	4
Boxing	2	1	0	6	5	4
Wrestling	2	1	0	6	5	4
Horse racing	2	1	0	6	5	4
Winter sports	2	1	0	6	5	4

53 Are there any other sports that you've been to watch as a spectator or watched on TV in the past 12 months?

Yes	1
No	0

IF YES (1) (a) What?
(b) How often?

What?	Spectator How often? 12+	1–11	Watched on TV How often? 12+	1–11
	2	1	6	5
	2	1	6	5
	2	1	6	5
	2	1	6	5
	2	1	6	5
	2	1	6	5
	2	1	6	5

54 Now some other leisure activities you might have done during the past 12 months.

	How often? 12+	1–11	Not
Go to cinema	2	1	0
Go to theatre	2	1	0
Go to museum	2	1	0
Go to art gallery	2	1	0
Go out for a meal NOT FOR LUNCH	2	1	0
Go to pub NOT FOR LUNCH	2	1	0
Attend church	2	1	0
Voluntary work	2	1	0
Billiards or snooker	2	1	0
Darts	2	1	0
Dancing	2	1	0
Go for a walk of a mile or more	2	1	0
Go for a drive in a car for pleasure	2	1	0

Camping	2	1	0
Caravanning	2	1	0

55 Are you an active member of any organisations or clubs? Any of these:

PROMPT CODE ALL THAT APPLY

Any club run by your firm IF WORKING	1
Sports club	2
Supporters club	3
Social club	4
Church group	5
Political party	6
Tenants, Ratepayers, Civic Group, Parents Association	7
Any other club or organisation (SPECIFY)	8
None	0

IF ANY (1–8) Are you an officer or committee member of it/any of them?

Yes	2
No	1

56 Are there any other leisure activities that you've done in the last 12 months and that we haven't included so far?

Yes	1
No	0

IF YES (a) What?
(b) How often?

What?	How often? 12+	1–11
	2	1
	2	1
	2	1
	2	1
	2	1
	2	1

57 Thinking of all the leisure activities that you have said you've done in the last year (including the ones you've added) which one would you say has given you the most enjoyment? IF DIFFICULT, Well just pick out one that you've enjoyed a lot.

WRITE IN
ONE
ACTIVITY

58 How *much* would you say you've enjoyed it?

WRITE IN
AND CODE

Enthusiastic answer	U
Other answer	L

59 IF NOT DONE AT HOME (a) Where did you go for that the last time?

DISTRICT OR TOWN

(b) Is that where you usually go or not?

Usually	7
Not	8

(c) And who were you with then (last time)?

Alone	0
Spouse only	1
Spouse + other h/hold members (+ others)	2
Other h/hold members (+ others)	3
Others only	4

(d) Do you usually go with the same people or not?

Usually	5
Not	6

60 TO THOSE WORKING FULL- OR PART-TIME Is there any way at all in which any of the leisure activities mentioned in the interview so far are linked to the kind of work you do? PROBE AND HELP

Yes 1
No 0

IF YES (1) LIST BELOW

(a) What is it/are they?	(b) How is it/are they linked to the kind of work you do?

61 TO ALL Can I ask this. What would you say is the difference between what you'd call 'work' and what you'd call 'leisure'?

No difference, 'same', 'merged', 'difficult to distinguish' 0
'Pleasure': Enjoy leisure, not work; work is 'hard', 'tiring', 'monotonous' 1
'Autonomy': Free in leisure, not in work; 'have to work' 2
Pay: Paid for work not leisure 3
Other (SPECIFY) 4

62 Do you regularly read a daily newspaper?

Yes 1
No 0

IF YES (1) (a) Which ones do you usually read?

Times 1
Financial Times 2
Guardian 3
D Telegraph 4
D Express 5
D Mail 6
D Mirror 7
Sun 8
D Sketch 9
Morning Star U
Other (SPECIFY) L

(b) What section of the paper do you usually read first? I don't mean just looking at the headlines?

Sports 2
Other 1

63 Do you think of yourself as a supporter of any particular team or teams – I mean a football team, rugby team, cricket club or anything like that?

Yes U
No 0

IF YES (U) What team is it/are they?

WRITE IN
AND CODE

Professional football club 1
Other football club 2
Rugby Union club 3
Other rugby club 4
County cricket club 5
Other cricket team 6
Other (SPECIFY SPORT) 7

IF PROFESSIONAL FOOTBALL CLUB
(1) Why do you support it?

CODE MAIN ONE ONLY
Near to present home 1
Near to former home 2
Through relative 3
Through friend 4
'Good team', 'Got good players' 5
Other (SPECIFY) 6

64 We are also interested in the part that relatives and friends play in people's leisure. I'd like to ask some questions about your family. IF PARENTS NOT IN SAME HOUSEHOLD Are your parents alive? IF ALIVE Have you met

your mother/father socially during the last week?

	Mother	Father
Dead	0	0
Alive, not met in week	1	1
Met in week	2	2

65 What is/was your father's (main) occupation?

66 IF MARRIED AND SPOUSE'S PARENTS NOT IN SAME HOUSEHOLD Are your parent's-in-law alive? IF ALIVE Have you met your mother-in-law/father-in-law socially during the last week?

	Mother-in-law	Father-in-law
Dead	0	0
Alive, not met in week	1	1
Met in week	2	2

67 IF MARRIED What is/was your husband's/wife father's (main) occupation?

68 IF MARRIED, WIDOWED, DIVORCED OR SEPARATED AND 30 OR OVER Have you any children (16 or over) living away from home?

Yes U
No L

IF YES (U) (a) Have you met him/her/any of them socially during the last week?

Yes 1
No 0

IF YES (1) How many?

____

(b) Are any of them married?

Yes U
No L

IF YES (U) Have you met any sons-in-law or daughters-in-law socially during the last week?

Yes 1
No 0

IF YES (1) How many?

__________ __

(c) Are any of your children living away from home sons who are in regular paid work?

Yes 3
No 2

IF YES (3) What is his/their present occupation?

____

____

____

____

69 TO ALL Are there any (other) relatives of your own (or your husband/wife) who you've met socially during the last week?

Yes 1
No 0

IF YES (1) How many? Count in a husband and wife as two people if you saw them both.

____

70 IF NO RELATIVE MET IN LAST WEEK When was the last time you did meet any relatives socially?

Over week – month 3
Over month – year 2
Over a year ago 1

IF OVER YEAR (1) SKIP TO Q 78

71 I'd like to ask a few questions about the last relative you met socially. (IF MORE THAN ONE AT SAME TIME Just pick the one you feel closest to) Who was it?

Mother 1
Father 2
Daughter 3
Son 4
Sister 5
Brother 6
Other female relative 7
Other male relative 8

CODE Sex M U
F L

72 Is he/she married or single?

Married 1
Single 2

Widowed	3
Divorced	4
Separated	5

73 About how old is he/she?

–24	1
25–29	2
30–39	3
40–49	4
50–59	5
60–69	6
70–79	7
80+	8

74 What is/was his/her present (or main) occupation?
OWN OCCUPATION FOR MAN OR SINGLE WOMAN

HUSBAND'S OCCUPATION FOR MARRIED, WIDOWED, DIVORCED OR SEPARATED WOMAN

75 Where does he/she live?

10 minutes walk	1

DISTRICT OR TOWN

76 Where did you last meet him/her? Was it:

PROMPT	Your home	7
	His/her home	8
	Somewhere else	9

77 IF SUBJECT MARRIED Was your husband/wife present then?

Yes	1
No	0

78 TO ALL As well as family and relatives, we're interested in non-relatives. First, have you any friends who live within ten minutes walk of here and who you've met socially during the last week, inside or outside the home?

Yes	1
No	0

IF YES (1) How many? Count in husband and wife as two people if you saw both of them.

____

79 IF WORKING FULL- OR PART-TIME Are there any friends from your work who you've met socially during the last week, inside or outside the home? (NOT LUNCH HOUR)

Yes	1
No	0

IF YES (1) How many? Count in the husbands or wives of your friends from work if you met them as well.

____

80 TO ALL Are there any other friends at all who you've met socially during the last week, inside or outside the home?

Yes	1
No	0

IF YES (1) How many?

____

81 IF NO FRIENDS MET IN LAST WEEK When was the last time you did meet any friends socially?

Over week – month	3
Over month – year	2
Over a year ago	1

IF OVER YEAR (1) SKIP TO Q 90 (IF MARRIED) OR Q 96 (IF NOT MARRIED)

82 I'd like to ask a few questions about the last friend you met socially. (IF MORE THAN ONE AT SAME TIME Just pick the one you feel closest to.) Was that friend a man or a woman?

Man	U
Woman	L

83 Is he/she married or single?

Married	1
Single	2
Widowed	3
Divorced	4
Separated	5

84 About how old is he/she?

–24	1
25–29	2

30–39 3
40–49 4
50–59 5
60–69 6
70–79 7
80+ 8

85 What is/was his/her present (or main) occupation?
OWN OCCUPATION FOR MAN OR SINGLE WOMAN

HUSBAND'S OCCUPATION FOR MARRIED, WIDOWED, DIVORCED OR SEPARATED WOMAN

86 Where does he/she live?
10 minutes walk 1
DISTRICT OR TOWN:

87 Where did you last meet him/her? Was it:
PROMPT Your home 7
His/her home 8
Somewhere else 9

88 IF SUBJECT MARRIED. Was your husband/wife present then?
Yes 1
No 0

89 How did you first meet him/her?
CODE ONE ONLY
Neighbour (met locally) U
Former neighbour L
Present or former work colleague 1
Services 2
Through past or present work/through professional interests 3
Present or former colleague of spouse/through spouse's past or present work/through spouse's professional interests 4
School/University/College 5
Club, association or other leisure interest 6
Through relative 7
Through friend 8
Through children 0
Other (SPECIFY) 9

SINGLE, WIDOWED, DIVORCED AND SEPARATED SUBJECTS SKIP TO Q 96

90 MARRIED SUBJECTS ONLY When was the last time you went out for the evening without your husband/wife. I mean going out for at least two hours, for pleasure or entertainment or to visit someone?
Yesterday evening 1
Within last week 2
Within last month 3
More than a month ago 4

91 When was the last time you went out for the evening *with* your husband/wife?
Yesterday evening 5
Within the last week 6
Within the last month 7
More than a month ago 8

IF WITHIN LAST MONTH (5, 6 or 7) AND IF ANY CHILDREN OF 12 OR UNDER Did you have to make any arrangements for baby-sitting/sitting-in?
Yes 1
No 0

IF YES (1) Would you go out more often if it was easier to get baby-sitters?
Yes 2
No 3

92 ASK MARRIED MEN ABOUT THEMSELVES AND MARRIED WOMEN ABOUT THEIR HUSBANDS Do you/does your husband help at least once a week with any household jobs like washing up, making beds, (helping with the children), ironing, cooking or cleaning?
None 0
Washing up 1
Making beds 2
Help with children 3
Ironing 4

Cooking 5
Cleaning 6
Other (SPECIFY) 7

93 TO MARRIED WOMEN SUBJECTS How many children have you had altogether? TO MARRIED MEN SUBJECTS How many children has your wife had altogether?

Number________

CHECK Are there any others that were born but not alive now? IF SO, INCLUDE THEM
IF WIFE 45 OR OVER SKIP TO Q 96

94 IF WIFE 44 OR UNDER Do you (couple) expect to have any (more) children?

Yes 1
No 0

IF YES (1) How many?

Number________

95 What do you think is the ideal number of children for couples like yourselves to have these days? (PROBE IF NECESSARY: Well what do you think, less than 3, 3, or more than 3?)

(No ideal, depends on circumstances L)

Number________

CHECK Probe used 1
Probe not used 0

IF NUMBER GIVEN, Why do you think that's a good number?

Finance (e.g. 'can't afford more', 'expense') 1
Children's interest, practical (e.g. 'more opportunity for them', 'can do more for them') 2
Children's interest, psychological (e.g. 'become better people', 'less self-centred') 3
Wife's interest (e.g. 'too hard for wife if more', 'wife too tired if more') 4
Family interest (e.g. 'a real family', 'better family life') 5
Other (SPECIFY) 6

96 TO ALL Here's a very general question: Do you think that in future most people will go on wanting to get more possessions?

Yes 1
No 0

IF YES (1) Do you think that you yourself are like most other people in that way?

Yes 1
No 2
Other (SPECIFY) 3

97 When was the last time you went to Central London?

Within last week 4
Over week – month 3
Over month – year 2
Over a year ago 1
Never 0

IF 'OVER A YEAR AGO' (1) OR 'NEVER' (0) SKIP TO Q 101

98 What was the main thing you did the last time you went there?

Work 1
Activities directly connected with work/business 2
Professional activities (e.g. professional meeting,
CODE conference) 3
ONE Shopping 4
ONLY Show, cinema, theatre, concert, dancing 5
Meal 6
Drinking 7
Meeting relatives 8
Meeting friends 9
Other (SPECIFY) 0

99 Now some questions about the traffic problem. Can you tell me whether you agree or disagree with this statement: 'It would be right to prevent so many cars going into Central London and leave more room on the streets for the buses.'

PROMPT Agree 3
Disagree 1
(Uncertain, can't say 2)

100 *Here's another statement I'd like to put to you: 'It would be wrong to add to existing restrictions on the use of cars in Central London.'

PROMPT Agree 6
Disagree 8
(Uncertain, can't say 7)

*After the first few interviews this question was deleted.

101 TO ALL Here is a list of things that the Government and local councils have to spend money on. (HAND SUBJECT LIST) You may think all those things are important. But, if you *had* to decide, which three things would you put at the top for spending more money on?

Improving primary education L
Improving secondary education 0
Giving more help to old people 1
Building more new homes 2
Building new motorways inside London 3
Providing more educational opportunities for young people 4
Improving the railways and underground 5
Improving the bus service 6
Controlling air pollution 7
Reducing noise 8
(Can't choose any) 9

102 We're nearly at the end now. I'd like to ask some standard questions. Which country were you born in? And your father?

	Subject	Father
England	L	L
Scotland	0	0
Wales	1	1
N Ireland	2	2
Eire	3	3
Cyprus	4	4
Europe (excluding above)	5	5
India/Pakistan/Ceylon	6	6
Carribean/W Indies	7	7
Other (SPECIFY)	8	8

103 Most people say they belong either to the middle or to the working class. If you had to make a choice, would you call yourself:

PROMPT Middle class 1
Working class 2
(Don't know, can't say 3)

104 How old were you when you finished your full-time education? And your husband/wife?

	Subject	Spouse
Years		
Still a full-time student	0	0
Don't know	9	9

IF NOT FULL-TIME STUDENT Are you taking any educational or training course at the moment?

Yes 1
No 0

IF YES (1) (a) What is that?
(b) CODE:
Correspondence 2
Attends Course 3

105 IF HAS EVER WORKED What was your occupation at the age of 16? IF STARTED LATER When you first started work?

WRITE IN

CHECK Working at 16 U
Started later L

SINGLE, WIDOWED, DIVORCED AND SEPARATED SUBJECTS SKIP TO Q 110

106 IF MARRIED Is your present marriage your first?

Yes 1
No 0

107 How old were you when you were (first) married?

Age

MARRIED WOMEN SKIP TO Q 110

108 IF MARRIED MAN Is your wife's marriage to you her first?

Yes	1
No	0

109 How old was she when she was (first) married?

Age

110 TO ALL May I ask which political party you think you will vote for in the next General Election?

Labour	1
Conservative	2
Liberal	3
Other party	4
Won't vote	5
Don't know	6

IF DON'T KNOW (6) Which party do you think you are most likely to vote for?

Labour	1
Conservative	2
Liberal	3
Other party	4
Still won't vote	5
Still don't know	6

111 TO MARRIED SUBJECTS LIVING WITH SPOUSE Could you tell me which figure on this card corresponds to your total *joint* income (you and your husband/wife) before tax. SHOW CARD AND CODE BELOW

TO ALL OTHERS Could you tell me which number on this card corresponds to your own total income before tax? SHOW CARD AND CODE BELOW

Under £500	1
£500<£1,000	2
£1,000<£1,500	3
£1,500<£2,000	4
£2,000<£3,000	5
£3,000<£4,000	6
£4,000<£5,000	7
£5,000 or more	8
Don't know	9

112 I wonder if you would help with this. (HAND SUBJECT LIST OF WORDS) It's a bit different from the rest of the questions. It will only take 3 or 4 minutes. We want to find out how familiar people are with different words. What I'd like you to do is look at the word in capital letters on each line. Then you look across the line and see which word comes closest in meaning to the word in capital letters.

113 I'd like to come back to the main question that our study is all about. Do you think there is a need for any more leisure facilities around here? I don't mean just for yourself but for people of other ages as well. EXPLORE

Thank you for your help (LEAVE LETTER) IF ELIGIBLE FOR DIARY (MARRIED AND AGED 30–49 INCLUSIVE) We are asking some of the people we are seeing to fill in a diary for a few days for a fee of £1. SHOW DIARY FORM AND EXPLAIN

Willing to do diary	1
Not willing	0

TO ALL You've been very helpful. If one of the directors of the study, who are writing a book about it all, wanted to come back to have a further talk, would you be willing?

Yes	2
No	0
Doubtful	1

IF YES (2) RECORD IF PARTICULARLY INTERESTING/ARTICULATE/HELPFUL SUBJECT

Yes, particularly good 6

Who present in interview?

Informant only 0

Spouse as well 1

Father/mother as well 2

Other person/people as well 3

Name:

Address:

Date:

Length of interview:

______hrs ______mins

APPENDIX 3

THE TIME BUDGET STUDY

Richard Mills

A time budget, as it is conventionally called, is a systematic record of a person's use of time over a given period. The basic information it contains is the duration of activities and their sequence and timing. The fact that it aims to provide a systematic account of time use is what primarily distinguishes it from the literary diary. Normally there is some subjective criterion of selection at work to determine which of his activities a literary diarist chooses to record, and this differs from one diarist to another. A literary diary ordinarily excludes full information on timing, duration and sequence.

The time budget aims to reduce such selectivity to a minimum. It may be expanded to include other aspects of behaviour besides sequence, timing and duration, and may record not only the activities themselves but the people with whom they were performed, and the location of activities. There may also be subjective assessments of activities, such as how far they were 'routine', or 'pleasurable', or how far the respondent would like to do them more or less often.

The time budget is a relatively new device, and one which has not so far been much used, probably because of the methodological problems outlined below. Only in recent years have the major pioneering studies,[1] mostly conducted in the United States in the 1930s, been followed in Britain, in studies to do with mass communication, transport and recreational planning, besides more general social analysis.[2]

The primary advantage of time budgets is their sheer compre-

[1] See, in particular, G. A. Lundberg *et al.*, *Leisure: A Suburban Study*, and P. A. Sorokin and C. Q. Berger, *Time Budgets of Human Behaviour*.

[2] Among recent studies, see, in particular, A. Szalai *et al.*, 'The Multi-national comparative time budget research project', and A. Szalai *et al.*, *The Use of Time*; also, among British studies, BBC Audience Research Department, *The People's Activities;* I. Cullen and V. Godson, *The Structure of Activity Patterns;* and the review article by J. Anderson, 'Space-time budgets and activity studies in urban geography and planning'.

hensiveness, even if the information is superficial. They have obvious advantages over ordinary questionnaires and 'check-lists': with these one can in practice ask only about a limited number of activities which must be precisely specified in advance. Relatively informal activities such as 'napping' and casual encounters, the undergrowth of a person's day, cannot easily be got at by interview, especially if one does not know in advance what to expect.

The second advantage is that duration is itself a criterion of the importance of different activities, though De Grazia's qualification is, of course, sound.[1]

> By using a strictly quantitative, assembly belt conception of time – time as a moving belt of equal units – one ignores the significance of most activity. A moment of awe in religion or ecstasy in love or orgasm in intercourse, a decisive blow to an enemy, relief in a sneeze, or death in a fall is treated as equal to a moment of riding on the bus, shovelling coal, or eating beans.

Even so, duration is at least one useful measure.

The third advantage of time budgets is that they provide information on the sequencing and scheduling of activities.

A fourth advantage for us was that with time budgets we could get a comprehensive account of the time spent on 'work' by housewives to compare with that of their husbands.

The elements which were added to the basic diary arose out of the special interests of the study. As well as description, duration and sequence, we asked: with whom else, if anyone, was each activity performed; whether it was performed 'at the same time as usual', to give a rough indication whether it was part of a weekday, Saturday or Sunday routine; and finally – by way of subjective evaluation – whether the respondent thought the activity was 'work', 'leisure', 'neither work nor leisure', or 'a mixture'.

The remainder of this appendix is devoted to a summarized description of the sample and research methods, a note on the problem of activity coding and analysis, and a brief discussion of some of the methodological problems that time budget studies raise.

Sample and research methods

A respondent had not only to have completed the main questionnaire, but also to be married and between the ages of thirty and forty-nine inclusive. Our main interest was in men and women in middle life,

[1] S. De Grazia, *Of Time, Work and Leisure*, pp. 347–8.

and particularly in housewives. The time budget sample is thus a fairly homogeneous one.

What period to cover? On the one hand, a single day may not be very typical, particularly if the day in question is a Saturday or Sunday. On the other hand, completing a diary is, for some respondents at least, sufficiently demanding for them to be unwilling to do it for more than a single day; their interest inevitably wanes. In the end we decided that the minimum requirement, and the maximum we could ask, for each respondent was a diary covering both weekend days and one weekday. The assumption was that one weekday for a married middle-aged respondent would be fairly representative of his others, because of the constraints imposed by normal work-time. We included both weekend days because of their difference and because of our special interest in leisure. The second assumption was that 400 such diaries would yield a reasonably representative picture.

Outside the day, we were concerned about the possibility of major variations from one weekday evening to another. So it was decided that respondents should be asked also to keep a log of any activities done *outside* their home on the other four evenings of the week. The trouble involved in keeping a detailed account of time use through three full days and four other evenings was such, we felt, that respondents should be paid a fee.

The next problem was the design of the diary form. It could not be so formidable that the respondent was discouraged. On the other hand it had to contain sufficient instructions to make completing it reasonably straightforward. The diary booklet as it was finally evolved is reproduced, together with the relevant section of the Interviewers' Instructions, at the end of this Appendix. It is for the most part self-explanatory, but a few additional points need to be made.

The diary was designed in such a way that a full day's record could be made on a single pair of facing pages: with no pages to turn over, the respondents' task each day was that much less daunting. A variable number of lines was left between hour markers. This was because piloting showed that there was a tendency for activities to be 'bunched' in particular periods of the day.

When the interviewer had completed the interview and confirmed that the respondent was eligible for inclusion in the time budget sample, she asked whether he was willing to complete the diary as well. If he was, the task was explained and if necessary the interviewer went through a short trial run in which, with the respondent, she completed a dummy form for the previous few hours. When leaving the form the interviewer would fill in on the front the respondent's name, address, telephone number and serial number, and also the days and evenings (normally starting the day after the interview) for which the diary was to be completed.

For the return and checking of the diary forms, various procedures can be adopted. The Multi-national Comparative Study had a second interview when the diary form was collected after the interviewer had checked through it for omissions and inconsistencies. We felt that the procedure was unnecessarily costly for the verification and additional information it provided. It was also questionable how useful such additional probing could be after a week had elapsed. Piloting suggested that with careful explanation to the interviewee and the incentive of the small fee the majority of diarists would both complete a diary that was sufficiently clear and full for analytical purposes and return it to us by post without the need for collection, and this procedure was therefore adopted. Any major omissions or logical inconsistencies could then be checked by telephone or post, or by call back if necessary. In fact less than a quarter of the diaries had the kind of omissions or inconsistencies that had to be referred back to the diarists.

A number of respondents who had agreed to complete the diary failed to return it. Reminder letters were then sent. If there was still no reply, the interviewer called back to check on the reason for the non-return and give further help with the completion of the form if the respondent still wanted to take part. As has been pointed out already, the total of 411 diaries was, on the main socio-demographic variables, similar to the corresponding section of the general sample.

The final response was as shown in Table A6.

TABLE A6 *Response in time budget study*

Refused to keep diary	274	
Agreed to keep diary, but failed to do so	12	
Diary kept but returned too late	1	
Diary kept but too poor for analysis	1	
TOTAL FAILURES		288
Diaries returned without reminder	337	
Returned after reminder or call back		
Completed with some help from interviewer	69	
Completed without help from interviewer	5	
TOTAL DIARIES FOR ANALYSIS		411
Eligible sub-sample from general survey		699

Appendix 3

The diary data

Some diarists failed to keep the diary for some part of the full period. The final information provided by the 411 diaries was:

Weekdays	*Saturday*	*Sunday*	*Four weekday evenings*
411	397	398	285

The discrepancy between the total of 411 and the other figures is accounted for by some diaries which were completed inadequately for Saturdays, Sundays, or evenings, with so many gaps and omissions that even with calls back they were unsuitable for analysis. Because the response was so low for weekday evenings, we have not used them in this book.

Table A7 shows the average numbers of activities recorded for the diary days. The first line is the 'unedited' total, that is the simple total of discrete activity episodes recorded by the diarists. The second line, the edited total, represents the number of activities for purposes of analysis. This differs from the former number, because in certain instances the diaries had to be edited to meet the requirements of the coding frame. For example, diarists might record as one activity episode (e.g. '9.30 – 10 a.m. made, ate and washed up breakfast') what the coding frame required to be separated into the different categories of preparing meals, eating and washing-up. Only in rare instances, however, was the amount of editing required at all substantial, and normally the edited total would be only one or two different from the unedited total.

TABLE A7 *Average numbers of recorded activities*

	Weekday	*Saturday*	*Sunday*
Unedited total	24·5	20·3	20·0
Edited total	25·3	21·9	21·7

The coding frame

In this study a person was recorded as doing only a single activity at a time. Wherever two were recorded as simultaneous the one was chosen which the diarist's description implied was paramount. Activities not described in this way – primarily watching TV, and listening to radio or records – are therefore not taken account of in the analysis. Another problem, the classification of activities, was dealt with by adopting (with minor adjustments) the codes developed for the Multi-national Comparative Time Budget Study. This was done partly for direct comparison with that study, but also so that our results might be more generally useful if, as is to be hoped, the multi-national codes are used in subsequent studies. Anyone familiar with the past body of time budget research will know the frustrations of being unable to compare findings when substantially different classifications have been used.

The multi-national code includes a hundred basic activity classifications, divided initially into ten broad categories. Our final coding frame, shown in Table A8, was the same as that of the multi-national study except for items 06, 13, 38, 45, 46, 47, 56, 71, 72, 73, 80, 81, 85, 86, 87, 90, 91, 92, 93, 94 and 97. The changes were matters of detail and do not affect the broad categories. The detailed categories were regrouped into the revised broad categories shown in Table A9, again in line with one of the groupings used in the multi-national study. A comparison of the London results with those of the thirteen surveys in the multi-national study is given in Table A10. As is pointed out in Chapter IV, the comparison should be interpreted with caution because the London time budget survey related only to married people aged thirty to forty-nine; at the time of writing comparable data were not available for the multi-national study and we had to compare with married people generally, who were of all ages between eighteen and sixty-four.

TABLE A8 *Codes used in time budget study (based upon those of the Multi-national Time Budget Study, and using essentially the same titles)*

WORK TIME AND TIME RELATED TO IT (00–09)

Code	*Activity*
00	Normal professional work (outside home)
01	Normal professional work at home or brought home
02	Overtime if it can be specifically isolated from 00
03	Displacements during work if they can be specifically isolated from 00
04	Any waiting or interruption during working time if it can be specifically isolated from work e.g. due to supply shortage, breakdown of machines, queueing for pay, etc.
05	Undeclared, auxiliary, etc., work
06	Meals between work periods
07	Time spent at the workplace before starting and after finishing work
08	Regular breaks and prescribed non-working periods during worktime

TABLE A8—*cont.*

Code	*Activity*
09	Travel to and from workplace, including waiting for means of transport

Note 07 is not to be used for activities incidentally related to the workplace, e.g. at a works club.

DOMESTIC WORK (10–19)

10	Preparation and cooking of food/drinks
11	Washing-up and putting away the dishes
12	Indoor and outdoor cleaning
13	Car maintenance and repairs
14	Laundry, ironing
15	Repair or upkeep of clothes, shoes, underwear, etc.
16	Repairs and home decorations
17	Gardening, animal care
18	Heat and water supplies – upkeep
19	Others (e.g. dealing with bills and various other papers, usual care to household members, etc.)

Note Gardening and animal care are to be recorded as 'domestic work' only if not part of professional work or gainful employment.

Note In the category of activities listed above no time for travelling is provided for. Trip to home is to be regarded as connected to the last activity performed before going home.

CARE OF CHILDREN (20–29)

20	Care to babies
21	Care to older children
22	Supervision of school work (exercises and lessons)
23	Reading of tales or other non-school books to children, conversations with children
24	Indoor games
25	Outdoor games and walks
26	Medical care (visiting the childrens' doctor or dentist, or other activities related to the health of children)
27	Others
28	Not to be used
29	Travel to accompany children including waiting for means of transport

TABLE A8—*cont.*

PURCHASING OF GOODS AND SERVICES (30–39)

Code	*Activity*
30	Purchasing of everyday consumer goods and products
31	Purchasing of durable consumer goods
32	Personal care outside home (e.g. hairdresser)
33	Medical care outside home
34	Administrative services, offices
35	Repair and other services (e.g. laundry, electricity, mechanics)
36	Waiting, queueing for the purchase of goods and services
37	Others
38	Visits to libraries
39	Travelling connected to the above-mentioned activities, including waiting for means of transport

PRIVATE NEEDS: MEALS AND SLEEP, etc. (40–49)

40	Personal hygiene, dressing (getting up, going to bed, etc.)
41	Personal medical care at home
42	Care given to adults, if not included in household work
43	Meals and snacks at home
44	Meals outside home and other than at work or between professional work periods
45	Sleep (essential)
46	'Nap' or rest
47	Having drinks, cups of tea
48	Private activities, non-specified, others
49	Travelling connected to the above-mentioned activities, including waiting for means of transport
Note	A number of special types of meals outside home and work have special codes, different from 44. See Entertainment, Social Life (70–79)
Note	Code 48 may include any time expenditure the respondent is unwilling or unable to give information on.

ADULT EDUCATION AND PROFESSIONAL TRAINING (50–59)

50	Full time attendance at classes (undergraduate or postgraduate student), studies being the principal activity
51	Reduced programme of professional or special training courses (including after-work classes organised by the plant or enterprise in question)
52	Attendance at lectures, evening classes, etc.
53	Programmes of political or union training courses

TABLE A8—*cont.*

Code	*Activity*
54	Home work prepared for different courses and lectures
55	Reading of scientific reviews or books for personal instruction
56	Driving lessons, others
57–58	Not to be used
59	Travelling connected to the above-mentioned activities, including waiting for means of transport
CIVIC AND COLLECTIVE PARTICIPATION ACTIVITIES (60–69)	
60	Participation as member of a party, or a union, etc.
61	Voluntary activity of an elected official of a social or political organisation
62	Participation in meetings other than those covered by 60 and 61
63	Non-paid collective civic activity (e.g. volunteers)
64	Participation in religious organisations
65	Prayers, religious practice and attending religious ceremonies
66	Participation in various factory councils (committees, com missions)
67	Participation in other associations
68	Voting, others, etc.
69	Travelling connected to the above-mentioned activities, including waiting for means of transport
ENTERTAINMENT, SOCIAL LIFE (70–79)	
70	Attending a sports event
71	Fair, circus
72	Pub
73	Theatre, concert, opera, cinema
74	Museum, exhibition
75	Receiving visit of friends or visiting friends and relatives
76	Party or reception with meal offered to or offered by friends, cocktail party
77	Cafe, tea-room, restaurant, social meals out
78	Attending receptions (other than those mentioned above), and others – social clubs, community centres, etc.
79	Travelling connected with the above-mentioned activities, including waiting for means of transport
SPORTS AND ACTIVE LEISURE (80–89)	
80	Sport and physical exercise, hunting and fishing
81	Excursions
82	Walks

TABLE A8—*cont.*

Code	*Activity*
83	Technical hobbies, collections (e.g. crosswords)
84	Needlework, dressmaking, knitting, etc.
85	Artistic creations (sculpture, painting, pottery, literature, playing a musical instrument, singing, etc.)
86	Bingo, whist drives, betting shops
87	Dancing, night club, etc.
88	Others – cards, monopoly, home games, etc.
89	Travelling connected to the above-mentioned activities, including waiting for means of transport
PASSIVE LEISURE (90–99)	
90	Passive leisure – mixed or unspecified
91	Listening to the radio
92	Watching television
93	Listening to records
94	Reading books, reading reviews, periodicals, pamphlets, etc.
95	Reading newspapers
96	Conversations, including telephone conversations
97	Reading or writing private correspondence
98	Relaxing, reflecting, thinking, planning, doing nothing, no visible activity
99	Travelling connected to the above-mentioned activities, including waiting for means of transport

The following kinds of analysis were employed. Activity frequencies yielded information, firstly, on how often activities were performed, by different categories of respondent, etc., and secondly, on the times at which different kinds of activities were begun, through the day, and distributed through the week, again by different categories of people. Subsequent statistical analysis yielded the data primarily quoted in this report – the average amounts of time spent on different kinds of activity by different groups of people. The only important kind of information which the data and the analysis techniques did not effectively yield was on the *sequencing* of activities.

As has been suggested by our questions, analyses could also be made of who the person was with at the time, whether the activity was considered 'work' or 'leisure', and whether it was done 'at the same time as usual'. Respondents were not asked to record where they were when a particular activity was performed, but we found that the general kind of location (e.g. own garden, friends' house, own work-

TABLE A9 *Regrouping of activities in time budget study*

Description used in this book	*Description used in Multi-national Study*	*Codes of activities included (see Table A8)*
Paid work	Working time	00 to 05
Travel to work	Trips to/from work	09
Household work	*Housework obligations*	
Housework	Housework	10 to 19
Child care	Child care	20 to 22, 26, 27
Shopping	Shopping	30, 31, 34 to 38
Subsistence	*Physiological needs*	
Personal care	Personal care	32, 33, 40, 41, 48
Eating	Eating	43, 44
Sleeping	Sleeping	45
Meals and breaks in connection with paid work*	Non-work time out of time related to work*	06 to 08
Leisure	*Free time*	
Adult education	Education	50 to 56
Civic and collective activities	Organisations	60 to 68
Entertainment	Spectator	70 to 74
Sports and walking	Sport, walking	25, 80 to 82
Other leisure	Other leisure	23, 24, 42, 46, 47, 75 to 78, 83 to 88, 90 to 98
Non-work travel	*Non-work trips*	29, 39, 49, 59, 69, 79, 89, 99

* The change that we made was to put these activities as part of Subsistence so as to put the time spent eating and having breaks during the working day on a par with the meals and breaks of wives not at work. In the multi-national study this category was grouped, along with working time and trips to/from work, under a general heading of 'time related to work'.

place, etc.) could be confidently inferred from the diary records, and the data were accordingly analysed in this way.

The major problems

We should now mention some of the chief qualifications which should be taken into account in assessing the results. The first is that there were inevitably differences in people's degree of commitment. Apart from boredom, disenchantment, forgetfulness and inaccurate recall (due to completing the whole diary in one sitting or varying intervals after the specific period of coverage had elapsed), there are other reasons for inaccuracy. Time budgets may be less prone to influence by interviewers than other methods of data collecting, depending of course on the structuring imposed by the time budget instructions. Respondents are at least free to fill out the time budget in their own time and in relative privacy, without direct intervention by an interviewer. But this very freedom inevitably allows some respondents to edit entries, and thus omit valuable material, or to enter only those activities which are of special importance to them.

Respondents clearly make assumptions about what is trivial in their lives and what is not. 'Seven minutes making coffee' may or may not be too minor to be entered at all. This leads to large amounts of 'lost time'. It is rare to find a time budget without some discrepancy, generally of the order of 5 per cent. Respondents also tend to 'round up' periods of time to the nearest five, ten or fifteen minutes. Further, there is a tendency to record several activities within, say, thirty minutes. It is quite common to come upon entries which lump together a sequence of events; '9.00–9.30; took the dog for a walk; made supper; ate supper; laid table for breakfast'. There is no alternative but to allocate an average amount of time from the total among the separate activities.

In the coding, one meets all the familiar problems of meaning that arise with interview questions and check lists: at what point, for example, does moving about on foot become the recreational activity of going for a walk? With time budgets the problems of meaning and categorization are more substantial. Respondents themselves are, simply by deciding what they record, 'coding' their behaviour. A person's definition of what he is doing can easily differ from an outside assessment. The researcher must then himself code these often highly compressed written accounts. Moreover, while a check-list procedure will have reference only to particular segments of behaviour which are open to relatively little misinterpretation, there are periods of the day when a person's behaviour can defy simple classification. In part it is

TABLE A10 *Use of time per day in hours and tenths of hours in London Region and in Multi-national Study (London Region, married men and women aged 30 to 49; Multi-national Study, married men and women aged 18 to 64)*

Married men	*London Region*	*Belgium*	*Bulgaria*	*France*	*Hungary*	*Poland*	*West Germany National*	*West Germany Osnabruck*	*Czechoslovakia*	*USSR*	*U.S.A. Cities*	*U.S.A. Jackson*	*Yugoslavia Kragujevac*	*Yugoslavia Maribor*
Paid work and travel to work	7·1	7·4	7·5	7·3	8·3	7·6	7·1	6·9	6·5	6·9	7·0	6·9	7·3	7·5
Household tasks	1·4	0·8	1·9	1·6	1·9	1·6	1·3	1·2	2·0	1·6	1·1	1·1	1·2	2·1
All 'work'	8·5	8·2	9·4	8·9	10·2	9·2	8·4	8·1	8·5	8·5	8·1	8·0	8·5	9·6
Subsistence	10·6	10·7	10·6	11·0	10·0	9·7	10·9	10·6	10·2	10·2	10·3	10·3	10·2	10·0
Leisure	4·5	4·7	3·4	3·7	3·5	4·7	4·4	4·9	4·8	4·6	4·8	4·9	4·6	3·9
Non-work travel	0·4	0·4	0·6	0·4	0·3	0·4	0·3	0·4	0·5	0·7	0·8	0·8	0·7	0·5
Married women working														
Paid work and travel to work	4·7	5·9	6·8	5·8	6·6	6·1	4·9	4·4	5·5	6·2	5·2	4·9	5·7	6·4
Household tasks	4·3	3·9	3·6	4·7	5·3	4·7	5·5	4·9	5·4	4·6	4·1	3·8	4·7	5·5
All 'work'	9·0	9·8	10·4	10·5	11·9	10·8	10·4	9·3	10·9	10·8	9·3	8·7	10·4	11·9
Subsistence	10·5	10·6	10·2	10·9	9·5	9·5	10·2	10·7	9·8	9·7	10·3	10·2	9·8	9·6
Leisure	4·1	3·2	2·8	2·3	2·2	3·1	3·2	3·6	3·0	2·6	3·7	4·1	3·3	2·1
Non-work travel	0·4	0·4	0·6	0·3	0·4	0·6	0·2	0·4	0·3	0·9	0·7	1·0	0·4	0·4

TABLE A10—*cont.*

Married women not in paid work														
Paid work and travel to work	0·0	0·3	0·2	0·1	0·8	0·0	0·2	0·1	0·2	0·1	0·1	0·1	0·2	0·2
Household tasks	6·5	7·2	7·9	8·0	9·3	8·5	7·8	7·5	7·9	7·9	6·9	6·8	7·2	10·2
All 'work'	6·5	7·5	8·1	8·1	10·1	8·5	8·0	7·6	8·1	8·0	7·0	6·9	7·4	10·4
Subsistence	10·6	11·0	10·6	11·2	10·4	10·4	11·0	11·1	11·0	10·3	10·2	10·2	10·2	10·3
Leisure	6·3	4·9	4·5	4·1	2·9	4·2	4·8	5·0	4·5	4·7	5·9	5·9	5·5	2·7
Non-work travel	0·6	0·6	0·8	0·6	0·6	0·9	0·2	0·3	0·4	1·0	0·9	1·0	0·9	0·6

The multi-national surveys were carried out in 1965–6. The figures for the multi-national study are for an average of the full seven-day week; for comparability the London Region data had to be recalculated, by multiplying the daily figures by five, adding Saturday and Sunday and then dividing by seven. In the multi-national study, but not in London, some women defined as 'not employed' were nevertheless recorded as doing some work; hence the apparent contradiction of non-working wives shown as working, for example, 0·3 hours in Belgium. The definition of an 'employed person' in the multi-national study was that it was someone who 'according to their declaration, pursued at the time of the survey, to a non-negligible degree, a bread-earning activity.'

the problem already referred to, that he can be doing several things at once: typewriting, composing a paper, intermittently looking out of the window and waiting for dinner. In part it is the problem that he can be doing nothing capable of finite definition in brief and conventional form.

Interviewers' instructions on time budgets

1. *Purpose of time diaries.* The purpose of the diaries is to gather detailed information on the way in which people used their time during a given period. We are interested in the whole range of activities in which people engage, not just one particular type of activity. Moreover it is not enough just to know that they did them: we want to know, with as much precision as possible, the amount of time that they gave to them, and the sequence in which they did them. Time diaries make it possible to gain this sort of information because, rather than ask the informant to recall what he did at some point in the past as one would do in the normal interview, we ask him to keep a continuous record of his activities *as he does them*.

2. *Need for skill.* Both because the information required is so detailed and because obtaining it requires more active participation from the informant, it follows that even more skill than usual will be needed from interviewers in eliciting interest and co-operation. While the diaries will place some additional demands on you there is no reason to approach them with any apprehension: the informant generally quite enjoys completing the diary and is often surprised to see how his time is spent.

3. *The sample.* We do not want all informants to complete a diary. To be eligible he or she must be married and aged 30–49 inclusive. We do of course want as many people as possible within that age range to complete a diary. Experience suggests that almost all of those who agree to be interviewed will be willing to go on and do the diary.

4. *Period covered.* We want each person who falls within the time diary sample to keep a detailed diary for one weekday and one weekend, and to provide some more limited information – just on away-from-home activities – for four weekday evenings. The intention is that there should thus be some information for each of seven consecutive days, which constitute the 'Diary Week' for the informant. His diary week will normally begin at midnight on the day of the interview. The first 24-hour period will constitute the full

diary weekday and the following Saturday and Sunday the full diary weekend. Weekday evenings between diary weekday and diary weekend and following weekday evenings, up to a total of four, make up the full diary week. For example, if you conduct the interview on a Tuesday, the informant will keep the full diary for the Wednesday, the evening diary for the Thursday, Friday, Monday and Tuesday, and the full diary for the intervening Saturday and Sunday.

5. *The diary form.* You will give each diarist a booklet in which to record their activities. Each booklet is made up as follows: two pages each for the diary weekday and the Saturday and Sunday, and a single page at the end for the four evenings.

6. *Return of diaries and payment.* Since the completion of a diary entails some time and effort on the part of the informant we shall pay everybody who completes a diary a fee of £1. Along with the diary booklet you will leave each diarist a pen (which he can keep) and a stamped addressed envelope in which to return the diary to the Institute office. The fee will be sent to him as soon as his diary is received.

7. *Introducing the diary.* You will ask the informant if he is willing to complete the diary when you have got to the end of the first interview. The best procedure is to tag it to an expression of thanks for co-operation in the interview:

   > Thank you for answering all these questions. It really is a great help to us. There is one other way in which we would like your help if you are willing. We need to know in some detail how people spend their time through the day, so we can compare the lives of people of different ages, different countries – that sort of thing. So we'd like the people we interview to fill in this diary for a few days for us – it's quite easy and straightforward. But it will take up a little bit of your time, so we are paying £1 to all the people who help us with this . . .

   Show the diary and, if the informant agrees or is hesitant (i.e. if he does not firmly say 'No'), continue with the explanation. Try not to give the impression that this is something we are asking only a few people to do, that it is a sort of optional extra. You should stress that it is an essential part of the study and that it is important that the particular informant should keep the diary if at all possible.

8. *Helping the informant to understand his task.* We suggest the following stages in explaining the diarist's task. First, explain the arrangement of the diary booklet. Then fill in a Practice Diary Page with the

informant and explain the various columns. Note that there is a full explanation of the various columns on the front of the diary. It is not necessary to go through all of this with the diarist, but you should tell him that it is there for his reference. You should, however, make the following points:

> *What did you do?* Use a separate line for each activity, and give a specific time for it. Try to avoid running activities together, such as 'cooked and ate dinner'. Treat each journey (to and from a destination) as a specific activity, separate from the purpose of the trip or activities at the destination.
> *With whom?* Personal names are not needed here. Relationships (sister, friend, colleague) are quite enough.

It is best to make these points, and give the explanation of the other columns, in the course of filling in a few lines of the practice diary. You should fill in the diary yourself, from information provided by the informant for any appropriate time period – say earlier in the day. If the informant has difficulty recalling a past period in sufficient detail, you should invent it, and stress that it is how the diary might have been completed. Do try to include a journey in this. The practice diary can then be left with the diarist. Continue with the practice diary only as long as is necessary for the diarist to understand clearly what he has to do.

9. *Filling out the diary cover*. Before leaving, fill in the informant's name, telephone number (if any), address and serial number on the front of the diary. Finally, tell the diarist that if he wants any further advice he is welcome to telephone us at the number on the front of the diary, and that the £1 fee will be posted to him as soon as the diary is received by us fully completed.

Appendix 3

INSTITUTE OF COMMUNITY STUDIES

STUDY OF EVERYDAY ACTIVITIES

DIARY

for

Weekday: ____________

Weekend: ____________

____

Weekday Evenings: ____________

____

____

____

____

We are grateful to you for agreeing to complete the diary. These notes may help you. The diary is in two parts. For the first, which covers the next weekday and next weekend, we would like you to keep a full record of all your activities. For the second, which covers four weekday evenings, we need to know only about away-from-home activities.

FULL WEEKDAY AND WEEKEND

We would like you to keep the full diary for the first weekday after your interview and for the first weekend after it.

- **What Did You Do?** First record in this column each of your activities through the day. Please try to record each activity separately and on a different line. Then record the time you started and completed each activity. A few examples of things you might write in are: 'got dressed', 'worked' 'cooked dinner', 'watched TV', 'had friends in for a chat', 'ate breakfast'
- **With Whom?** If you were doing an activity with someone else you should write in who it was. If you were watching television with your son you would write 'son' in this column. Some other examples of what you might write in are: 'wife and child', '3 friends', '2 relatives', '8 work colleagues'.
- **Same Time as Usual?** Then, for the weekday, we would like you to record for each activity whether you did it at the same time as usual on weekdays. If you did, please write 'S'. If you did not, please write 'D'. Do the same thing for the weekend: if you did the activity at the same time as usual on a Saturday (or for Sunday activities the same time as usual on a Sunday) record an 'S', and if not record a 'D'.
- **'Work' or 'Leisure'** You remember that one of the questions we asked you in the interview was about what you thought made the difference between work and leisure. We would be grateful if you would go through all the activities you record in the diary, and put a 'W' in the column against those activities you think of as work and an 'L' against those you think of as leisure. If you think that some of the activities are a mixture of both, put an 'M' in the column. And if you think some activities are neither work nor leisure nor a mixture of both, put an 'N' in the column. Everyone will have different ideas about whether an activity is work or leisure, a mixture or neither. There are no right answers. Please just label the activities *how you feel*. It is what *you* think that counts.

Please try to fill in the diary at several times during the day, as it is so easy to forget things if you leave it all to the end of the day.

WEEKDAY EVENINGS

For the other weekday evenings we need information only on those activities you do *away from your home*. We would like you to start keeping the record from 6 p.m. and continue until you go to bed.

- It may happen that on some or all evenings you will stay at home all the time. If so, just write 'at home all evening'.
- If you are at work in the time between 6 p.m. and midnight, just write in 'at work'. There is no need to give more details.

Name: ____________

Tel. No. (if any): ____________

Address: ____________

RETURNING THE DIARY

When you have completed the final section of the diary, please post it to us in the stamped addressed envelope. We will then post the £1 fee to you.

THANK YOU FOR YOUR HELP

Appendix 3

Weekday

TIME	WHAT DID YOU DO? (no more than one activity on each line)	TIME BEGUN	TIME ENDED	WITH WHOM?	WAS ACTIVITY DONE AT SAME TIME AS USUAL ON WEEKDAYS? S = SAME D = DIFFERENT	W = Work L = Leisure M = Mixed N = Neither
Midnight		Midnight				
1a.m.						
2a.m.						
3a.m.						
4a.m.						
5a.m.						
6a.m.						
7a.m.						
8a.m.						
9 a.m.						
10a.m.						
11a.m.						
Noon						
1p.m.						

Appendix 3

Weekday

TIME	WHAT DID YOU DO? (no more than one activity on each line)	TIME BEGUN	TIME ENDED	WITH WHOM?	WAS ACTIVITY DONE AT SAME TIME AS USUAL ON WEEKDAYS? S = SAME D = DIFFERENT	W = Work L = Leisure M = Mixed N = Neither
1p.m.						
2p.m.						
3p.m.						
4p.m.						
5p.m.						
6p.m.						
7p.m.						
8p.m.						
9p.m.						
10p.m.						
11p.m.						
Midnight			Midnight			

Saturday

TIME	WHAT DID YOU DO? (no more than one activity on each line)	TIME BEGUN	TIME ENDED	WITH WHOM?	WAS ACTIVITY DONE AT SAME TIME AS USUAL ON A SATURDAY? S=SAME D = DIFFERENT	W = Work L = Leisure M = Mixed N = Neither
Midnight		Midnight				
1a.m.						
2a.m.						
3a.m.						
4a.m.						
5a.m.						
6a.m.						
7a.m.						
8a.m.						
9 a.m.						
10a.m.						
11a.m.						
Noon						
1p.m.						

Saturday

TIME	WHAT DID YOU DO? (no more than one activity on each line)	TIME BEGUN	TIME ENDED	WITH WHOM?	WAS ACTIVITY DONE AT SAME TIME AS USUAL ON A SATURDAY? S = SAME D = DIFFERENT	W = Work L = Leisure M = Mixed N = Neither
1 p.m.						
2 p.m.						
3 p.m.						
4 p.m.						
5 p.m.						
6 p.m.						
7 p.m.						
8 p.m.						
9 p.m.						
10 p.m.						
11 p.m.						
Midnight			Midnight			

Sunday

TIME	WHAT DID YOU DO? (no more than one activity on each line)	TIME BEGUN	TIME ENDED	WITH WHOM?	WAS ACTIVITY DONE AT SAME TIME AS USUAL ON A SUNDAY? S = SAME D = DIFFERENT	W = Work L = Leisure M = Mixed N = Neither
Midnight		Midnight				
1a.m.						
2a.m.						
3a.m.						
4a.m.						
5a.m.						
6a.m.						
7a.m.						
8a.m.						
9 a.m.						
10a.m.						
11a.m.						
Noon						
1p.m.						

Appendix 3

Sunday

TIME	WHAT DID YOU DO? (no more than one activity on each line)	TIME BEGUN	TIME ENDED	WITH WHOM?	WAS ACTIVITY DONE AT SAME TIME AS USUAL ON A SUNDAY? S = SAME D = DIFFERENT	W = Work L = Leisure M = Mixed N = Neither
1p.m.						
2p.m.						
3p.m.						
4p.m.						
5p.m.						
6p.m.						
7p.m.						
8p.m.						
9p.m.						
10p.m.						
11p.m.						
Midnight			Midnight			

Appendix 3

Evening Activities (from 6p.m. to midnight)

DAY	WHAT DID YOU DO? (You need only record activities *outside your home*)	TIME BEGUN	TIME ENDED	WITH WHOM?
		6 p.m.		
			Midnight	
		6 p.m.		
			Midnight	
		6 p.m.		
			Midnight	
		6 p.m.		
			Midnight	

APPENDIX 4

CHANGES IN AGES AT MARRIAGE, CHILDBEARING AND DEATH: PREPARATION OF ESTIMATES

P. R. Cox

At the request of the authors, estimates were prepared of the average ages at certain vital events in England and Wales, classified according to the year of birth of the persons to whom those events occurred. Some of the results are shown in Chapter IV; the full results are in Table A11.

Table A11 *Some demographic changes over a century*

	Year of birth					
	1850	*1870*	*1890*	*1910*	*1930*	*1950*
1. *First marriage*						
Men	27	27	28	27	26	24
Women	26	26	26	25	24	22
2. *Birth of first child*						
Men	29	29	30	29	28	26
Women	28	28	28	27	26	24
3. *Birth of last child*						
Men	37	36	35	32	30	28
Women	36	35	33	30	28	26
4. *Spouse's death*						
Men	56	60	62	64	66	68
Women	55	58	61	63	65	67
5. *Own death as widow or widower*						
Men	75	77	79	80	81	82
Women	75	79	81	81	82	83

Appendix 4

Although vital events are well recorded in England and Wales, and relevant statistics have been published for over a century, a number of problems arose in preparing these estimates, and there are various reasons why this should be so. First, some of the figures involve an element of forecasting, while others relate to happenings which are formally registered today but went unrecorded in the past. Secondly, the published data may be incomplete, or need to be interpolated or call for special understanding. Thirdly, on some subjects direct evidence is not available. Finally, alternative interpretations are occasionally possible, and a choice of presentation needs to be made. The following notes outline the salient points successively for marriage, childbearing and death, considered in each case first from the point of view of the experience at given times and then in relation to the history of generations.

Age at first marriage

The numbers of marriages of men and women, classified by age and prior marital status, have been tabulated in the Registrar-General's Annual Reports since about 1840. Until the 1890s, however, the data were incomplete because many couples did not state their ages. In the absence of direct evidence of any inaccuracy from this cause, the average ages have been calculated from the published figures for bachelors and spinsters marrying, without any adjustment. The rise in the mean age to a peak in 1911 is well established. An alternative set of results could have been obtained from the marriage rates in the given years by using a life-table technique. The published statistics can be arranged without difficulty to show the experience of generations, but for those born in 1950, in 1930 and even in 1910 not all first marriages can yet have taken place. An element of forecasting, based on extrapolation from the past, therefore had to be included in the assessments.

Age at birth of first and last child

The age at birth for the first child is shown as two years later than the average age at first marriage, for all generations. Data giving particulars of first legitimate births are available only from 1938 onwards. For earlier years the duration since marriage needs to be inferred from less specific statistical information of various kinds, but the scope for variation is small, as the ages are quoted to the nearest integer.

As the average size of family has fallen, from perhaps five or six children for women born in 1850 to little more than two children for those born in 1950, the difference between the age at marriage and the age at the birth of the last child must naturally have diminished considerably. But data for a precise assessment of the amount of the change are not available.

In 1911, detailed questions about the numbers of children borne by women were asked for the first time at a census in this country. Between 1911 and 1945 a similar censal inquiry was not held but since the second world war various items of information about families have been obtained in official statistical investigations. Also, from the recent birth registrations, there are statistics of the ages of mothers on bearing their first child, second child and so on.

The results shown in section 3 of Table A11 have been estimated from all the available data, using more than one method as a check. The average time-spacing between children probably rose between the middle of the Victorian era and the turn of the century but has subsequently diminished appreciably.

Age at death of spouse

An alternative expression, which has not been evaluated, is the average age of a married man on his death, if he should predecease his wife, or on her death if that should occur before his. This seems a less satisfactory index of social change than the average age of the surviving spouse at the death of the partner, having regard to its complement of the age at death as a widower, mentioned below. In any event, there is not much difference in the level or trend of the results according to the two interpretations.

Age-distributions of newly-widowed men and women have been published for England and Wales since 1938. For earlier years they can be estimated from census data showing the ages of husbands and wives in combination, by applying suitable mortality rates. For intervening periods, figures can be assessed from general considerations. As for marriages, the method used produces results different from those which would have been obtained by the use of life tables based on rates experienced in the various years. The history of generations can be constructed by a judicious combination of these methods, but the figures must be more speculative in some degree, because for no year of birth is there a complete record of data. For people born in 1950, forecasts of mortality as far as the year 2050 are required for the estimate; for this purpose the same assumptions have been made as in the official population projections. No allowance has been made for the possibility of divorce as a factor terminating marriage, but this is not very important as many divorced people remarry fairly quickly.

Age at death as a widower or widow

The number of widows dying each year, classified by age, has been published for very many decades, but the corresponding information for men has been available only since 1938. Nevertheless, an estimate can be made for any census year before then, by applying suitable male mortality rates to the number of widowers enumerated. For the generation assessment, some interpolation and reassembly of the estimates is necessary, and the element of forecasting is even more prominent than it was for the age at bereavement.

For all the events described, there is a considerable dispersion of ages about the means and the distributions are skew. The median age at first marriage is about one-and-a-half years younger than the mean, but for the items relating to deaths the median age is about a year older than the mean age.

APPENDIX 5

LEISURE FORECASTS[1]

Like any other forecasts, those reported in this appendix are nothing more than estimates of what can be expected to happen in the future on certain assumptions. Our first was based upon the Principle which has figured in the main text. Briefly, the reasoning goes like this. We know that in 1970 some people did some things more than other people did: for example, people with cars and those in high-class jobs were more keen on sport. It is expected that by 2001 more people will have cars and more will be in such jobs. If in 2001 these people behave as their counterparts did in 1970 there will be more active sportsmen. To apply this formula to particular sports or other leisure activities and thus produce a set of quantitative estimates, one needs to know how people differed from each other in their participation in 1970 and – another important assumption – how the social structure of 2001 is likely to differ from that of 1970. Our information about differences in leisure came from our main survey, which we were anyway using for many different sorts of analysis, and our forecasts of changes in the population were based upon figures from Census reports and similar sources. To distinguish these two sets of information, we use the term 'leisure variables' for the different leisure activities and 'population variables' for the characteristics of the population included in the forecasts.

The first step was to select these population variables. We have already mentioned two – car-ownership and occupational class. We added three others that, as is shown by Table 44 on p. 225, were important – age, income and terminal education age. We next looked to see how in detail these population variables were correlated with all of the different leisure variables from the main survey. We took

[1] This appendix is based on a study carried out by Roger Mitton at the Institute of Community Studies for the Long-Range Studies Division of Post Office Telecommunications. This study was undertaken by contract and the views expressed are not necessarily those of the Post Office. We are grateful to Post Office Telecommunications for permission to draw upon the study for this summary.

participation once or more in the previous year as the index, rather than twelve times or more, because with some activities there were so few participants that they would otherwise have had to be ruled out from this analysis.

One problem was to decide how much weight to attach to each population variable. People in higher-class jobs and people with cars play more sport, but there are more car-owners in the higher social classes, so one cannot tell from the straightforward analyses whether it is the jobs or the cars that make the difference. To decide this, the activity rates of people in the same class with and without cars were compared and weights given to the two according to their relative influence. This sort of procedure had to be followed for combinations of all the five population variables and with each leisure variable separately.

For each leisure activity, we then had three sets of data. The first was the proportion by age group, by class, among car-owners and non-owners, and so on, shown by the survey as doing the activity in the previous year. The second, which was the same for every activity, was the predicted distribution of the population of 2001 in terms of the population variables – class, age, income, education and car-ownership. The third was the weightings for each population variable, reflecting its influence upon participation in the particular activity. These sets of data made it possible to calculate the proportion of the adult population doing each activity at least once a year – the participation rates, as they could be called – for 1970 and for 2001, and to see how participation was likely to increase or decrease in each of the leisure activities.

Our forecasts of changes in the population variables were for the United Kingdom rather than for the London Region. This was because the Post Office wanted estimates of changes in leisure for the country as a whole. The expected changes between 1970 and 2001 are shown in Table A12. Since the participation rates were from our survey for the London Region rather than the UK, we had to make a series of estimates of the UK rates for 1970, using the London rates and allowing for the differences in the composition of the two populations. The London Region population was higher in class, richer, more educated and had more cars – that is, contained more of the people who were most active in leisure – and so the UK estimates came out as lower than the actual participation rates in the London Region sample – 5 per cent lower on average. There are, of course, regional variations beyond this. More golf is played in Scotland, for example, and this is not explained by the differences in population variables, but in making our forecasts we assumed that such regional variations would remain fairly constant.

TABLE A12 *Forecasts of changes in the United Kingdom in the five population variables (percentages)*

		1970	*2001*
Age	18–24	15	15
	25–29	9	10
	30–39	16	19
	40–49	17	17
	50–59	17	16
	60 or over	26	23
Income (2001 incomes at 1970 prices)	Under £1,000 a year	44	8
	£1,000 or more but less than £2,000	44	28
	£2,000 or more but less than £3,000	8	27
	£3,000 or more but less than £4,000	2	23
	£4,000 or more but less than £5,000	1	6
	£5,000 or more	1	8
Occupational class	Professional	5	19
	Managerial	17	14
	Clerical	10	7
	Skilled	41	44
	Semi-skilled	19	11
	Unskilled	8	5
Age of finishing full-time education	16 or under	84	55
	17–19	9	29
	20 or over	7	16
Car-ownership (in household)	No car	50	18
	One car	42	58
	Two or more cars	8	24

Sources: Age: Central Statistical Office, *Social Trends*, no. 1, p. 31. Income: C. Leicester, *Britain 2001 A.D.*, p. 33 (middle projection) (report as published for the Post Office, 1972). Occupational class: extrapolation from Census reports, allowing for changes in classification; for division between 'clerical' and 'skilled', G. Routh, *Occupation and Pay in Great Britain 1906–1960*. Education: extrapolation from Census reports. Cars: extrapolation from *Readers Digest European Surveys* 1963 and 1970 and Road Research Laboratory (A. H. Tulpule, *Forecasts of Vehicles and Traffic in Great Britain*).

In this table, as in the rest of the forecasting exercise, the proportion aged 18 to 24 was taken rather than 17 to 24. This was to compensate for the under-representation of young people in the London Region main sample, as reported in Appendix 1.

Because even the 1970 rates for the UK are only estimates, the exact percentages shown as participating at both dates are less reliable than the ratio between the estimate for 1970 and the forecast for 2001. This ratio shows, regardless of regional variations like those just mentioned, what effect on leisure activities the changes in the population variables might be expected to have in the UK by 2001. Since the changes in these five variables are expected to be of roughly the same order in the London Region, these ratios can be taken to apply broadly to the London Region as well. When we show, as we do in Table A13, the figures of 1.2–1.3 for swimming, this means that the proportion of people doing so in 2001 is expected to increase in the ratio of between 1.2 and 1.3 of the base level of 1.0 for 1970. Such ratios should apply in broad terms to the population of both the London Region and the United Kingdom, the difference being that the proportion doing most things was higher in the London Region in 1970 than in the whole country and is likewise expected to be higher in 2001. If the population of the London Region were to change its structure in a different way from that of the whole country over the next thirty years, this would alter the picture, but it does not look as if this is likely to happen to a dramatic extent.[1]

The results

Tables A13–A17 present the forecasts for the leisure variables. The first two columns show the proportions of the UK adult population estimated as doing the activity at least once in 1970 and then in 2001. They are rounded to the nearest one per cent, or the nearest half per cent for small ones. Any below one per cent are shown as: –. As explained, these figures should not be taken as precise proportions but as giving an indication of the relative popularity of activities. The third column shows the change between 1970 and 2001 in the proportion doing each activity. As a reminder that the ratio is intended as an indication of the likely change, not as a precise forecast, it is expressed in terms of a range around one decimal point, for example 1·1–1·2. A ratio of 1·4–1·5 on a particular leisure variable means that an increase of 40–50 per cent is forecast. The figures were calculated from those in columns 1 and 2 before the rounding off, so it is possible to get, for example:

	% in 1970	% in 2001	Change in proportion
	–	–	1·3–1·4
or	3	4½	1·4–1·5

[1] South East Joint Planning Team, *Strategic Plan for the South East, Studies*, vol. 1: *Population and Employment*, p. 36.

TABLE A13 *Forecasts of changes in active sports (adult men and women in UK)*

	% doing the activity 1970	*% doing the activity 2001*	*Change in the proportion doing the activity*
Swimming	29	37	1·2 –1·3
Sailing	3	4½	1·4 –1·5
Golf	7	10	1·35–1·45
Fishing (all kinds)	9	10	1·1 –1·2
Association football	6	7	1·05–1·15
Cricket	4½	5	1·05–1·15
Tennis	8	10	1·25–1·35
Table tennis	11	13	1·1 –1·2
Bowls	2	2	1·0 –1·1
Ten-pin bowling	9	10	1·05–1·15
Athletics	2	2	0·95–1·05
Badminton and squash	3	4½	1·5 –1·6
Rugby football	–	1	1·1 –1·2
Boating	1½	1½	1·0 –1·1
Motor cruising	–	–	0·75–0·85
Water ski-ing	–	–	1·35–1·45
Skating	1½	1½	1·0 –1·1
Boxing, judo, karate, wrestling	–	–	0·9 –1·0
Fencing, archery, shooting	–	–	0·9 –1·0
Hiking, climbing, rambling	–	–	0·95–1·05
Horseriding, pony trekking, hunting	1	1½	1·15–1·25
Motor sports	–	–	1·05–1·15
Any sport	44	52	1·15–1·25

TABLE A14 *Forecasts of changes in spectator sports (adults in UK)*

Spectator sports	*% in 1970*	*% in 2001*	*Change in proportion*
Swimming	6	6½	1·05–1·15
Golf	2½	3	1·25–1·35
Football	20	22	1·0 –1·1
Rugby Union	3½	4½	1·25–1·35
Cricket	10	13	1·25–1·35
Tennis	5½	7½	1·25–1·35
Athletics	3	3½	1·1 –1·2
Motor sports	7	8	1·05–1·15
Boxing	3	3	0.95–1·05
Wrestling	4	4	1·0 –1·1
Horseracing	5½	7	1·25–1·35
Winter sports	–	1	1·45–1·55
Show jumping	2	2½	1·3 –1·4
Any sport	40	45	1·1 –1·2

With minority activities, it must be remembered that the forecasts are based on the characteristics of only a few people (one per cent of the main sample was about twenty) and are therefore less reliable. The reader should also bear in mind that the ratio is of the change in the proportion of the adult population participating. Since the adult population is expected to increase in size by about 15–20 per cent, the growth in absolute demand, for example for swimming pools or golf courses, will be greater than is suggested by the participation rates alone.

There is one notable leisure activity missing from the tables – television viewing. Almost everyone in the sample watched television many times a year, so the percentage of people watching it at least once (about 98 per cent) would not be a useful figure. A forecast was, however, produced from the time budgets. The average time spent watching television could be calculated for men, women, different income groups, etc. Because richer, higher-class and more educated people watched less television in 1970 a fall is forecast to a ratio of 0·8–0·9. As the sample of time-diarists was composed entirely of

TABLE A15 *Forecasts of changes in home-based activities (adults in UK)*

	% *in 1970*	% *in 2001*	*Change in proportion*
Listening to music on radio, record player or tape recorder	68	70	0·95–1·05
Playing an instrument	9	11½	1·15–1·25
Home decorations or repairs	60	66	1·05–1·15
Car maintenance	20½	27	1·25–1·35
Car cleaning	33	50	1·45–1·55
Knitting or sewing	46	44	0·9 –1·0
Reading	67	74	1·05–1·15
Gardening	63	67	1·05–1·15
Model-building	5½	6½	1·15–1·25
Collecting stamps or other objects	12	13½	1·1 –1·2
Handicrafts	5	5½	1·05–1·15
Technical hobbies	5	6	1·2 –1·3
Playing cards or chess	8½	11½	1·3 –1·4
Crosswords	3	4	1·25–1·35
Cooking	2½	3½	1·25–1·35
Painting and sculpture	3	4½	1·5 –1·6
Working at home*	4½	7½	1·5 –1·6

* The percentage of full-time workers who did five or more hours work at home in the week prior to the survey, not counting those whose work was at home.

married people aged between 30 and 49, the television-viewing times do not apply to the whole population, though comparisons with BBC data[1] suggest that the class and other differences in viewing in this age group apply to the rest of the population, so that our forecasts should not be so far out on this score. The results are shown in Table A18.

[1] BBC Audience Research Department, *The People's Activities*.

TABLE A16 *Forecasts of changes in other leisure activities (adults in UK)*

	% in 1970	*% in 2001*	*Change in proportion*
Cinema	53	58	1·05–1·15
Theatre	37	45	1·15–1·25
Museum	25	32	1·25–1·35
Art gallery	17	25	1·4 –1·5
Going out for a meal (not lunch)	62	70	1·1 –1·2
Going to pub	62	69	1·05–1·15
Attending church	37	41	1·05–1·15
Voluntary work	15	19	1·2 –1·3
Billiards or snooker	12	12½	1·0 –1·1
Playing darts	21	22	1·0 –1·1
Dancing	31	35	1·05–1·15
Going for 'a walk of a mile or more'	65	68	1·0 –1·1
Going for 'a drive in a car for pleasure'	68	78	1·1 –1·2
Camping	7	8	1·1 –1·2
Caravanning	10	11	1·05–1·15
Bingo	3½	3	0·9 –1·0
Adult education	3½	6½	1·8 –1·9
Politics	–	–	0·95–1.05

The outstanding feature of the forecasts is that almost everything is likely to increase. This is a reflection of the main finding of the survey – that richer, higher-status, more educated, car-owning people did more of almost everything. Since we assume that people will be richer, more educated, doing higher-status jobs and owning more cars, it follows that almost every activity should have more participants in 2001.

One way of summarizing the forecasts is to take groups of activities and calculate their collective growth. The 1970 percentages for sports, for example, can be combined, then those for 2001, and the second

TABLE A17 *Some additional forecasts (adults in UK)*

	% *in 1970*	% *in 2001*	*Change in proportion*
Owning second homes	5½	9	1·55–1·65
Members of a club	42	51	1·15–1·25
Seeing five or more relatives per week	20	20	0·95–1·05
Five miles or more from home when seeing a relative	42	49	1·1 –1·2
Seeing five or more friends per week	35	39	1·05–1·15
Five miles or more from their home when seeing a friend	18	22	1·2 –1·3

TABLE A18 *Forecasts of changes in television viewing*

		Average time in hours	
		1970	*2001*
Men:	Weekday	1·6	1·4
	Saturday	2·7	2·3
	Sunday	2·5	2·4
Women not working:	Weekday	1·9	1·8
	Saturday	1·9	1·8
	Sunday	2·3	2·1
Women working:	Weekday	1·5	1·3
	Saturday	1·9	1·8
	Sunday	1·8	1·8
All, per week:		12·9	11·1

divided by the first. This is done for various groups of activities in Table A19.

The forecasts are, of course, based entirely on the five population variables – age, income, social class, education and car-ownership. They are simply estimates of the effect on leisure activities that changes

TABLE A19 *Expected proportionate changes in various categories of leisure*

Average growth over all activities in the proportion of people participating	1·15
Cultural pursuits*	1·33
Water sports	1·24
All sports	1·22
Spectator sports	1·18
Team games	1·15
Home-based activities	1·14
Passive activities†	1·10

* Playing an instrument, collecting stamps, etc., technical hobbies, cards and chess, crosswords, painting or sculpture, museums, art galleries, adult education, politics.
† Spectator sports, listening to music, reading, cinema, theatre, eating out, pubs, church, bingo. Television viewing is also in this category, of course, but cannot be included in this calculation.

in these five variables might be expected to have in the next thirty years and they do not allow for the influence of other variables. Nor do they make any allowance for possible changes in trend – staggering of holidays for example – that we discuss in Chapter X. What is more, even within its own limits, this exercise did not take into account the supply of facilities for leisure activities, although there could not, for example, be a very large increase in water ski-ing if there was not enough water for the extra people to ski on.

Unfortunately the data on leisure facilities are poor and no adequate attempt to take this into account could be made in these forecasts. It seems reasonable to expect that supply will expand to meet demand in those activities likely to be commercially profitable. Cinemas, bingo halls and ten-pin bowling alleys, for example, were built quickly when demand for them was rising. Squash courts and indoor golf ranges might be provided at a similar rate. There were, and are, many demands that could be met by private enterprise with comparatively small demands on open space. Where open space is needed, public authorities also have to play a part. For activities which require much space an upper limit may be reached before demand is fully met. Our guess is that this will, for example, happen with sailing (especially on inland water), water ski-ing and swimming.[1]

[1] For more detail on this point see the reports on water recreation prepared for the Sports Council by Michael Dower of the Dartington Amenity Research Trust. Sports Council, *Water Recreation Research Studies*.

Even allowing for the limitations of these forecasts and taking supply constraints into account, the broad direction of trends is clear. To sum up, people's leisure in 2001 will probably be more varied and more active, with sports and cultural participation particularly growing in popularity.

REFERENCES

ANDERSON, J., 'Space-time budgets and activity studies in urban geography and planning', *Environment and Planning*, vol. 3 (4) (1971), pp. 353–68.

ANDERSON, M., *Family Structure in Nineteenth Century Lancashire*. Cambridge University Press, 1971.

ARENDT, H., *The Human Condition*. New York, Doubleday Anchor Books, 1959.

ARVILL, R. (pseud.), *Man and Environment*. Harmondsworth, Penguin Books, 1967.

ASHTON, T. S., *The Industrial Revolution, 1760–1830*. Oxford University Press, 1968.

ASHWORTH, W., 'Types of social and economic development in suburban Essex', in Centre for Urban Studies, *London: Aspects of Change*, pp. 62–90.

BAKER, J. and YOUNG, M., *The Hornsey Plan, A Role for Neighbourhood Councils in the New Local Government*. 3rd ed. London, Association for Neighbourhood Councils, 1971.

BANHAM, R., 'Household godjets', *New Society*, no. 381 (15 January 1970), pp. 100–1.

BANKS, J. A., *Prosperity and Parenthood*. London, Routledge & Kegan Paul, 1954.

BARFIELD, R. and MORGAN, J., *Early Retirement: the Decision and the Experience*. Ann Arbor, Michigan, Institute for Social Research, University of Michigan, 1969.

BARTLETT, F. C., *Remembering*. Cambridge University Press, 1961.

BBC Audience Research Department, *The People's Activities*. British Broadcasting Corporation, 1965.

BECHHOFER, F., 'Occupations', in C. M. STACEY (ed.), *Comparability in Social Research*. London, British Sociological Association and Social Science Research Council, Heinemann, 1969.

BECKERMAN, W., *The British Economy in 1975*. Cambridge University Press, 1965.

BECKERMAN, W., 'The future growth of national product', in W. BECKERMAN, *The British Economy in 1975*, pp. 73–106.

BELBIN, R. M. and CLARKE, F. L., 'The relationship between retirement patterns and work as revealed by the British Census', *Industrial Gerontology* (Winter 1970), pp. 12–26.

BELL, D., *The End of Ideology*. New York, Free Press, 1962.

BELL, D., 'The year 2000 – the trajectory of an idea', *Daedalus* (Summer 1967), pp. 639–51.

BESANT, W., *East London*. London, Chatto & Windus, 1901.

BEST, G., *Mid-Victorian Britain 1851–75*. London, Weidenfeld & Nicolson, 1971.

BIENEFELD, M. A., 'A study of the course of change in the customary and in the specified or normal hours of work for manual workers in certain British Industries and of the factors affecting changes in the specified or normal hours from the eighteenth century to the present day', Ph.D. thesis, University of London, 1964. Later published as BIENEFELD, M. A., *Working Hours in British Industry*. London, Weidenfeld & Nicolson, 1972.

BLAUNER, R., *Alienation and Freedom*. University of Chicago Press, 1964.

Board of Trade, *Consumption of Food and Cost of Living of Working Classes in the United Kingdom and Certain Foreign Countries*. Cd. 1761, London, HMSO, 1903.

Board of Trade, *Report of an Enquiry into the Earnings and Hours of Labour of the Workpeople of the U.K.* London, HMSO, 1906.

BOLTON, J. H., *Flexible Working Hours*. London, Anchor Publications, 1971.

BOOTH, C., *Life and Labour of the People in London*. 17 vols. London, Macmillan, 1902.

BOSANQUET, H., *Rich and Poor*. London, Macmillan, 1899.

BOTT, E., *Family and Social Network*. London, Tavistock Publications, 1957.

BOTTOMORE, T. B., 'Social stratification in voluntary organisations', in D. V. GLASS (ed.), *Social Mobility in Britain*, pp. 349–82.

BRIGGS, A., 'The language of "class" in early nineteenth century England', in A. BRIGGS and J. SAVILLE (eds), *Essays in Labour History*. London, Macmillan, 1967, pp. 43–73.

BRIGGS, A., *Victorian Cities*. Harmondsworth, Penguin Books, 1968.

BRONFENBRENNER, U., *Two Worlds of Childhood*. New York, Russell Sage Foundation, 1970.

BROWN, D. G., 'Hours and output', in A. C. E. DANKERT, F. C. MANN and H. R. NORTHRUP (eds), *Hours of Work*, New York, Harper & Row, 1965, pp. 147–60.

BROWN, E. H. PHELPS and BROWNE, M. H., 'Hours of work', in D. L. SILLS (ed.), *International Encyclopedia of the Social Sciences*, vol. 8. New York, Macmillan and Free Press, 1958, pp. 340–4.

BURGESS, E. W., 'The growth of the city: an introduction to a research project', in R. E. PARK *et al.*, *The City*, pp. 47–62.

BURGESS, E. W. and LOCKE, H. J., *The Family: From Institution to Companionship*. 2nd ed., New York, American Book Co., 1953.

BURNS, T., 'Management in action', *Operational Research Quarterly*, vol. 8 (2), June 1957.

BUTLER, D. and STOKES, D., *Political Change in Britain*. London, Macmillan, 1969.

CARTER, H. and GLICK, P. C., *Marriage and Divorce: A Social and Economic Study*. Harvard University Press, 1970.

CARTWRIGHT, A., *Parents and Family Planning Services*. London, Routledge & Kegan Paul, 1970.

CAUTER, T. S. and DOWNHAM, J. S., *The Communication of Ideas*. London, Chatto & Windus, 1954.

Central Statistical Office, *Social Trends*. no. 1, London, HMSO, 1970.

Central Statistical Office, *Social Trends*. no. 2, London, HMSO, 1971.

Central Statistical Office, *Standard Industrial Classification*. London, HMSO, 1968.

Centre for Urban Studies, *London: Aspects of Change*. London, MacGibbon & Kee, 1964.

CHEKHOV, A., *Uncle Vanya*. London, Duckworth, 1912.

CHESTER, R., 'Contemporary trends in the stability of English marriage', *Journal of Biosocial Sciences*, vol. 3 (4) (October 1971), pp. 389–402.

CHILD, J. and MACMILLAN, B., 'Managerial leisure in British and American contexts', *Journal of Management Studies* (May 1972), pp. 182–95.

CLARK, C., *The Conditions of Economic Progress*. 3rd ed., London, Macmillan, 1957.

CLARK, C., 'The economics of housework', *Bulletin of the Oxford Institute of Statistics*, vol. 20 (2) (May 1958), pp. 205–11.

CLEGG, H., *Implications of the Shorter Working Week for Management*. London, British Institute of Management, 1962.

COHEN, E., *The Growth of the British Civil Service 1780–1939*. London, Allen & Unwin, 1941.

COPEMAN, G., LINGH, H. and HANIKA, F. DE P., *How the Executive Spends His Time*. London, Business Publications, 1963.

COPPOCK, J. T., 'A general view of London and its environs', in J. T. COPPOCK and H. C. PRINCE (eds), *Greater London*, pp. 19–41.

COPPOCK, J. T. and PRINCE, H. C. (eds), *Greater London*. London, Faber, 1964.

CULLEN, I. and GODSON, V., *The Structure of Activity Patterns*. Research Paper No. 1, London, Joint Unit for Planning Research, January 1972.

DAVIE, R., BUTLER, N. R. and GOLDSTEIN, H., *From Birth to Seven*. London, Longmans, 1972.

DEANE, P. and COLE, W. A., *British Economic Growth*. 2nd ed., Cambridge University Press, 1967.

DEFOE, D., *The Life and Strange Surprizing Adventures of Robinson Crusoe, of York, Mariner*. vol. I, London, W. Taylor, 1719.

DEFOE, D., *A Tour Through Great Britain*. vol. III, London, G. Strahan, 1727.

DE GRAZIA, S., *Of Time, Work and Leisure*. New York, Twentieth Century Fund, 1962.

Department of Employment, *Department of Employment Gazette*. London, HMSO, February 1973.

Department of Employment, 'Family Expenditure Survey: subsidiary occupations', *Department of Employment Gazette*, London, HMSO, June 1972. pp. 528–34.

Department of Employment and Productivity, *British Labour Statistics: Historical Abstracts 1886–1968*. London, HMSO, 1971.

Department of Health and Social Security, *Supplementary Benefits Handbook*. London, HMSO, 1971.

DICKENS, C., *Sketches by Boz*. Oxford University Press, 1957.

DIXON, W. J. (ed.), *Biomedical Computer Programs*. Berkeley and Los Angeles, University of California Press, 1968.

DOBBS, A. E., *Education and Social Movements, 1700–1850*. London, Longmans, 1919.

DONNISON, D., *The Government of Housing*. Harmondsworth, Penguin Books, 1967.

DOUGLAS, J. W. B. and BLOMFIELD, J. M., *Children Under Five*. London, Allen & Unwin, 1958.

DOWER, M., 'Fourth wave: the challenge of leisure', *Architects' Journal*, 20 January 1965, pp. 123–90.

DUBIN, R., 'Industrial workers' worlds: a study of the central life interest of industrial workers', *Social Problems*, vol. 3 (3) (January 1956), pp. 131–42.

DUMAZEDIER, J., *Toward a Society of Leisure*. New York, Free Press, 1967.

DUNNING, J. H. and MORGAN, E. V., *An Economic Study of the City of London*. London, Allen & Unwin, 1971.

DURANT, H., *The Problem of Leisure*. London, George Routledge, 1938.

DURKHEIM, E., *The Division of Labour in Society*. Chicago, Free Press, 1933.

DYOS, H. J., *Victorian Suburb*. Leicester University Press, 1966.

ENGELS, F., *The Condition of the Working Class in England.* Oxford, Blackwell, 1971.

EVERSLEY, D., 'Old cities, falling populations and rising costs', *G.L.C. Intelligence Unit Quarterly Bulletin*, no. 18 (March 1972), pp. 5–17.

FAIRCHILD, H. P. (ed.), *Dictionary of Sociology.* New Jersey, Littlefield, Adams, 1964.

FIREY, W., *Land Use in Central Boston.* Harvard University Press, 1947.

FOGARTY, M. P. and RAPOPORT, R. and R. N., *Sex, Career and Family.* London, Allen & Unwin, 1971.

FOGARTY, M. P. and RAPOPORT, R. and R. N., *Women and Top Jobs: The Next Move.* London, PEP Broadsheet 535, March 1972.

FORSHAW, J. H. and ABERCROMBIE, P., *County of London Plan.* London. Macmillan, 1943.

FOSTER, E. and BULL, G. (eds), *The Director, His Money and His Job.* New York, McGraw-Hill, 1970.

FRIEDMANN, G., *Industrial Society.* New York, Free Press, 1955.

FUCHS, V. R., *The Service Economy.* New York, National Bureau of Economic Research, 1968.

General Register Office, *Census of 1911 – Occupations and Industries.* vol. X, part 1, London, HMSO, 1914.

General Register Office, *Census 1931 – General Report.* London, HMSO, 1950.

General Register Office, *Census 1951 – Fertility Report.* London, HMSO, 1956.

General Register Office, *Census 1961 – Fertility Tables.* London, HMSO, 1966.

General Register Office, *Classification of Occupations 1966.* London, HMSO, 1966.

General Register Office, *The Registrar-General's Statistical Review of England and Wales for the Year 1967.* Part II, London, HMSO, 1969.

General Register Office, *Sample Census 1966 – Economic Activity Tables.* Part III, London, HMSO, 1969.

General Register Office, *Sample Census 1966 – Household Composition Tables.* London, HMSO, 1968.

GLASS, D. V., 'Fertility trends in Europe since the second world war', *Population Studies*, vol. XXII (1968), pp. 103–46.

GLASS, D. V. (ed.), *Social Mobility in Britain.* London, Routledge & Kegan Paul, 1954.

GLASS, R., 'Aspects of change', in Centre for Urban Studies, *London: Aspects of Change*, pp. xii–xlii.

GOFFMAN, E., *The Presentation of Self in Everyday Life.* London, Allen Lane, 1969.

GOLDTHORPE, J. H., LOCKWOOD, D., BECHHOFER, F. and PLATT, J.,

The Affluent Worker: Industrial Attitudes and Behaviour. Cambridge University Press, 1968.

GOLDTHORPE, J. H., LOCKWOOD, D., BECHHOFER, F. and PLATT, J., *The Affluent Worker in the Class Structure.* Cambridge University Press, 1969.

GOODE, W. J., *World Revolution and Family Patterns.* New York, Free Press, 1963.

GORER, G., *Sex and Marriage in England Today.* London, Nelson, 1971.

GOVAERTS, F., *Loisirs des femmes et temps libre.* Brussels, Editions de l'Institut de Sociologie, 1969.

Government Social Survey, *Family Expenditure Survey Report for 1969.* London, HMSO, 1970.

Greater London Development Plan, Report of Studies. London, County Hall, 1969.

Greater London Development Plan, Subject Evidence – Stage 1: General Strategy and Implementation. London, County Hall, May 1971.

GREENWOOD, J., *Seven Curses of London.* London, 1869.

'The growth of longer vacations', *American Federationist* (November 1967).

HABAKKUK, H. J., *Population Growth and Economic Development since 1750.* Leicester University Press, 1971.

HALÉVY, E., *A History of the English People in 1815.* London, T. Fisher Unwin, 1924.

HALL, P., 'The development of communications', in J. T. COPPOCK and H. C. PRINCE (eds), *Greater London.*

HALL, P., GRACEY, H., DREWETT, R. and THOMAS, R., *The Containment of Urban England.* vols. I and II, London, Allen & Unwin, 1973.

HALSEY, A. H. (ed.), *Trends in British Society since 1900.* London, Macmillan, 1972.

HAMMOND, J. L. and B., *Lord Shaftesbury.* London, Constable, 1923.

HARRISON, J. F. C., *The Early Victorians, 1832–1851.* London, Weidenfeld & Nicolson, 1971.

HARRISON, J. F. C., *Robert Owen and the Owenties in Britain and America.* London, Routledge & Kegan Paul, 1969.

HECKSCHER, A. and de GRAZIA, S., 'Executive leisure', *Harvard Business Review*, July-August 1959, pp. 6–19.

HILL, C., *Reformation to Industrial Revolution.* London, Weidenfeld & Nicolson, 1967.

HOBSBAWM, E. J., *Industry and Empire.* London, Weidenfeld & Nicolson, 1968.

HORNE, J. H. and LUPTON, T., 'The work activities of "middle" managers', *Journal of Management Studies*, vol. 1 (2) (February 1965), pp. 14–33.

HOYT, H., 'The pattern of movement of residential rental neighbourhoods', in H. M. MAYER and C. F. KAHN (eds), *Readings in Urban Geography*. University of Chicago Press, 1959, pp. 499–510.

HUIZINGA, J., *Homo Ludens*. London, Paladin, 1970.

HUMPHREYS, B. V., *Clerical Unions in the Civil Service*. London, Blackwell & North, 1958.

HUNT, A., *A Survey of Women's Employment*. London, HMSO, 1968.

ILLICH, I. D., *Deschooling Society*. New York, Calder & Boyars, 1971.

Institute of Directors, 'The Director Observed', *Director*, April 1966, pp. 82–6.

Institute of Directors, 'The Director Observed Away From the Desk', *Director*, May 1966, pp. 270-3.

JAHODA, M., LAZARSFELD, P. F. and ZEISEL, H., *Marienthal*. London, Tavistock Publications, 1972.

JENKINS, R., *Mr Attlee*. London, Heinemann, 1948.

JEPHCOTT, P., *Married Women Working*. London, Allen & Unwin, 1962.

JOHNSTON, J., *Econometric Methods*. New York, McGraw-Hill, 1963.

JOINER, D., 'Office territory', *New Society*, no. 471 (7 October 1971), pp. 660–3.

JONES, D. CARADOG (ed.), *The Social Survey of Merseyside*. University Press of Liverpool, 1934.

JONES, G. S., *Outcast London*. Oxford, Clarendon Press, 1971.

KAPLAN, M., *Leisure in America*. New York, Wiley, 1960.

KROPOTKIN, P., *Mutual Aid*. Harmondsworth, Penguin Books, 1939.

KUZNETS, S., *Economic Growth*. Chicago, Free Press, 1959.

LAMB, C., *The Essays of Elia*. London, Blackie, 1959.

LANSBURY, G., *Looking Backwards and Forwards*. London, Blackie, 1935.

LASLETT, P., *The World We Have Lost*. London, Methuen, 1965.

LEICESTER, C., *Britain 2001 A.D*. London, HMSO, 1972.

Leisure in the North West. Salford, North West Sports Council, no date.

'Longer hours for executives', *Financial Times* (9 December 1969).

LORENZ, K., *On Aggression*. London, Methuen, 1965.

LUNDBERG, G. A., KOMAROVSKY, M. and MCINERY, M. A., *Leisure: A Suburban Study*. New York, Columbia University Press, 1934.

MCGREGOR, O. R., *Divorce in England*. London, Heinemann, 1957.

MCKENZIE, R. D., 'The ecological approach to the study of the human community', in R. E. PARK *et al*., *The City*, pp. 63–79.

MADGE, C., *War-Time Pattern of Saving and Spending*. Cambridge, National Institute of Economic and Social Research, 1943.

MALTHUS, T. R., *Principles of Political Economy*. 2nd ed., London, John Murray, 1820.

MARRIS, P., *Widows and Their Families*. London, Routledge & Kegan Paul, 1958.

MARRIS, R., *The Economics of Capital Utilization*. Cambridge University Press, 1964.

MARSHALL, T. H., 'Citizenship and social class', in T. H. MARSHALL, *Sociology at the Crossroads*. London, Heinemann, 1963, pp. 67–127.

MARX, K., *Capital*. London, J. M. Dent, 1946.

MARX, K. and ENGELS, F., *The German Ideology*. London, Lawrence & Wishart, 1965.

MATHIAS, P., *The First Industrial Nation*. London, Methuen, 1969.

MAYHEW, H., *London Labour and the London Poor*. vol. 1, London, George Woodfall, 1851.

MEAD, M., *Male and Female*. London, Gollancz, 1949.

MEADOWS, D. H., *The Limits to Growth*. New York, Earth Island Publishing Co., 1972.

MEARNS, J., *The Bitter Cry of Outcast London*. London, Clarke, 1883.

MERRETT, A. J., 'How well off are directors?' in E. FORSTER and G. BULL (eds), *The Director, His Money and His Job*, pp. 3–6.

MEYERSOHN, R., 'Television and the rest of leisure', *Public Opinion Quarterly*, vol. 32 (1) (1968), pp. 102–12.

MILL, J. S., *The Subjection of Women*. London, Longmans, 1909.

MINER, J. B., *Intelligence in the United States*. New York, Springer Publishing Company, 1957.

Ministry of Labour and National Service, *The Length of Working Life of Males in Great Britain*. London, HMSO, 1959.

Ministry of Pensions and National Insurance, *Reasons Given for Retiring or Continuing at Work*. London, HMSO, 1954.

MISHAN, E. J., *The Costs of Economic Growth*. London, Pelican Books, 1969.

MITCHELL, J. CLYDE, 'The concept and use of social networks', in J. CLYDE MITCHELL (ed.), *Social Networks in Urban Situations*, pp. 1–50.

MITCHELL, J. CLYDE, *Social Networks in Urban Situations*. Manchester University Press, 1969.

MORRIS, W., *News from Nowhere*. London, Reeves & Turner, 1892.

MORRIS, W., *On Art and Socialism*. London, Lehmann, 1947.

MORRISON, A., *Child of the Jago*. London, MacGibbon & Kee, 1969.

National Board for Prices and Incomes, *Hours of Work, Overtime and Shiftworking*. Report No. 161, Cmnd. 4554, London, HMSO, 1970.

OAKLEY, A., *Sex, Gender and Society*. London, Temple Smith, 1972.

Office of Population Censuses and Surveys, *Census 1971 – Preliminary Report*. London, HMSO, 1971.

Office of Population Censuses and Surveys, *Census 1971 – Advance Analysis*. London, HMSO, 1972.

Office of Population Censuses and Surveys, *The Registrar-General's*

Decennial Supplement, England and Wales, 1961. Occupational Mortality Tables. London, HMSO, 1971.

OGBURN, W. F. and NIMKOFF, M. F., *Technology and the Changing Family*. Boston, Houghton Mifflin, 1955.

OPIE, I. and P., *The Lore and Language of Schoolchildren*. Oxford, Clarendon Press, 1959.

OSBORNE, E. E., *The Output of Women Workers in Relation to Hours of Work in Shellmaking*. United Kingdom Industrial Fatigue Research Board, Report No. 3, London, HMSO, 1919.

OWEN, J. D., *The Price of Leisure*. Rotterdam University Press, 1969.

PAHL, J. M. and R. E., *Managers and their Wives*. London, Allen Lane, 1971.

PAHL, R. E., 'Poverty and the urban system', in M. CHISHOLM and L. MANNERS (eds), *Spatial Policy Problems of the British Economy*. Cambridge University Press, 1971, pp. 126–45.

PARK, R. E., BURGESS, E. W. and MCKFNZIE, R. D., *The City*. University of Chicago Press, 1966.

PARKER, S., *The Future of Work and Leisure*. London, MacGibbon & Kee, 1971.

PARSONS, T., 'Age and sex in the social structure of the United States', in T. PARSONS, *Essays in Sociological Theory*, Chicago, Free Press, 1954, pp. 89–103.

PARSONS, T., *The Social System*. Chicago, Free Press, 1951.

PIEPER, J., *Leisure: the Basis of Culture*. London, Faber, 1952.

Pilgrims' Trust Fund, *Men Without Work*. London, Pilgrims' Trust, 1938.

PIMLOTT, J. A. R., *The Englishman's Holiday*. London, Faber, 1947.

PIMLOTT, J. A. R., *Recreations*. London, Studio Vista, 1968.

PINCHBECK, I., *Women Workers and the Industrial Revolution, 1750–1850*. London, George Routledge, 1930.

POLLARD, S., *The Genesis of Modern Management*. Harmondsworth, Penguin Books, 1968.

POLLINS, H., 'Transport lines and social divisions', in Centre for Urban Studies, *London: Aspects of Change*, pp. 29–61.

POTTER, B., 'The tailoring trade', in C. BOOTH, *Life and Labour of the People in London*, vol. 4, pp. 37–68.

POWER, E., *Medieval People*. London, Methuen, 1924.

PREST, J., *The Industrial Revolution in Coventry*. Oxford University Press, 1960.

QUENNELL, M. and C. H. B., *History of Everyday Things in England*. vol. IV, London, Batsford, 1941.

RAPOPORT, R. and R. N., *Dual Career Families*. Harmondsworth, Penguin Books, 1971.

RASMUSSEN, S., *London: The Unique City*. 3rd ed., London, Cape, 1948.

READ, H., 'Atrophied muscles and empty art', in N. CALDER (ed.), *The World in 1984*, vol. 2, Harmondsworth, Penguin Books, 1965, pp. 88–92.

Reader's Digest European Surveys. London, Reader's Digest Association, 1963, 1970.

REEVES, M. S., *Round About a Pound a Week*. London, Bell, 1913.

REISSMAN, L., 'Class, leisure and social participation', *American Sociological Review*, vol. 19 (1) (February 1954) pp. 76–84.

'Report of the Changing Nature of Residential Areas.' London, Borough of Enfield (duplicated), 1969.

RODGERS, H. B., *The Pilot National Recreational Survey: Report No. 1*. British Travel Association, University of Keele, July 1967.

ROSE, E. J. B. *et al.*, *Colour and Citizenship*. Oxford University Press, 1969.

ROSS, J. M., BUNTON, W. J., EVISON, P. and ROBERTSON, T. S., *A Critical Appraisal of Comprehensive Education*. Windsor, National Foundation for Educational Research, 1972.

ROUTH, G., *Occupation and Pay in Great Britain 1906–60*. Cambridge, University Press, 1965.

ROWE, D. A., 'Private consumption', in W. BECKERMAN, *The British Economy in 1975*, pp. 177–200.

ROWNTREE, B. S., *Poverty: A Study of Town Life*. London, Macmillan, 1901.

RUNCIMAN, W. G., *Relative Deprivation and Social Justice*. London, Routledge & Kegan Paul, 1966.

RUSSELL, B., *In Praise of Idleness and Other Essays*. London, Allen & Unwin, 1935.

SALAIS, R. and MICHAL, M.-G., 'L' activité des femmes mariées', *Economie et Statistique*, no. 26 (September 1971), pp. 27–36.

SHARMA, U., *Rampal and His Family*. London, Collins, 1971.

SHERIDAN, G., 'Flexing time', *New Society*, no. 526 (2 November 1972), pp. 273–9.

SILLITOE, K. K., *Planning for Leisure*. London, HMSO, 1969.

SMELSER, N. J., *Social Change in the Industrial Revolution*. London, Routledge & Kegan Paul, 1959.

SMITH, A., *The Wealth of Nations*. vols. I and II, London, Methuen, 1904.

SMITH, H. L., *The New Survey of London Life and Labour*. 9 vols, London, P. S. King, 1935.

SOFER, C., *Men in Mid-Career: A Study of British Managers and Technical Specialists*. Cambridge University Press, 1970.

SOROKIN, P. A. and BERGER, C. Q., *Time Budgets of Human Behaviour*. Cambridge, Mass., Harvard University Press, 1939.

SOUTAR, M. S., WILKINS, E. H. and SARGENT FLORENCE, F. P., *Nutrition and Size of Family*. London, Allen & Unwin, 1942.

South East Joint Planning Team, *Strategic Plan for the South East. A Framework*. London, HMSO, 1970.

South East Joint Planning Team, *Strategic Plan for the South East, Studies, Volume 1: Population and Employment*. London, HMSO, 1971.

Sports Council, *Water Recreation Research Studies*, nos 3, 4, 5 and 6. London, 1973.

SPRING RICE, M., *Working-Class Wives*. Harmondsworth, Penguin Books, 1939.

STENTON, D. M., *The English Woman in History*. London, Allen & Unwin, 1957.

STEWART, R., *Managers and their Jobs*. London, Macmillan, 1967.

SZALAI, A. *et al.*, *The Use of Time*. The Hague, Mouton, 1972.

SZALAI, A. *et al.*, 'The multi-national comparative time budget research project', *American Behavioural Scientists*, vol. 10 (4), (December 1966).

THOMPSON, E. P., *The Making of the English Working Class*. London, Gollancz, 1963.

THOMPSON, E. P. and YEO, E., *The Unknown Mayhew*. London, Merlin Press, 1971.

TITMUSS, R. M., 'The position of women', in R. M. TITMUSS, *Essays on the 'Welfare State'*. London, Unwin University Books, 1958, pp. 88–103.

TOCQUEVILLE, A. DE, *Democracy in America*. vols. I and II, New York, Vintage Books, 1945.

TÖNNIES, F., *Community and Association*. London, Routledge & Kegan Paul, 1955.

TOUT, H., *The Standard of Living in Bristol*. London, Arrowsmith, 1938.

TOWNSEND, P., *The Family Life of Old People*. London, Routledge & Kegan Paul, 1957.

TULPULE, A. H., *Forecasts of Vehicles and Traffic in Great Britain*. Report L.R. 288, Road Research Laboratory, 1969.

VEBLEN, T., *The Theory of the Leisure Class*. New York, New American Library, 1959.

VERNON, H. M., *Fatigue and Efficiency in the Iron and Steel Industry*. United Kingdom Industrial Fatigue Research Board, Report No. 5, London, HMSO, 1920.

WEBER, M., *The Theory of Social and Economic Organisation*. Chicago, Free Press, 1947.

WEDGE, P. J., 'Working mothers' children', in preparation.

WESTERGAARD, J. H., 'The Structure of Greater London', in Centre for Urban Studies, *London: Aspects of Change*, pp. 91–144.

WILENSKY, H. L., 'The uneven distribution of leisure: the impact of economic growth on "free time" ', *Social Problems*, vol. 9 (1), (Summer 1961), pp. 32–55.

WILENSKY, H. L., 'Work, careers and social integration', *International Social Science Journal*, vol. XII (4) (1960), pp. 543–60.

WILENSKY, H. L., 'Work as a social problem', in H. S. BECKER (ed.), *Social Problems: A Modern Approach*, New York, Wiley, 1969.

WILLIAMS, R., *Culture and Society 1780–1950*. London, Chatto & Windus, 1958.

WILLMOTT, P., *Adolescent Boys of East London*. London, Routledge & Kegan Paul, 1966.

WILLMOTT, P., *The Evolution of a Community*. London, Routledge & Kegan Paul, 1963.

WILLMOTT, P., 'Family, work and leisure conflicts among male employees: some preliminary findings', *Human Relations*, vol. 2 (6) (December 1971), pp. 575–84.

WILLMOTT, P. and YOUNG, M., *Family and Class in a London Suburb*. London, Routledge & Kegan Paul, 1960.

WILLMOTT, P. and YOUNG, M., 'How urgent are London's motorways', *New Society*, no. 426 (10 December 1970), pp. 1036–8.

WILLMOTT, P. and YOUNG, M., 'Social class and geography', in D. EVERSLEY and D. V. DONNISON (eds), *London: Urban Patterns, Problems and Policies*, London, Heinemann, 1973.

WOHL, A. S., 'The housing of the working class in London', in S. D. Chapman (ed.), *The History of Working-Class Housing*. Newton Abbot, David & Charles, 1971.

WOMAN and the National Market. London, Odhams Press, 1956 and 1967.

WRIGHT, H. B. and PINCHERLE, G., 'Profile of the coronary man', in E. FORSTER and G. BULL (eds.), *The Director, His Money and His Job*, pp. 329–38.

WRONG, D. H., *Population and Society*. 2nd ed., New York, Random House, 1961.

YOUNG, A., *A Six Months Tour Through the North of England*. 2nd ed., vol. III, London, 1771.

YOUNG, M., 'Distribution of income within the family', *British Journal of Sociology*, vol. III (1952), pp. 305–21.

YOUNG, M. BENJAMIN, B. and WALLIS, C., 'The mortality of widowers', *Lancet*, vol. II (1963), pp. 454–6.

YOUNG, M. and WILLMOTT, P., *Family and Kinship in East London*. London, Routledge & Kegan Paul, 1957.

YOUNG, M. and ZIMAN, J., 'Cycles in social behaviour', *Nature*, vol. 229, no. 5280 (1971), pp. 91-5.

ZWEIG, F., *Labour, Life and Poverty*. London, Gollancz, 1949.
ZWEIG, F., *Men in the Pits*. London, Gollancz, 1949.

INDEX

ABOUT THE AUTHORS

Michael Young and Peter Willmott are codirectors of London's famous Institute of Community Studies and the joint authors of the highly praised *Family and Kinship in East London,* among other titles. Michael Young has also written *The Rise of the Meritocracy,* and Peter Willmott *Adolescent Boys of East London.* Michael Young is a former chairman of the British Social Science Research Council, president of the British Consumers Association, and originator of the plan for Britain's Open University. Peter Willmott is a part-time professor at the School of Environmental Studies of the University College of London and has been Visiting Professor at the University of Paris, where he is currently directing research on urban poverty.